Suturing the City

Living Together
in Congo's Urban Worlds

Filip De Boeck & **Sammy Baloji**

text   photography

LEUVEN UNIVERSITY PRESS

TABLE OF CONTENTS

Je suis riche	I am rich
Tu es pauvre	You are poor
Il est célibataire	He is single
Elle est belle	She is pretty
Nous sommes à l'église	We are in church
Vous êtes les bakongo	You are bakongo
Ils sont au bureau	They are in the office
Elles sont au marché	They are at the market

1. Preface: Suturing the City. Living Together in Congo's Urban Worlds.

'Inhabiting only that ocular ground in which the country appeared out of nothing and vanished again into nothing, tree and rock and the darkening mountains beyond, all of it contained and itself containing only what was needed and nothing more.' (McCarthy 2002: 542)

'Our purpose has been to recognize in the zero number the suturing stand-in for the lack.' (Miller 2012 [1966]: 99)

A TALE OF THREE MOUNTAINS:

Kinshasa, the capital of the Democratic Republic of Congo and home to at least ten million inhabitants, is growing at an alarming speed. It is bordered on its north flank by the Malebo Pool, the vast inner sea that the Congo River becomes at this point, and thus has no alternative but to expand to the west and south of its old colonial core in direction of the Lower Congo, and to the east, where a vast sandy plain stretches from the southern bank of the Malebo Pool to the foot of the imposing Mount Mangengenge, the eastern gateway to the city for newcomers coming from its rural hinterlands.

Let us now enter the city like these rural migrants from the vantage point of Mount Mangengenge, and start this book about Kinshasa with the figure of the mountain.

Rising up into the sky like the white cliffs of Dover, Mount Mangengenge has always been held sacred. In precolonial times, it was a site of ancestral worship for the local Bateke, Bahumbu and Banfunu populations that inhabited the area long before the arrival of Bula Matari, 'breaker of rocks', as the local population dubbed Henry Morton Stanley, who represented and embodied King Leopold's harsh colonial rule. The colonial intrusion and occupation that Stanley set in motion when he first arrived in the Pool in 1877 greatly disturbed the world of its inhabitants and would forever change the existing political and spiritual geography of the Pool.

Mount Mangengenge bears the marks of that process of transformation. Due to the impact of the new world that was introduced by the Belgian colonisation, Mount Mangengenge gradually lost its former spiritual significance as an ancestral site to become a Christian place of worship, close to the Almighty God that the white missionaries

had brought along with them. Over the years, the mountain became an established pilgrimage site for Kinshasa's Catholics. And today, it is in the process of being re-colonised yet again; this time by Kinshasa's rapidly growing army of Pentecostals. In the process, Mount Mangengenge has now become Mount Tabor in reference to the place where Jesus started to shine with bright rays of light. This miraculous event on the Mount of Transfiguration is an important episode in the New Testament (Matthew 17:1-9, Mark 9:2-8, Luke 9:28-36) and of crucial importance in Pentecostal theology.

February 2013: Sammy Baloji and I climb the path that leads up to the top of Mount Mangengenge. The path is punctuated by the Stations of the Cross, which were inaugurated in the early 1990s by Cardinal Frédéric Etsou Nzabi Bamungwabi, the Archbishop of Kinshasa from 1991 until his death in 2007. On reaching the windswept mountain top, we follow a narrow sandy trail that leads to a rudimentary prayer camp, built around a huge cement cross. The camp overlooks a large portion of the Malebo Pool, and Kinshasa's landmark Sozacom Tower glitters in the distance. The contours of the downtown city centre are blurred in the afternoon heat and a yellowish haze of dust and pollution seems to envelop the whole city. Up here on clearer days, you can see the skyline of Brazzaville on the opposite side of the Pool, but today Kinshasa's mirror city has evaporated in the opalescent light.

In the prayer camp itself, voices rise above the low moan of the wind. People have begun to shake as they go into a trance while singing, praying and preaching in ardent, high-pitched tones. Some will remain here for days or even weeks to fast and meditate. High above our heads, an eagle is circling in slow motion around the mountain, as if the Holy Spirit itself has decided to descend from heaven to listen to the people praying. On the slopes of one of the nearby mountain ranges that descend into the green emptiness of Bandundu province, I can distinguish tiny, motionless solitary figures. Some are dressed in white robes. Some are crouching in the sand while others are kneeling, with their arms raised towards the sky and their palms turned upwards. All these men and women are in deep, concentrated prayer in a fervent attempt to retreat from the urban pool of sin and its temptations, problems and disillusions. They pray to purify themselves of the omnivorous giant called Kinshasa that is rapidly approaching the foot of the mountain and engulfing the once empty sand-plains now overrun with thousands of small rudimentary rectangular constructions, which are often merely shelters. Their grey cement brick walls are barely distinguishable from the sand of the plains, and it is only the recently added glistening sheets of corrugated iron roofs that expose their presence. But before long, these sheets will start to rust and the houses will blend in with the colour of the sand and sink back into the landscape.

———————

If today the provisional endpoint of Kinshasa, which spreads along the southern bank of the Malebo Pool, is Mount Mangengenge to the east, the actual starting point of the city was another mountain, Mount Khonzo Ikulu. Located near the rapids where the Pool narrows to become a river again, Khonzo Ikulu was chosen by Stanley as the site to set up camp shortly after his return to the Malebo Pool in 1880, three years after the epic transcontinental journey that brought him worldwide fame. Soon renamed Leopold Hill, Khonzo Ikulu was a salubrious and easily defendable site that overlooked the small bay of Kintambo, a short distance from the market-village of Kintambo (also called Ntamo or Kintamo), one of the most important precolonial Teke villages of the Pool. In Stanley's wake, the Arthington Mission of the Baptist Church established a mission station at the top of Leopold Hill in July 1882.

Only months before on 9 April 1882, Stanley was at the top of Leopold Hill and looked over what he would later describe as 'the glories of the Pool and its encircling ring of hill and mountain', 'bright and clear' under 'opalesque skies':

'That broad low plain — from Kintamo south, to the foot of Mabengu mountain — which forms the western shore of the Pool, is to me full of promise and beauty. Even now it is almost idyllic in appearance, yet there is only the grass huts from Kintamo conspicuously in view; the rest is literally only a wilderness of grass, shrubs and tree-foliage. But my mind, when I survey the view, always reverts to the possibilities of the future. It is like looking at the fair intelligent face of a promising child; we find nought in it but innocence, and we fondly imagine that we see the germs of a future great genius; perhaps a legislator, a savant, a warrior, or a poet. Supposing the rich fertile soil of that plain, well-watered as it is by many running streams, were cultivated, how would it reward the husbandman! How would it be bursting with fullness and plenty!' (Stanley 2011 [1885]: 391)

A year later in 1883, Stanley and his Association concluded an important treaty with a confederation of local chiefs including the powerful Teke chief Ngaliema, who lived in a hamlet near Kintambo village. From then onwards and for many years to come, the flag of the Association would fly from the summit of Leopold Hill on important occasions, while all the surrounding villages were ordered to hoist the same flag on Sundays, signalling their obedience to the new colonial rule.

March 2014: Sammy and I stand on almost the exact same spot on Leopold Hill where Stanley viewed the bay and its surrounding mountain ring over a century ago. In front of us lie Kintambo Bay and the Chanic shipyard, which replaced the original port in Leopoldville, as Kinshasa was then called. The water surface still reflects the same opalesque skies as in Stanley's days. But where Stanley saw promise and future, the landscape that now unfolds below us seems to point mainly to the past. The shipyard, once the Bay's industrious heart bustling with life and activity, is now a sorry sight filled with decaying and half sunken ships. In the distance three canoes with fishermen glide by.

Just a few metres away from us lies a larger-than-life bronze statue of Stanley in the grass. His feet are missing: they broke off when Mobutu ordered the statue to be removed from the commemorative site where the Belgian coloniser honoured the colonial pioneers. The statue had been erected in 1950 on the very same location where chief Ngaliema's court had once been, and where some of Stanley's companions still lie buried. Mobutu well understood the political importance of symbolic grand gestures. Not only did he remove Stanley's statue but in line with the anti-colonial and nationalist 'return to authenticity' campaign that he launched in the early 1970s, Mobutu also built a new presidential palace on top of Leopold Hill, which was officially renamed Mount Ngaliema, in honour of this former Teke chief. Alongside the new presidential palace, Mobutu also constructed a number of warehouses that would become the *Institut des Museés Nationaux du Congo* (IMNC), a new ethnographic museum meant to

replace Leopoldville's former colonial *Musée de la vie indigène*.[1] Placing the ethnographic museum and its collection of 'traditional' power objects within the walls of the new presidential compound was Mobutu's way of stressing that he, and he alone, was Ngaliema's legitimate heir.

In 1997, when Kabila's troops were already at the city's gates, Mobutu exhumed the mortal remains of a few of his family members who had been buried in the Mount Ngaliema presidential graveyard, and fled to Morocco in their company. Shortly afterwards, Kabila's soldiers looted the presidential grounds and converted the palace building into army barracks.

Against all odds, Kabila's looting troops left the museum intact. As Sammy and I stroll through the main exhibition room, our attention is caught by an object that stands out amongst the masks and power objects on display. It is one of Mobutu's thrones and seems to have miraculously survived the looting spree in the palace. Covered with a leopard's skin, its overall shape seems to be a vague imitation of a Louis XV chair. This iconoclastic quality well illustrates the fact that Mobutu considered himself not only heir to Ngaliema's legacy but paradoxically also to that of King Leopold II, the Belgian

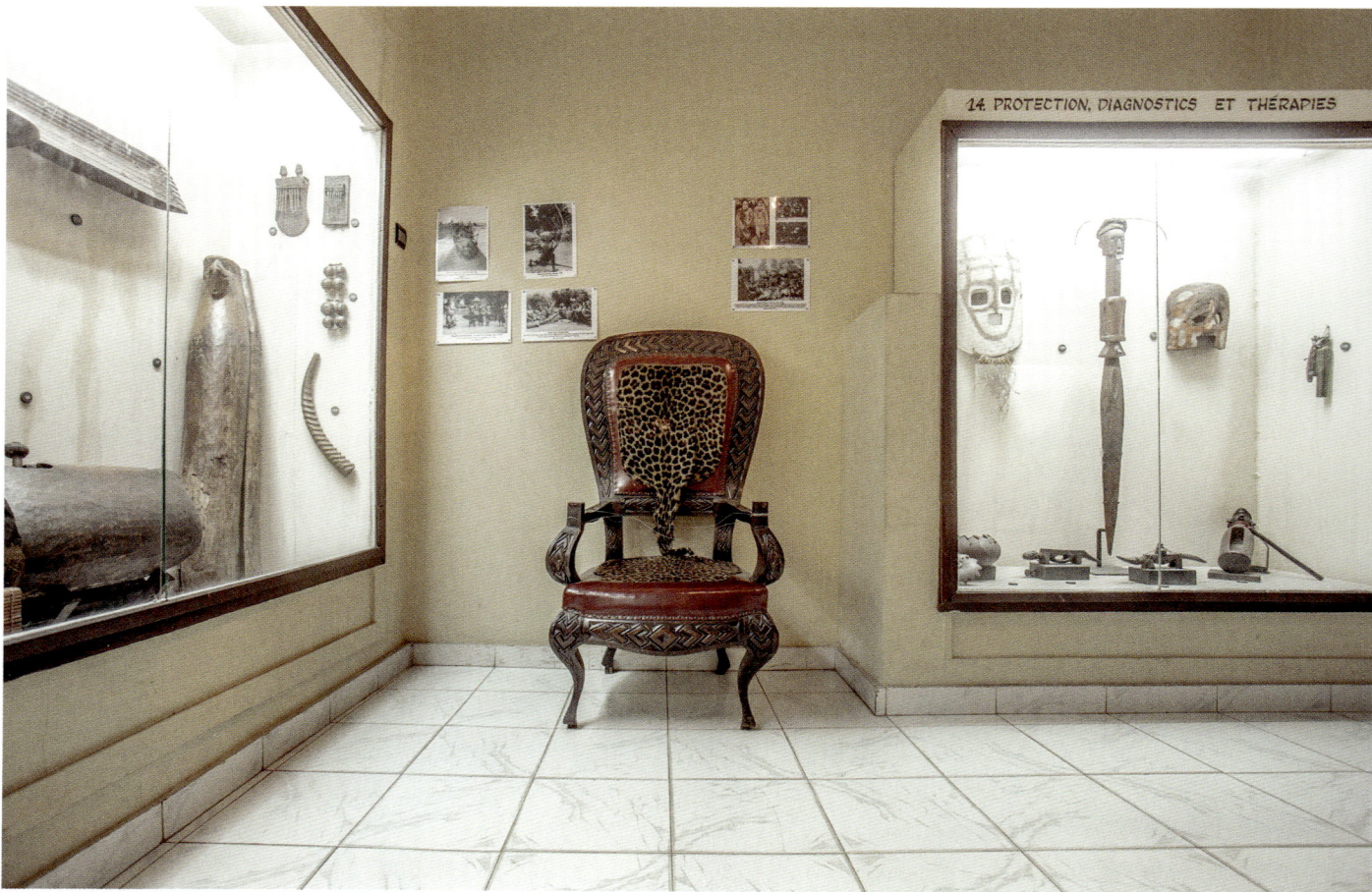

sovereign whose absolutist style of personal rule served as another source of inspiration for Mobutu's patrimonial state project (cf. Young and Turner 1985). Sammy takes a picture of the leopard skin throne, and we continue our walk through an otherwise silent and deserted museum. When we ask a museum attendant why there are no other visitors, she explains that school children, who used to visit the museum, no longer come because they have all converted to charismatic Christianity, which, in its attempt to break with autochthonous pasts (cf. Engelke 2010), considers the museum's collection of ancestral objects and 'fetishes' to be diabolical and satanic.

———

Like Mounts Mangengenge and Khonzo Ikulu, many of the Pool's surrounding mountains underwent profound transfigurations during colonial and postcolonial times. As the geographical emanation of local notions of sovereignty and ancestral authority, the mountains had once been important places in the topography of precolonial political and ritual power constellations. They were then transformed into sites that came to symbolise the superiority of the new colonial powers. The colonial intruders colonised the mountains through military might and missionary zeal. They planted their flag or cross on the mountain tops, and by renaming the mountains they erased their former connotations and inscribed new meanings on their surface: new notions of sovereignty and governance, new power and knowledge regimes and the new ideologies of colonialist modernity and Christian faith (which in turn are being redefined today by the agendas of neo-liberalism and charismatic Christianity).

The last mountain site that the Belgians converted into a glorification of their colonial endeavour was Mount Amba. This mountain had been an important place, like Mount Mangengenge, for ancestor worship before colonisers arrived. Its slopes had been ancestral burial grounds and access to them was once guarded by Lemba, one of the most important chiefs and land custodians of the precolonial landscape that would become Kinshasa. In the early 1950s towards the end of the Belgian colonial period, the Catholic University of Leuven in Belgium started on its plans to build a campus on Mount Amba, which was part of the Kimwenza plateau above the main city.[2] To this end, Mgr. Luc Gillon, a Belgian priest and nuclear scientist with a Princeton University degree, was sent to Congo, where he managed to conclude a land deal with a local Humbu land guardian, chief Matsanga Kintete, and obtain a large plot of land on Mount Amba on which the campus of the University of Lovanium was then built. Gillon himself became the first rector of this university in 1954, a position he occupied till 1967. And in this capacity, he founded one of the grandest and most spectacular modernist campus infrastructures of the African continent with large faculty buildings, lecture halls, a cathedral, cafeterias, a swimming pool, tennis courts, spacious villas and bungalows for professors and academic staff, and even a nuclear reactor for research purposes. Today, the reactor is threatened by the soil erosion that is eating up the sandy slopes of Mount Amba, and the university campus itself is increasingly surrounded by several slum areas. In one of these encroaching slums, a neighbourhood known as Tchad, land chief David Ebalavo, a descendant of Matsanga Kintete and head of the Mbuku Mvemba Mavuba clan, continues to contest the land deal that his forefather signed with Mgr. Gillon.

OF MOUNTAINS AND HOLES:
___

The histories of the autochthonous Humbu and Teke courts, the Belgian colonial enterprise and Mobutu's postcolonial state project of Zaire were to a great extent connected, within the setting of the Malebo Pool, by the fact that they all 'thought like a mountain' (cf. Pandian 2014) in their own individual ways. All these actors (chiefs, colonisers and postcolonial nationalists) turned the topography of the mountain into a powerful metaphor to convey and give form to how each of them understood governance, sovereignty, domination, control and coercion. The figure of the mountain anchored in all these historical time frames the specific (and often conflicting) meanings given to notions of colonisation, territorialisation and occupation. And today, the mountains surrounding the city of Kinshasa continue, like living palimpsests, to carry within them these various pasts.

In colonial times, the topographical framework offered by the mountain also provided the conceptual ground that enabled the birth of the colonial city. The mountain not only symbolised the panoptical and authoritarian ambitions of the colonial state but its vertical dimension also formed the perfect illustration of the ambitious dreams of colonialist modernity. The emerging physical landscape of the post-World War II colonial city symbolised these dreams to the full. In the period following World War II, the sky was the limit for Leopoldville, and the colonial image of the mountain was reinforced by and translated into the vertical propositions of tropical modernist architecture. In 1946, the Forescom Tower, Central Africa's first skyscraper, was built in the centre of Leopoldville, and epitomised colonialism's triumph. After independence, colonialism's vertical topographies were re-appropriated by the Mobutist state. Renaming and reclaiming Leopold Hill, the Mobutist regime also constructed its own skyscraper alongside the Forescom Tower. This postcolonial skyscraper was the Sozacom Tower, which was built on the central *Boulevard du 30 Juin* between 1969 and 1977. Higher and more imposing than its colonial predecessor, it became the city's new landmark.

However, many of the dreams that the city engendered have become disappointments. Even though the image of the skyscraper is recycled in the new urban overhaul that is taking place in Kinshasa today (see Chapter Two and Seven), and even though it still functions as a powerful topos that embodies the current regime's aspirations of insertion into a more modern and global world, the raw urgencies of living in the physical and social environments of Congo's capital constantly belie these dreams. There is a large gap between official urban planning projects and management policies and the reality of everyday lives in the shadow of the colonial and postcolonial towers. The political, economic and cultural structures and processes that have caused this gap are multiple and, as will become apparent throughout this book, they not only have deep historical roots but they are also exacerbated nowadays by the extractive nature of neo-colonial economies at play throughout Congo, as well as by increased global processes of financial speculation, a growing democratic deficit and quite simply a profound lack of concern on behalf of the state as to whether its citizens live or die. Participatory urban planning strategies are non-existent, the legal frameworks concerning land rights, property value, and zoning rules are completely non-transparent, and basic infrastructural services such as the supply of water and electricity are utterly neglected by the state. Moreover, there seems to be a general lack of genuine interest on the part of decision-makers to know more about what actually constitutes everyday life for the majority of people trying to survive in the often harsh realities of the existing urban environment. In the face of all this, Congo's urban residents have long since stopped thinking that their cities are glorious mountains, for the only mountains that appear on the horizon of their urban worlds are ones made up of garbage piles that urban authorities have ceased to collect. Instead, in their attempts to make sense of the life that the city imposes on them, urban denizens have turned to opposite topographical figures: the sinking ground and the hole.

In Kinshasa as in Congo's other cities, the concept of hole, or *libulu* in Lingala (which is the city's lingua franca), has come to define the wretched, dreary place that the city has become for many of its inhabitants. 'Hole' has become a local master trope, a conceptual figure, to express the dismal quality of urban life in the postcolonial city. In the minds of many, the city has quite literally become 'hollowed land'. This should not be confused with Eyal Weizman's use of the term to describe the sophisticated tunnel infrastructure that Israel employs in its late-modern colonial occupation of the West Bank (Weizman 2012), but should be understood in a much more immediate and less sophisticated way. Postcolonial urban living in Congo *literally* means living with potholes as generic urban infrastructures (Chapter Three). It also means living with the constant danger of soil erosion after heavy rainstorms, which create giant holes and ravines that swallow houses, streets and people. Living in the postcolonial hole also means surviving on the meagre livelihoods provided by artisanal mining holes. Finally, the image of the hole refers to the ultimate hole of the grave and to the city itself as a death-world and a 'cemetery of the living' (Mavinga 2011) (see also Chapter Five).

The concept of holes that urban residents revert to in order to express the quality of their lives in the setting of the city refers to the tangible physical depressions on its surface as well as to the black hole of urban living, the dark matter of the urban praxis itself. It is used as a metaphor to describe all of the shady deals that urban residents have to rely on in order to survive in the city's informal economy, and all the impromptu movements into often uncharted spatial, social and mental territory that the city obliges them to make. As Joshua Walker observes in his anthropological analysis of the diamond mining city of Mbuji Mayi, holes are both symptom and metaphor 'for an experience of loss that is simultaneously material and moral. Erosion itself signifies not only the city's physical decline; it also informs discourses about the corrosion of wealth and values (...)' (Walker 2014: 76). Holes, in other words, have become potent local tropes by means of which Congo's urban residents encapsulate their experience of living in what they often describe themselves as a 'multi-crisis'. At the same time, Walker rightly reminds us that 'discourses of holes — which imply removal and the empty spaces it produces — are deeply problematic' in that they suggest that urban existence is solely defined by 'depletion, as if the processes of extraction were not, themselves, productive

in any sense besides the depletive' (Walker 2014: 31). Indeed, the hole is never just a black hole. It is never merely hollow or emptied of content. Holes also have the capacity to metaphorically elide how life continues through, and despite, decline. And even if living the experience of the hole considerably complicates life and often degrades its quality, the hole itself also offers an aperture, an opening, a possibility, at least for those who know how to read an alternative meaning into its blackness.

HOLES AS POINTS OF SUTURE:

In Congo's postcolonial urban worlds, the hole is therefore the city's baseline, its ground zero. And in this sense, the hole is also a suture. In a recent publication, Nancy Rose Hunt uses the concept of suture in order to join together different colonial medical histories in Congo in new ways (Hunt 2013). Suturing, she argues, suggests closing a wound, making an incision, or stitching together parts, locations and points of view; as such it points to new kinds of creativity with sources, evidence and interactivity. I would like to pick up on this idea and extend the notion of suture as closure, as junction and as a seam, to the way in which, often against all odds, the inhabitants of Congo's urban landscapes read meaning into the black hole of the city; the way they use material, but also mental and moral holes, as suture points to fill the gaps, overcome the hiatus, design realignments and thereby redefine the zero — that is, the impossible circum- stances of living in the kind of urban environment that Congo's cities offer — into a possibility, a something else, a surplus. Taken like this, the notion of suture remains close to how Jacques-Alain Miller, who first introduced the concept of suture in Lacanian psychoanalysis, originally interpreted it. For him, suture is always between zero as a lack, as something impossible to conceptualise, and zero as a number, as 'one'. It is in that sense that the hole as suture both represents lack while also placing and 'suturing' it:

> 'Suture names the relation of the subject to the chain of its discourse; we shall see that it figures there as the element which is lacking, in the form of a stand-in (*tenant-lieu*). For, while there lacking, it is not purely and simply absent. Suture, by extension — the general relation of lack to the structure — of which it is an element, inasmuch as it implies the position of a taking-the-place-of (*tenant-lieu*).' (Miller 2012: 93)

In a short text that accompanied the recent publication of Sammy Baloji's photographic essay on Kolwezi's artisanal miners and postcolonial mining holes, Achille Mbembe also refers to the zero's potential to reformulate lack. 'In this zero world,' he writes, 'neither the material nor life come to an absolute end. They do not become nothing. They simply move on towards something else, and in every case the end is deferred and the question of finiteness remains unanswered.' (Mbembe 2014)

Subsequently, what this book aims to capture and understand is how urban residents do exactly that: how they manage — with varying degrees of success — to turn the zero into a one; how they read potential, promise and prospect into the blackness of the hole; how they throw themselves — their words and their own bodies — into this daily struggle with the city's madness; and how it is the hole itself that propels them to do that.

In this sense, tropes of hole and suture tell us something about the changes that have taken place in how urbanity is imagined and lived in the Democratic Republic of Congo today. '(...) [W]hat sort of collective life and what sort of knowledge is to be gathered,' Latour asks, '(...) once modernity has been thrown into doubt while the task of finding the ways to inhabit remains more important than ever?' (Latour 2005a: 16-17). To a great extent, this book is one long exploration of that very question. If the notion of the hole offers a kind of meta-concept that people use to reflect on the material degradation of the city's infrastructure and rework the closures and often dismal quality of the social life that has followed the material ruination of the colonial city, then this book explores the question of how this 'reworking' and reassembling takes place, and how this postcolonial hole is filled in the experience of Congolese urban residents. What possible answers does Kinshasa come up with in response to the challenge posed by the hole? If the city has transformed into a 'zero world' or a black hole that makes any clear assessment of it simply disappear by the force of its gravity, then how can this hole be 'illuminated' so as to remain and become the 'animated space' (Amin 2015) that enables living, and *living together* in the city?

I refer here to the notion of 'living together' in the sense of Derrida's *vivre ensemble*: a living together that can only exist where the whole, the assemblage, is not fully formed and is not closed (Derrida 2013). For *living together* always implies a contestation about how a social body, a collective, completes itself; it is a process that is never completely finished. It never sums up or is never fully identical with itself. And through it, to evoke Latour again, 'An entirely new set of questions has now emerged: "Can we cohabitate with you? Is there a way to survive together while none of our contradictory claims, interests, and passions can be eliminated?"' (Latour 2005b: 30). These are questions that relate to any urban context, of course, but they seem to be particularly urgent in a city such as Kinshasa, where the gap between the topographies of mountain and hole is so conspicuous, where pleasure and poignancy always go hand in hand, and where the hiatus itself has become the topological framework to map out any existence in the city.

For Latour, the possibility of cohabitation situates itself in the time of simultaneity. The time of cohabitation is the contemporary, in which 'space has replaced time

as the ordering principle' (idem). By lifting the opposition between time and space, or between history and world, the question for Latour is no longer: 'Are you going to disappear soon? Are you the telltale sign of something new coming to replace everything else? Is this the seventh seal of the Book of Apocalypse that you are now breaking?' (ibidem). While it is certainly true that much of Kinshasa's drive is 'anti-teleological' by its very nature (cf. Malaquais 2011), and even if most of urban life in this context is lived in the temporality of the moment without a yesterday or tomorrow, nevertheless both the future and the past are not so easily evacuated. In spite (or even because) of the urgency of the contemporary that animates this city, it also very much lives in the anticipatory time-frame of the apocalyptic interlude (cf. De Boeck 2005a) while various pasts are constantly brought back and revived in a multitude of different, and indeed simultaneous, intertwined ways that make the cohabitation always a deeply uneasy and even 'illicit' one (cf. Mbembe 1992:4).

On the other hand, Derrida's answer to the question of how people can live together is located in a future-oriented ethics of unconditional hospitality (Derrida 2000, 2013). But what does such ethical humanism mean in a city such as Kinshasa? We commonly conceive of a city not only as a place where people attempt to chart out a life for themselves, but also where living becomes living together with others. And we therefore expect the city to be an entity with the capacity to stabilise itself so that we can inhabit and experience it in predictable ways, and turn inhabitation into cohabitation. And yet, even if there is no other choice but to live together, as Derrida puts it, in an urban environment such as Kinshasa's, there always seems to be something that refuses such stabilisation, that makes all possibilities of inhabitation at least partially uninhabitable, and all gestures of hospitality and attempts at cohabitation at least partially suspect. Something about this kind of urban context eludes any attempt to tie it down, or to make it act in a predictable way. In light of the many clashes, frictions, suspicions, accusations, and contradictions that accompany any kind of life in the Congolese urban context, proposing an ethics of hospitality as a condition for living together does not, therefore, seem to fully cover the problem either.

So what can be posited against that dispersal, that refusal to remain in place, that unpredictability? What, in the end, does the nebulous notion of 'living together' in a city like Kinshasa still mean today? As family, kinship and neighbourhood solidarities are often eroded or stretched to the limit and residents desperately search for new viable experiences of being together, what new forms of collective life are emerging? Where and how do people stitch their lacks and losses together to 'suture' the folds, gaps and holes of the city, close its wounds, generate realignments and open up alternatives? What kinds of creativity with (both spatial *and* temporal) beginnings, and new forms of interactivity and sociability does this entail?

'ACUPUNCTURING' THE CITY THROUGH ANTHROPOLOGY AND PHOTOGRAPHY:

These questions are of particular importance if one wants to understand the nature of urban life in Congo's cities today, and in this book Sammy Baloji and I provide what can only be partial and provisional answers. Focusing upon the 'urban now' (cf. Robinson 2013), a moment suspended between the shattered wreckage of precolonial worlds, the broken dreams of a colonial past and the as yet unfulfilled promises of neoliberal futures, Sammy's photographs and my texts aim to work together as a form of 'urban acupuncture', a delicate puncturing of the city's surface in order to understand some of its underlying dynamics. In Chapter Two I will return to the notion of 'acupuncture' at greater length, but suffice it to say for now that we use the instruments of pen and photographic lens as analytical needles to stick into what we believe to be some of Kinshasa's meaningful sites and suturing points. They could be certain buildings, or else a market, graveyard, mountain, pothole, or a new city extension. They could be various different places that form important though sometimes materially barely visible nodes in the city: sites in which the city invents and reveals its own rhythms most fully or places in which the city reworks the histories (often forgotten but nonetheless very present) that give it its specific character.

As a combination of two ways of 'seeing' that brings together ethnography and photography, this book is the outcome of a long collaborative work that began several years ago when we were offered the opportunity that arose within the context of a larger research project on new urban extensions, satellite cities and gated communities. Thanks to this project Sammy and I travelled not only to the Democratic Republic of Congo but also to Ghana and Kenya in order to document and create a visual archive of some of these emerging urban sites in Accra and Takoradi (together with my colleague and partner Ann Cassiman and her doctoral student, Geertrui Vannoppen), as well as in Nairobi (with Jan Van den Broeck, whose doctoral research I was guiding at the time). The Congo leg of the research soon started to have its own life. It developed into two longer research trips that took Sammy and me to Kinshasa, where I have worked as an anthropologist for over twenty years, and two shorter trips to the Katangese mining towns of Fungurume and Lubumbashi, Sammy's home town. Our joint field research took place between February 2013 and March 2015, and most of this book's visual archive was produced in that period. Our reading of the city, however, builds on a much longer knowledge of the sites that will be discussed throughout the book. Born in Lubumbashi, Sammy has been photographing mining sites and cities in Katanga for most of his professional career as a photographer. As for myself, I have been working as an anthropologist in Congo since 1987. My first long-term field research was carried out in Nzofu, a Lunda village in a remote rural area along the borderline between Congo and Angola. Over the years and in a similar manner that many Congolese discover the city upon leaving their villages, I started to follow in the tracks of my Lunda informants to some of the region's secondary towns, such as Kikwit. And as in the case of many of my rural acquaintances, this journey finally led me to Kinshasa.

What Sammy and I had in common from the start was a shared fascination for 'the mirror', the spectacle of money and its impact on the 'specular' development of cities in Congo (see Chapter Seven). There is also the way in which people, on the level of their everyday lives, move beyond their own fascination with this mirror and the different kinds of — colonial and postcolonial — modernities that it reflects in order to construct more tangible and liveable, inhabitable urban lives and futures for themselves.

In my view, the combination of ethnography and photography provides a particularly powerful tool to delve into these dimensions, even though we have perhaps not yet fully understood and explored all the possibilities of such a combination in general. For me personally, Documenta 11, which Okwui Enwezor curated in 2002, proved a formative moment in which it became clear to what extent contemporary artists (and especially photographers, video artists and other producers of visual culture) had appropriated ethnographic methods of observation to capture, document and comment upon what Enwezor called 'the black box' of our contemporary world, which is being increasingly shaped, united *and* divided by powerful spectatorial regimes, each with their specific (necessarily fractal but simultaneously often very authoritarian) aesthetics (Enwezor 2002b). This somehow already strongly resonated with my own work when Enwezor invited me to the Documenta's Platform 4 meeting in Lagos (Enwezor 2002a) because I had already started to move in the opposite direction, from anthropology to photography and video, in my own ethnographic practice. By then, I had nearly finished writing my first Kinshasa book, a collaborative project with photographer Marie-Françoise Plissart (De Boeck and Plissart 2004), in which we both tried to find a form and a language for our increasingly shared awareness of how important it was to combine the ethnographic fact and its politics of representation if one wants to say something meaningful about urban life.

Personally, I find it hard to conceive of an ethnography of 'cityness', of a truly urban anthropology, without photography. To say that the 'modern' city is a visual thing is stating the obvious. As Geoff Dyer remarks in his captivating meditations on the history of urban photography (Dyer 2012), in many ways the city only exists through the photographic image. In the same way, photography itself could not have developed without the city. It is very likely that the images that immediately come to mind when we think of Paris, for example, were shaped and fashioned by Brassaï's photographs. Similarly, the New York in our mind's eye would not exist without Walker Evans or Paul Strand, nor would our image of Istanbul exist without the photographic work of Ara Güler, the 'eye of Istanbul'. Jean Depara's photographs of Leopoldville — or more recently Kiripi

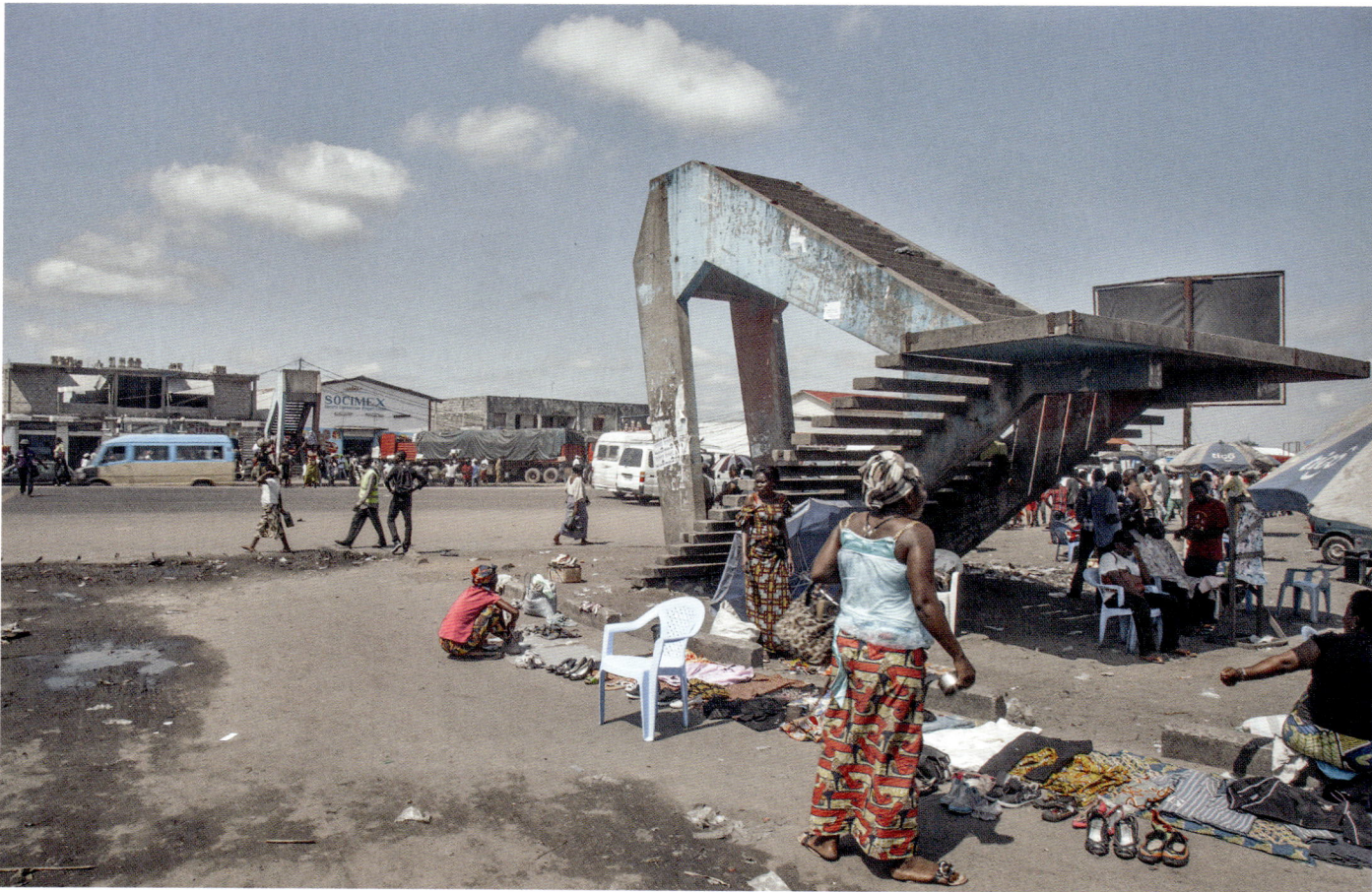

Katembo Siku's photos of Kinshasa as a broken mirror, reflected in the puddles and potholes of its streets — have likewise become our collective image of this city.

The present study is both a textual narrative of life and place in the urban setting as well as a visual study of things that defy verbal narration: the city's affective landscapes, its moods and the ways in which it 'touches' its inhabitants. This is completely different from a verbal narration, from what people themselves say about their city and what I, as an anthropologist, can narratively capture about the city. It is a dimension that photography can provide. It is said that photographs objectify, render static and freeze. Depending on how the medium is used, however, they can also do the opposite: they can make the city a particular kind of fluid, living subject. In this way, Sammy Baloji's photographs have helped me to take in and understand — and render — the feel of the city. They have helped me to bridge the gap between theory and the lived experience of the city and construct an analysis or a narrative of the paradoxes of urban life as an oscillation between the simultaneous character in which life in the city unfolds, that is on one hand, the dissolution of a linear continuation between past, present and future in the kind of spacing out of time that Latour commented on,

and, on the other, the particular ways in which the dimension of time (and history) is constantly re-introduced and re-inscribed in the urban space.

The possibility of combining both dimensions in novel and alternative ways entails the different compositional possibilities of text and image. A straightforward linear narrative of the city seems somehow impossible because the city — and certainly an urban context such as Kinshasa — refuses to be captured in one single master narrative. But at the same time, a narrative is always implied in what one writes. Subsequently, there is this inevitable tension between the successive time that a narrative imposes and the simultaneous time in which the city happens and unfolds. Here photography has helped us to overcome this difficulty and make chronology subordinate to the analytic/narrative demands of the sequence. Photography carries within itself the possibility to negate chronology. It has indeed the capacity to impose a visual narrative that invents its own sequences. For example, it can represent simultaneity through working with paradox and random juxtapositions. In that sense, it is extremely well suited to cover an urban landscape such as Kinshasa in which juxtaposition and paradox are omni-present. Employing these visualising strategies enables a different kind of narrative to

emerge away from more standardised and strictly linear records that are actually not at all suited to this kind of city. Instead, we have tried to generate a narration of the city as a set of interdependencies between figures, places, segments, colours, shades, moods and affects. In that sense I have learnt a great deal from the photographer. It is perhaps no coincidence that Sammy Baloji started out as a creator of comic strips, a genre in which visual chronology evidently plays a very important role. The question of chronology and sequence is therefore something that is very much on his mind in his own artistic practice, and it has been something that has connected the two of us in what we have tried to do and say.

Photography does many other things too. First of all, it is a surface intervention in that it is horizontal and therefore well suited for capturing the fluid geography of a city such as Kinshasa that constantly negates and transcends matters of the map as well as attempts at more formal planning. On the other hand, photography can also be vertical. Photos allow access to an inside, an interior, or what Walter Benjamin famously described as an 'optical unconscious' (Benjamin 1972). That is why the night is so prominently present in the work of many photographers who try to capture urban reality.

Photos have the potential to reveal the inside of darkness, make the content of the shadow and the hole visible and 'illuminate the shadow', as the artist William Kentridge would say (see Chapter Two). This is an idea that shaped my previous collaboration with photographer Marie-Françoise Plissart. Our book, *Kinshasa: Tales of the Invisible City* was in many ways a vertical examination of the city as a space of the unseen and the occult: the invisible forces that drive the city forward and 'beyond' the hardware of its architecture and infrastructure. It was about the city as 'zero degree infrastructure' (De Boeck and Plissart 2004: 242); the city as it exists as a mental space, a mirror of the mind, a specific form originating from autochthonous and more global imaginations. It was a book that wanted to render darkness — the hidden underneath of the city — visible. To a certain extent, the present book advances from the opposite direction. It is a much more horizontal book, an exploration of the surface of the city, not beyond but within its various topographies and material appearances, its current infrastructures and architectures, the various stages of dilapidation or emergence in which they find themselves, and the different ways in which such spaces animate life in the city and are themselves animated by it. Our horizontal exploration of this cityscape thus becomes an investigation into the qualities of a surface that includes both 'mountain' and 'hole', and thus inevitably re-introduces the vertical.

The vertical is always there in terms of the temporal layers, the historical palimpsests that have contributed to the creation of the city's contemporary surface. Sammy Baloji has been very attentive to these layers and to 'the anxiety of history made invisible' (Arndt 2013) in all his photographic and artistic work (see also Jewsiewicki 2010, 2014). His art is basically about how different times convert into the space of the now. He is rightly famous for his photo collages that reveal so clearly the presence of various pasts and strive to unravel the palimpsest of the city through photographic work on themes such as memory, history and nostalgia. In this sense, I see his work as a collecting and recollecting of urban pasts in the present, and the possible futures one can live in from that point on.

In conclusion, the joint effort of bringing together our textual and visual urban acupunctures is about the spacing of time and the timing of space. On a first level, it lays bare the horizontal and synchronic lines that spatially connect the various sites of the city and sometimes branch out far beyond its actual geographical limits to include other urban (and rural) sites within Congo and beyond. But these acupunctures also work vertically, blending space and time. They are more 'archaeological' acts, diachronic test drillings that bore into the various historical sedimentations that have made 'living together' in the city what it is today. These layers have not crystallised or fossilised into the solidity of dead matter. They form the organic material, the humus that feeds the living organism of the city. They are the compost, or 'rubble' as Gordillo (2014) has called it, in which various precolonial and colonial pasts decompose and are recycled in order to fertilise the present with new, hybrid, and palimpsestual meanings that often distort older contents, but also provide a certain continuity (albeit shaky and not always in recognisable or illuminating ways). Our urban acupunctures, therefore, never become an autopsy. Instead, they enable us to encounter and describe emerging urban assemblages as living bodies in alternative and novel ways.

ACKNOWLEDGEMENTS:

The collaboration between Sammy Baloji and myself was made possible thanks to a research grant from the Research Fund of the University of Leuven within the framework of a larger project on satellite cities in Africa that was co-funded by the Fund for Scientific Research-Flanders (FWO), and that I coordinated together with two other colleagues from the Institute for Anthropological Research in Africa (IARA), Ann Cassiman and Steven Van Wolputte. I would like to thank both of them for their continued help and support. Sammy and I also thank our London publisher, Autograph ABP, its director, Mark Sealy, and all his staff. Not only did they host an exhibition of some of the book's photographs in an early stage of this project but without their further logistic and financial backing and intellectual input this book would not have seen the light of day. Thanks are also due to Imane Farès Gallery in Paris for contributing financially towards the publication of this book, as well as to the Brussels-based Wiels Contemporary Art Centre and its director, Dirk Snauwaert, for providing a venue to present the visual outcome of the work Sammy and I collaborated on.[3] Finally we thank Jean Loup Pivin for kindly providing a photo of Bylex's *Cité Touristique*, and Ilan Weiss for assisting us with the photo work.

Many people also helped us during our research stays in Kinshasa and Lubumbashi. I want to express my sincere thanks to my colleague and friend Professor Jacob Sabakinu Kivilu from the University of Kinshasa for his unwavering support over the years. I am also extremely grateful to Zephyrin Muyika, my long-time research assistant in Kinshasa, and all his family for their hospitality and friendship. I also extend my gratitude to Charles Naweji, who generously welcomed us to his home during our last research stay in March 2015. Many other people offered their assistance and the pleasure of their company and conversations during our different research periods in Kinshasa. I would like to thank three of them in particular: first of all, Kinshasa-based painter Pathy Tshindele, who guided us to the location of the Doctor's Tower (see Chapter Seven), secondly, the artist Bylex, whose work continues to be a major source of inspiration and finally, the photographer Kiripi Katembo, who facilitated our research in numerous ways and without whom our various stays in Kinshasa would not have been the same. His unexpected death in August 2015 came as a shock, and it is to his memory that we want to dedicate this book. In Lubumbashi we particularly thank

the Picha ASBL for its logistic support, and the artist Jean Katambayi for his artistic contribution to this book.

A substantial part of this book was conceived during a two-month writing retreat in Lisbon, where I landed in the old downtown neighbourhood of Mouraria that, as it name indicates, turned out to be a perfect place to write about cities and black holes. Many people contributed to making my stay in Lisbon a productive and wonderful period. I would first of all like to thank Professor Eduardo Costa Dias, who kindly provided me with an office at the Lisbon University Institute (ISCTE-IUL). I extend my thanks to Professor Clara Carvalho, the director of the university's Centro de Estudos Internacionais for her support, as well as to Jürgen Bock, the director of the Maumaus School of Visual Arts, who hosted both Sammy and me on various occasions, and to Joana Gomes Cardoso, Joana Vasconcelos, Lorenzo Bordonaro and Arne Kaiser, who all shared their city so generously with me. A very special thanks goes to my Mouraria neighbour, Carole Garton, who not only proved to be the perfect guide to Lisbon and its rich history but also kindly accepted to edit the book manuscript in its various stages of becoming.

This book could not have existed without the numerous academic exchanges that I was lucky to engage in over the years. Directly or indirectly, many of my colleagues and friends have helped me in shaping the ideas and arguments that are expounded in this book in many ways: by reading and commenting on the chapter's draft versions, by offering me a platform to try out some of my ideas in seminars and conferences, by inviting me to contribute to books and journals and by enriching me with the wealth of their own research. For their feedback, comments, questions, criticisms and ideas I am particularly grateful to (in alphabetical order): Ash Amin, Arjun Appadurai, Julie Archambault, Sylvie Ayimpam, Jean-François Bayart, Asaf Bayat, Gautam Bhan, Jochen Becker, Luce Beeckmans, Bjorn Enge Bertselsen, Jesper Bjarnesen, Peter Bloom, Jacky Bouju, Lindsay Bremner, Lard Buurman, Teresa Caldeira, Andrea Ceriana Mayneri, Brenda Chalfin, Armando Cutolo, Veena Das, Bruno De Meulder, Hansjörg Dilger, Andreas Eckert, Johannes Fabian, Angela Ferreira, Kristien Geenen, Wenzel Geissler, Peter Geschiere, Knut Graw, Kim Gurney, Jane Guyer, Amanda Hammar, Thomas Hendriks, Mathieu Hilgers, James Holston, Nancy Rose Hunt, Deborah James, Bogumil Jewsiewicki, Luca Jourdan, Joanna Kusiak, Jean La Fontaine, Johan Lagae, Michael Lambek, Peter Lambertz, Brian Larkin, Christian Lund, Colin McFarlane, Dominique Malaquais, Bettina Malcomess, Adeline Masquelier, Achille Mbembe, Elikia M'Bokolo, Birgit Meyer, Pedro Monaville, Valentin Mudimbe, Martin Murray, Garth Myers, Morten Nielsen, Thierry Nlandu, Joël Noret, Sarah Nuttall, Juan Obarrio, Stefania Pandolfo, Sue Parnell, Pierre Petit, Edgar Pieterse, Steve Pile, Charles Piot, Kacper Poblocki, Ruth Prince, Katrien Pype, Vyjayanthi Rao, Jennifer Robinson, Clara Saraiva, Ramon Sarro, Surabhi Sharma, Abdoumaliq Simone, Annika Teppo, Antonio Tomas, Joseph Tonda, Noémi Tousignant, Erik Trovalla, Ulrika Trovalla, Léon Tsambu, Mats Utas, Jan Van den Broeck, Geertrui Vannoppen, David Van Reybrouck, Koen Van Synghel, Joshua Walker, Vanessa Watson, Mathew Wilhelm-Solomon, Eric Worby, James Williams, André Yoka Lye Mudaba and Austin Zeiderman.

Finally, there is home, our own ground zero, without which no departures and no returns would be possible. Ann and Rosa, thanks for having given us the space, time, love and encouragement that made it all possible.

Excerpts from this book have already been published, although often in rather different forms. Part of Chapter Two was previously published in *Global Horizon. Expectations of migration in Africa and the Middle East*, a book volume edited by Knut Graw and Samuli Schielke (Leuven University Press, 2012). Chapter Three is loosely based on three separate recent publications. One appeared in a special issue on 'confusion' that was guest edited by Jane Guyer for the journal *Social Dynamics* (2015); another was published in a special issue that Veena Das and Shalini Randeria guest edited for *Current Anthropology* (2015), while a third part of the chapter is a much expanded version of a short commentary I wrote for a curated collection on 'infrastructure' that was co-edited by Jessica Lockrem and Adonia Lugo for *Cultural Anthropology* (2012). Chapter Five went through several metamorphoses of which various versions made it to print, most recently in Veena Das and Clara Han's *Living and Dying in the Contemporary World: A Compendium* (University of California Press 2015). Finally, an embryonic version of the Bylex section in Chapter Seven was co-authored by Koen Van Synghel and published in the book *Rogue Urbanism: Emergent African Cities*, co-edited by Edgar Pieterse and Abdoumaliq Simone (Jacana / African Centre for Cities, 2013). A much shorter first version of the Tower section in the same chapter was published in the book catalogue *Africa. Architecture, Culture, Identity* (2015) on the occasion of the AFRICA exhibition that took place at the Louisiana Museum of Modern Art from 25 June to 25 October 2015.

2. The Last Post: Congo, (Post)colonialism and Urban Tales of Unrest

FIRST POST, also called 'Reveille', is a military bugle call, used to wake soldiers at sunrise. The name comes from 'réveille' (or 'réveil'), the French word for 'wake up'.

LAST POST was originally a bugle call used in British army camps to signal the end of the day. The name derives from the practice of playing a bugle call at all the sentry posts around such a camp at the end of the day. Today the 'Last Post' is played as a final farewell at military funerals, symbolizing the fact that the duty of the dead soldier is over and that he can rest in peace.

'The world of the living contains enough marvels and mysteries as it is; marvels and mysteries acting upon our emotions and intelligence in ways so inexplicable that it would almost justify the conception of life as an enchanted state.' (Conrad 1962 [1917]: v)

REVEILLE: THE FIRST POST, AN OUTPOST OF PROGRESS

Joseph Conrad wrote *An Outpost of Progress* in 1896, just a few years before his celebrated novel *The Heart of Darkness* came out in 1902. He first fictionalised some of his life experiences in Congo in this short story and it was included in his *Tales of Unrest* collection (Conrad 1898). As poignant as its famous successor, *An Outpost of Progress* can be read as a psychological thriller as well as a political statement undermining the very idea of empire. Conrad gives the reader an account of two white traders, Kayerts and Carlier, who are put in charge of an ivory trading station along an unnamed river easily identified as the Congo River. In all likelihood, the station itself was modelled on *Léopoldville*, a trading post founded by Henry Morton Stanley in 1882 next to Kinshasa, a small village under the authority of chief Ngobila.

This historical colonial context forms the backdrop of Conrad's fictional narrative, but as will become apparent, fiction and fact are often tightly intertwined in the context of Congo. Kayerts and Carlier begin to feel slightly uneasy and on their own soon after the steamer that had brought them disappears over the horizon of Stanley Pool, the vast inland sea that the Congo River forms at this point. At first, they enjoy discussing the few books they have with them and from time to time they receive the visit of 'Gobila', the old chief of the neighbouring village, with whom they get on well. They also find some old copies of a 'home paper' left by the previous stationmaster, who died of a fever and lies buried in the yard.

> 'That print discussed what it was pleased to call "Our Colonial Expansion" in high-flown language. It spoke much of the rights and duties of civilization, of the sacredness of the civilizing work, and extolled the merits of those who went about bringing light, and faith and commerce to the dark places of the earth. Carlier and Kayerts read, wondered, and began to think better of themselves. Carlier said one evening, waving his hand about, "In a hundred years, there will be perhaps a town here. Quays, and warehouses, and barracks, and — and — billiard-rooms. Civilization, my boy, and virtue — and all. And then, chaps will read that two good fellows, Kayerts and Carlier, were the first civilized men to live in this very spot!"' (Conrad 1961 [1898]: 94-95)

In spite of this comforting thought, it soon becomes painfully clear that Kayerts and Carlier are not really up to the job. They have no idea how to go about the heavenly mission of 'bringing light, and faith and commerce to the dark places of the earth.' In a way they prefigure Vladimir and Estragon, the tragicomic characters from Beckett's play 'Waiting for Godot', as all Kayerts and Carlier seem able to do is to sit and wait for the steamer to return. A deep silence falls between them and, as time goes by, they grow increasingly aware that they are out of their depth, not in control of events and totally dependent on their 'nigger', Makola, (who maintains that his name is Henry Price), their very own Caliban or Friday, who, 'taciturn and impenetrable', despises his two white bosses.

> 'They lived like blind men in a large room, aware only of what came in contact with them (and of that only imperfectly), but unable to see the general aspect of things. The river, the forest, all the great land throbbing with life, were like a great emptiness. Even the brilliant sunshine disclosed nothing intelligible. Things appeared and disappeared before their eyes in an unconnected and aimless kind of way. The river seemed to come from nowhere and flow nowhither. It flowed through a void.' (Conrad 1961 [1898]: 92)

Foreshadowing the fate of Conrad's best-known character, the infamous Mr. Kurtz in *The Heart of Darkness*, Carlier and Kayerts are overtaken by what they call 'the unusual' and slowly go out of their minds.

It is this Africa of the second half of the nineteenth century that has become the most powerful and emblematic topos in the Western collective imagination and representation of the historical process of colonisation. It is not only the Africa of Joseph

Conrad's Congo and his characters Carlier, Kayerts and Kurtz, but also that of Henry Morton Stanley, Livingstone, Casement and Morel, Leopold II of Belgium, the 1878 Berlin conference and the ensuing 'Scramble for Africa.' As Kevin Dunn (2003) has pointed out, it is the screen of the 'discursive landscape' of this nineteenth-century Congo that still haunts Western imaginings and re-imaginings of Congo and therefore of Africa as a whole. Through this discourse, one can draw a straight line from the first to the last post: from the beginning of the colonial era, when Congo is depicted as a hopelessly backward, cruel and savage 'heart of darkness', a ruthless colonial enterprise, a place where rubber is soaked in blood (Vangroenweghe 1986) and where European travellers, explorers and administrative agents go 'out of their minds', to paraphrase Fabian (2000), all the way across to the postcolonial present, wedged between 'hope and despair' (Deibert 2013). Here Congo is still largely perceived as a country that continues 'in the footsteps of Mr. Kurtz' (Wrong 2001), still haunted by Leopold's ghost (Hochschild 1998) and its Mobutist reincarnation (Michel 1999); a violent land now defined as 'Africa's broken heart', where blood continues to run through its many rivers (Butcher 2007) and the neo-colonial horror of a New Barbarism continues to thrive; where people keep 'dancing in the glory of monsters' and warlords (Stearns 2011); where the forces of neo-liberal globalisation rage in their most brutal and unchecked forms and the dead have by now become so numerous they can no longer be put to rest.[1]

If colonialism is to be understood as a space producing both physical and cultural death (Taussig 1992), then all recent books, films and articles on the subject catering mainly to larger non-academic audiences seem to suggest that the colonial enterprise produced its ultimate mass grave in Congo. With a few exceptions (see for example Van Reybrouck 2014), they also seem to indicate that Congo's postcolonial reality is best

The impossible is not Congolese

defined as an endless afterlife, a *post mortem* world (De Boeck 1998) situated beyond the grave of colonisation and born from the tomb of its assassinated first post-independence leader, Patrice Lumumba, that other spectre from the past that continues to haunt the present.[2] In darker moments of doubt, it appears as if more than five decades after the short period of *réveil*, from the Fanonian *grande nuit* to the sunrise of independence, the only possibility open to Congolese citizens consists of picking up a bugle and playing the Last Post over this postcolonial graveyard as it rots away in the 'shadow' of the neo-liberal global world order (cf. Ferguson 2006).

In many respects, the legacy of the nineteenth-century discursive landscape about Congo, with the strength of stereotypical imaginings of Africa, is so powerful that it can render the real physical reality of Africa invisible and make it as impossible for us as it was for Kayerts and Carlier to see 'the general aspect of all things' as they really are in contemporary Congo. In that respect, Conrad's *An Outpost of Progress*, and later *The Heart of Darkness*, proved to be almost visionary, programmatic texts in which the author does not just describe a specific historical moment of colonisation in Central Africa. Above all else, these texts deal with a number of key themes that were crucial to the colonial encounter but have also retained their relevance in the ambivalent postcolonial universe that has emerged in Congo since. Essentially, these themes linger over issues concerning identity, alterity, inequality and diversity. These are issues that also involve the significance of belonging, place and displacement, as well as the meanings attached to the never-ending production of margins, difference and the hybrid, in an increasingly globalising world where the intrusion of colonialism formed an earlier but decisive moment. Generally speaking, what is covered and foreshadowed here are the ambiguities, paradoxes, struggles, attractions, fears, fantasies, hidden conflicts and open clashes; the complex interplay between hegemonic and counter-hegemonic practices and discourses that punctuate and define power relations in the laborious cohabitation between the West and this part of Africa.

If Leopold's Congo Free State epitomised the brutal workings of nineteenth-century colonialism to the full, the Belgian colonial era that followed this period (from 1908 to 1960) also constituted a textbook example of what the enterprise of formal colonisation stood for. Subsequently, Congo became the most important icon of the decolonisation struggle, but only for a brief moment. As such, it occupies a special place in the writings of Aimé Césaire, Frantz Fanon and others in the foundational gene-ration of the postcolonial theoretical canon. The euphoric moment of Congo's independence — a historic moment that crystallised around the prophet-like figure of Lumumba — presented a whole continent with the chance to dream of alternative African futures; a possibility that continues to inspire many, even if the dream has often been transformed into a nightmare since then. But let us start with the Belgian colonial period first.

THE POSTMAN ALWAYS RINGS TWICE:
FROM LEOPOLD'S CONGO FREE STATE TO THE BELGIAN CONGO

Congo went through fifty (1908-1960) formative but, at various levels, also very destructive years of formal Belgian colonisation between its infamous Leopoldian beginnings and its often bleak present; between the emblematic image of a brutal nineteenth-century trading post economy and the violent economies of extraction that Mobutu's long and ruinous reign put in place and which still mark life in today's postcolonial state.

It is perhaps Congolese writer and scholar V.Y. Mudimbe who has best succeeded in dissecting the workings and methods of colonialism as applied to the Belgian Congo. A number of his widely acclaimed books, such as *The Invention of Africa* (1988) and *The Idea of Africa* (1994a), attest to this. But Mudimbe's lucid analysis of Belgian colonial politics also remains very informative in his internationally less known French writings, such as *L'odeur du père* (1982), and the fascinating autobiographical *Le corps glorieux des mots et des êtres* (1994b). Even though the formal Belgian colonial period represented but a brief moment in the history of Congo (and Africa), it created the possibility of radically new types of discourse about African traditions and cultures, and these are the discourses Mudimbe lays bare.

In essence, according to Mudimbe,[3] colonising means organising, classifying and ordering (from the Latin *colere*: to design, to cultivate). The practice of colonisers (those exploiting a territory by dominating a local majority) was strongly marked by the tendency to redefine non-European societies and turn them into fundamentally European constructs. In a Foucauldian reading of this colonising effort, Mudimbe anatomises that process by focussing on three phases which play a crucial role in any colonising process: acquisition, domination and exploitation of physical space; domestication and reformation of the colonial subjects' mental space; and transformation along Western lines of precolonial modes of political and, above all, economic organisation. These are what constitute the core of the structure of colonisation. Each is accompanied by specific technologies of domination and control. Obviously, these technologies often imply the use of brute force. It is no coincidence, for example, that the '*chicotte*', which is a specific kind of whip, occupies a central place in the Congolese collective memory of the Belgian colonial presence in the Congo Free State and later (cf. Peffer 2013).

Even more importantly, colonising techniques involved a much more covert, symbolic violence through their use of different sorts of 'sequestrating' methods to control, punish and reward colonial subjects and, in the process, colonise their minds and redefine their thoughts. A colonising tool that proved much more powerful and effective in achieving this than the whip was the 'colonial library' (Mudimbe, 1994a: 213), the West's knowledge production, which was deposited in and transmitted through the technology of the 'book'. In this way, the Bible became a very effective colonising instrument, together with maps, for example, or the totalising register of the census. The last two effectively allowed colonisers to take hold of and tie down a dominated territory in one document, thereby localising, categorising and ranking 'tribes', races and belief systems, and eventually redefining 'culture' in terms of governance and administration. In this respect, more than physical violence grafted onto the bodies of unruly colonial subjects, colonial violence was essentially a mental violation, characterised by the alienating violence of the mimetic, inherent in the attempt to redefine Africans along Western lines.

This more diffuse colonial violence manifested itself in the imposition of new modes of spatial organisation, new time frames (imposed by state and church), a new labour division and work ethics, and new moral matrices which intervened in the most intimate aspects of indigenous life, its social organisation, belief systems and the moral economy of its body politics (in terms of hygiene, sexuality, clothing and diet). It was, in short, the violence of being turned into 'mimic men' (Naipaul 1969) and 'black skins with white masks' (Fanon 1952), and of being matriculated as '*évolués*', a specific status for 'advanced' blacks in the Belgian Congo, granted by the *Commission du Statut des Congolais civilisés* (Sohier 1949; see also Maquet 1949).

In this way, Mudimbe lays bare the foundations of colonial discourse as an apparatus to define racial, cultural and historical differences and create a 'subordinate' space. This strategy is authorised by the Western production of a certain 'Africanist' knowledge concerning a stereotypical but antithetically defined relationship between coloniser and colonised. In such Africanist discourse the African continent is defined by means of negative statements which lead to a definition of Africa as a pathological case and a field of lack, thereby enabling the construction of a colonial master-and-subordinate relationship that allows the coloniser to define the colonised as inferior, or inadequate, and therefore in need of being colonised. Mudimbe thus reveals how Africa is 'invented' in the West. His work localises the epistemological locus of that invention, and its continuing relevance for contemporary (Western and African) discourses about Africa in general and Congo in particular.

While plantation and labour camps are certainly crucial spaces of investigation to understand the deep impact of all these colonising strategies and moves, it is perhaps the city that exemplifies most strongly the Belgian colonial attempt to transform and re-programme Central Africa in its own image. In the first half of the twentieth century, the urban setting becomes the main scene on which the colonial intervention is played out most forcefully. Kayerts and Carlier were right about one thing. Even though their own story failed to end well, the river *did* stop flowing through a void and their modest 'outpost of progress' next to the grave of the first station master became a town indeed, and what a town it is. Kinshasa is a vibrant city that has grown into one of the African continent's largest urban conglomerations today. In the literature about urban Africa, this megalopolis 'that does not respond to reason' and in which 'everything that cannot exist flourishes', as the Angolan writer José Edouardo Agualusa puts it in his novel *Barroco Tropical* (Agualusa 2009: 250), this urban giant which others have described as 'the quintessential postcolonial African city' (Pieterse, 2010: 1) and 'one of the most drastic cities of the world' (Simone 2010a: 291), has emerged as the trope of tropical baroque *par excellence*, a radical instance of the superlative, of excess and the 'too much'. Home to a population of more than ten million today, which makes it Africa's second largest city south of the Sahara, Kinshasa is also the fastest-growing African city in absolute terms with 4 million more inhabitants expected by 2020, a 46 per cent increase over its 2010 population of 8.7 million (cf. UN Habitat 2010).

None of this unbridled growth was foreseeable in 1878, when Stanley started to set up four stations along the Congo River that were to be manned by 150 European and American officials and supplied by four steamers. In these early years, while Savorgnan de Brazza was busy claiming land on the opposite bank of the Congo River in the name

of the French, the most important post, the Stanley Pool trading station, quickly grew into a thriving model station and became the administrative centre of the Stanley Pool District in 1886.

In fact, Stanley's first posts were far from isolated, and the villages surrounding them far less pristine than Conrad's description of chief Gobila's village leads us to believe. The trading stations were erected at what was actually a major meeting point between caravans coming from the Lower Congo and the navigable upstream part of the river that reaches deep into the heart of Central Africa. Already at the beginning of the nineteenth century, and even centuries before as testified by the writings of seventeenth-century Italian missionaries in search of the Teke king, Makoko, the villages around the Pool formed the regional core of a large market system with wide-ranging connections, a bustling place where goats, fish, salt and also slaves and European goods were traded by the local populations.

But all this activity was a far cry from the town that these trading stations were soon to become. In Conrad's *Outpost of Progress*, the storehouse of the station manned by Kayerts and Carlier is called 'the fetish' and this, as Conrad remarks, is 'because of the spirit of civilization it contained'. In the next decades, the spirit of this new civilisational fetish called 'colonial capitalism' was indeed unleashed in full force. Between 1885 and the First World War, the heart of present-day Kinshasa rapidly formed around an axis of about ten kilometres long between two sites close to where Stanley and his men first set foot: the military and commercial centre of Ngaliema/Kintambo to the west and Kalina (now known as Gombe) to the east.[4]

By the end of the nineteenth century, the Kintambo and Kalina outposts had developed from small trading stations into the booming towns of Leopoldville and Kinshasa, or Léo-Ouest and Léo-Est respectively. By 1900, this Leopoldville-Kinshasa agglomeration, already connected by a railway and a road, which became Kinshasa's main *Boulevard du 30 juin* after Congo's independence from Belgium in 1960, had considerably expanded. Not only had it engulfed the former fishermen's villages of Kintambo and Kinshasa, but it was also steadily pushing its way east toward Ndolo, turning that whole riverine zone along the left bank of the Stanley (now Malebo) Pool district into an industrial area and a trans-shipment hub for goods and raw materials to be dispatched to the Belgian metropole. Meanwhile, the white population, most of which consisted of men, had grown to a thousand. By the early 1920s, the riverbank was lined with at least eighty storehouses, belonging to several industrial enterprises and trading companies . And when this sprawling city finally became the administrative capital of the Belgian Congo after the colonial administration was transferred from Boma in 1929, all that was left of the 'pristine' village of chief Gobila was its name. Today's infrastructurally derelict but lively port of Beach Ngobila continues to be one of the main gateways to Kinshasa.

The industrial growth of the city required increasing quantities of cheap labour from the rural hinterlands and attracted people from all over the Belgian Congo. From 1907 onwards, this population was housed in a rapidly expanding number of camps and 'indigenous' living areas, which were conceived as huge labour reservoirs for the emerging industrial activities along Stanley Pool as well as the commercial, administrative and residential 'white' urban areas of Gombe and Kitambo. The indigenous zones that emerged between 1907 and 1930 included Saint Jean (now Lingwala), Kinshasa and Barumbu on the eastern side, and Kintambo to the west (Fumunzanza 2011: 102). They were spatially demarcated from the city centre by the railway line between Gombe and Kintambo and an intricate patchwork of other spaces including strategically placed army barracks (such as the 1924 Leopold II garrison that would become notorious as Camp Militaire Lt. Col. Kokolo in the Mobutist period), cemeteries, a market, a zoo and large tracts of nondescript and empty no-man's-land. All these spaces were conceived by colonial urban planners as 'zones neutres' and 'zones tampons' (Beeckmans 2013; Toulier, Lagae and Gemoets 2010: 127). They drew a divisive line between various living areas, and formed effective buffers between *La Ville* (Gombe) and its 'indigenous' periphery, *La Cité* (cf. also De Boeck and Plissart 2004: 30ff; De Meulder 2000).

These zones of separation were largely responsible for the fact that the city spread out over a vast distance. Even today, in the historical heart of Kinshasa, many of these empty pockets of land have not yet undergone housing and construction densification. But in the colonial period, these buffers were above all meant to inscribe a spatial colour bar onto the city surface, even though from the 1930s onwards, the need for this segregationist colonial policy was often framed not in terms of race but through the lens of a sanitary discourse and in terms of public health.[5]

In 1932, *Les Editions de l'avenir colonial belge*, a publisher based in Leopoldville, published a satirical 'oriental tale' called *Chroniques de Stinkopolis* (a word coined from the Dutch 'stinken' [to reek] and the Greek 'polis'). In this tale the author, a certain Irneh-Bin-Desireh (the *nom de plume* of Henri Stevelinck, a Belgian working in Leopoldville at the time) urges the urban authorities, and more specifically the *Comité Urbain de Léopoldville*, to create a 'clean, nice and healthy city' (*une ville propre, agréable et saine*) and tackle 'the wrong that the actual state of things causes the city', namely the fact that its 'inferior population' (*population inférieure*, also referred to as the 'sons of Cham') was endangering the health of the urban residents by openly selling and preparing indigenous foodstuffs 'as nutritive as they are nauseating' (*aussi alimentaires que nauséabondes*). Calling for a ban on such sales in the city's streets, 'especially where they were undesirable' (*particulièrement là où ils étaient indésirables*), Stevelinck's cautionary tale presents a plea for the construction of modern 'abattoirs' and 'extra-muros entrepôts'.[6]

The desire to rid the city of activities and people deemed 'unhygienic' is also reflected in the official discourse of the colonial urban planners with regard to their

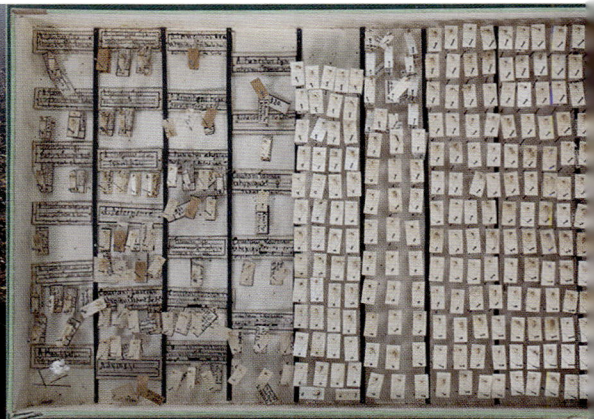

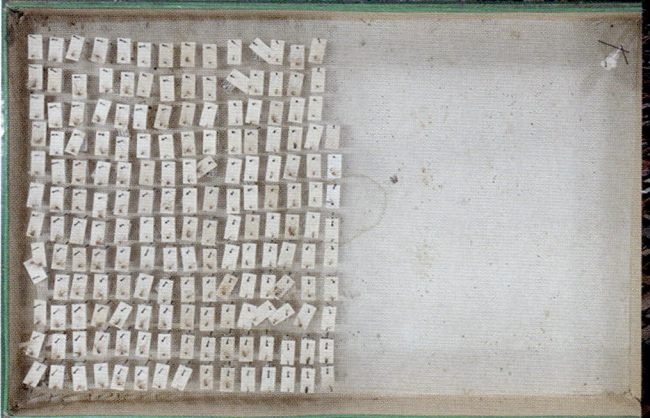

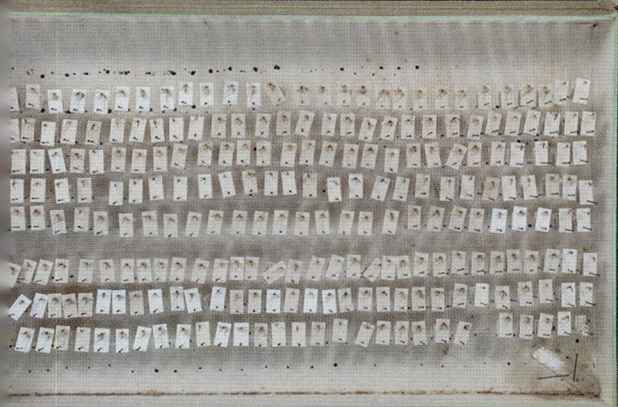

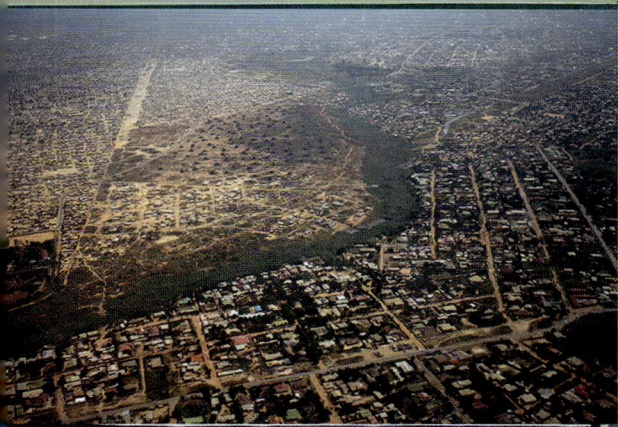

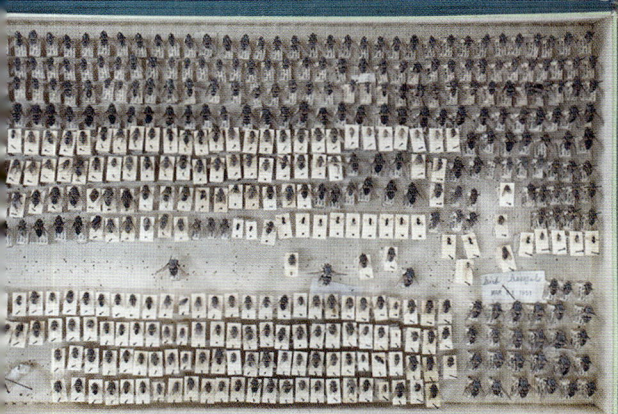

LUBUMBASH NO1
1929
lutte contre les mouches : chaque travailleur
à la distribution quotidienne de la ration
doit apporter 50 mouches.
30 octobre 1929.

Anti-mosquito campaign: each worker has to bring in 50 mosqu toes during the daily food distribution. Lubumbashi 30 October 1929 zoning strategies as from the 1930s. In many cities in the Belgian Congo, for example, the width of the corridors separating European and African living quarters was often determined by the distance mosquitoes can supposedly fly so as to prevent the transmission of 'indigenous' diseases such as malaria to the white residential areas. This is well illustrated on a 1929 photo from the Gécamines archives in Lubumbashi. It shows two Congolese workers next to a heap of dead flies and mosquitoes. In those days, every Gécamines employee had to bring in fifty dead mosquitoes a day or else would not receive his daily ration of food.

Contemporary aerial photos of Lubumbashi show how the presence of these corridors remains very visible in the geography of today's cityscape. In Leopoldville too, the corridors literally became '*cordons sanitaires*' to prevent the spread of tropical diseases. Even the underlying racial rationale was medicalised in this way, because the 'intermingling' of races was likewise deemed 'promiscuous', unhygienic and a danger to (white) public health.[7] And even though the borders between the two mirroring parts of the city, the European centre and the African periphery, were porous in the sense that Congolese were allowed into *La Ville* as 'boys', workers, watchmen, manual labourers and so on, the Congolese *main-d'oeuvre* or workers needed special permits to stay in the centre at night, or else they had to retreat to their own neighbourhoods at the end of the day. To this effect and until the Second World War, a night curfew was imposed on the city's inhabitants. It was announced by a bugle call, like a real Last Post, barring the city's African population from entering European neighbourhoods after 10pm (and vice versa to large extent).

In the first half of the twentieth century, Leopoldville thus rapidly grew into what was essentially a racially segregated, Janus-faced city; a city like a Bounty candy bar with a white heart and a surrounding layer of rapidly growing African satellite *cités* [indigenous quarters]. Throughout the colonial period, this growing presence was perceived not only as an economic necessity but also as a potential problem (cf. Capelle 1947). The African *cité* was closely monitored by the colonial administration while it remained, at the same time, a prime target of various missionary interventions.

Between the end of the Second World War and the final days of the Belgian colonial presence, Leopoldville's population multiplied tenfold: from 46,884 in 1940 to approximately 400,000 in 1960. By 1959, the African *cités* included Dendale (present-day Kasavubu), Ngiri-Ngiri, Bandalungwa, Kalamu, Lemba, Matete and Ndjili. These new neighbourhoods were the result of a large-scale housing scheme launched in 1949 by the Belgian colonial administration as part of their broader *Plan décennal pour le développement économique et social du Congo*. In less than ten years, between 1952 and 1960, more than 32,000 houses were built by the urban planners and architects of the newly-created *Office de Cités Africaines* (OCA) in an impressive effort to respond to the demographic explosion of the city and the increasing social unrest it engendered after the Second

World War. Although the white and more residential areas of Gombe were partly extended into Limete in the 1940s and 1950s, *La Ville* did not expand to the same extent after 1960, caught as it was between the Congo River on the city's western and northern side, and the growing belt of satellite *cités* on its eastern and south-western borders.

REVEILLE II: *DEBOUT CONGOLAIS*? [8]

As Fanon famously remarked in *The Wretched of the Earth* (1961), a book that quickly became the bible of the decolonisation movement, Africa is shaped like a revolver, and Congo is its trigger. Therefore, whoever has their finger on the trigger controls Africa. For a brief moment after it achieved its independence from Belgium, Congo became the hopeful icon of change for a whole generation of African nationalists, even more so than Algeria, where the liberation struggle had turned into such a bloody nightmare. It epitomised the possibility of independence and the promises embedded in the magical word *dipenda*, 'independence': the promise of freedom and a radical tabula rasa, and a totally new start. Independence brought about the longed-for materialisation of a 'post' in the literal sense of the word. It seemed to offer a clear break with the past and with the project of colonialism as a historical moment, a cultural practice and a mentality (cf. Appiah 1992).

Political leaders such as the legendary Lumumba, who became for a brief moment Congo's first post-independence prime minister, exemplified to the full the winds of change sweeping through the continent over half a century ago. Patrice Lumumba embodied the hopes that the decolonisation process brought to the African continent as a whole. *Dipenda* created such a powerful trope of hope that when Laurent Kabila took power in 1997, he returned to the politics and aesthetics of that defining moment in an attempt to force history into a loop to re-run the country's past in an alternative future; almost as if Congo were a huge Monopoly board game and history offered chance cards to return to 'start'.

But together with these hopes and dreams, Congo also exemplified the dark side: the disillusion, tragedy and despair that accompanied the postcolonial dream right from the start. Aimé Césaire described the tragic figure of Patrice Lumumba in *A Season in Congo*, a play that premiered in the Brussels municipality of Anderlecht in 1967. In this play, Lumumba is portrayed as a poet-leader who heightened African awareness, but failed to unify his own country, and control Africa's trigger. In describing Lumumba's assassination, Césaire prophetically envisions all the failures and disappointments still to come: dictatorship, corruption, ruin, 'The horror!'.

There are different ways to think about these failures. For Mudimbe, the structure of colonisation created a system of paradigmatic oppositions (between tradition and modernity, for example, or between oral and written culture, agrarian and industrial societies, countryside and city, or subsistence economies and capitalism) that inescapably continues to structure the way in which we reflect upon processes of modernisation and progress, and thus upon the place of 'Africa' in the world today. A great deal of attention continues to focus on this passage from past to future in Marxist theories that were so fashionable in Africa in the 1960s and 70s, as well as in today's mainstream development ideologies. But according to Mudimbe (1988:4), this presupposed evolutionary jump from one extreme to another is actually misleading and fails to provide us with an accurate picture of evolutions on the African continent today. Indeed, progress and development sometimes seem to lie buried in an irretrievable past rather than in a future filled with promise. Consider, for example, the case of the Congolese (and Zambian) Copperbelt. As Sammy Baloji and Faustin Linyekula so powerfully illustrate in their 2007 video piece *Mémoire*, which highlights Katanga's post-industrial landscape, little now remains of the infrastructures created by industrial developments that shot up in mining towns such as Lubumbashi, Kolwezi and Likasi during the 1920s and 30s. (Baloji 2007. See also Ferguson 1999; Mususa 2012). Faced with these post-developmental worlds, in which the usual horizon of the future has been replaced by something else, the conventional notions of 'development' and 'progress' no longer offer workable solutions. All they seem to do is to lock the here and now of African realities into a realm of impossibility, projecting classic ideologies and standardised forms of solution and teleology onto an imagined but non-existent future. And that, for Mudimbe, seems to be where Africa has landed ever since the start of colonisation: in a diffuse, intermediary and marginalising space, a non-place, a paradoxical locus between a so-called African tradition that is often no more than a faint echo of an irretrievably distant past and a colonialist modernity that only offers the illusion of development. For him, this intermediary space is that of the slum, poverty, malnourishment, illiteracy, demographic instability, the breakdown of stabilising family and kinship structures, sharp social and economic disparities, dictatorial regimes operating under the flag of 'democracy', lost religious traditions and new religious regimes that re-colonise the African mind.

THE LAST POST: URBAN LIFE, THE LEGACIES OF URBAN COLONIAL MODERNITY AND THE ADVENT OF NEO-LIBERAL URBAN DEVELOPMENTS

If the first post of colonialism was an outpost, its last post and most important final legacy was — and remains — the city. In a similar vein to Mudimbe's reading, a considerable number of policymakers, politicians, urban planners, architects, sociologists and demographers seem to consider this legacy to be a predominantly negative one. Seen as a shadow of its former colonial self, a *Kin la poubelle* (Kin, the rubbish bin) rather than the *Kin la belle* (Kin, the beautiful) it used to be, many people appear to have given up on the city itself. It is as if Kinshasa has become what Charles Piot called elsewhere a place of 'remoteness' (Piot 1999); as if cities such as Kinshasa, overarched by the figure of the 'slum', have become 'shadow cities' (Neuwirth 2006) that have somehow fallen off the map of the global cityscape. At best, Kinshasa and other cities in Congo, and more widely across the African continent, only seem to exist as eccentric landmarks in a planetary geography of slums, filled with 'excess' or 'surplus humanity' (Davis 2006). At worst, they are considered ungoverned and ungovernable 'population bombs' that pose a major 'security threat' to the global community (Liotta and Miskel 2012). Along similar lines, Kilcullen (2013) sees the 'peri-urban slum settlements' of the Middle East, Africa, Latin America and Asia as the scene for a 'coming age of urban guerrilla', a bold claim that Kilcullen enforces by a quote from Attali according to whom 'mafias will control immense zones outside the law (this is already the case) in Rio, Lagos, Kinshasa and Manilla.' (Attali 2011: 132). Kilcullen, Davis, and Liotta and Miskell all explicitly use Kinshasa, along with Lagos and other urban centres in the Global South, as examples that epitomise dangerous and disastrous urban environments. Their harsh, dystopian and apocalyptic reading of the urbanscape in the Global South is remarkably similar, although Davis approaches urban life from a radically opposed ideological direction in comparison to Liotta, Miskell and Kilcullen.[9] Whereas the analyses presented by the latter three portray the urban resident of the Global South as the ultimate embodiment of a newly emerging ultra-dangerous terrorist figure in an increasingly Mad Max-like world that is also taking over the cities of the Global North, Davis tends to see the same urban resident as the victim of corrupt leadership, institutional failure and disastrous IMF policies. More curative approaches to the postcolonial urban space (mostly from the urban development policy literature) have also tended to construct the inhabitants of these urban worlds as vulnerable and 'passive victims of inexorably structural processes beyond their control' (Murray and Myers 2006: 3; cf. also Beall and Fox 2009). In these approaches, urban dwellers are often reduced to powerlessness and alienation, remaining strangely devoid of agency and the possibility for enunciation, creative potential and communal action.

It could indeed be argued that the Congolese city has never fully belonged to its inhabitants. It has never grown clear, for example, what the notion of the term 'polis', with its double meaning of urban community and of political community, might actually mean in this particular context, because a majority of Kinois have never enjoyed any officially recognised right to the city. As mentioned before, access to the city was carefully controlled and regulated by the urban authorities during the colonial period. And in many ways the segregationist colonial city continued to retain some of its former meanings even after the sun of independence rose over the country. As will be discussed in more detail elsewhere in this book, much of the new urban development taking place in Kinshasa and other cities in Congo clearly illustrates the fact that the polis was and often continues to be a place of exclusion.

If the Congolese have never been fully recognised as '*citadins*' or city-dwellers, they have never been granted the full status of '*citoyens*' or citizens either. Under Belgian colonial rule the Congolese were defined not as citizens but as subjects (see Mamdani 1996), and were thereby excluded from full participation in the political life of the polis. In Mobutu's Zaire, a new and seemingly more inclusive notion of '*citoyenneté*' or citizenship was generated, but at the same time, Mobutu presented himself as the ultimate sovereign in a country in which the law remained in force but gradually lost all substantive meaning. This produced a displacement both of state and citizens; a displacement and a dislocation of the polis that continues to reverberate nowadays on many levels of everyday life in Congo. In an attempt to sail into the neo-liberal wind that is currently blowing across the continent, the Congolese state has tried to reinvent itself in recent years. Or at least, it has been making gestures to demonstrate the possibility of such a makeover; but in the process, it seems to share with many of the neo-liberal urban reform and development plans it so eagerly embraces, the tendency to obliterate — conceptually if not physically — the local reality of its citizens' lives. Time and again, a number of common assumptions are evident in these policy engagements, governance practices and private investment frameworks. Above all, they are marked by a profound lack of attention to and total disregard for the small-scale connections, negotiations and decisions that people engage in on a daily basis in order to make a living and survive in the urban context. These concerns and policy challenges are exacerbated by the unintended effects of economic change, inadequate utilisation of empirical information in strategic management decisions and a complete indifference to the complexities of poverty and the myriad connections between and across divergent urban (and rural) spaces.

How does this translate into the current reality of the city? Until very recently, the 1949 Belgian *plan décennal,* or ten-year plan, was never followed by a further formalised governmental attempt to control, steer and guide Kinshasa's development. Compared to the 32.000 houses built by the colonial regime between 1952 and 1960, only 800 new houses were constructed by the Office National de Logement in 1971, and another 442 and 674 houses, in the *Cité Verte* and the *Cité Mama Mobutu* respectively, were added to that in 1986. Yet, after 1960, the city's population grew tremendously, and the number of *cités* and rural-urban municipalities (*communes urbano-rurales*) increased drastically. Existing *cités* further densified and expanded, while others were added: Selembao, Mont Ngafula, Makala, Ngaba, Kisenso, Malweka, Masina, Kimbanseke and Kinkole among others. Some of these post-1960s expansions, such as Kinkole, had already been planned by the Belgian colonial administration, but many others were added onto the existing urban core in a rather unplanned, chaotic fashion. This was not for lack of

urban master plans. Luce Beeckmans recently wrote in great detail about the history of the many postcolonial master plans that were conceived for Kinshasa between 1960 and today (Beeckmans 2013; see also Beeckmans and Lagae 2015). However, as becomes abundantly clear from her account, none of these plans and maps has ever been fully, if at all, implemented. And in the rare cases in which they were partially realised, they have never succeeded to produce the desired effect and proactively steer and engineer the city. At every attempt, the city itself seems to have overtaken and run away with the plans. Kinshasa, this indomitable beast, has been changing in size and direction at a far greater speed and on a much more impressive scale than these plans could ever have handled. In the end, most master plans have been bypassed and swept away by this tsunami of a city. Chasing after unrealisable urban utopias, they remained locked within the realm of the imaginary, and often never even left the offices of the urban planners who conceived them. Unknown and invisible to the city's residents, they often did not produce the desired effect on the ground.

In the meantime the city is unstoppable. With an estimated annual housing deficit of 240.000 (a housing shortage that amounted to two million units between 1999 and 2010), it continues to spread and expand west and south towards the Lower Congo, and east far beyond Ndjili, Kinshasa's national airport, towards the foot of the impressive Mangengenge mountain, the eastern gateway to the city. Unfolding as it does in a dis-organised, unplanned, chaotic, often random and ad hoc manner, this expansion has greatly impacted the quality of urban life in general, leaving the majority of a rapidly growing number of urban residents to fend for themselves. Erratic access to unreliable urban infrastructures and amenities, such as electricity and particularly water — a pre-cious commodity that many Kinois (the inhabitants of Kinshasa) have to struggle for on a daily basis — has also contributed to an increasing ruralisation of the city. Reaching across the formation period of high colonialism and its modernist ideals, Kinshasa has rejoined, to some extent, its earlier rural roots. Aided by a never-ending political and economic crisis, the city has ruralised, or re-ruralised, not only in terms of its social infrastructures and spheres of social interaction but also in terms of its economic survival and coping strategies, engendering various new types of agrarian urbanity.

La Ville remained a rather exclusive and expensive part of town after independ-ence, although today the divisions between *Ville* and *Cité* are no longer as clear-cut as they once were in colonial times. Even so, *La Ville* is still where the country's political and economical power centres are located, as are embassies, international hotels, fancy supermarkets and residential areas for expatriates and local political and economical elites. Many of Kinshasa's inhabitants still feel they are crossing an invisible but very tangible line when accessing the city centre (even if today the line is more strongly de-fined in social and economic terms than in terms of racial divisions). When trying to explain this feeling of trespassing to me, many of the residents of Masina, Ndjili and

other parts of the peripheral city I spoke to referred to a statue of Lumumba that was erected a decade ago at the *Échangeur* of Limete, a major roundabout on Boulevard Lumumba, the main road leading into *La Ville*. The statue portrays Lumumba with a raised hand to greet, salute and welcome the inhabitants to the city. However, for many of my interlocutors the statue conveyed a radically different message. For them, Lumumba was put there by the urban authorities as the gatekeeper to the city, raising his hand and telling the inhabitants of the surrounding *cités* in a loud, clear voice: 'You will not enter!' (*Okokota te*!). Stopping them in their tracks, the people's hero Lumumba, by an ironic twist of fate, thus prevents the slum dwellers of Kinshasa from crossing the borderline into the 'real' city, a place where they do not belong and which will never be theirs.

The exclusionist logic that informed colonial urban planning was never totally abandoned and, as will be further outlined in Chapter Seven, it has even made a spectacular return in recent years.

On 20 December 2013 FRANCE 24 journalist Alexandre Capron reported from downtown Kinshasa:

> 'Authorities in Kinshasa have launched a crackdown on street vendors who sell their wares along the capital's avenues. Though this was presented as a "pedagogical" operation, police ended up destroying and burning stalls on Wednesday morning. (...) Launched on December 11, this operation is part of a citywide cleanup effort meant to make the capital more attractive. The goal is to get rid of all the street markets where unlicensed vendors have set up shop. The authorities have said that they plan to replace these markets with green spaces.'[10]

The same press article also presented the account of an eyewitness:

> 'I heard screaming, and saw a huge fire blazing down the street. When I got closer, I saw several policemen turn over stalls and tear apart bags of flour, rice, and other food items. Others were stomping on the merchants' wares. An elderly woman was clinging to a wooden table in order to stop them from throwing it into the fire, while a policeman was pushing her violently. (...) Police officers even took crates of sardines and put them in one of their vehicles.'

Similar stories are regularly reported in local newspapers. For many years now, successive city governors have vowed to disrupt street life in order to 'clean up' the city. As the example above illustrates, and as I have personally witnessed on numerous occasions, this 'pedagogical' cleansing, this *assainissement des moeurs* [11] through a spatial rewriting of the street, often boils down to hard-handed and repressive politics of erasure by destroying 'irregular', 'anarchic' and unruly housing constructions, bulldozing street bars considered to be too close to the roadside, and banning from the street all containers, which Kinois regularly convert into little shops. The same happens to the small improvised street restaurants known as *malewa*. The women who work these *malewa* stalls are constantly harassed and chased off the street by policemen, and their stalls are destroyed (even though they often constitute these women's only source of income).

Having to suffer regularly the same fate are the many other makeshift and minimal infrastructures (usually no more than a plastic chair, a small table or a parasol) that allow urban dwellers to survive in a volatile street vendors' economy (selling cell phone credit cards and second-hand clothes, charging cell phone batteries, changing money, repairing cars). Urban authorities started to wage a war not only against these 'illegal' structures and activities but also against the very bodies of the people who perform or embody them. Kinshasa's street children (*bashege*) were among the first to fall victim to the state's renewed effort to sanitise and re-colonise the city by rewriting the city's public spaces and redefining who has a right or not to the street and to the city. In more ways than one, street kids embody and constitute the very physicality of Kinshasa's public space. That is why they sing: 'Our bodies belong to the state, but our souls to God' (*Nzoto ya Leta, molimo ya Nzambe*). When the state inscribes its violence onto the bodies of street children and street vendors, it is domesticating and recolonising the city's public spaces and imprinting it with its own revisionist logic.

'Sweeping the poor away' (Watson 2009) means that the same exclusionist dynamics are fuelling an even more outspoken attempt at redefining what a 'proper' city means today. During the campaign leading up to the 2006 presidential elections, President Kabila launched his *Cinq Chantiers* (Five Public Works) programme, which was renamed *Révolution de la modernité* (Revolution of Modernity) after the 2011 presidential elections. For the first time after decades of official neglect with regard to urban planning, and fifty years after the Belgian *plan décennal* ground to a halt, the *Cinq Chantiers* concept presented an outline of some sort of inclusive recovery plan for Congo as a whole, and summarised the government's pledge to modernise education, health care, road infrastructure, housing and access to electricity in the DRC. Predictably, these plans were welcomed with the necessary scepticism, but at the same time they also generated broad-based new feelings of hope, expectation and anticipation, as well as a certain collective willingness to suspend judgement concerning the government's capacity to tackle some of the most urgent infrastructural problems that cities in Congo have been facing for many decades. As attested by the anti-Kabila riots that swept through the streets of Kinshasa in February 2015, this suspension of disbelief was rather short-lived but it was definitely there in 2010, for this was the year in which Congo celebrated the fiftieth anniversary of its independence from Belgian colonial rule, and the *chantiers* appeared to be in full swing.

Downtown Kinshasa went through a radical facelift, which is still ongoing albeit at a slower pace, under the guidance of Chinese, Indian, Japanese, Korean and Pakistani architects, engineers and construction workers. All the trees on the main boulevards and major traffic arteries, such as the aforementioned Boulevard Lumumba, were cut down and adjacent gardens and fields destroyed. Roads and boulevards were widened to become eight-lane highways leading straight into the heart of the city. Some landmark buildings were embellished or restored, while others made way for new construction sites on an unprecedented scale, promising to bring new luxurious hotels, apartments, shopping malls and conference centres to the city centre. There even exists a

plan, so the city's rumour mill has it, to build a new viaduct connecting an upgraded Ndjili International airport with *La Ville* (and more precisely with its Pullman Grand Hotel, one of the two international hotels of downtown Kinshasa). The viaduct will follow the Congo river, and run over and above the heads of the hundreds of thousands of impoverished inhabitants of the municipality of Masina, commonly referred to as '*Chine Populaire*', the People's Republic of China, because it is so over-populated.

These attempts at a large scale infrastructural overhaul (part of which has indeed been realised in the meantime) went hand in hand with another new development. In Kinshasa, as elsewhere on the African continent (De Boeck 2011; Watson 2013), international investment funds and real estate groups have been pouring huge amounts of money into the construction of satellite cities, often built from scratch alongside existing cities. Similar developments are taking place or are being envisaged in some of Congo's other major cities, such as Lubumbashi. In reality, these new segregationist infrastructural spaces that are called 'cities' operate as zones of what Easterling terms 'extrastatecraft', a portmanteau term that describes 'the often undisclosed activities outside of, in addition to, and sometimes even in partnership with statecraft.' (Easterling 2014: 15). These spaces are built alongside existing urbanscapes, which are thereby defined as 'not cities'. Mainly conceived as huge gated communities run by means of specific bylaws for a newly emerging, but still largely hypothetical, African middle class that is supposed to be the beneficiary of the current economic Afro-optimism (cf. Ellis 2011) these new 'free zones' thus effectively generate new radical geographies of inclusion and exclusion.[12]

In Chapter Seven I will discuss in greater detail the birth of one such new city in Kinshasa: the *Cité du Fleuve* (along with other examples from Lubumbashi and other areas in Katanga). Declared by the government to be one of the flagships of its 'revolution of modernity', this private initiative consists of two artificial islands in the Congo River. These islands will supposedly become the new administrative and commercial city centre of Kinshasa, and as such will contribute significantly towards redefining the existing city with its ten million inhabitants as an urban fringe, a 'slum' or even 'village'. The implications of such an effort present interesting continuities as well as inversions from older colonial conceptualisations and bipolar models (cf. D'Ascenzo 2013).

In the Belgian Congo, the problem that the colonial administration faced was how to turn villagers into urbanites (even if these urbanites in reality became the inhabitants of a specific kind of inferior urban peripheries). In the colonial mindset, the 'village' was invariably constructed as a dark and static shadow-part of a dynamically developing city, imagined by the Belgian colonial administration as a *centre extra-coutumier*, a centre that defined itself as 'extra-local,' that is, as 'outside tradition'. This was an attempt to escape the weight of what was perceived by the coloniser to be the dark forces of autochthony and ethnicity; and an attempt at a new start for a radically different, more

enlightened type of urban society and a new kind of de-ethnicised urban denizen. The current neo-liberal developments that inscribe themselves on the surface of cities such as Kinshasa, however, seem to spring from the opposite starting point. Far from trying to work towards 'slum upgrading' and making gestures towards participatory urban planning strategies — even further removed from the policies of forced urbanisation that may currently be witnessed in the Chinese context, for example — the kickoff premise here seems to be how to get urban dwellers off the premises; how to write the masses of increasingly pauperised and 'villagised' urban dwellers out of the city; and how to reconvert them, at least conceptually if not physically, into villagers so as to evacuate the scene and set it up for a renewed, 'purer' and more exclusive modern urban setting in which the neo-liberal exurbia may become the central *urbs*.

In this respect, it is interesting to look at the website of Congo-Forêt, a private agro-business with close links to the *Cité du Fleuve* project.[13] Congo-Fôret holds a regional agricultural portfolio and its activities consist of converting 'virgin' savannah land into rubber plantations in Bandundu Province along the Kasai River, near the town of Dima, where the rubber-producing *Compagnie du Kasai* used to be based in colonial times. Congo-Forêt promotes its agricultural activities to possible investors in terms of responsible village-level ecological and human resources management. The latter consists of 'community involvement' aimed at upgrading the local living environment of 3,000 villagers. In 2011, the website of Congo-Forêt phrased it as follows:

'During 2010, Congo-Forêt opened a store (Meikles Dima) and small club that is accessible by the whole community on the property overlooking the Kasai River. This meeting place has grown in popularity over the past few months and often crowded with families who bring their children for entertainment. Judging from the distances that people are travelling to our property, it is clear that there are very few places that people can go to and certainly no place that offers entertainment for the children. Our vision is to expand the store and entertainment area to offer families a safe play area for their children and a means for them to interact and develop their special awareness abilities (which are severely lacking according to UNICEF) on simple apparatus.'[14]

So this means that we are back where we started: more than fifty years after Congo's independence, its cities are being reframed and re-conceptualised in neo-colonial segregationist terms as residual spaces. Similarly, the 'threat' posed by its urban citizens is neutralised by redefining them as childlike villagers. As such, they are conceptually barred from the future of the *Cité du Fleuve* and relegated to the past of the outpost and the village. Physically, they are subjected to forced relocations that also aim at triggering 'shadow evacuations' to rural hinterlands. These then serve as the renewed decor for reinvented *comptoir* economies with strong Leopoldian overtones.[15]

The concepts of 'village' or 'slum' as used in current debates about the possibilities of urban reform (cf. Rao 2006; Roy 2011) often function as huge black holes that suck in and completely obliterate their content, namely the resourcefulness and determination of millions of urban residents who, much like black South Africans under Apartheid, are being reduced to invisibility. They become 'shadow people' (Pillay 2007), subjected to the harsh cleansing methods of their own government and to the modes of 'shadow governing' (Wedel 2011) that neo-liberal urban reform plans and neoconservative governance policies seem to favour.

And yet, somehow, between these two obliterating machines, the urban dwellers themselves are never fully effaced. They manage, on the contrary, to negotiate success-fully everyday life in multiple urban locales and through often complex urban tactics and strategies that succeed to 'displace' the state and thereby change these powerful modes of urban governance in the process. If there is still a strong tendency to frame cities in the Global South as 'urban shadows' on the 'edges of urban theory' (McFarlane 2008: 341; see also De Boeck, Cassiman and Van Wolputte 2010), there is also a growing body of literature that attempts to re-centre the city and make 'the shadows smaller' (Herrick 2014: 556) by focusing on the ways in which people actively imagine and construct meaningful urban lives for themselves.[16] As this recent literature suggests

and documents, it is in these southern urban arenas that people most actively re-territorialise and reclaim space, develop their own specific forms of urbanism, remake and reinvent notions of community building, and infuse the order of the city more generally with their own praxis, values, moralities and temporal dynamics.

In the decades of the post-independence period, this process, which started on the margins of Kinshasa, has engulfed the city as a whole, signalling a move away from the physical and mental mimetic 'place' of colonialism (its spatial layout, work ethos, time-management and language, which is French). Unhampered by any kind of formal industrialisation or economic development, the city has also bypassed, redefined or smashed the post-independence nationalist rhetorics that were stamped onto its surface. It has done so spatially, in terms of its architectural and urban development, as well as in terms of its socio-cultural and economic imprint, making us question standard ideologies and teleologies of urban development, and forcing us to reconsider familiar notions of (post-)colonialist modernity. As I will discuss later, the city also compels the neo-liberal dynamics that are currently reframing urban (and rural) sites throughout Congo to adapt to the on-the-ground realities of the Congolese cityscape. It is the city itself that forces us to look 'beyond neo-liberalism', thereby inviting us to re-theorise it in a different way (Parnell and Robinson 2012).

In the remainder of this introductory chapter, I will outline how this book intends to contribute to these theoretical re-workings by offering some possible routes for 'bringing the city back in' and rethinking the 'partial connections' and 'shifting contexts', as Marilyn Strathern (1991, 1995) once termed them, between different scales, sites and times; various material, mental, moral and affective worlds; various cultural sites and economic and political territories in which people's lives unfold; contexts in which they move and from which they attempt to create collectivities, publics and shared 'platforms of engagement' (Ernstson, Lawton and Duminy 2014) with each other, with the city itself, and with the rural and the more global worlds beyond its immediate horizon. First, I will discuss the possibilities of what I refer to as a 'theory of shadow', and how this might help us to reduce urban 'darkness'. Second, I will say something about the process of the line (or the network as a complex intersection of lines). By way of conclusion, I will briefly reflect on possible strategies for capturing and containing these shadows and lines, and the local urban worlds they generate by introducing the notion of 'urban acupuncture'.

BRINGING CITY LIFE BACK IN: INVESTIGATIONS OF SHADOW

More than ever before, I consider it to be one of anthropology's crucial public roles to counteract the previously described annihilating strategies by theoretically re-inhabiting the notion of the everyday, reinvesting the urban locale with meaning and making the lives lived 'in the shadow of the Sheraton' (Moyer 2003) more visible again in all of their resourcefulness, hopes, sorrows and pains.

To be defined as visible or invisible has everything to do with the power constellations in which one is inscribed and entangled, as well as with the (im)possibility to construct and put into broader circulation an objectified identity of oneself. Unable to give a more global voice to its own identity constructions and in spite of its considerable size, Kinshasa, like many other non-Western cities, remains a 'black hole of informational capitalism', to cite Castells, who, in the third volume of his Information Age trilogy, applied this label to the whole of the African continent (Castells 2000). As the ultimate trope for urban dystopia and 'noir urbanism' (Prakash 2010), Kinshasa continues to occupy a very weak, peripheral and invisible position on the official map of world cities that form the nodes in a global network of transnational flows of capital, people and ideas, a central notion to the neo-liberal agenda.

Yet urbanscapes such as Kinshasa's often take the lead within more invisible global networks. Interconnected, entangled and transposed by more informal social structures, cultural imaginaries and economies of desire, Kinshasa's inhabitants constantly generate new forms of urbanity, sociality and mobility, and thereby 'world' the city in ways that also deeply mark and change the rest of the global urban community (Simone

2001; Roy and Ong 2011). They are, for example, increasingly embedded in complex and often very mobile networks of exchange and interdependence that channel flows of people, remittances, goods, words and ideas between Kinshasa, its local rural hinterlands and its transnational diasporas from Brussels, Paris and New York to southern and western Africa, and also to the Emirates, Guanzhou and other cities in the Pearl River Delta.[17]

Rather than being poor pre- or post-urban outposts territorially anchored outside the globalised network of the new information age, these urban networks constantly interconnect various geographical spaces. They form open-ended sites of mobility, flux, contact, transmission, circulation and migration. This does not necessarily mean that they reconfigure the standard constellations between culture and capital, or between politics and religion, along the lines of the new technology paradigms described in Castells' sociology of cities in the age of information. The kind of urban living I want to focus on here remains difficult to pin down within the historicist approaches of modernity and its accompanying ideologies and teleologies of linear development, progress and accumulation. This is why memories and imaginaries of these forms of cityness often remain diffuse and opaque. And yet cities such as Kinshasa increasingly share many of the main dimensions of social change that constitute Castells' 'new society': they are often radically global, though not necessarily in terms of their material, technological or institutional capacity; they are the living illustration of the demise of the sovereign nation-state and the crisis in the family and in patriarchy; and they are an important site for the redefinition of identity around religion, history, nation, ethnicity and locality.

There is therefore still a need to explore the social fabric and the unexpected ways in which material transformations and various new infrastructural and technological uses are generated and given form and content in this type of urban context. It is by documenting and investigating the various forms of this urban social machine, with all its destabilisations and thickenings of urban and rural, global and local, or present and past, that the 'black hole' may acquire a different dimension. The hole seems to remain black not only because of a lack of 'local' content (whether that 'local' means place, quality, mentality or morality) but mainly because of a lack of knowledge about essential characteristics of various kinds of cultural material (new socialities or specific forms of aesthetics, commerce, movement, authority, violence, combat and crisis) that remain permanently hidden in the shadow or are difficult to grasp and comprehend when looked at by means of the more conventional tropes and categories many of us still use to describe social life in the kind of post-developmental worlds we are discussing here.

Different interpretations of the notion of 'black hole' and 'shadow' may help us achieve this. The black hole image referred to above continues, of course, the longstanding Conradian discursive tradition this chapter opened with; a tradition in which Africa is erected as a dark continent, a heart of darkness and an *Afrique fantôme*. But instead of dismissing the black hole analogy as yet another statement reconfirming the hegemonic and colonising discourses that underpin the disconnection, or at least the specific hierarchies through which the African urban site is connected to a wider global world, I suggest that we need a re-appraisal of the notion of the shadow, somewhat along the lines that Ferguson proposed in his *Global Shadows: Africa in the Neoliberal World Order* (2006). Ferguson urges us to try and read into the possibilities of 'blackness' and into the forceful realities of the 'shadow' that so far have remained unexplored, even though metaphors of shadow have been pervasive, for example, in scholarly work about African shadow economies and shadow networks (Duffield 2002); shadow states (Reno 1995); shadows of war (Nordstrom 2004); shadow globalisation (Jung 2003); twilight institutions (Lund 2007); twilight policing (Diphoorn 2015) and postcolonial realities characterised by informality, irregularity, clandestinity, illegality and occult practices 'in the shadow of the law' (see Spyer 2006; Comaroff & Comaroff 2006: 16ff). In the work of all these scholars, the postcolony is portrayed as a world where the shadow and the invisible have become, as it were, institutionalised (cf. Nordstrom 2004).

I was reminded of Ferguson's advice when watching *Drawing Lesson One: In Praise of Shadows*, a recording of a 2012 lecture by William Kentridge.[18] This lecture about the qualities of the shadow also reminded me of Kentridge's 'Black Box / Chambre Noire' installation, which I saw at the Johannesburg Art Gallery in the summer of 2006. The Black Box project is a marvellous piece of work, a veritable theatre of shadows, bringing together puppets, animated film and Mozart's Magic Flute, in order to reflect on the Herero genocide, colonialism, the idea of Enlightenment, violence, destruction, loss and *Trauer Arbeit*, amongst other things. Shadows and their endless variations play a key role in the aesthetics of Kentridge's work. In the Black Box piece, as in much of his other work,[19] the artist probes the depths of darkness by exploring the versatility of light and its absence, and creating a true encyclopaedia of shadows, elusive at times and almost palpable at others. In *Black Box: Between the Lens and the Eyepiece*, a short text he wrote in the catalogue of the original Black Box exhibition in Berlin, Kentridge reflects upon Plato's allegory of the cave, the nature of film as 'shadowgraphy', the art of shadows that transform themselves, and 'the child who plays with shadows, delighting not just in seeing the image of the creature on the wall but also in watching and grasping the illusion' (Kentridge 2005: 47). He asks what it is that we learn from shadows: what can be clarified through the obscurity of shadows and if obscurity really is so obscure or if it depends on how you reframe what takes place between the lens and the eyepiece. One of the metaphors that Kentridge is playing with here is that of the *illuminating shadow*: 'If you have an image, and a shadow across it, you invert what is light and what is dark, and the shadow itself functions as a kind of spotlight' (Kentridge, 2005: 51).

He goes on to say that the shadow's ability to transform itself is one of the key elements for understanding it. A shadow forces one to think differently about dimensionality and relationality, for example. It is not a solid object: its essence is lack of dimensionality. Shadows, therefore, are essentially shape-shifting realities, resisting objectification, colonisation, synthesis and summary.

In the end, something about shadows makes us very conscious of the activity of seeing and perceiving. Shadows challenge us to reframe the reality we perceive, and to develop a specific kind of ethnographic imagination, a 'negative anthropology' as it were, an ethnography of 'shadows' that makes us aware of how we shape meaning through this 'inescapable need to make sense of shapes' (Kentridge 2005: 47).

It is clear that the shadow is 'good to think with', and I would therefore like to highlight the need to reconsider the notion of the shadow and of (in)visibility in order to understand better the more hidden realities and dynamics of city life and the specific modes of connection and disconnection that give shape to different networks acting on each other and intervening on different levels of social life within the urban context. A shadow, Kentridge and Ferguson remind us, is not only a dim or empty likeness, it also implies a bond and a relationship. A shadow is not a copy; it is not only negative space, or a space of absence.

Taking 'shadow' as an analytical starting point to understand local urban worlds in a country such as Congo not only offers the possibility to reflect differently on the place that Congolese cities and their inhabitants occupy in our imagination of the global world, it also offers the possibility to reconsider the specific ways in which these inhabitants' bodies, words, practices, dreams, desires and imaginaries (are made to) move and connect in a more global world, and the specific ways in which embodiment displays and is able to rework certain (geo-)political and economic hierarchies.

KINSHASA'S LOCAL SHADOWS

In the urban realities that I have been analysing over the past two decades, the only way to capture and interpret the forms of local life that the city generates is by taking the notion of the shadow and the invisible quite literally (cf. De Boeck & Plissart 2004). In Congo's cities local reality is defined by the *occultus*, in its double sense: the processes that structure urban local lives are not only often clandestine and therefore remain hidden and unrecognised by more formal economic and political frameworks, but local urban reality itself has become impossible without a 'knowledge of the hidden' and of the spiritual world beyond the physical reality of everyday life. Indeed, in a city such as Kinshasa, people continuously switch between two modes of existence: the reality of the first world, the diurnal one, and that of a more invisible urban world that exists in what Kinois themselves refer to as the nocturnal 'second' world, or second city, an occult city of the shadow, forming a topography and historiography of the local Congo-lese imaginary that is no less real than its physical counterpart. This constant slippage between visible and invisible, between diurnal and nocturnal, between the dead and the living, and between reality and its double, shadow, reflection or image, heavily impacts the ways in which social relationships and co-presences are shaped in the urban context. This slippage also leads to a constant religious transfiguration of local reality, a trans-formation that is enhanced in the re-enchanting spaces of Christian fundamentalism, for example, with their ceaseless emphasis on the existence of the devil and the witch. These shifts between surface and shadow are also evidenced by what people perceive as the constant invasion of the space of the living by the dead. As I will discuss in Chapter Five, the changed nature of death in the urban context has also led to new ways of death management, and it has also contributed to the deepening of intergenerational rifts that are played out, for example, in novel forms of witchcraft accusations that parents and elders direct at their children and grandchildren (cf. De Boeck 2009b).

In short, an important part of local urban experience seems above all to be gener-ated in the folds and shadows of the city, which itself exists as a huge friction zone, marked by a generalised feeling of uncannyness and various forms of material, spiritual and ontological insecurity. Instead of offering a steady ground, an unchanging back-ground or canvas against which to read the passage of time and make sense of one's life, thereby enabling one to generate a sense of stability from which to interpret change and transformation, a city such as Kinshasa has the tendency to manifest itself as a hole filled with quicksand, a place in which life itself turns out to be as unstable as the sandy hills upon which Kinshasa is constructed.

This is not only true with regard to the level of an unmoored *imaginaire,* but also with regard to the very materiality that determines people's lives. My interlocutors in Kinshasa frequently tell me: 'When I leave home in the morning, I don't know if I'll make it back alive in the evening. And each day, when I *do* come home in the evening, I tell myself, "It is a real miracle!"' Between morning and evening, between leaving home and returning, there are so many material and logistical obstacles, so many lurking dangers and changing parameters, that the risk of sudden disappearance and imminent death is ever present. The local realities of one's own street or neighbourhood never seem to offer a stable setting for one's daily activities. The familiar always unravels into something else. In the few hours between the time one goes to bed and the time one gets up again in the morning, the world as one knows it might have vanished. Over-night, one's own street might have turned into unknown territory and a social mine-field; prices might have changed and one's francs might have mysteriously devaluated; soldiers might have erected roadblocks on all the roads giving access to the neigh-bourhood; power relations might have switched between neighbourhood gangs (with names such as *Zoulou, Armée Rouge, Salopards, Antichrist, Mbeli-mbeli, Les Anglais, Les*

Allemands, Bana Bolafa, Onu-Britanique, Les Rois de Bengazi...); the man selling Coca-Cola in the kiosk across the street might have been necklaced because he was caught stealing in an adjacent compound at night; overnight neighbours and friends might have become foes and are now accusing each other's children of being witches; sudden and inexplicable deaths might have occurred; a building might have collapsed, or erosion due to heavy rainfall or deficient drainage might have swept away a neighbour's house; electricity might have been switched off only to return three hours or three weeks later; and the main electricity cables or water pipes feeding the neighbourhood might have been stolen by the very people supposed to fix them. In this city, where every item seems to be still in use and recycled long after its expiration date, most objects and buildings have been touched, soiled and tainted by thousands of eager hands, like a decrepit, worn-out house where too large a family have been living for far too long. The material infrastructures of the city are mostly marked by shortage, deprivation, lack and incompleteness. Often, these constitute the main qualities that determine the daily rhythms of urban life for the vast majority of people living in the city. And the very architectures of degradation and decay that constitute the physical life of local

urbanity, the technologies of fixing and repairing that such architectures generate, everything adds to the feeling that to venture forth into the local world of one's own street in the morning is to venture into a vast, increasingly exotic, unknown world. '*Terrain eza miné!*', 'the terrain is full of landmines', as urban dwellers often exclaim, thereby indicating that one is never quite sure where to step, or which move to make next in such an urban context.

To understand locally grounded cityness, therefore, requires a combined reading of the diverse territorial, material and physical experiences of the city *and* of the individual and collective dimensions of the social, affective, haptic, mental energies that run through the city. All of these constitute and are constituted by each other, and it is through this complex interplay between fragments of built material forms, individual dreams and collective architectures of the imaginary, and the relationships between individuals and smaller collectives that local urban worlds are turned into a collective subject . Each intention reveals its apparatus and each apparatus its intention. By looking at apparatus and intention, at material transformations and at the social machine generating them (and being generated by them), what appeared as a black hole and as shadow no longer sucks in these locally situated lives and narratives, rendering them invisible in the process; instead, the hole itself reveals 'the thing', the very content of the dark matter of the urban. The black hole, in other words, becomes the powerful producer of individual narratives, collective experiences and the various material and spiritual lines that connect both.

THE LOCAL AND THE LINE: LOCATING TRACES OF URBAN LIVING

This brings me to a second point, that of the line or the 'shadow lines' — to paraphrase the title of one of Joseph Conrad's later novels (Conrad 1917) — the threads and traces of which constantly shape new forms of local sociality. A theory of the shadow necessitates a methodology of lines, and an understanding of their 'entanglement' (Nuttall 2009) and the ways in which they might become lines of flight and open up possibilities.[20] As Fanon famously stated in *The Wretched of the Earth*, the colonial world was a compartmentalised, dichotomous world, consisting of the city of the coloniser and the city of the colonised (Fanon 1961). Today, we cannot continue to look at postcolonial realities by means of the same compartmentalising linearities that applied to the centre-periphery, rural-urban or local-global oppositions of the colonial world, even though projects such as *Cité du Fleuve* try to revive it. If, as I stated earlier, the shadow is about doubling, about a bond and a relationship, it means that in order to perceive it, we have to develop new ways of perception; new ways, above all, of perceiving connectedness. As with Kentridge's idea of the illuminating shadow, we have to learn to adjust our lens and our focus in order to see other hitherto more invisible lines that establish these connections, networks and numerous strands of transposed meaning and action in the multiple but simultaneous territories between local and global, urban and rural, or past, present and future that mark the world today.

How can we uncover some of these other lines that are usually excluded in the figures that our analytical models commonly map out to determine and capture the spaces in the practice of everyday life? The ordinariness of many of the lines and connections we make analytically is often responsible for creating the black hole itself. By contrast, the lines and connections drawn out by people in the context of the everyday movements of their lives often defy such closure and exclusion, and call into question established notions of flexibility and fixture.

Let me return at this point to Mudimbe, who, in a more recent text on lines and the paradoxes inherent in allegories of identity and alterity, states: 'Our physical geography, the whole domain of our culture, including mental configurations and our relations to nature, are topographies structured by lines' (Mudimbe 2008: 25). In his essay, he starts off with the idea that lines generated by the movements and physical interactions of people, ideas, commodities and so on, can no longer be described or interpreted as *straight* lines. Indeed, the lives of postcolonial subjects no longer unfold as 'straight stories', to paraphrase the title of one of David Lynch's well-known films (Lynch 1999). In Congo's popular cultural practices and narratives, linearity has come to mean something else. Local biographies and physical interactions are not, and have probably never been, generated as straight lines. Instead, they develop into cultural topologies that are basically more like non-linear 'lost highways' (cf. Lynch 1997): that is, they are marked by deviations from straightness, negations of unambiguous closure and instability (in economic terms certainly, but certainly also politically and morally). Living in the local reality of the city often means that one cannot afford to rely on the safety net of stability, predictability and durability. Local urbanities are anything but static in this respect and often turn out to be rather alienating realities instead.

Consider the complexity of the lines described by ordinary Congolese citizens throughout their lifetimes. The biographies of many of my acquaintances in Kinshasa, such as Trésor, come to mind:

Kinshasa, February 2012: As a kid Trésor[21] grew up in Masina, a crowded municipality in Kinshasa where most inhabitants trace their roots to neighbouring Bandundu province, and many share a Yaka ethnic background, as does Trésor himself. He was thirteen years old in 1993, at the time of the second wave of looting that swept through Kinshasa and the country as a whole [the first 'pillages' took place in 1991]. Trésor and his friends participated with great enthusiasm in the looting frenzy, and got away with lots of goods he managed to drag out of some industrial plants not far from where he lived. With the money he made out of this, Trésor decided to leave home. He paid his way to the Angolan border and crossed into Lunda Norte in search of dollars and diamonds, as so many young people did during those years. At the UNITA checkpoint on the border he was directed to a UNITA diamond mine along the Kwango River, where he celebrated his fifteenth birthday. There was not much else to celebrate though, for Trésor failed to find any diamonds. Instead he became very ill, due to the harsh treatment and the unhealthy working conditions in the mine he was sent to. Desperate, he spent the last of his money on transport to return to the Congolese side of the border. More dead than alive he made it to the border town of Kaungula, where one of his uncles lived. The latter took him in and there he was slowly nourished back to life. But when it became clear that he had not returned from Angola with money, he was told by his uncle he could no longer stay. Trésor had no choice but to make his way back to Kinshasa, which he did with great difficulty. Stuck in Kinshasa, he celebrated his seventeenth birthday in May 1997, at same time that Laurent Kabila's troops marched into the capital. Seeing the young rubber-booted *kadogos,* Kabila's infamous child-soldiers, walk through the city with their guns, Trésor decided to join the army. When the second war broke out a year later, and Rwandan troops tried to take Kinshasa while rebel movements in the east gained control over a large part of the country, Trésor was sent to the front near Mbuji Mayi, the capital of eastern Kasai province, in the central western area of Congo. When after a couple of years, his relatives in Kinshasa still had not received any news from Trésor, they assumed that he had died and a mourning ritual was organised. And then, all of sudden, thirteen years after his departure, Trésor miraculously showed up on the doorstep of one of his other uncles in Kinshasa. Trésor had lived all these years a soldier's life at the front, but one day he decided that 'war does not build a country' and, in an attempt also to save himself from his own war traumas, he deserted from the army, leaving a wife and two children behind in the outback where he had been stationed for the past four years. With the little money he had managed to set aside over the years, he started to make his way from distant Kasai back to Kinshasa. When I met him in March 2012, he had been living at his uncle's for three months. Penniless, he was waiting for the latter to set up a meeting with a local police officer in the hope of joining the police force and making enough money for his family to follow him to the capital. Increasingly frustrated and impatient with his situation, however, Trésor started to drink more. One night, when totally drunk, he was arrested after a row in a bar where he had insulted a high ranking army officer. When I left Kinshasa in early April, Trésor had just been released from a week in jail, where he had been severely beaten. Three months later he was still waiting to join the police force.

Seen within the Congolese context, Trésor's story is by no means exceptional. Other people's lives are often even more complex and unpredictable than his. Consider, for example, the life stories of Shayibunda and his uncle.[22] The lines of their lives do not start in Kinshasa but somewhere on the borderlands between Congo and Angola, a site where I conducted field research between 1987 and 1994, and which will continue to resonate and echo in various chapters of this book:

Shayibunda was born in Congo in the mid-1950s, the son of an important Lunda paramount title-holder who had thirty-two wives and over fifty children in the course of his lifetime. As a boy he was sent to a Catholic boarding school run by Belgian missionaries in southwestern Congo. There he completed his primary education and the first three years of secondary school, making him one of the first Lunda 'intellectuals' in the area. He then returned to his father's village and started living in a number of other villages in the border area between Congo and Angola. His father died in the early 1980s and his maternal uncle, Kasongo Lunda, was enthroned and became paramount title-holder Kateend II in 1984. In this new capacity, Kateend set up a royal village, situated in Congo's Upper

Kwango area in the province of Bandundu. Kateend, who was also born in the Belgian Congo, had never received a formal school education and could barely read, write or speak French, although he mastered a smattering of rudimentary Portuguese. As a young man, he moved to Angola to become a soldier in the Portuguese colonial army. It was said that he was even sent to Portugal for a brief period for military training. After the independence of Angola in 1975, Kateend, an authoritarian but intelligent man, was appointed *regedor*[23] in Lunda Norte by the Angolan authorities, but he later got into trouble because of his UNITA sympathies. The MPLA killed one of his sons, and when he sought revenge by capturing and executing an MPLA soldier, he had to flee to Congo. There he became locally famous as a renowned elephant hunter, before becoming a paramount title-holder. In this capacity he also made quite a name for himself and was eventually made Knight in the National Order of the Leopard by Mobutu, who even invited him to the presidential palace in Gbadolite in the late 1980s. In the meantime, riding on the waves of a newly developing diamond traffic in the early 1980s, Shayibunda started to travel between Lunda Norte, Kinshasa and Brazzaville, trading diamonds. Along the way he married his first wife, a Mbala girl from the town of Kikwit, where he bought a house with the money from his diamond transactions. After a couple of years, he returned to the village, bringing her back with him. By then, he had also started a career in local Lunda politics, as an advisor to the new paramount title-holder, his maternal uncle. Because of this, the royal court pressured him into marrying a second wife,

one of his own matrilineal cross cousins, a daughter of Kateend II. Shayibunda agreed to marry her, but insisted that she should first be sent to Kinshasa for a couple of years to become a nurse. Upon her return, a conflict broke out between Shayibunda's two co-wives. As a result, his first wife, together with her children, moved back to the house in Kikwit, while his second wife moved out of the village and set up a household in the local border town of Kulindji, where Shayibunda built a new house for her. This forced him to divide his time between his uncle's village and the households of his two wives, each of which were hundreds of kilometres apart (not easy distances to bridge in Congo today). Then, in the early 1990s, he was sent by the royal court to Kinshasa to act as a representative of the Lunda paramount ruler at the National Sovereign Conference that was held when the country was opening up towards a multi-party system. Contrary to what he had expected, his stay in Kinshasa lasted not three weeks but three years, during which he was unable to visit his wives and children, mainly because he lacked the means to do so. As a result, his senior wife, who lived in total poverty in Kikwit, abandoned her five children and left for Tshikapa in the Kasai region, where she remarried and got pregnant again soon afterwards. In the meantime, Shayibunda himself got involved with another woman in Kinshasa. Then, in the late 1990s, he finally managed to move back to his uncle's village, and from there he started travelling again between Angola and the household of his second wife, who refused to return to the royal village with him. In 2002, after a long political struggle and much lobbying during

another long stay in Kinshasa, he was appointed local district commissioner by the central government, which enabled him to move to the town of Kulindji and pick up his life with his second wife again. He also started to try and reassemble the children from his first marriage. They were by now dispersed between Kikwit, Kinshasa and some villages along the border with Angola. Two years later, his uncle, paramount Kateend II, died after a long illness. His death left his royal court weakened and divided. Shayibunda, in spite of his reluctance and even his refusal to become the new paramount, became entangled in a fierce succession fight with two of his own brothers (who through their mothers had different political allegiances and were backed by different clans within the royal lineage). In 2004, Shayibunda was on the road again on his way to Angola, when he suffered what appears to have been a massive heart attack. Fighting for his life in a Canadian Mennonite hospital on the border with Angola, he miraculously recovered after he left hospital and started treatment with a local healer (even though he had become a born-again Christian in the meantime). In 2005, however, he suddenly collapsed again and died while on his way to his office in Kulindji. Inevitably, it was whispered that his political adversaries had poisoned or bewitched him.

It could be argued that Shayibunda's or Kateend's sense of social mooring and belonging were firmly rooted in the Lunda village world and the local politics of the royal lineage. Yet their worlds were not confined to that reality alone. Throughout his life,

Shayibunda struggled hard to avoid being totally swallowed by that 'local' world: for example, he refused the role of paramount ruler for which he seemed to be predestined long before his uncle's death. He tried to expand his horizons and break out of their confines; he travelled between Angola, Brazzaville, Kikwit and Kinshasa and got involved in broader economic and political processes by becoming a born-again Christian and a state administrator. His life, which we would hardly think of as 'cosmopolitan', became increasingly caught up in numerous different trajectories and codes, roles, moralities and languages (in Shayibunda's case at least nine different languages), war and peace, Congolese and Angolan politics, the local and translocal, rural and urban worlds, exogamous and endogamous marriages, gifts and money, ethnic and other identities, ancestors, Neo-Pentecostalists, traditions and modernities. His life story also reads, rather tragically, as an increasingly unsuccessful attempt to connect all these threads and steer the course of his own life so that it would remain intact despite the constant threats of dispersal.

Many Congolese biographies, I would argue, share the same complexity. The lines described in the course of such biographies connect figures of a praxis in their dimension of a negation of standard, straight lines. They set off from unexpected points of departure, whether in an urban or a more rural context (and often the two have become hard to distinguish), and often these lines are formed in more or less successful attempts to steer the course of a person's life unharmed through it all and fight the constant threat of dispersal. As 'an opening up to the unexpected', to use Mudimbe's expression (2008: 26), these lines often overrun all known boundaries (gender, belief systems, ethnicity, rural-urban divisions, etc.), forcing people to live simultaneously in multiple territories and making of each of them a community unto themselves (idem: 28).

LINES AND RHYTHMS

The issue is not so much to make the now overly familiar point concerning the celebrated capacity of postcolonial subjects to use strategically multiple identities in various contexts. The issue I want to raise instead is that all of this never seems to be carefully planned in advance. The line of one's life is almost never unidirectional; on the contrary, it is fundamentally rhizomatic and 'anti-teleological' (Malaquais 2011) because of the often instantaneous, spontaneous, improvised and random nature of the unfolding lines throughout individual biographies and also because of the equally unplanned and accidental ways in which these individual biographies get caught up and become entangled in other lines and networks of physical and mental contact with other people, places, discourses, practices and ideas.

In other words, there never is a straight line between today and tomorrow in these lives; or between here and there, the possible and the impossible, success and failure, or life and death. This also means that the lines of people's lives unfold within a different kind of temporality. People are, of course, conscious actors and participants in their own lives, struggling to some extent to stay in control. They are therefore always on the lookout and ready to anticipate, seize, secure and hold onto opportunities to reinvent and re-imagine their lives in different ways. But at the same time these processes of seizure remain highly unpredictable, transient and ephemeral because opportunities can often only be framed within the temporality of an equally unpredictable moment.

Instead of existing through habit and routine, or of being formatted by the temporalities of the static and the unchanging, the ascertainable and the planned, such lives are often shaped through movements of the unforeseen, which constantly seem to steer local actors off course, launching them into new orbits but often also condemning them to immobility. Such lives, therefore, are never fully autonomous projects either. The velocity of a person's life is constantly being determined by external factors over which one has little or no control. As a result, urban living seems to consist of constant stops and starts, directed by chance and misfortune, or 'miracle' and 'fate'. It is shaped around the specific tempos of anticipation and expectation, but it is also configured around boredom, apathy and ennui, around the cadences of inactivity and of pointless waiting, that then often becomes an activity in itself. People have to be always in an anticipatory mode, always on the lookout, ready to be on the go, alert and open to the opportunity any moment might offer; but without necessarily knowing if or when that moment is going to present itself or what it might bring, or what exactly that particular window of opportunity might consist of. And when that favourable moment arrives, it always comes suddenly, always uncomfortably wedged between the immobility of endless waiting that precedes it and the often short-lived effervescence of sudden activity and movement that it generates. And because of that, the opportunity is often also lost.

In short, living in the anticipatory time frame of the transient and impermanent speeds up and slows down time in unpredictable ways, and renders urban lives unstable, as the biographies of Trésor and Shayibunda testify. To live in the city is often a matter of having to cope with the fact of 'being stuck'. And the only way to overcome this state of strandedness and get things moving again is to be a *cascadeur*, as the Kinois would say: that is, a daredevil, someone with courage, ready to take risks and deal with life's risks This also necessitates permanent speculating and betting on things. Driven by mobilities of 'searching' (*koluka*) in order to survive, urban life certainly generates opportunities and openings, but it also causes sudden cuts and closures, producing a great deal of fallout and collateral damage along the way (as the dispersals of Shayibunda's and Trésor's families also show). The disabling factors that constantly impact urban dwellers' lives force them to be flexible and master the tricky skills of improvisation and excel in the mental gymnastics necessary to transcend or outlive the moment and survive on a daily basis.

Many urban residents seem to be very good at doing exactly that: at opening up to the 'unexpected' that often reveals itself to be outside the known pathways that constitute life as many of us know it. Although urban inhabitants rarely know where they will end up, they are highly skilled at discovering itineraries beyond the obvious, at exploiting more invisible paths and clandestine possibilities that lie hidden in the folds of urban domains and experiences. Out of necessity, city dwellers have trained themselves to tap successfully into the imbroglio of urban life and exploit to the full the possibilities its juxtapositions offer. Trained to look out for feasibility within what is seemingly unfeasible, they are continually engaged in designing new ways to escape from the economic impositions and excesses that urban life imposes on them.

Taking all these levels into account, the emerging figure of the city dweller changes from being a poor and passive victim into an active participant with his or her own social, economic, political and religious agendas, and these are often situated far beyond the level of mere survival. This generates a specific agency in a specific urban experience; an agency that cannot possibly be considered ideal, but that is not less tangible or real because of this.

URBAN ACUPUNCTURES

In order to understand this agency, and the reality of city life as experienced every day by millions like Trésor and Shayibunda, I believe it is absolutely necessary to stay close to the specific rhythms of the spatial and temporal lines these meandering lives inscribe onto the urban surface, and also close to the conjunctures and conjectures of sudden action and passivity, power and powerlessness, expectation and disappointment that these rhythms generate.

Throughout this book, the combination of my textual analysis and Sammy Baloji's photographs attempts to activate and render visible the lines of urban dwellers' lives by applying a methodological tool that I refer to as 'urban acupunctures'. Both Bärbel Müller and Ariel Osterweis Scott use the notion of 'acupuncture' to describe the dance performances of Congolese choreographer Faustin Linyekula (Müller 2009; Scott 2010). Scott analyses Linyekula's dance as a form of 'geo-choreography', an embodied practice that demands a continual reordering of the spaces of the urban landscape without colonising them. Scott claims that Linyekula's artistic interventions establish a network of corporeal and architectural sites, such as his Kisangani-based Studios Kabako, within that landscape in an endeavour to 'connect the dots', to use the artist's own words, and thereby re-contextualise and 'heal' or 'appease' the body of the city, with its multiple spaces and forms of cultural production (Scott 2010: 21). Similarly, for Müller, the small-scale spatial, temporal and programmatic interventions that are initiated by Studios Kabako have the capacity to activate 'waypoints' or 'acupuncture points' within urban space, thereby negotiating and transforming the urban tissue both in terms of space and time, as well as through operations that are relational as well as reactive, and create new 'networks of characteristic energy levels with catalytic effects on the urban fabric' (Müller 2009 : 207).

The notion of 'urban acupuncture' itself originated in the 'weak architecture' movement associated with Catalan architect de Solà-Morales, who first coined the term (cf. Ellin 2006: 124). The concept was further developed by architectural environmental theorist and urban planner Marco Casagrande (Elkjaer 2010). Building on his involvement with an illegal urban farming settlement in Treasure Hill in Taipei, Taiwan, Casagrande conceptualises urban acupuncture as a strategy for micro-urbanistic interventions in weak and vulnerable parts of cities. In line with a longstanding tradition (cf. Sennett 1994), he sees cities as living, breathing organisms. Architects and planners manipulate what Casagrande refers to as 'the collective sensuous intellect'[24] of this urban organism or body. They stick their needles in the city's neural tracts and pathways, in carefully chosen local urban nuclei, nodes and pinpoint areas that are damaged, endangered or in need of repair. By 'opening up the blockages along "urban meridians", just as acupuncture and other forms of bioenergetic healing open up blockages along the energy meridians of our bodies' (Ellin 2006: 10), this intervention is aimed at activating and healing problematic parts of the urban body in an attempt to revitalise the urban corpus as a whole, to liberate its 'life force' (Ellin 2006: 10) and turn its negative energies into positive ones. These interventions are often minimal. As stated on the Casagrande laboratory website: 'A weed will root into the smallest crack in the asphalt and eventually break the city. Urban acupuncture is the weed and the acupuncture point is the crack.'[25]

While this book does not immediately share any of the therapeutic, healing or appeasing intentions and aspirations of Linyekula's geo-choreographies or Casagrande's urban acupunctures, I find their respectful and delicate approach to the city theoretically enriching and methodologically helpful. Focusing on the city's less visible layers, cracks and folds rather than on its planned and rational surface, they are attentive to the city as lived environment. They tap into its fluxes and rhythms and are open to the streams of energy pumping through the arteries of the city, to the affective, tactile and haptic dimensions of this urban body and the action potential of its neural system. They privilege the human scale of the incorporated over the distant scale of the master plan, improvisation over colonisation, interstitial connectivity over fragmentation, and continuity over radical break (even though, as I noted before, that continuity between past and present never actually materialises as a linear narrative). As such, their artistic or planning strategies seem to formulate two possible answers to the question that de Solà-Morales asked with regard to architectural practice:

'How can architecture act in the *terrain vague* without becoming an aggressive instrument of power and abstract reason? Undoubtedly, through attention to continuity: not the continuity of the planned, efficient, and legitimized city, but of the flows, the energies, the rhythms established by the passing of time and the loss of limits... we should treat the residual city with a contradictory complicity that will not shatter the elements that maintain its continuity in time and space' (de Solà-Morales 1995: 123).

Likewise in this book, I use methodologically the metaphor of urban acupuncture to stick analytical needles (in the form of textual and photographic analyses) into specific urban sites that constitute important, though sometimes materially barely noticeable, nodes within the city: sites in which the city switches on and off, where quickenings and thickenings of goods, people and publics are generated and the various lines and connections between them become visible. These sites range from mountains to pot-holes, from markets to streets, from specific buildings to fields and gardens, from cemeteries to new city extensions, and from electrical wires to the human body. Each of the following chapters in this book is constructed around one or more of these sites. Through a detailed anthropological and photographic analysis of their quality and dynamics, we intend not so much to 'break the city', or change, heal or intervene in it, but rather to 'break open' the city, to make it visible and reveal it, connect the dots between the different sites that constitute it and activate the desire lines that run through it. The registers of textual analysis and visual reflection thus act as forms of trailblazing or way marking that contribute to a better understanding of the often elusive manner in which people in this kind of city context manage not only to survive individually but also transcend that basic level of bare life, and build a more inclusive urban co-presence and 'togetherness' where the possibilities of collective action and dreams of a shared future may be explored.

3. The Urban Politics of Syncopation

SYNCOPATION, a musical effect caused by a syncope, missed beat or off-the-beat stress (also referred to as *suspension*)

SYNCOPE: In phonology, syncope (Greek: *syn-* + *koptein*, meaning 'to strike, cut off') is the loss of one or more sounds from the interior of a word, especially the loss of an unstressed vowel. A loss of sounds from the end of a word is an *apocope* (from *apo-* meaning 'away from' and *koptein* meaning 'to cut').

SYNCOPE is also the medical term for fainting, and is defined as a transient loss of consciousness and postural tone.

Teka masanga na yo! — Sell your corn,
Soki olandi mibela ya lelo, — If you follow today's husbands,
Oya koteka liputa ya chinois! — You risk selling your Chinese loincloth! [1]
Teka, teka, teka! — Sell, sell, sell!
Mibali ya lelo basalaka te. — Today's husbands don't have a job,
Soki olandi bango, — And if you follow them,
Okoya kobamba liputa ya chinois! — You risk wearing a second-hand Chinese loincloth!
Teka, teka, teka nguba na yo! — Sell, sell, sell your groundnuts!
Mibali ya lelo basalaka te. — Today's husbands have no work
Soki olandi bango, — And if you follow them,
Okoya kozanga elamba ya kolata! — You won't have a loincloth to wear at all!

[Popular song among Kinshasa's market women]

RHYTHMS OF URBAN POVERTY: OF SYNCOPATION AND SUSPENSION

Sell, sell, sell! But who has money to buy anything? In Kinshasa, *nzombo le soir* ('evening *nzombo*') is a specific buying strategy in markets. In the late evening just before a market closes, unsold perishable foodstuff, such as *nzombo*, a kind of freshwater fish (*Protopterus* or African lungfish), is sold outside the market at a reduced price by women

known as *bamama bitula*. Customers wait for that last and very brief window of opportunity to buy something affordable for their families to eat that night. *Nzombo le soir* has now grown to mean an unexpected opportunity or windfall under general conditions of lack and want. However, for many people with little money, even survival tactics such as *nzombo le soir* cannot be pursued on a daily basis.

As in multiple other urban settings across the Global South (cf. Jones and Nelson 1999; Mitlin and Satterthwaite 2013), the extremely low income level in Congo's urban centres, where most inhabitants survive on less than 2 US$ a day,[2] imposes a specific temporality on everyday life that deeply affects the rhythm of the day by syncopating its temporal framework. Hence *nzombo le soir* or, to give another example, *kanga journée*, which is what a small bread baguette is called in Kinshasa. Produced by large, often Lebanese-owned industrial bakeries, such as Pain Victoire, these breads are collected very early in the morning by thousands of women who spend the rest of the day selling them in the city's markets and streets. Although bread did not use to be a common part of the Kinois staple diet, for the last two decades it has increasingly come to replace other (often more expensive) sources of nutrition, such as cassava and corn flour. The term *kanga journée* ('to close the day,' an expression consisting of the Lingala verb –*kanga,* 'to close' but also 'to catch, to grab, to hold back, to remember, to understand', and the French word for 'day') marks the fact that many Kinois have replaced a more elaborate evening meal with a simple piece of bread, a bitter reminder of, and a sour comment on, a day unsuccessfully spent in search of money to buy food.

In these very immediate and physical ways, poverty constantly generates time- and energy-consuming blockages, suspensions and deviations, and thereby limits and reduces options on all practical levels of everyday life. But not only does it change one's experience of time, often condemning one to a quasi permanent condition of 'wait-hood' (Honwana 2012), it also deeply modifies the very language that urban dwellers use to make sense of this life. To keep to the market example: when people go to the market in search of chicken meat, they no longer buy *nsoso* (the usual term for chicken in Lingala), they buy *nso* instead. *Nso* has become the common term to refer to the tiny portions of chicken skin that most of Kinshasa's inhabitants can still afford. Not that chickens themselves have become scarce. Again, it is more because most people lack the means to buy a sizeable portion of chicken meat that the apocope *nso* — as an evocation of the concept of chicken, and a reminder of its flavour and smell — has come to replace the materiality of the 'real thing'.

What kind of crisis underlies the fact that not only time but even language becomes syncopated and rationed? What does this verbal amputation mean in a city where speech is such an important tool for self-making, and where one has to master fully the art of rhetoric and know '*ce que parler veut dire*' (Bourdieu 1982) in order to survive, to exist socially and become someone with social status and 'weight' (*mwana ya kilo*) in the domains of public and family life? Rooted in and moored down by the body, words, in

the form of speech, song and prayer, are are not only important tools for self-making, they also create the city itself. Indeed, the urban form is often principally an acoustic one, one of verbal and musical architectures (cf. De Boeck 2006). Particularly in the context of Kinshasa, one could argue that both the city's built material form and its lived form have been shaped by the fabulous music that it has engendered (see Stewart 2000; White & Yoka 2010). In the 1940s and 50s, the city created a new form of music, the *rumba ya lingala* that came of age with musicians such as Franco and Tabu Ley. Simultaneously, a novel form of urban space came into being with new iconic places, such as bars and *ngandas*. These were spaces of leisure that did not exist as such prior to the birth of the city, but that gradually emerged with the new labour and leisure time regimes imposed by the colonial city. It is in these profoundly urban spaces that Leopoldville invented its own musical rhythm and generated its urban speak and its very identity and soul. It is there, around the bars' orchestras, that new forms of associational life emerged in the form of *mozikis* and other voluntary associations (cf La Fontaine 1970: 153ff). It is also in the space of the bar that a first generation of nationalists invented its own political voice. It is there that Lumumba, who worked for a brewery at the time and frequented the *cité*'s bars to sell Polar beer, held his first political rallies.

In their current shape, the vibrating rhythms of the city's music and its lyrics seem less political, even though they match and reflect perfectly the deep rumblings and delirious explosions of what is going on in the city. A 'precarious balance between noise, sound and scream' (Mbembe 2006: 76), Kinshasa's music expands and contracts with strong and often irregular movements, while the slogans shouted by the *atalaku*, the orchestra's animators, who enhance the audience with their rhetorical talents and strongly determine the form and quality of the city's acoustic scape (cf. White 2008: 59), fluctuate between hopeful and abject. Known as *génériques* (cf. Nadeau-Bernatchez 2012: 221), the *atalaku*'s verbal interventions become signatures, vignettes that summarize the feeling of a particular moment in the history of the city. His shouts accompany the city at a particular point of its existence. They become 'signs of the times', sound bites that mark an epoch and thereby offer a reference point against which the flow of urban time can be measured and particular events that mark city life can be turned into a collective memory. The *atalaku*'s voice stops the flux of the city and breaks time open into a splintering moment of bodies dancing and meeting. Hard, sharp, metallic and fragmented, this music not only constitutes the perfect soundtrack to accompany the disorderly and contradictory nature of the city, it *is* the city itself; it fastens down and 'scapes' the city in what Binyavanga Wainana describes so well as 'the sound of all the clang, the rang-tang-tang, tinny clamor of agitated building, selling, and the multilingual clash of mouth cymbals, lifting up and down, jaws working, eating, trading, laughing.' (Wainaina 2011: 77). And in this musical moment of the *générique*, bodies become animated entities, while language itself rapidly unravels.

Typically, the *atalaku*'s shouted interventions often abandon the linearity of regular grammar and syntax. Their performances are exercises in linguistic disintegration. In imitation of the glossolalia so common in the context of prayer meetings, they strip language of its meaning, they gut out words and cut them up until they dissolve into the non-sensical or are reduced to onomatopoeia or pure noise, as if to say that this is the only level in which language can still make sense in and of a city that is itself constantly disintegrating and falling apart. In the end, it is not so much the poverty that the city imposes upon the majority of its inhabitants, but the unstable material and social nature of the city itself that reduces or 'cuts away' the capacity of one's language to reveal, demystify, clarify or explain the unsteady ground of one's life in the urban setting.

In his acclaimed history of modern art, *The Shock of the New*, Robert Hughes reflects on the horrors of mechanised trench warfare in World War I:

'In the Somme valley the back of language broke. It could no longer carry its former meanings. World War I changed the life of words and images in art, radically and forever. It brought our culture into the age of mass-produced, industrialized death. This, at first, was indescribable.' (Hughes 2013 (1981): 57)

Of course, Kinshasa is not the Somme valley and even though Congo has experienced more than its fair share of violence and warfare throughout its history, the daily wars that must be waged in the city in order to survive are mostly of a different order. They have, however, also deeply impacted the possibility to describe and make sense of the daily hardships of urban life. It is not as if the violence of material insecurity has 'broken the back of language' or totally diminished denizens' powers to reflect on or speak about the conditions they live in. It is more that it has created specific urban vocabularies and verbal regimes, as the expression *kanga journée* illustrates, in order to give that reflection a form that fits the vagaries of urban life better. If city life within the context of Central Africa is often characterised by its edginess and unpredictability, the language of the city is inevitably affected by this and becomes an unstable discursive borderland 'where contradictory discourses overlap, or where discrepant links of meaning-making converge' (Tsing 1994: 279).

Not only has the city greatly impacted the language of its residents, it has also generated novel words and expressions and thoroughly modified residents' capacity to order these urban vocabularies into comprehensible syntaxes. The city, in fact, constantly generates verbal diarrhoea, a swelling army of words or little soldiers that people deploy to confront and fight the chaos of their daily existence, or then to overcome and rearrange that chaos into an alternative order. Despite the wit and humour that is frequently involved in these verbal and grammatical skirmishes with an overwhelming reality, these attempts to attenuate its violence frequently remain futile. In this way, urban living is constantly punctuated by a semantic over-production, an 'overheating' of meaning, a veritable 'speaking in tongues' that eventually renders the world even more complex. There is an excess of often incomprehensible and always strangely coded messages. I already mentioned the often meaningless string of words shouted out by the *atalaku*. Similarly, Kinois seem to have an irrepressible urge to scribble or paint words and messages on almost every car and wall in the city. This overproduction of words points to the possibility of a certain agency in an attempt to capture the deeper meanings of city life while also simultaneously laying bare the futility of such an endeavour. Inasmuch as it elucidates the urban world, 'urban speak' also operates as a mystifying machine, complicating one's capacity to read order into the urban site.

Indeed, the words 'disorder' and 'confusion' rather than 'order' spring to mind to describe the rhythms and flows of the urban surface and the specific forms of life it generates. These concepts have not only been used analytically in the writings of social and political scientists, urban thinkers and policy makers (cf. Chabal and Daloz 1999; Comaroff and Comaroff 2006; Rakodi 2002; Trefon 2004; Urdal & Hoelscher 2009), they also belong to the daily vocabularies of the inhabitants on the unstable terrains of urban life in this part of the world. As will be illustrated elsewhere in this book, 'order' and to a great extent its opposite 'disorder' are terms that are commonly used by

members of Kinshasa's youth gangs, for example, to define themselves as 'children of disorder' (*bana désordre*), and to describe the unruly 'law' they try to impose on the streets and neighbourhoods of Kinshasa. Similarly, in the towns and cities of neighbouring Angola, *confusão* is often used to describe the increasing sense of lack of direction and orientation that characterises everyday life in the urban context.

What this social poetics of the disorderly translates is a growing incapacity to make sense of the urban site and understand the rules that govern life beyond the immediacy of its chaotic appearance, which would then give life a purpose and finality other than one of mere survival. An often heard phrase in Kinshasa is 'I don't see clear' (Lingala: *namoni clair te*), or *eza trouble*: 'It [and this 'it' might be a specific event as well as one's reading of it] is murky', i.e. indistinct, turbid, disturbed and indeed 'troubled'. In Congo's urban context, people routinely translate this sense of confusion into the word *mystique* (or *mistik*). People, things and situations are commonly designated *mystique*, that is to say, difficult to place, interpret, fully fathom or understand. As one of the organising tropes of Central Africa's city life, the word *mystique* seems to capture rather well the overall quality of urban existence in all its opaqueness and elusiveness, and its often uncanny nature and ontological ambivalence. It conveys well the draining nature of the demands the city places on its residents, and indicates their constant, intensive efforts to overcome the city's disorder and the ensuing ambiguities. It also denotes the effort of having to engage in an almost daily 'divinatory' act in an attempt to guess the meaning that lies hidden within the fluid parameters of urban life; to unveil the city's unreliability and steer clear of its many unpredictable events; to cruise unscathed the length of the day; and to make sense of one's own pathways of adversity or luck. This daily labour is often structured around the activity of 'searching' (Lingala: *koluka*), a term urbanites commonly use to describe their daily quest for food, money, jobs, contacts and opportunities. One can easily lose oneself in this desperate 'searching for the (good) life' (*koluka vie*), yet, at the same time, it involves the potential interpretive capacity to discover and grasp opportunities in the gaps that invariably open up between, or even within, things, events and persons. These gaps constitute the essential quality of unpredictability that defines this kind of urban life. Due to the influence of Neo-Pentecostal and other religious (Catholic, Protestant, Charismatic and Kimbanguist) vocabularies, the impossibility to foretell and foresee what today and tomorrow will bring is often translated into terms of 'fate', the 'occult' or the 'miraculous' (see also Goldstone 2011).

To meander successfully through all the contradictions, impossible possibilities and changes of pace and rhythm that urban life constantly generates, and to calculate one's chances and know when to cut one's losses, demands a quality of judgment and a capacity to multitask that Kinois commonly refer to as *matematik* (mathematics), a term also picked up and developed by In Koli Jean Bofane in his novel *Mathématiques congolaises* (2008). In another artistic work called *Pylone 53*, a cardboard representation of a transmission tower for electricity and ideas, Lubumbashi-based artist Jean Katambayi translates these mathematics into a navigational exercise around three axes: *coupure / facture / culture* (cut / invoice / culture), with which all other parameters of one's life interact and intersect, often generating a great deal of tension and friction in the process. Part of this artwork is a plastic screen in the middle of the transmission tower on which the artist wrote a summary of all these other parameters: privatisation, group, independence, hotel, heating, arrangements, deals, lover, rest, meal, health, salary, wedding, church...

And indeed, to get a deep insight into the complex dynamics of (social) transmission seems to demand an advanced knowledge of higher mathematics and matters such as chaos, fractals, mobility and vectorial capacity so that the course of one's life can be steered unharmed through every pitfall, every possible and constantly changing parameter of daily existence. One may then stand a chance of successfully networking, connecting and inserting oneself into as many collectivities as possible and thus increase the odds of obtaining food, work, money, (wo)men and so on.

Urban dwellers are frequently driven to the brink of insanity because of the constant networking and 'branching out' (locally referred to as *branchement*)[3] they need to survive in the city and also because of the unceasing decisions, often having to be made within a fraction of a second, as to whether or not they should seize an opportunity to connect or insert themselves. It is no coincidence that a mentally disturbed person (*moto ya liboma*) is said to be *na ba-réseaux*: 's/he got (too many) networks (in

République Démocratique du Congo
PYLONE 53

coupure
culture
repas
hotel
Famille
indépendance
télévision

his/her head)', like cell-phones with several SIM-cards that people use to switch between different providers, a *conditio sine qua non* to branch out, extend and stretch one's social networks as far as possible in order to improve one's chances of success in the city. But madness is also the very opposite of this: it may result from the fact that one's 'network is cut off' (*réseau ekimi*), that one does not know how to connect and is therefore in danger of growing too isolated to survive in the city.[4]

In this chapter, I want to explore further the rhythms of the syncopated, the excessive and the suspended by means of an ethnographic 'urban acupuncture' of a specific site within the city. How do these rhythms influence people's *branchements*, their (in) capacity to plug in and connect? And how does this contribute to creating publics and the notion of a shared public sphere? As we know from Amartya Sen's social choice theory, poverty, as a rhythm of syncopation, often constitutes a cutting off. It reduces the number of alternatives available for choice, and therefore regularly leads to 'a life within limits' (Jackson 2011); it leads to deviations as well as transient or more permanent blockages and losses (of time, energy, social possibilities and the capacity to express oneself). However, I will also argue that these suspensions and missed beats — generated by the syncopal and staccato rhythms of the social, material and mental lines that people's lives are forced to describe in the urban terrain — also generate new and often unexpected accents that form openings into the 'something else' of the off-beat track, and hint at the possibility of suturing cuts and ruptures, and hence of creating new publics and public spaces.

But before further exploring this, let me say something about the notion of 'poverty' itself, as well as the notion of 'the urban poor' in the context of Kinshasa.

NZALA: POVERTY AS (SOCIAL) 'HUNGER'

Even though Lingala has a number of words to denote the idea of 'poverty' (for example, *bobola*, which can mean indigence, poverty, misery and neediness), they are hardly ever used because people tend to use the French words *pauvre* or *pauvreté* instead. Most Lingala words for poverty are far less abstract. They relate almost always to a concrete situation, such as a lack of social autonomy, or then social dependency (*bosenga* from -*senge*: 'to ask, to beg or to request assistance), mostly seen as a dependency on other people's food (and food may mean foodstuff itself but also money or other forms of material and social assistance). In a Central African context, food has always been a common medium through which people define relations of reciprocity, exchange and social control, and thereby manipulate notions of rank, status, politics and prestige. Being dependent on eating the 'food' of others (without being able to reciprocate) not only makes one socially feeble, it also puts one at constant risk of becoming 'bewitched' or 'poisoned' (-*senga*) through that food. Above all, this 'poverty' is usually precisely that: the (weakening and often dangerous) incapacity to reciprocate, or to position oneself in the role of giver.

If idioms of eating and feeding cover a wide range of both positive and negative practices and experiences related to the fields of political power, sexuality and witch-craft, they can also express emotional states of satisfaction, solidarity and contentment, or, on the contrary, frustration, conflict and anger. 'Poverty' is always translated into these registers as well. It is not a fixed abstract state unrelated to personal and/or communal experience. Instead, it is a 'lack of food' (*bokeleli*) that is usually described and talked about as a generalised state of 'hunger' (*nzala*). Redefined as 'hunger' (whether physical, social and/or mental), poverty is therefore always rooted in an immediate lived expe-rience; it is localised in a time and space that relates to one's own body and life as well as to a larger social body and one's capacity to generate social contacts and carve out one's place in the world (cf. De Boeck 1994a). More than denoting a state of material want, poverty as 'hunger' is about violence (physical and mystical), the threats to social cohesion and the importance (and dangers) of ties with others. It is also a political idiom, as part of a moral discourse to discuss and criticise the state apparatus and the political elites who run it and have reduced the country to its present state of 'hunger'. In short, 'hunger' enables one to comment on one's own individual well-being or lack of it, and also allows one to discuss the state of the wider social, cultural and political landscape. 'Hunger' becomes a commentary about the quality of the public sphere. As a pivotal and transformative point between individual and societal breakdown and stability, 'hunger' introduces new boundaries and carves up that public sphere, while also generating new publics and new public spaces. I will further explore these now.

THE 'URBAN POOR'

To talk about 'the urban poor' as a general denominator of a specific social class within the city of Kinshasa does not clarify much. First, in the Congolese context the notion of 'class' has never been a major organisational principle. Second, for a long time urban poverty was an almost non-existing category. There are many historical reasons for both these points. As mentioned before, Leopoldville grew out of a small trading post set up by Stanley and his men in the late nineteenth century. At the start of the twentieth century, this post had already grown into an important industrial hub. This means that except for its commercial and residential white heart, the city was mainly made up of camp-like neighbourhoods that served as reservoirs for cheap and unskilled manual labour. In Leopoldville, as in many other towns and cities in Congo, such as the industrial copper capital Elisabethville (nowadays Lubumbashi), this newly created African 'working class' was imported from the rural hinterlands and housed in a rapidly expanding number of labour camps and 'indigenous' living areas.

The creation of industrial wage labour for a new (and until the end of World War II generally male) urban working class, generated previously non-existing forms of rural poverty throughout the country, and radically redefined the content and meaning of 'poverty' itself. The villages, lineages and households that fathers and husbands left behind when they were recruited by colonial authorities to work in the city were often weakened in the process, especially because the colonial introduction of a cash economy in Congo's rural areas created new forms of dependency on money that had not existed before. Between 1910 and 1935, rural areas became increasingly dependent on the city due to the emerging food trade with these rapidly growing urban centres, a process that also radically changed the nature of time, labour and agricultural production in the countryside (cf. Vellut 1977, 1987: 153. See also Hendriks 2013 on the nature of wage labour in the Belgian Congo). In the urban centres, on the contrary, structural poverty was absent, at least officially. It was not as if the urban workers (often ruthlessly recruited) did not suffer privation in the camps and quarters in which they were housed; for example, to feed themselves they usually continued to depend on products from the countryside or had to rely on whatever food the city's own ecology could offer. Nor was it the case that there was no unemployment in Leopoldville seeing that, especially from the mid-1950s onwards, the number of urban unemployed steadily rose to 20 % in Leopoldville by 1960 (Iliffe 1987: 171). But overall, the real wages of Leopoldville's unskilled labourers were rather high, and the colonial authorities only allowed Congolese to live in the city if they could prove they had a job. Unemployed migrants were identified and rounded up by the urban authorities to be deported back out to the countryside.

In the political crisis that arose around the country's independence in 1960, unemployment suddenly rose to 52 % in the capital (Iliffe 1987: 169ff). This crisis also gave rise to new forms of juvenile delinquency and urban youth street culture that continues to exert its influence to this day. To some extent, however, this 1960 crisis was conjunctural rather than structural, and between 1960 and the early 1970s, Kinshasa went through a period of relative prosperity, even though its population more than doubled from 400,000 in 1960 to 1,000,000 in 1970. In spite of this growth, many continued to find employment as manual labourers. At the same time, numerous urban residents accessed new labour markets from which they had been barred under colonial rule. In this way, a significant number of people were drawn into the state apparatus as civil servants, while others became teachers, doctors and lawyers, or joined the world of commerce and trade, especially after Mobutu's 'Zairianisaton,' a large scale nationalization process of the private and commercial sectors (cf. MacGaffey 1987). Up until 1973, these had remained mainly in Belgian hands or were outsourced to other groups, most notably Greek and Portuguese ones. The Portuguese constituted an important segment of the colony's commercial middle class, both in the colony's capital and its provincial and secondary towns. Many of these *commerçants* continued their businesses after independence until they were dispossessed of their shops and enterprises by the Mobutist state. Although Zairianisation, as part of Mobutu's famous 'authenticity campaign', was aimed at generating local upward social mobility by creating an autochthonous commercial middle class of shop owners, traders and businessmen, it actually produced the opposite effect. It was a total economic disaster and sparked the beginning of an economic and political crisis the country has yet to recover from fully. Instead of creating a local middle class, it set off a process of generalised pauperisation that affected the city's manual labour force as well as its new army of white-collar workers. The latter started to work for the post-independence state administration in the late 1960s and early 1970s, but as the economic crisis became more pronounced by the end of the 1970s and the early 1980s, they did not have time to consolidate their new status and solidify their position as a new (upper) middle class. Instead, Lebanese and Pakistanis started to fill up the void left after the departure of the Greek and Portuguese in the 1970s, and more recently the Chinese joined the ranks of this expatriate middle class.

In the early 1990s, following the dissolution of Mobutu's MPR party and the political turmoil that the start of a slow democratisation process inaugurated, inflation rates started to reach 8,000% on a yearly basis. The two waves of looting that swept through the city of Kinshasa and the country as a whole in 1991 and 1993 killed off whatever was still left of the national economic infrastructure and activity (cf. Devisch 1995). Towards the mid-1990s, only between 5% and 10% of Kinshasa's population was estimated to participate in the formal economy; a situation that condemned everybody else to the informal survival strategies and small scale corruption that became famous as *madesu ya bana* ('beans for the children'), *kobeta libanga* ('breaking stones'), *kosala nzingnzong*, *kosala shay*, or *Article 15* (an imaginary article of the Zairean Civil Code that says: *Débrouillez-vous*! [Shift for yourselves]) (see also de Villers 1996).

Already by the mid-1980s and increasingly afterwards, this downward spiral forced many Congolese into a diaspora existence, first in Europe (Tipo-Tipo 1995; Garbin and Pambu 2009) but soon afterwards in the rest of Africa and the world as a whole. But the vast majority of Kinois, for whom such an outward bound trajectory has never been an option, continues to struggle for survival at home, where the outlook for any economic improvement appears rather bleak seeing that most monetary indicators of well-being and poverty indicate a continuing downward levelling of different parts of the capital city (cf. De Herdt and Marivoet 2011). Within such a context of generalised pauperisation and 'precariat' (Standing 2011) that affects all layers of society and from which only a relatively small political and economical elite manages to escape (Freund 2009), the concept of 'urban poor' to designate a separate social class loses most of its explanatory strength because it basically encompasses the majority of the city's inhabitants. Here, the notion of 'poverty' itself comes to mean something totally different.

A place where these histories of continued decline and pauperisation have sedimented is Cielux OCPT (*Office Congolais de Poste et Télécommunication*), colloquially known as 'the Building' (*le Bâtiment*). The Building is located in the neighbourhood of Sans Fil ('Wireless'), a neighbourhood of the populous municipality of Masina, itself part of Tshangu, Kinshasa's riverine district that extends east of the colonial heart of the city.

The Cielux site was constructed in the mid-1950s as one of many *succursales* (branches) of the major post office in the central downtown municipality of Gombe. A grand modernist, L-shaped building situated in a large walled compound, it housed a section of the national radio and functioned as an outgoing relay station for international telephone and telegraph communications (hence the name 'Wireless', which now refers to the whole neighbourhood). In those years, the Building thus literally connected Leopoldville to the outside world, even though the site lay outside the city at the time of its construction.

After 1960, Masina rapidly developed into an immense and illegally occupied *zone annexe* of the municipality of Ndjili, one of the last municipalities to be developed by Belgian urban planners before independence (cf. Fumunzanza 2008: 54). In 1968, Masina's population had grown so extensively that the whole area was officially elevated to the status of municipality (idem: 227). From then on, it quickly developed into a *Chine populaire*, a 'People's Republic of China', so nicknamed because of its extremely high population density (estimated today at 50,000 inhabitants per km²).[5] In the years immediately following independence, the peripheral squatter areas of Masina mainly attracted (unemployed) workers from other more crowded neighbourhoods of the city. However, they were soon joined by newcomers from Kinshasa's adjacent rural areas (especially from the neighbouring province of Bandundu, where many are of Yaka ethnic origin).[6] These rural migrants in search of a better life in the city started to populate what has now become Masina I, II and III. And because of this history of massive migration from the countryside to Kinshasa, Masina's inhabitants often continue to be labelled as 'backward' and as 'villagers' by the rest of the city.[7]

Untouched by the swelling tide of new urban inhabitants and their improvised dwellings, which often lacked (and continue to lack) even the most basic urban infrastructures (water, electricity, sewage and so on), the area of Masina Sans Fil, surrounded as it was by a long wall that protected the Building and the land around it against intruders, remained virginally empty till the early 1980s. But then, the OCPT gave in to mounting pressure from staff at the Building and ended up opening a small part of the site and parcelling out a number of lots for its employees as compensation for all the years they had not, or only partially, been paid. Inevitably, however, once the wall

was breached, and even though the site continued to belong to the OCPT officially, it did not take long for other actors to move in as well (often because of their very good *branchement* with politicians, or members of the national secret service, for instance). Before long, the whole Cielux site was invaded. With surprising speed, the once pristine OCPT land turned into a chaotic jigsaw puzzle of lots, without much intervention by the city's cadastral services, or without even the semblance of an urban zoning plan.

After this first wave of random occupation and land grabbing, it was not long before a number of businessmen, lawyers, doctors and civil servants started to buy houses and tracts of land from OCPT employees who had been the first to receive a plot. In the late 1980s and early 1990s they were joined by *chitantistes* and *Bana Lunda* diamond traffickers, who had managed to make a quick fortune in the diamond-rich Kasai province or the Angolan diamond fields of Lunda Norte; and for a while this influx led to a certain 'gentrification' of Sans Fil.

But while the inhabitants of the Sans Fil neighbourhood were — in terms of income or because of their university degree and professional identity — originally more

of a 'middle class' than the rural migrants who occupied other parts of Masina, and while their houses in Sans Fil were often more spacious and luxurious, their fortunes were frequently very short-lived. Today, some twenty years later, little distinguishes this area in infrastructural or material terms from the rest of the Masina municipality or most of the city. The asphalt of the *Avenue Matankumu*, which had been laid in colonial times to connect the Cielux site to the N1 road (today known as the Boulevard Lumumba, the city's main road connecting the airport in the eastern periphery of the city to the city's centre), has by now completely disappeared. No other street in Sans Fil was ever asphalted. Instead the neighbourhood's roads are covered with layers of dirt and mud. Overall, the hasty, chaotic occupation of the area has left deep marks. Streets are often too narrow for a car to pass and many of them come to a dead end. Because no basic infrastructure was implemented before the area was occupied, the wastewater of most compounds is evacuated into the street. This means that many streets have become open sewers with large potholes that render car access to the neighbourhood very difficult and at times even impossible, especially during the rainy season. Due to increasing demographic pressure and the growing financial needs of the neighbourhood's inhabitants, the original tracts of land that were bought by the first generation of inhabitants have been re-parcelled into ever smaller plots; and because of this continuing atomisation of land and densification of space, Sans Fil too is rapidly becoming as over-populated as the rest of 'China.'

In terms of water supply, only half of Kinshasa's population has direct access to drinkable water, and Masina Sans Fil is no exception.[8] In spite of the proximity of the Malebo Pool, four to five compounds usually have to share the irregular water supply of one water point, which the national water company REGIDESO (*Régie de Distribution d'Eau*) does not install in a publicly accessible space but rather in someone's private compound. This not only occasions a lot of coming and going of children with buckets between neighbouring houses, but also generates frequent quarrels between neighbours as to the payment of the water invoice as well as about who actually has a right of access to the water point, and who is allowed to cross the boundaries between public street and private compound.

As for the neighbourhood's electricity supply, this typically consists of the infamous system of *délestage* or load sharing that SNEL, Kinshasa's electricity company, applies throughout most, if not all, parts of the city (De Boeck and Plissart 2004: 230). Like the irregular water supply, *délestage* is a good example of 'syncopated' infrastructure. It means that electricity is switched off in one neighbourhood during certain hours or days in order to feed other sectors in the city instead. The problem is that the rhythm of these cuts is totally unpredictable and apparently random. Some areas receive electricity most of the time, most receive electricity some of the time (though at hours that vary every day and never for the same duration), while some neighbourhoods or even streets within a neighbourhood do not get any electricity for days, weeks or even months. In the case of Sans Fil or 'Wireless', the very name of the neighbourhood has proved to portend the kind of volatile electricity supply that characterises this area of the city. But people are even worse off elsewhere, for numerous neighbourhoods are not even connected to the city's electrical network.[9]

In Kinshasa's urban speak, the *délestages* have also become a metaphor to speak about family food rationing and the fact that adults and children in many households often eat on alternating days because there is simply not enough for everyone to eat a meal on a daily basis. They have to rotate meals in the same way that SNEL rotates electricity around town. Syncopated infrastructures thus become models to think about the difficulties one encounters in daily life, while the imperfections of the grid offer blueprints for the invention of multiple new forms of social networking. Material and social infrastructures have become analogies of each other.

An easy way to explore the social geographies that result from the precarious nature of infrastructural elements is to follow the meandering trajectories of electricity cables. Not only do people start to 'bend' the power lines towards their own compounds and tap electricity from official posts, poles and cables, but the erratic rhythm of the electricity supply and the instability of the electric current itself (often worsened by this informal bending) also sets in motion a carrousel of people in search of light with which to read or write, of power for the refrigerator or to get the generator to work, or they simply seek an opportunity to connect a laptop or watch a soccer game on TV. In the streets of every neighbourhood, numerous shops equipped with privately-owned generators provide people with the chance to recharge the batteries of their cell phones if they leave them there in the morning and pick them up again in the evening. Watching TV often becomes a collective street happening when the lucky owner of a TV set *and* a generator puts his TV out in the street. All these infrastructural and 'technological indeterminacies' (de Abreu 2013), gaps, absences, silences and sudden stops and starts, which so strongly characterise the syncopated nature of the city's public infrastructure, thus generate new coping strategies and, above all, new spheres of social interaction. If, as Howe recently argued (Howe et al. 2015), ruin, as a paradox of infrastructure, suggests that even as infrastructure is generative, it degenerates, the opposite is equally true: as infrastructure degenerates, it also creates new prospects and points of opening.

In Sans Fil, the heart of all these interactions is situated around the Building that towers over the houses, shops, bars, cassava milling apparatuses and market stalls that invaded and have taken over the OCPT compound and the Building's immediate surroundings. In sharp contrast with the 'human' scale of most adjacent constructions (almost none has two storeys, for example), the Building dominates the whole neighbourhood with its sheer size, as if, after all this time, this colonial architecture remains an alien body in a postcolonial environment, a Gulliver surrounded by Lilliputians.

Yet, although it has kept some of its modernist elegance, the Building has not escaped the overall material degradation that has come to mark the rest of the Sans Fil neighbourhood. And it is on stepping inside the Building that one realises the full extent of its material degradation.

When the land surrounding the Building started to be taken over and occupied in the 1980s, it was already clear that the Building itself was also going to succumb to the pressure. And indeed, although the industrial infrastructure of the site is totally unfit for any kind of housing, the OCPT allowed some of its employees to move in, by way of an advance on unpaid salaries or as a kind of pension for some of its retiring employees. Numerous OCPT employees started to inhabit the site with their wives, children and other family members. Their example was quickly followed by employees of the national radio and television broadcasting corporation (formerly *Office Zaïrois de Radiodiffusion et de Télévision* [OZRT], today *Radio-Télévision Nationale Congolaise* [RTNC]), housed in another wing (referred to as Wing A) of the same building. Most of these people continue to be officially employed by both these companies, but I spoke to some of inhabitants who had not been paid for 150 (!) months, while others had only been paid a tenth of their monthly salaries, amounting to no more than a sum between 10 and 15 USD in most cases (March 2013). And although they are all supposed to present themselves every morning at the OCPT representative's office (see below), the equipment that would have allowed them to work in the Building has long since disappeared. When the first occupants moved in, the Building had already been badly damaged in the two waves of generalised looting and popular uprising that hit Kinshasa in 1991 and 1993 and destroyed a major part of the city's and country's industrial and commercial infrastructure. These two looting sprees also contributed substantially to the Building's infrastructural degradation: looters removed water pipes, electricity cables, elevator equipment and also stole a substantial part of the power turbines and the other electrical equipment. Other machines and motor parts were sold by corrupt OZRT officials during and after the lootings. Only the machinery that was too heavy to move, or was considered to be of no immediate practical use, was left in the Building, and remains a silent reminder of the site's more glorious past.

Today the Building is occupied by several families, totalling more than 300 people. In theory, access to and 'ownership' of an 'apartment' in the Building is arranged, supervised and controlled by an agent of the OCPT who does not actually live there himself, but comes to his office in the Building every day. Known as 'ADGA' ('Assistant of the Deputy General Director') he is the one who knows who has a right to live in the Building, and he is also the person who manages the inhabitants' conflicts and daily problems. If necessary, the ADGA will also report problems to his OCPT superiors at the ministry (*Ministère des Postes et Télécommunications*) in the city's central Gombe district. The ADGA's authority, however, is limited. While some families arrived rather recently, some other families have now been living in the Building for so long that the 'ownership' of the 'legal' squats they occupy within the building has *de facto* been passed on to the next generation. Many children of the original occupants continue to live in the Building and have already become parents themselves, so that now several generations inhabit this squatters' 'village', together with a growing number of in-laws and other dependents. Other occupants have brought their parents or grandparents along. Parts of the site are also occupied by a number of single elderly people, mostly former OCPT employees, as well as by some young orphaned children of deceased OCPT employees. The Building's least occupied areas, such as the machine room in Wing A, have been broken into by street children seeking shelter, and by other, even more unwanted guests, such as members of Kinshasa violent *kuluna* youth gangs.

In its current use, the word *kuluna* (or *kuluneur*) denotes gang youths; these gangs often have their roots in neighbourhood martial arts clubs. The members of these sports associations are also known as 'strong people' (*bato ya makasi*), *pomba* or *yanke* (from 'Yankee', a term that originates in the youth street culture known as 'Billism').[10] Today, the word *kuluna* has come to overshadow these other terms. The etymological genealogy of the word is complex but interesting. It refers to the Lingala verb *kolona*, which means 'to plant, to sow or to cultivate' and as such also resonates with the French *coloniser*. Simultaneously, it refers to a military column (as in an infantry column on foot patrol) and hence 'escort, pack or posse'. With this meaning, the word *kuluna* is

the Lingala transformation of the Portuguese *coluna*, which is imported from Angola. In the last decade of Angola's bloody civil war until the death of Savimbi in 2002, and before the DRC fell out with Angola over the often brutal and still ongoing expulsion of illegal Congolese migrants (to which Congo has retaliated by kicking out illegal Angolan migrants too), it is in the diamond-rich northern regions of the Angolan province of Lunda Norte that thousands of Congolese traffickers and artisanal miners or *garimpeiros* — many from Kinshasa — used to earn a living.[11] In the context of Kinshasa, the French/Lingala transformation of *coluna* into *kuluneurs* designates people who take part in a posse or pack that carries out 'military *kuluna*' raids to occupy, appropriate, colonise and re-territorialise streets and neighbourhood in Kinshasa.

Mainly a phenomenon that appeared in the past ten years, the *kuluna* are believed to have started in the municipality of Kalamu, and more precisely in Yolo, a neighbour-

hood famous for its boxers and wrestlers. From there the *kuluna* phenomenon has gradually engulfed the whole city, and now it is thought to have spread to sixteen of Kinshasa's twenty-four municipalities. In the early years of their existence, *kuluna* gangs were sometimes viewed in their neighbourhoods as a sort of vigilante, enhancing safety in the streets. But given the increasingly violent nature of their activities,[12] they have completely lost the sympathy of the public and are now viewed, above all, as a serious urban security threat and a concern to everybody in the city.

The graffiti that the inhabitants have written on the walls in the Building leave no doubt as to their anti-*kuluna* feelings. They warn gang members in no uncertain terms not to trespass: '*Kuluna* watch out, we will catch you! We will know you in death' (*Kuluna keba, tokokanga bino. Na liwa toyebi bino*). Testifying to the sense of insecurity that often reigns in the Building, especially at night, these warnings are not mere rhetoric. This was illustrated by an incident that took place in March 2013 in an adjacent street, when boys from the neighbourhood killed a *kuluna* intruder from a different neighbourhood because he had attacked someone from Sans Fil. Members of his gang then launched a counter-attack in the streets of Sans Fil.[13] More recently in March 2014, observers reported an increase in *kuluna* related violence in other neighbourhoods of the Tshangu district, in areas such as Mikondo, Disasi, Mayengela, Mapela and Ngamazita, in spite of the fact that only months before in November 2013, the police launched a large scale operation known as *Likofi* (*Coup de poing* or 'Punch') to sweep Kinshasa's streets clean of *kuluna* gangs.[14]

Given the increasingly brutal and violent nature of street life in the Sans Fil neighbourhood (which had been spared the worst in terms of gang violence for a long time), the Building's inhabitants have been trying to organise their own security measures, even though (and maybe also partly because) the local police is stationed on the ground floor of the Building.

As well as this police station, the ADGA's offices and the 'apartments' of the inhabitants, the Building also houses a bar, a restaurant, a cellular phone repair shop (rather fitting for a building called 'Wireless'), a Pentecostal church (with the optimistic name *Le Tremplin*, 'The Springboard'), and more recently since September 2012, a local community Pentecostal radio station called *Le Coq*, owned and run by some students who are themselves children of the families living in the Building. All these activities generate a constant coming and going of inhabitants and visitors, and this adds to what the inhabitants themselves describe as the Building's 'promiscuity' (*promiscuité*), a term that echoes the 'sanitary discourse' of earlier colonial times. The wear and tear caused by all these bodies, hands and feet inevitably adds to the material strain the building undergoes. Without any sanitation blocks, toilets, bathrooms, kitchens or access to tap water inside the Building, the overall hygienic conditions are far from ideal: many corners of the building smell strongly of urine, the elevator shafts are used as toilets,

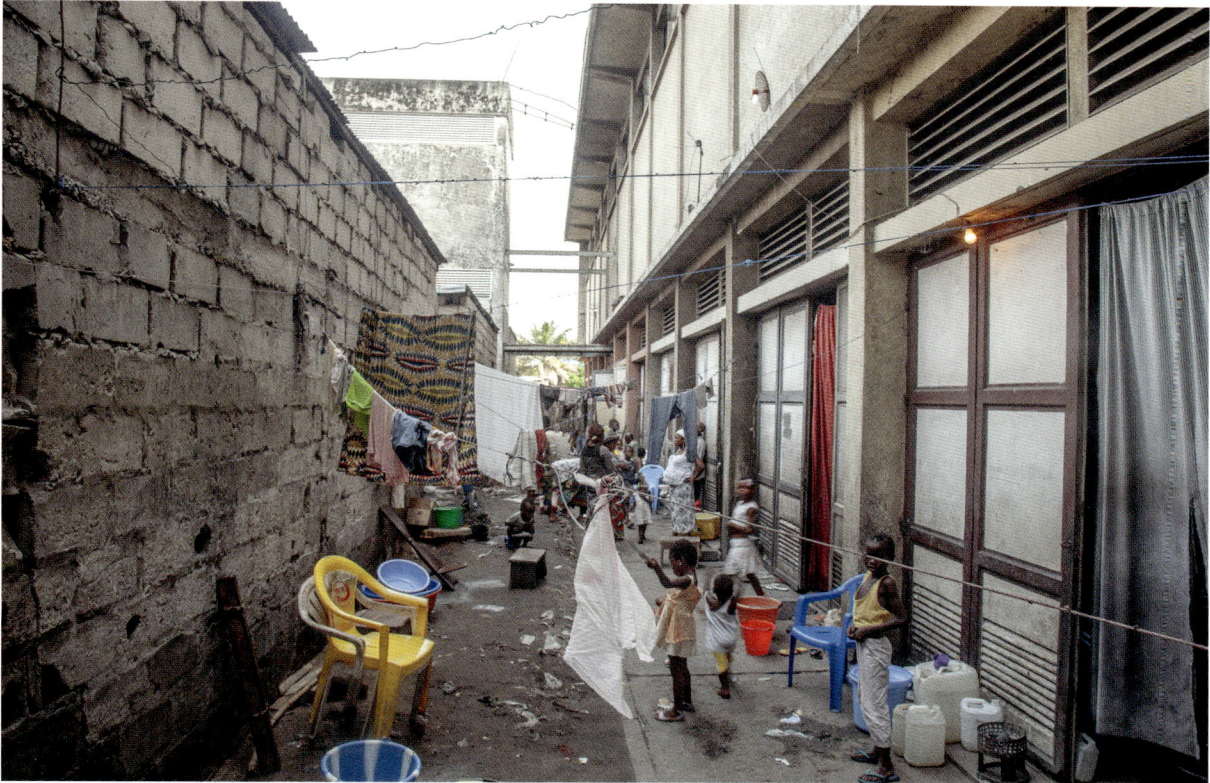

and the water from buckets that children have to carry upstairs to different living quarters constantly seeps back down to the street level again through the broken pipes of a decrepit drainage system, or via the stairs.

POVERTY, POTHOLES AND AN ANTHROPOLOGY OF INFRASTRUCTURE

The example of the Building is by no means an isolated case. Many other government buildings and sites in Kinshasa endure a similar fate. For example, most of the city's army barracks, such as Camp Kokolo — the city's best-known military garrison — are home to thousands of active-duty but also retired army personnel as well as disabled war veterans. Many of these people have been living there with their extended families for generations in conditions similar to those in the Building, and this in spite of the fact that the government has tried to evict them several times in the recent past. Government sites all over the city function in similar ways as urban microcosms that epitomise Kinshasa's popular 'urban politics' and its particular invention of specific forms and modes of semi-public/semi-private life beyond the official state vision of what the city ought to be. In fact, in Kinshasa, urban inhabitants give little or no credence to these official claims; nor is there much to give credence to either. The absence of a pro-active governmental urbanisation and housing policy leaves a lot of room for other dynamics to emerge instead. Actively re-territorialising and reclaiming the available urban space, urban residents develop their own specific forms of urbanism and infuse the city with their own praxis, values, moralities and temporal dynamics. The small-scale modes of action that punctuate such urban living provide residents with an urban politics of the possible. Often these unsteady, provisional and continually shifting possibilities and action schemes are all that is available to urban dwellers; it is, therefore, impossible to underestimate their importance.

It is in sites such as the Building, or in local zones and spaces such as wastelands, fields, cemeteries, markets, streets, bars and churches, with their myriad activities and complex webs of 'informal' economies that centre on the local production, marketing and consumption of goods and services, that the city most fully illustrates its own production, and generates the possibility of economic survival and of social life. The city reveals itself here not so much as the product of careful planning or engineering but as the outcome of a randomly produced and occupied living space belonging to whoever grabs, generates and uses it (cf. Piermay 1997). Of course, this occupation always comes with the threat of expulsion and eviction. The random occupation of urban space almost always engenders conflicts with the urban authorities. Yet, it is this organic approach to the production of the city and its spaces that eventually enables many city dwellers to survive at all, in spite of such conflicting interests and the uncertainties and constant renegotiations that these clashes entail.

Partly as a result of this organic occupation of space, everyday lives in Kinshasa are to a large extent conceived around architectures that are defined by lack and absence on a material level; many activities in the city become possible not because there is a well-developed infrastructure available to sustain them, but because that infrastructure is *not* there, or only exists through its degradation and 'absent presence'. As in the Building, people's lives in large parts of the city unfold around truncated urban forms, fragments and figments of imported urban technologies, echoes of built environments from the colonial period and recycled levels of older infrastructural accommodation. Although these infrastructures might have originated as the product of careful engineering of the urban space, they often no longer function along these lines today.

Paradoxically, the syncopated rhythms that Kinshasa's material landscape, with its physical condition punctuated by constant breakdown, lack, paucity, failure, recycling and repair, imposes on its denizens, in turn also generate new possibilities and opportunities, as well as different kinds of spaces, all of which are important to investigate and understand. As has been pointed out by many, infrastructure is usually invisible, i.e. taken for granted and therefore largely unnoticed until it breaks down, at which point it becomes very present in its absence. The switching between absence and presence, or between visibility and invisibility of infrastructure, is of a complex and unpredictable nature, and therefore involves a whole 'range of visibilities' (Larkin 2013: 336).

As just one example of this, the potholes or pools of water on the public road underneath the Building may become enabling infrastructural elements in themselves. For years, I would pass the Building on my way to a friend's house, and even during the dry season when the mud in other streets in the neighbourhood had dried and hardened enough for the streets to be used, this particular point was impossible for me to pass through as the water was too deep and the mud too excessive. Pedestrians were forced to walk to the side of the street and pass underneath the pillars of the Building's ground floor, while drivers would have to stop and leave their cars in front of the Building's police office, in order to continue their way on foot . The cause of all this inconvenience and misery was obvious: the Building had a broken rain gutter and pipe through which the sewage from its bowels flowed non-stop into the street. 'How much can it cost to repair a rain pipe,' I often wondered, 'and how eroded can the feeling of community be if the inhabitants of the Building and its surroundings can't even get together to raise the small sum needed to repair such a minor thing that has become such a nuisance to everyone day in, day out?' It finally dawned on me that nobody *wanted* to fix the broken pipe, because by repairing it, a whole part of the social and economic tissue in and around the Building would be disrupted. In fact, everyone was preoccupied not with repairing the water pipe, but with the question of how to maintain the mud-filled potholes. Not only did they generate an extra income for the policemen who would keep an eye on the cars left in front of the police station in return for a small 'gift', but the potholes would also generate customers, and therefore a source of income for the numerous women who had managed to grab a place to set up their market stalls between the pillars beneath the Building. Thanks to the potholes, this space was perceived to be a commercially viable spot; consequently, these women, some of whom lived in the Building or else were the wives, daughters and girlfriends of the Building's policemen, had to make small regular payments (to the ADGA, for example) in return for the privilege of 'owning' such a strategic spot.

Elements such as potholes are infrastructurally invisible, because we do not tend to think about them as constructive elements. But they represent not only 'infrastructures in reverse' or 'negative' infrastructures, they are also 'reverse' infrastructures, or 'negatives' of infrastructures that, in Kentridge-like fashion, become visible only when one manages to invert the negation and 'illuminate the shadow' (see Chapter Two). It is only when one starts to think of potholes as *instructure* rather than 'infrastructure', that they start to reveal their potential, to create publics, for instance, and to offer the possibility of drawing pedestrians to them or 'thickening' and slowing these pedestrians down and thereby converting them into potential customers. As car drivers in Kinshasa well know, this is the way in which potholes function everywhere in the city. In many a

street, young men are busy with shovels filling up potholes with sand and gravel. Doing so enables them to stop cars and ask drivers for a small contribution in return for their 'service', i.e. in recognition of the fact that their road repair facilitates the drivers' mobility and thus improves their well-being. Again, it is important to be able to claim a pothole at a particularly busy point in the street as one's own, for this will generate more income. Similarly, it is of utmost importance to hold on to that pothole for as long as possible. They have to make sure, therefore, that the pothole never gets filled up. That is why the same men, at night, will empty the pothole they had been busy filling the previous day, in order to secure some earnings, however small, the next day. I know people who have been filling the same potholes on the same street corner for almost ten years. In Kinshasa and Congo more generally, the word 'hole' therefore no longer primarily denotes a physical pit, cavity, crater, depression or hollow. Instead it has become a metaphor to denote an opening, an aperture that offers a possibility or an opportunity. Along these lines, for example, people sometimes use the word *mena* (which literally means 'hole' in Chokwe, one of the languages spoken in Southern Congo and Angola) to speak about the money changers (also known as *cambistes*) that one

commonly encounters on markets and in busy streets. One has to know how to approach and address them, how to enter these 'holes' in order to negotiate a good rate and come out of this encounter, this descent into the 'hole', with a little extra money in hand, like a diamond digger who emerges from his mining pit with some valuable diamonds.

What this illustrates is that the form that city life takes is not only imposed by the rhythms of the city's failing material infrastructures and the 'confusion' that the decrepit nature of these infrastructural simulacra constantly generates, but that the city is as much shaped by mental and social landscapes. As Stoler remarks, ruinations simultaneously are about 'the material and social afterlife of structures, sensibilities, and things. Such effects reside in the corroded hollows of landscapes, in the gutted infrastructures of segregated cityscapes and in the microecologies of matter and mind' (Stoler 2008: 194). In short, these vulnerable infrastructures impose their own spatial and temporal logic on the city. They close off many possibilities, but they also create new social infrastructures, alternative spheres of social interaction, and different coping strategies and regimes of knowledge and power, which in turn change the meaning and the degree of visibility of the infrastructure itself.

All of this forces us to look at city life differently and to question standard urban paradigms and prevailing notions of 'slum' life and urban dystopia, without forgetting, however, that this level of urban functioning outside of the official frameworks of formal urban management and planning is indeed also strongly defined and characterised by poverty, precariousness, hardship and necessity. Yet to some extent, this way of being in and with the city also allows urbanites to become local producers and controllers of infrastructure and technology rather than local consumers of technology imported from elsewhere. It transforms city dwellers from passive victims into active participants with their own social, economic, political and religious agendas, which are often situated way beyond the sphere of mere survival. Far from allowing them to 'enjoy poverty', as film-maker Renzo Martens provocatively put it (Martens 2009; cf. also Demos and Van Gelder 2012), it actually offers them instead considerable freedom to seize and hold onto the sudden possibilities opened up by unexpected occasions that are generated by the synergies and frictions of urban life.

THE (UN)MAKING OF THE PUBLIC SPHERE:
POLITICS, PUBLICS AND VIOLENCE IN THE CITY

In recent years and even more so than before, everyday urban life, with its shifting appropriations of public space, has taken on the dimension of an existential and also deeply political, struggle for day-to-day survival. Kinshasa is currently being reframed by neoliberal urban reform and development plans that radically relocate people's rights to the city, as it currently does all over the Global South (see, for example, Kaminer, Robles-Duràn and Sohn 2011; Künkel and Mayer 2012; Samara, He and Chen 2013). As I noted in Chapter Two, in Kinshasa the implied teleological futurities of these urban reforms have a tendency to obliterate physically and conceptually the reality of millions of local lives. A focus on 'infrastructure' is therefore becoming increasingly 'political': it is a means to reflect on the changing connotations of what constitutes the public sphere and the meaning of the categories of public and private and of 'diversity' in the urban locale.

If one of a state's founding conditions is the way in which it defines and implements the categories of public and private, then these categories are in need of a profound redefinition, certainly (but not only) in postcolonial contexts such as the DR Congo, where the state does not hold the monopoly over how these categories are defined and where it no longer constitutes (if it ever did) the sole core of power to orchestrate its contents. The state, in the realities of its everyday governance, constantly needs to negotiate its place to the same extent as all the other actors (cf. Hagman and Péclard 2011; De Herdt and Olivier de Sardan 2015); this is illustrated by the role of the AGDA in the Building and by the fact that the policeman stationed in the Building has to adapt his street interventions around the Building if he does not want his wife to lose her place or her customers at the little market beneath the Building. In such contexts, the lines between public and private remain blurred or are constantly given new meanings (in terms of the spaces, infrastructures, body politics and the specific conditions of the sort of modernities and informalities in which these categories are erected and transform their meaning). Urban existence in the Global South more generally, and in Kinshasa more specifically, often seems to consist of various publics in various specific (distinct yet often interrelated) locations (the already mentioned gardens, fields, bars, buildings, cemeteries, churches, streets and markets) that are often situated outside or not totally within the grasp of political institutions, even though they might be partly modelled by them. The result is not one public realm, but a diversity of publics and public spaces, things (material infrastructures), words (verbal architectures) and bodily functions. Together, all these elements make up the social machine of the public realm as the sum of different collective experiences in which individual survival is made possible or, on the contrary, constantly made impossible.

The important issue of *diversity* in the city should first and foremost apply to this diverse notion of the public itself (and its association with political life). As already noted, 'class' has never been a strong marker to delineate publics and public spheres in Congolese urban life, notwithstanding the much heralded, but still largely illusory, birth of a new African upper middle class. When discussing an urban context such as Kinshasa's, we are not exactly dealing here with a Habermasian model of a single and 'rhetorically constituted bourgeois public sphere of self-conscious political deliberation' (Chalfin 2014: 101). What Chalfin vividly describes in relation to the context of public toilets in Tema, a planned city in Ghana, goes for Kinshasa as well: instead of presenting itself as one unified dominant space, Tema's (as well as Kinshasa's) public sphere consists of an entanglement between the classic notion of such a space and a different, much vaster, realm of everyday 'co-presence' (Amin and Graham 1997: 417–18), embedded in 'embodied' and 'practical discourse enabling individual and social life' (Chalfin 2014: 101). This is perhaps what scholars like Swyngedouw mean by the 'post-political' city. Within such post-political moments, the urban space is no longer capable of acting as a single meaningful space for the construction of political subjectivities and new modes of political decision-making: 'While the city is alive and thriving (at least in some of its spaces),' Swyngedouw remarks, 'the polis, conceived in the idealised Greek sense as the site for public political encounter and democratic negotiation, the spacing of (often radical) dissent, and disagreement, and the place where political subjectivation literally takes place, seems moribund.' (2007: 59; see also Wilson and Swyngedouw 2014).

Swyngedouw is discussing urban contexts in the West, but in many cities in the Global South, the *res publica* seems even less made up of one dominant ethical or normative space. On the contrary, if only because of its colonial and precolonial pasts, it is always already diversified through various different, often conflicting, views on what collectivity, sociality, solidarity, collaboration or the associational might mean. Various publics, from within and across various (often entangled) spaces, constantly offer a ground for questioning, recalling, bypassing or resisting official definitions of the public 'thing'. It should be added, however, that this does not exclude a consensus with, a simultaneous adherence or conforming to, or even a yearning for the realization of the official definitions.

At the same time, mobilisation of diversity in these urban contexts is often rather paradoxically played out in somewhat monolithic ways. One the one hand, urban life is always generating openings, divergences, possibilities and lines of flight, while on the other, it never ceases to generate closures and exclusions on other levels by creating fake dichotomies, oppositions and potential choices that are a pretence of diversity, but in fact spring from an extremely limited number of options that generate an overwhelming sense of uniformity. As already mentioned, this is true for the State itself as a negotiated entity, but also for the various publics in their attempts to constitute collectivities and groups, and through them individual identities. One's membership of a certain collectivity or group might be less well defined by the fluid and volatile category of class, but it certainly is defined — to a greater or lesser extent and at varying moments in time — by ethnic belonging, either along regional or territorial lines, or else along generational or religious lines, or then by belonging to a trade or smuggling network, fan club, rotational saving bank, student club, youth gang, and so on. According to the various needs or the relevance of the moment, each of these 'belongings' might be strategically activated or slip into 'sleep' mode. There can be a combination of different memberships, but the ethical spaces that each of these groups generate usually seems to exist as mutually exclusive: a supporter of Vita Club (one of the two famous football clubs in Kinshasa) can in no way make this known in a neighbourhood where people support Vita's rival club, Motema Pembe (see also Simone 2010b:141). One either listens to the music of Werrason or JB Mpiana, but it would be unthinkable to admit to liking both, even though their music sounds rather similar. In the same vein, one drinks either Primus or Skol beer, in spite of their tasting almost exactly the same, and the bars where both are served simultaneously, or by the same waitress, are rare because the two brands are mutually exclusive: waitresses who serve Skol even belong to a different 'tribe' from those who serve Primus (the first one is called 'Princesse' and the other 'Amazone'). Similarly, if one uses Vodacom as a mobile telephony provider rather than Zain or Airtel for instance, it makes one part of a certain constituency, a specific public (even though, in reality, and for obvious reasons of connectivity and networking, several memberships and access to several networks are needed simultaneously, and therefore a phone with several SIM cards must be used). But even so, here too a strong sense of uniformity creates an obligation to conform to your public (and often, on meeting someone for the first time, the very questions that are asked are about which club you support, which music you like, what kind of beer you drink, which cell phone provider you use). The answers determine the likelihood of a longer relationship, they place one within a specific moral or aesthetic universe, and offer the sense of being able to 'know', 'place' and 'read' the person in question. But when scrutinised more closely, this 'knowing' is often merely based on a (performative) pretence of difference. And the more impossible it is to establish a public or even imagine the likelihood of a public, the greater the pretence and the simulacrum of difference.

This is also, in part, how the city produces its own specific forms of social violence. Even if, all things considered, Kinshasa has been a relatively non-violent urban space in terms of overt physical violence for most of its existence (which is perhaps surprising given the harshness of life in this city on the material and social levels, its formidable scale and the multiple imperfections of its administrative, military and policing structures), there has been an undeniable sharp rise in extreme violence in the city; a violence and sense of insecurity resulting from the territorial warfare between a growing number

of *kuluna* gangs who not only fight each other but also terrorise the inhabitants of the neighbourhoods they have territorialised and colonised (as can be seen in the examples above), or are hired as thugs by politicians to attack political opponents.[15]

But most people's experience of everyday violence is less spectacular and lies elsewhere. It is the violence of daily survival, which everyone resorts to and directs mainly at each other (instead of at the political and economical elites that exploit and abuse them). In fact, all cleavages in Kinshasa (in terms of class, ethnic background, political adherence, generational rifts etc.) are constantly overcome by a fracturing of the city's public space, which produces a violence of proximity but also manages to overcome that violence because of that same proximity (or 'promiscuity' as the Building's inhabitants call it). Kinshasa's public space is a conglomerate of multiple spaces that are constantly being 'privatised' in various degrees and with varying levels of success. Public space is constantly fractured and parcelled out by an array of individual actors, by means of intricate processes of seizing hold and taking possession of public space. This goes hand in hand with a process of individualisation and a refutation of group identity, which is expressed in a number of phrases that have become very popular in

Kinshasa in recent years: 'Mind your own business!' (*Kipe ya yo!*)[16] and 'What's yours is yours, what's mine is mine' (*Ya yo ya yo, ya ngai ya ngai*). Concurrently, the same individual actors are constantly made to identify with a very specific group and public. A woman working in the market is not just a market woman, for example. In the beginning of this chapter, I mentioned the expression *mama bitula*, the name given to a specific kind of market woman (a vendor of unsold goods at reduced prices outside the market in the evening). This is a totally different category of market woman from the category of *mama benz*, for example, or *mama manoeuvre*, *mama bipupula*, *mama trieuse*, *mama mitelengano* and the *bamama baboya toli*, not to mention the multiple different categories of specialisation existing for men and children in and around the market.

Mama manoeuvre is a small-scale retailer who resells goods and food that she buys from large suppliers (referred to as *mama benz* because they usually drive in a Mercedes Benz and sell quality textiles). *Mama manoeuvre* divides everything she sells into as many small quantities as possible in order to make more of a profit. She does not specialise in one specific product. *Mama bipupula*, on the other hand, is a 'scavenger' who searches for food scraps and leftovers from the market and resells at even more reduced prices.

Mama bipupula and *mama trieuse* are hired by more powerful merchants to sieve flour or clean vegetables and are paid for these services with a small quantity of these items. *Mama mitelengano* (from the Lingala verb *-telengana*: 'to vagabond, tramp, meander') roams about the market in search of something edible or some task, such as washing clothes, delivering food at a home, helping buyers to get a good price with sellers, and so on. *Bamama baboya toli* ('the mothers who refuse [their husbands'] counsel') are successful market women who, thanks to the relative financial independence they enjoy and the social power that comes with it, refuse to recognise that their husbands have any authority over them and demand and claim the position of heads of their households.[17]

The income and survival of each of these individual women and groups of women and their survival depends on their sticking to their specificity and particular skill, while they re-inforce the lines of their professional identity and group as they stake their claim, mark their territory and stand their ground; because they all have to fight, first between themselves and then as a group against other groups of 'mamas' for their place in the market and for the same clients (who themselves are most likely to have similar professional occupations). These demarcations, therefore, go hand in hand with a great deal of social violence, verbal abuse and even physical aggression. 'Everything becomes a fight' (*nionso ezali bitumba*), as one market woman told Kamba (2008: 348): 'To get into a bus, minibus, taxi or make some money, eat, everything turns into violence. If you are not awake and alert, if you are too passive, you'll die before you know it and then they'll bury you. It's like a jungle. When you are weak, you are eaten by those who are stronger.' (2008: 348)[18]

As a result, the public space becomes the sum total of a myriad of narrowly defined identities and small parcelled lots that are temporarily, and rather fleetingly, owned by individuals and small, often ad hoc, collectivities. These have to keep constant guard over the boundaries of their temporary ownership of a small piece of space within the city's streets and markets, and to negotiate nonstop their right to be there with a multitude of others, whether they be neighbours, passersby, street gangs, police, civil servants and so on. All these instances never fully enter into the game as institutional or collective entities, because they always also step into the arena as individual actors, men and women with whom they might establish (often very provisional and temporary) bonds and relationships of trust, reciprocity, interest and mutual gain; they become each other's 'field' (*elanga*) and therefore also need each other, whether they like it or not. A common expression in Kinshasa compares citizens to 'fields' that soldiers, or 'the State', regularly harvest in order to 'feed' themselves (*Civil azali elanga ya soda*) (Kamba 2008: 350). But this utilitarian interpretation of what co-presence and interdependence means has increasingly become an inalienable part of urban society in general.

The absolute and constant necessity to renegotiate these links, to inscribe oneself in as many networks as possible and engage in as many relationships as possible, offers a mechanism through which strangers and others may be redefined, however briefly, in terms of relatedness, kinship, friendship and autochthony (and possibly also vice versa). The endless lifting of the anomaly of anonymity also requires ceaseless construction of a promiscuous public social life that takes place on a very localised scale and by means — out of necessity — of a very physical proximity. This, in turn, then imposes the reductive material and social scale of the local onto things and people, which can make it impossible for people to break out and take themselves to a different, broader plane of action.

This does not mean that these conceptualising manoeuvres of relatedness, or the necessity of proximity and promiscuity, do not pose problems or dangers. On the contrary, they are usually even more dangerous: accusations of witchcraft are far more common amongst close kin than between strangers, for example (cf. Geschiere 2013; see also Ayimpam 2014b). But at least they offer the possibility of a performance of potential *ad hoc* sociabilities and convivialities. This performance is more usually conditional or *pro forma*, and sometimes very short-lived; but at least it indicates a possible overcoming of differences and generating of temporary co-presences, or at least the intention of doing so. That is why interpersonal conflicts and disputes (over money, access to a field or 'ownership' of a lover) are always played out in public. This 'playing out' invariably takes place in very theatrical ways, which always involve verbal and often even physical attacks; it is the performance, the theatricality of the way in which the conflict is acted out, that draws a crowd and forms a public that eventually and inevitably ends up intervening and preventing the conflict from further escalating,

even if only temporarily. The same goes for witchcraft accusations because while they can fracture a collectivity, they also bring the conflict out into the open, and by making it public, provide possibilities for re-assembling and for what Simone refers to as the 'setting of the screen' for a possible public:

'For example, one striking aspect of everyday life in Kinshasa — that vast rambling almost ungovernable megacity of the Congo — is just how often strangers intervene into scenarios on the verge of getting out of hand and come up with the right sense of things in order to steer them in another direction'. (…)
'But in contexts where the legitimacy of actions of all kinds can be incessantly contested, where people are always looking out for instances of self-aggrandize-ment and where veracity has long disappeared as an essential component of believability, the screen must always carry with it the traces of elsewheres — i.e. something inserted that is familiar, desired or reliable. Of course, the person who 'sets the screen' — who 'screens' — cannot be expected to be aware or in control of this. In this way the screen acts as a kind of 'graft', an image of momentary integrity and completeness that comes from the outside but is capable of acting as if it had been inside of the scenario in question the whole time. An imposition can take place — a different way of keeping things moving, a change in the anticipated story line, where individuals feel variation in the way they experience they are in matters — but with the sense that everything is taking place in the same 'neighbourhood', at the same time, in the same world (…).' (Simone 2012a: 212)

The performative nature of public space is therefore always marked by three inter-related processes. Firstly, the 'morcellation'[19] or 'informal' privatisation of that space, that is, the setting up of boundaries to demarcate a piece of that space as one's own by seizing, holding onto and taking possession. This can be helped by infrastructural imperfections (see the pothole example above) and is signalled in tangible and material ways by means of makeshift shacks, fences, trees and so on. Secondly, given the permeability of borders and the ever-present option, almost the right and obligation, to interfere in other people's matters (even if that right is immediately contested as well), one's property has to be guarded by relentlessly (re)negotiating these boundaries (which in and of themselves not only generate power and control and thus income, but also the possibility of identity construction and establishing a public to which one can belong). Thirdly, given the precarious nature of the reality of property claims, there is always the possibility of having to resign oneself to letting go, moving on and becoming mobile again and later returning perhaps at the right time to repossess the place that had to be relinquished. As such, movement becomes a form of property in and of itself seeing that urban residents usually have no stable or lasting proprietary relationship to anything they may own — even the space they appropriate, occupy and inhabit.

Here the corporeal infrastructure becomes important again, for the body is always with you and it is mobile. It may be beaten and violated but it can never be stolen or taken away from you (unless, of course, one enters the realm of the occult, where the

'stealing' of bodies or their 'doubles' is common practice, as most bodies are considered to have a double life [cf. Bernault 2013]). The likelihood and frequent necessity of physically moving away and coming back, retreating, waiting (and determining the exact time needed to wait), and then returning to stake a claim again, must be taken into account to understand the spatial and temporal politics of urban poverty and public space, and the precise ways in which these take shape in an urban environment such as in Kinshasa.

In these urban worlds, diversity eventually mutates into something else. While offering the possibility to constitute a collectivity and form a group, it also creates boundaries and differences that, lacking a difference in content and because of the interchangeability of publics, seem to be established and played out along totally arbitrary lines that prevent different publics, i.e. different groups of individuals, to constitute a general public (as the overarching totality of such groupings). The possibility (or a simulacrum) of the freedom to chose in an environment of poverty that does not otherwise offer many real choices and options is indicative of the unceasing tension between the public thing and its various publics. Whatever the case may be, the urban context by means of these mechanisms continually generates fixity, conformity and homogenising uniformity that can also be seen in the monotony of the built environment itself, which is often marked by its strongly generic quality. Simultaneously, in so doing, it also generates incessant heterogeneity and dispersal.

On the one hand, then, the urban world is the space where (political) subjectivation takes place. It imposes a strong and dominant necessity to conform in order to exist socially and/or politically within the city. But at the same time, this conformity is always double-edged and continually unravels in a disorderly, often playful but sometimes also violent plurality, which seems to be an equally necessary prerequisite in order to survive. Hand in hand with flow, flux, opening up, excess, fragmentation, dissipation, difference, mobility and multiplicity goes an often fanatical adherence to arbitrary rules, laws and legal frameworks in a lawless world[20]; or at least a world where laws always seems to shape-shift into something else. There is a longing to believe in absolute truths in a world where truth is volatile, arbitrary, easy to manipulate and always multiple; and a strong tendency to generate a monolithic high moral ground in a world that often seems to be devoid of morality. Similarly, the need to singularise and thereby realise oneself by becoming a member of an exclusive group always coexists with the impossibility of being exclusive: if exclusive membership of a group seems an absolute prerequisite in order to become visible and exist socially in the urban site, this only works if one can inscribe oneself into as many groups and networks as possible; it is this capacity to insert oneself, to belong and belong together, that also determines the possibility to survive physically, socially, economically and politically. The tension between singularisation and exclusivity, and the need to conform to and be part of as many collectivities as possible is played out on all levels and makes *and* undermines the public realm.

In order to understand the tensions and complex complicities between the individual and the collective, between publics and the public, that are inherent to this urban life, it is important to reflect more profoundly on specific modes of singularisation, self-realisation and self-making within the often very limited existing possibilities of forming groups (and therefore public realm or realms) in these urban contexts. A good starting point for such an exercise seems to be to reflect on the possibilities and, above all, the *im*possibilities of accumulation. It brings us back to reflecting on the apocope *nso* (tiny portions of chicken skin) with which this chapter started. As Foucault (1995: 220-221) pointed out, the accumulation of capital or goods and the accumulation of people (the forming of groups and constituting of publics) are two processes that cannot be viewed separately. This seems to apply all the more in a universe where wealth in people and wealth in things often reinforce each other or are even interchangeable. The processes by which goods and people can be seized, held, immobilised and accumulated go hand in hand with processes of circulation, mobility, expenditure and a non-directional or non-teleological temporality. It is this double dynamic that offers the possibility of making and claiming identity and place in an urban context, and generates specific ways in which the public good, in terms of resources and resource control, is imagined and managed. But it is also this possibility that is most at risk

because of the conditions and the staccato rhythms of syncopation and suspension that the city imposes on social life in general.

This brings us back to the theme of rhythm that I introduced in the beginning of this paper and which I would like to expand by way of conclusion. I have argued that as a basic 'structure' of feeling and experience, to paraphrase Williams (1977), the 'form' that permeates the *mistik* of Kinshasa's urban topographies may best be described as *rhythm*: the rhythms, paces, tones and echoes pulsating through the city's social life and its accompanying acts of *koluka,* of 'searching'; its metrical contradictions and syncopal deviations, the quickenings and thickenings of time and people that shape the surface of everyday life, with its releases and restraints, its sudden opportunities and eternal postponements, its ejaculations and constipations, patterns of conspicuous consumption and enduring abstention.

DIVINING URBAN RHYTHMS: THE CITY AS LIMIT-EXPERIENCE:

Suspensions and missed beats, occasioned by the staccato cadences and all the literal and figurative outages the city imposes on its inhabitants sometimes offer the possibility to discover, explore and invent unexpected accents. The syncopal off-the-beat produces openings into the 'something else' off the beaten track. But above all, they generate interminable questions of an almost divinatory nature, even if it is only because people are always searching for the reasons behind, for example, the erratic power supply (to return to the notion of the already mentioned *délestage*). In this sense, the city's material infrastructure actually becomes a divinatory tool that allows one to read spiritual and ontological insecurities into infrastructural breakdowns, and vice versa.[21] And, as is common protocol in a divinatory ritual séance, they try to come up with a causal explanation for present wrongs by tracing them back to (a chain of) events in the past. Establishing complex etiological grids of this kind represents spontaneous attempts to individuate the dysfunctionalities in the city, and the State, and thereby question, re-assemble, understand and transform their disjointed and often random nature. 'Why does the street next to ours receive electricity, and we do not? Why did SNEL decide to change our electricity regime from a couple of hours per day to half a day every week? Which neighbour could possibly have influenced that decision? Why do they hold a grudge against us? Did we (me, my wife, my children, my cousin, my uncle) possibly do something to upset them, and if so, what could that have been? Did someone in the neighbourhood annoy the authorities? Isn't the next-door neighbour rumoured to be sleeping with the wife of the personal assistant of the director of the local sector of SNEL? And isn't the other neighbour politically active in a party that opposes the party to which the minister responsible for the electricity company belongs? Could that be why thieves always steal our street's electricity cables? If not, who else sent them to do so?' These questions become all the more poignant if, as is frequently the case, houses burn down and people die because the power cables were not correctly connected, or merely because of the poor quality of the electrical wiring, or a sudden overvoltage that causes cables to melt and household appliances to explode.[22]

The disjointed infrastructural figments and fragments that make up the urban landscape are consequently embedded in other rhythms and temporalities, in totally different layers of socially networked infrastructures, punctuated by various spatial, temporal and affective oscillations: these vary between connectedness and disconnection, situated in the waxing and waning movements between foreground and background or underground; between surface, fold and gap; between the visible and the invisible, darkness and light, movement and motionlessness, continuity and discontinuity, flow and blockage, opening and closure. As such, urban living is ceaselessly rhythmed by its excesses and scarcities; its dispersals and immobilizations; its homogeneity and heterogeneity; its total boundlessness and the totalitarian nature of its endless restrictions; its frequent moments of violent effervescence and the boredom of endless waiting that also characterise urban life.

It takes a great deal of perseverance, courage and tactical skills to live the 'limit-experience' of the city on a daily basis. I am using here the concept of 'limit-experience' in its Foucauldian sense of an experience which, in terms of its intensity and seeming impossibility, leads a person to life's edge by 'seeing to it that the subject is no longer itself, that it is brought to its annihilation or its demolition' (Foucault as quoted in Sluga 2005: 224). This is also one of the reasons why people, in their quest to convert this 'living on the edge' into something more enduring, often turn to ritual specialists for assistance and help. To a considerable extent, this role has been taken on by the preachers and pastors of Kinshasa's Pentecostal churches. However, diviners, who make use of older local divinatory traditions and techniques, also continue to be consulted.[23]

Take, for example, the case of Makila, a policeman who was assigned to the Building's police station in Sans Fil.[24] When off duty, Makila lived with his family in a small compound in Bibwa, on the eastern outskirts of Kinshasa. In 2012, when I paid a visit to his house, Makila introduced me to a Suku diviner who lived nearby.[25] He had already told me how they had met some years earlier. One night, Makila, together with another policeman, were supposed to keep watch over a car that they had confiscated and then parked in front of the Building's police station. The two policemen fell asleep and when they woke up a couple of hours later, the car was gone. As a result, Makila was accused by his superiors of having stolen the car. He was arrested and jailed. From prison he managed to send a message to his wife, telling her to contact the diviner in question and ask for help. Makila's wife hurried to the diviner's house and during the ensuing divinatory session, the diviner traced the whereabouts of the stolen car, or at least, he told the wife in which specific neighbourhood of the city the car could probably be located, adding that, in all likelihood, it had by now been repainted another colour. With this information, and after a search that lasted three days, Makila's wife and her sister managed to find the stolen vehicle (which had not only been repainted but its engine had already been removed and sold) near the area that the diviner had indicated. As a result of this successful search, Makila was released and the real culprits of the car theft were arrested. Ever since then, the diviner has continued to play an important role in many of the decisions Makila makes on a daily basis in his private and professional life.

Judging from the number of visitors waiting to consult this diviner every time I visit him in his compound, Makila is by no means an exception. Whatever the situation may be — whether illness, misfortune, witchcraft attacks, professional setbacks, troubled marriages, problematic relationships, the weight of city life, and so on — the divinatory oracle identifies and re-formulates the problem in question by embedding it in a different, less closed and more constructive narrative that always suggests the possibility of agency, that of acting on and thereby transforming and opening up the problematic limit-experience that is responsible for 'wrenching the subject from itself' (Foucault as quoted in Sluga 2005: 224). This revelatory breaking open of the problem at hand, and the suggestion of a possible line of action, counters the subject's breaking away from itself; it brings one back to oneself and reconfigures the (social) boundaries between oneself and the surrounding world. This is what Silva describes so beautifully when she states that through (basket) divination, objectified individuals (and by 'objectification' she means a 'sense of existential powerlessness, uncertainty and diminution') attempt to de-objectify themselves (Silva 2011: 6).

In other words, a divinatory consultation allows clients to re-insert themselves into the world in an alternative way and through a transformative ritual movement, as properly re-assembled subjects. It should be noted that the diviner also undergoes a similar transformation. This happens during an initiatory trance possession that Devisch, in the context of Yaka divinatory rituals, describes as a form of 'self delivery' or 'auto release' (2013: 36). In other words, to become a diviner one first has to become 'ill', i.e. become 'possessed' by the divining spirit, *ngoombu* or *ngombo*. And this 'illness', this 'suffering' that can best be described as an experience of self-dispersal, of being 'wrenched' from oneself, of being annihilated and, indeed, 'objectified' in Silva's sense, is a necessary moment in order to be able to de-objectify afterwards. Interestingly, the Yaka term for this initiatory trance possession or moment of self-dispersal is *kaluka* (Devisch 2013: 36ff), which etymologically links the initiatory trance experience of a diviner (a moment that also involves his 'searching' for a hidden object in order to prove his clairvoyant capacities — see also De Boeck & Devisch 1994) to the way in which urban residents move and 'search' (*koluka*) their way through the city. Two screens, two different kinds of landscape, are thus superimposed and melt to become one. In a divination ritual, the diviner's searching is metaphorically likened to that of a hunter, or a hunting dog, searching for game in the bush or the forest.[26] On the other hand, in the collective social instituting imaginary of its inhabitants, the city itself is often also conceived in terms of a forest. As I have elaborated elsewhere (De Boeck and Plissart 2004: 41), this is why Werrason, Kinshasa's most popular musician, is nicknamed 'King of the Forest' (*le roi de la forêt*), for example. The (precolonial) hunter's landscape, which is that of the potentially dangerous, frontier-like fringe, is thus constantly merging with and mapped onto the urban landscape. In order to survive and thrive in this urban jungle, one needs to be able, like a hunter and a diviner, to read all the traces left behind and follow the right tracks and trails.

In the end, what do divinatory practices tell us specifically about the *form* of the urban drive, and the particular energies of suffering, disillusionment, ailing, healing and hope that run through the city?

RHYTHMS OF AMALGAMATION AND KNOTS AS LIMIT-SITUATION:

Characterised by the specific nature of the chaotic rhythms that determine people's lives within the urban terrain, with all its 'bumpy incoherent surfaces and inexplicable narrow bottlenecks' (Guyer 2011: 477), the urban world consists of complex divisions and/or conflations of space, time, frequency and codes that make and mark the form of urban life, and are shaped by the multiple modes of transference, channelling, networking and *branchement* discussed earlier. Social scientists, architects and urban planners have applied a myriad of metaphors and images to capture analytically the often paradoxical and rarely unidirectional or teleological movements the city experiences, or to describe the thick layeredness of matter and time that so greatly characterises the form that urban existence can take. Think, for example, of the forms of the rhizomatically non-orientable, the palimpsestual, or the multiplex, of Amselle's *branchements* (Amselle 2001), of Tsing's connections and articulations in global zones of engagement (Tsing 2005), of assemblages (McFarlane 2011 a/b), or the notion of 'entanglement' as advanced by Sarah Nuttall (2009). In ways that strongly resonate with my own reading of Kinshasa, Nuttall distinguishes between historical entanglement, temporal entanglement, entanglement of the seam and complicity, entanglement of people and things and racial entanglement (Nuttall 2009: 2-9). What all of these different forms and entanglements seem to have in common with each other is the quality (or process) of *amalgamation*, i.e. of combining or uniting multiple entities into one form.

In Central African cultural registers, the ideas of amalgamation and combination have always been expressed by the form of the knot, and through processes of knotting, tying, connecting, weaving and intertwining. As 'limit situations' (and here I borrow the term from Eliade 1952), knots are both conjuncts and disjuncts. They may simul-

130

taneously express the idea of interlinking, connecting, border-crossing and the trans-position of meaning from one field to another. Or they might, on the contrary, express acts or states of disconnection and the untying of integrative links. They may also represent closure, blockage and suffocation. Throughout large areas of Central Africa, the notion of the knot and the act of knotting are often used as metaphors to express states of physical health, social well-being, physical and social reproduction and, more metaphorically, acts of 'world-making', i.e. the establishment and replenishing of social and cultural orders, through ritual, for example. But the notion of the knot might also simultaneously express and designate the opposite of all this: it might refer to physical illness, bondage and slavery, social disintegration, witchcraft, conflict and death. In many Bantu languages, words for the form of the knot or the idea of interlinking often derive from the proto-Bantu *-dungu. In Central Africa, the notion of 'underworld' (*kalunga*), or the name commonly given to the idea of a supreme being or energetic force-field (*nzambi mpungu*), share the same proto-Bantu root. Similarly, the idea of life and of life force (*mooyi*, or variations of the word) is invariably conceptualised in terms of the joining or knotting together of male and female complementary opposites.

I suggest that the knot, as a polymorphic form of amalgamation and as 'limit situation', perfectly captures the rhythm of the city's limit-experiences. It offers us the material form of an autochthonous conceptual meta-discourse about the specific nature of the rhythms of (urban) life, which is in itself force rather than form.[27]

SUTURING THE CITY: DIVINATORY KNOTS, MOEBIUS STRIPS AND BORROMEAN RINGS:

Knots bring us back to processes of divination and to the divinatory apparatus itself, to the baskets or bags that diviners in this part of the world have always used (see also Laranjeira 1985; Turner 1975; Werbner 2015), and, as the afore-mentioned case illustrated, continue to use in the urban context. Like urban existence itself, these containers consist of a border-crossing amalgamation of various objects, materials and substances of human, animal and vegetal origin. Though often in a more hidden or subterfuge way because of the hegemony of Neo-Pentecostalist discourses and prac-tices, diviners continue to operate in the city, and in doing so they have incorporated, amalgamated and 'knotted' the city into their baskets by integrating many of the com-modities or objects the urban world produces (for example, photos, padlocks, plastic dolls, car parts and many other items, including batteries or cell phone parts that metonymically represent the 'modern' urban world).[28] These items allow the diviner to say something about the impact of that world on a person's physical and mental state.[29] Secondly, they allow the diviner, who often also acts as healer of identified problems, to exert a transformative influence on the world, by opening up possible therapeutic paths and suggesting possible (ritualistic) ways to counter and undo, to 'untie' and 'unknot' the blockages in one's life.

That is again why the inalienable part of the material object repertoire of the baskets that diviners use during their divinatory séances all over southern Congo and large parts of northern Angola and Zambia is a particular form of knot, known as *kata* (a Chokwe word that refers to entwinement and enclosure as well as the idea of rupture). In the divinatory context, this particular *kata* is of crucial importance as a representation of the rhythms of the flow of life, energy, breath and vitality. The knot in question is Moebius-shaped and consists of twisted strips of palm leaves which are woven into a single whole. These knots often appear in pairs, representing the knot's double nature of the already-mentioned flow and closure.

The Webster's dictionary describes the Moebius strip or band as
> 'a mathematical object, or a physical representation of it, which is a
> two-dimensional sheet with only one surface. It is constructed or visualised
> as a rectangle, one end of which is held fixed while the opposite end
> is twisted through a 180-degree angle and joined to the fixed end. It is
> a two-dimensional object that can only exist in a three-dimensional space.'

Kata, the indispensible part of the divination baskets that are used throughout Southern Congo, Angola and Zambia. (From Filip De Boeck's collection)

132

The divinatory knot is not a pure Moebius shape as its two surfaces reveal, on close inspection, that it has more than one side and one rim, but it still seems to share the Moebius strip's mathematical property of being non-orientable, endless and without origin. When one examines the divinatory knot, one can see that it *does* have an origin: a specific starting point for the winding of the various layers of the parallel lines that are woven into a knot. This origin is not easy to perceive, however. It is seemingly 'forgotten' and therefore the knot seems to be arranged as a ruled surface, i.e. a surface in affine space. An affine space is what is left of a vector space when its point of origin is unknown.

In other words, such a Moebius-like shape or geometric structure forms a translation or permutation of the Euclidian map, generalising the affine properties (the properties of parallel lines) within Euclidian space, offering projective maps to chart the particular rhythms of parallel, spiralling and yet intersecting lines without origin or end.

Such a Moebius form, therefore, seems to fit and describe the plane of the city rather well: its instable topology and the miraculous unfolding of the non-orientable lines of people's lives within it. Non-orientable, never 'straight', and therefore constantly involving all the 'mathematics' that is entailed when living in constant confusion and improvisation. Translating the necessity to connect and knot oneself to as many networks as possible, the knot also expresses the possible dangers that every connection may bring. Here, the divinatory knot refers less to the structural properties of the Moebius ring, which so greatly inspired someone like Lévi-Strauss, and more to the topological operation of inter-knotting that the Borromean rings represented for Lacan: urban living in the shape of a Lacanian *suture*, a constant attempt to find ways to 'stitch' and 'sew up' lack and losses (cf. Miller 2012). Sutures suggest the possibility of closing wounds, generating realignments and opening up alternatives, because sutures also point to new kinds of creativity with (spatial and temporal) beginnings, and therefore with new forms of interactivity, as Nancy Hunt (2013) reminds us. Lack needs and demands to be overcome in order to survive and form a collectivity in the city. But the same lack also drives individual and collective desire, and therefore the very rhythm of the city itself, as dream and nightmare, the theatre of rise and fall.

Les **PIONNIERS BATISSEURS DU CONGO** Belge

NOMS	NE(e) à	FONCTION	DECÈS	NATIONALITE	NOMS	NE(e) à	FONCTION	DECÈS	NATIONALITE
BERTHELINS, CAN.	14-7-1865, S.	Cap. de Steam	19-5-1897	SUÉDOISE	STRAND, K.J.	STOCKHOLM	Chaudronnie	30-3-1899	SUÉDOISE
BOSTYN, D.L.A.J.	BRUXELLES	Agent com.	5-6-1897	Belge	LARDINOY, R.J.F.	MALINES	S.O/F.P	21-5-1899	Belge
THOMASSEN, V.	21-7-1870	Trappiste	26-6-1897	Belge	BARBIER, J.J.D.P	WAVRE	S.O/F.P.	25-5-1899	- " -
SCHON, A.		S. Intendant	6-9-1897		ANSIAUX, A.L.V.	LIÈGE	S.O/F.P.	21-6-1899	- " -
CAPPUYNS, L.E.	LOUVAIN	S. Intendant	2-11-1897	Belge	MAGNUSON, A.F.	KARLSHRONA	Capt. Adj.	22-8-1899	SUÉDOISE
NELSSON, R.T.A.	HOOR	Dr./Médecine	5-11-1897	SUÉDOISE	ANELLI, L.	MILLAN	Médecin	4-9-1899	Italienne
DAHLSTEIN, J.R.	LEDSOIR	Cap. STEAMER	21-2-1898	- " -	WOOLING, S.	1872, LONDRE		30-9-1899	BRITANIQUE
BERG, W.C.	FREDERICKSTAD.	Cap. Steamer	5-3-1898	NORVÉGIEN	MILANTS, A.M.F.	LOUVAIN	Commis	6-10-1899	Belge
MAYER, J.A.	BRUXELLES	Commis	30-3-1898	Belge	MEUNIER	LIEGE	Sgt.	13-12-1899	Belge
VAN DER VAEREN	GROENENDAEL	Paseur/Télég.	28-4-1898	- " -	SCHONROCK,		Mécanicien	15-1-1900	ALLEMANDE
JURGENSEN, J.			18-8-1898	Allemande	ZUCCARO, N.J.A		Médecin	19-4-1900	AUTRICIEN
ANDERSON, A.J.G.	WESTERVIX	Charpentier	1-9-1898	SUÉDOISE	SERVIAS, E.S.	Jette St. Pierre	Commis	5-3-1900	Belge
LANSBERG, J.C.	SART-LEZ-SPA	Lt.	30-9-1898	Belge	WANCAMPS	LESSINES	S.Lt/F.P	10-3-1900	- " -
ANDERSON, C.A	FJORNFAGERF.	Charpentier	6-11-1898	SUÉDOISE	JOHANNSON		Mécanicien	26-3-1900	SUÉDOISE
SJORSTROM, F.P.	LAXEVAAG	Mécanicien.	11-11-1898	NORVÉGIEN	HENDRICKX	TIRLEMONT	Commis	22-4-1900	Belge
ANDERSON, J.G.A	STOCKHOLM	Machiniste	2-12-1898	SUÉDOISE	MARCHETTINI		Charpentier	6-6-1900	Italienne
BERNARD, 1.	MOLENBEEK		2-12-1898	Belge	MERCELSEN	Christiana	Cap. Adj.	12-6-1900	NORVÉGIEN
KARLSON, A	STOCKHOLM	Agisteur	11-12-1898	SUÉDOISE	DESIMONY	St. Joseph Ten		2-7-1900	Belge
D'HONDT, A.	HOBOKEN	Officier/M.	10-1-1899	Belge	MALAIRE	NAMUR	Commis	21-9-1900	Belge
ANDERSON, B.A.			13-1-1899	SUÉDOISE	BORNS, P.				- " -
GETTEMAN, A	LAMAIN-1875	S.Lt/F	14-1-1899	Belge	GLEICHMAN				
OFFREDON, H.			22-2-1899	Française	DEBAUM				

4. Mountains I: Pic Sörensen

It is a cold and rainy winter morning in 2008. I sit down at a desk in the public reading room of the Danske Utvandrerarkiv, the Danish Emigration Archives in Aalborg. Memories of more prosperous industrial times linger in this small coastal town of northern Jutland as they do in many towns in Congo: but the comparison ends here for no place could be more removed from the heart of Africa than this sleepy port. And yet, however unlikely it seems, it is in this nondescript provincial town that some of Central Africa's most turbulent colonial history is waiting to be uncovered. It is here in Aalborg's Emigration Archives that the lives of all the Danes who ever served in King Leopold II of Belgium's colonial enterprise are carefully filed, archived and stowed away in rows of uniform cardboard boxes, the scriptural tombs of what were often adventurous biographies.[1] In front of me lies a letter that I retrieved from one of these boxes. The thin paper on which it is written has turned a dirty yellow, like a newspaper that has been exposed to the sun for too long. The colour of the ink has faded too, but the forceful, even jaunty, handwriting is still very legible. Dated 18 January 1913 and unceremoniously addressed to 'Dear Jürgensen', the letter is written and signed by a certain S. Sörensen.

To my surprise, I see that Mr. Sörensen wrote this letter from a village called Kashinakashi.[2] The name immediately takes me back to a morning in 1987 and to my 26-year-old self sitting next to a few men in a small hut in Kashinakashi, then a tiny Lunda hamlet in the southernmost point of Kwango, a district on the current Congo-Angola border. Shivering from cold that morning, we all squat around a fire inside the hut. Palm wine is passed around. It must have been the rainy season for the firewood is wet. My eyes begin to smart from the smoke in the room and I can smell the moisture of the damp mud walls in the hut.

As I look out of the library's window opposite me, I can see the cold daybreak fog slowly retreating from Aalborg's grey streets, and again I am taken back to that chilly morning on the Angolan border, where the rising sun starts to dissolve the wisps of mist, wrapped like scarves around the mountain ranges of Lunda Norte as if they needed protection from the cold. I recall an eagle taking off from its perch in a nearby forest. Here, high above Aalborg, seagulls soar in the pale sky. As they slowly fly away and out of sight, I look down again at Sörensen's letter, and my mind starts to drift again. I am transported across space and time to both Sörensen's past and my own and the gap of a century closes.

18 January 1913. A thousand kilometres south of Leopoldville, near the still largely putative and constantly shifting borderline by the Kwango River between the Belgian and Portuguese colonial territories, Sören Sörensen sat down in his tent in Kashinakishi to write to his old friend, Captain Jürgen Peter Jürgensen. The two men must have known each other since their Merchant Navy days more than twenty years before. Sörensen, who was only twelve when he lost his father in 1885, passed the Merchant Navy entrance test at the age of sixteen in 1889. He completed his training and was promoted to the rank of second lieutenant in Frederikshavn in 1897. The following year (Sörensen had just turned 25 and Jürgensen was barely a year older), the two men decided to follow the example of many other young Danes in the second half of the nineteenth century: they enlisted in the *Force Publique*, the armed force of Leopold II's Congo Free State, and were both sent as sub-lieutenants to Congo in the late summer that year.

I do not know whether the two young officers made the journey in each other's company or not. If they did, they must have travelled on the steamship Albertville, the ship that Jürgensen boarded in Frederikshavn on 6 September. Whatever the case, they would have been separated upon arrival in Boma, a port town on the Congo River that had become the capital of the Congo Free State in 1886. Jürgensen was briefly stationed in Zambi, a training camp upstream from Boma, before being sent to Stanleyfalls.[3] Sörensen, after a first brief period as *chef de poste* or head of the mission in M'Toa in Katanga, continued his career in the *Force Publique* under the command of Dhanis,[4] who he accompanied during one of the expeditions against the rebellious Batetela. Sörensen was one of the few to return from that expedition alive.

Over the years, the paths of Sörensen and Jürgensen continued to cross several times; at least enough times for them to establish and maintain a close friendship. When in 1906 Jürgensen decided to return to Denmark, his departure marked the start of a long correspondence between the two friends, a correspondence that ended only in 1933 with Sörensen's death in Algiers, where he had retired after resigning from active colonial service in 1925. The only photo of Sörensen that the Aalborg archives contain is the one used in his obituary and which was published in the *Bulletin de l'association des vétérans coloniaux*. It shows him at the height of his colonial career. He must have been in his early forties when this picture was taken. Sitting on an ornamental chair, he is dressed in a white uniform, most likely that of a district commissioner. Posing rather awkwardly, his crossed legs turn away from the camera, while his upper body and expressionless face are turned towards the camera, his eyes staring blankly at us. He has a high forehead with a slightly receding hairline, a forceful nose and a large black moustache. His dark hair is neatly cut and shows no sign of ageing yet. His left arm lies on the chair's armrest and he holds a sabre in his left hand. But more greatly than all these details, it is the photo's visual centre that directs the viewer's attention to two rows of decorations pinned on the left side of Sörensen's breast. There are seven in all: the

Croix d'Officier de l'Ordre de la Couronne, the *Croix d'Officier de l'Ordre Royal du Lion, Officier de l'Ordre de la Couronne d'Italie, Chevalier de la Légion d'honneur, Chevalier de l'Ordre de Danebrog du Danemark, Etoile de Service en or avec quatre raies* and the *Médaille des Vétérans*.

Unlike Jürgensen, Sörensen continued a successful Congo career after the Congo Free State was officially handed over to Belgium in 1908. In 1903 he was promoted to the rank of captain, then left the *Force Publique* in 1904 and started to work his way up the colonial administration's complex hierarchical ladder. As the photograph suggests, he succeeded with panache. Appointed *chef de secteur de 1e classe* and then *chef de zone de 2e classe* in 1904, he quickly rose to the rank of *adjoint supérieur de 2e classe* in 1905, *adjoint supérieur de 1e classe* in 1908 and *commissionaire de district ad interim* in 1906. In 1912, Sörensen was finally promoted to the full rank of District Commissioner. In this new capacity, he was immediately sent to the troublesome Kwango district where, as he himself reported to Jürgensen in a letter dated 22 June 1913, 'work' was not yet finished as there remained in the district's southwestern part, 'a tribe, well-armed and supported by dubious people of the same tribe in Angola, who are not willing to obey Bula Matari'.[5]

Between 1912 and 1914, and again between 1919 and 1924, Sörensen embodied colonial authority and enforced it on Kwango, a vast territory of 128,000 km² with an estimated population of 800,000 inhabitants in 1912. The world that Sörensen encountered in his capacity of executive civilian and military colonial authority was in great turmoil. The Kwango countryside had been devastated by many decades of interethnic warfare, widespread famines, massive and very violent slave-raiding and smuggling activities, as well as by repressive and equally violent colonial intrusions: the Belgians from the north and the Portuguese from the south.

Indeed, ever since the 1884-1885 Berlin conference, both these colonial powers had been engaged in a fierce competition to establish control over the greater Lunda area that incorporated the Kwango region. A recent article by Belgian historian Jean-Luc Vellut provides a fascinating account of Leopold II's annexation of the Kwango area, and offers vivid details of both the local history of the 'invention of the Lunda frontier' and the wider geopolitical ambitions that shaped the borderline between Congo and Angola (Vellut 2006). In 1889, four years after the end of the Berlin conference, Leopold II sent a first expedition to the Kwango to explore the still largely unknown region with a view to concluding a treaty with Mwene Putu Kasongo, the paramount king (*kyaamvu*) of Lunda descent, whose line still rules over Kwango's Yaka population, the region's most dominant ethnic group and an important segment of Kinshasa's demographic make-up today. Because of the *kyaamvu*'s fierce resistance to the colonial intrusion, the expedition was unable to advance south and stopped at Kasongo Lunda, the royal village that has remained the seat of the *kyaamvu*'s royal court to this day (Vellut 2006: 165).

Around that time, the Lunda area in general had become the focus of an increasingly intense diplomatic struggle between Belgium and Portugal. In 1890, the Portuguese and the British endeavoured to reach an agreement and sign a treaty defining the borders of Angola as part of a larger deal that would also settle their border disputes in south-east Africa. The Portuguese position on Angola, however, conflicted with Leopold II's own aspirations: he considered the Kwango River to be the natural border between Angola and the Congo Free State. At variance with Portuguese claims, this meant that a major part of the Lunda area would be incorporated into Leopold II's already very considerable Congolese territory. As Vellut illustrates, the Portuguese tended to justify their territorial claims with the notion of a historically founded 'sphere of influence'. In their view, Lunda, including the Kwango region, was considered to belong historically to Angola's 'natural' hinterland. It was therefore viewed as an inalienable part of the Portuguese overseas territories, even if it had never actually been formally colonised and annexed as such by the Portuguese colonial powers. Radically opposing this Portuguese interpretation, both Leopold II and the British increasingly tried to justify their own territorial dreams by resorting to a different concept, namely that of 'effective occupation'. On the diplomatic front, therefore, Leopold II started to look for British support to achieve his own ambitions with regard to the Kwango region, while simultaneously attempting to strengthen the Congo Free State's 'effective occupation' on the ground. To this end, he sent a new expedition to the Kwango region in 1890. Headed by Francis Dhanis, the expedition was supposed to advance south of Kasongo Lunda, sign treaties with local chiefs and establish military stations in the Kwango regions's most eastern parts, thereby cutting off the access to Angola of any possible Portuguese outposts (Vellut 2006: 169).

It was, however, not Dhanis but Lerman, a Croatian officer in the service of the Congo Free State, who was able to push south of Kasongo Lunda into the area between the Kwango and Wamba rivers. In 1893, Lerman reported terrifying accounts from this area of an ongoing war waged by over eight thousand Chokwe warriors against Kaungula, the stronghold of an important Lunda chief, whose recent death had enfeebled his court (Vellut 2006: 177). At around the same time, the Portuguese Sarmento-Teixeira expedition moved from Angola into the area east of the Wamba valley (Vellut 2006: 177), close to where the Lunda royal village or *musuumb* of Nzofu is situated today. Leopold quickly dispatched the British missionary George Grenfell to reinforce the Belgian expedition in southern Kwango. In the Lunda borderlands Grenfell eventually met up with the Portuguese mission, headed by Lieutenant Sarmento. Surprisingly quickly, both men managed to reach a compromise, and together they negotiated the outline of a more final border, one that has survived *grosso modo* till today, even though renewed border disputes continued to surface between Belgium and Portugal as late as 1934 (Vellut 2006: 180). Similar disputes have haunted relations between Congo and

Angola in postcolonial times. In 2007, for example, Angolan troops crossed the border east of Nzofu, near the town of Kahemba, and planted the Angolan flag in the village of Shayimbwanda on Congolese soil. This invasion escalated into a major diplomatic incident between both countries (cf. De Boeck 2012b).

In 1912, some twenty years after the Grenfell-Sarmento agreement, Sörensen started to make his way towards the borderland frontier between southern Kwango and Lunda Norte. At that time, the borderline had not yet solidified and the whole area was still not completely pacified. Quite the contrary, in fact. Sörensen entered a war zone and often had to literally fight his way through. In one letter to Jürgensen, dated 22 June 1913, Sörensen mentions that he engaged in 25 battles before reaching the border. Yet, unlike Conrad's characters Kayerts and Carlier, he seems to enjoy the simplicity of this rough frontier life, and his accounts to Jürgensen abound with romanticising depictions of nature's beauty and the special comradery that he experiences with his soldiers:

> 'These eight months out here have been very happy.' (...) It was a nice life together with my people, and it reminded me of the old days. We felt like one person during fights, in the rain, and in the swamps, and we were glad we had each other's company. And when we finally established peace, even the natives received me with a warm heart.'

It took Sörensen several months before he managed to reach and follow the Kwango's southernmost border with Angola. Rather phlegmatically (he described his own letters as 'dry and boring'), he reported some of these difficulties to Jürgensen in the letter written from Kashinakashi:

> 'Dear Jürgensen,
>
> (...) in the last months I have mostly been alone with my soldiers and books up here at the Portuguese border. On Christmas Day, I engaged in some small fights with Batchoko (Kiok)[6] who have not surrendered yet. They are armed with guns and I am told that they are being set up against us by Portuguese smugglers.
>
> Earlier, in September, one of the commanders of my guard, a Belgian reserve-lieutenant, arrived at a trade settlement illegally set up on Belgian soil by Portuguese smugglers from Angola, and there he was attacked and got wounded. Two of our soldiers were killed, as well as one Portuguese, six workers and two natives. Thereupon our whites withdrew.
>
> When news about this incident reached me in Bandundu, I decided to attack this trading post, and on November 9 I started to march towards it, in the company of Judge Wergerland-Petersen (...), a Belgian lieutenant and 125 soldiers. We lost one Italian officer on the way.

When we arrived at the trade settlement, the natives had just burnt it down. We had to sleep without firewood, for we were still on the plains where there is no wood, and the poor soldiers and carriers became soaking wet from the pouring rain. When I woke up that night, I found that my tent was filled with carriers who were seeking shelter from the storm. Quickly, I pulled my nose back into the mosquito-net.

The next day, we continued in southern direction until we reached a new trading station that had been built by the Portuguese but was occupied by the natives. Here we were attacked and the judge was severely wounded. Two bullets pierced his right thigh. I removed one bullet, actually it almost fell out by itself. Another bullet had hit his right hand, so unfortunately he will lose some fingers. But otherwise he feels rather well. The next day I gave the lieutenant the order to return with him, while I continued to push back the natives, who were still shooting at us.

Eight days later the lieutenant started to suffer from haematuria, and I remained alone at our little fort. And just when everything started to go well and the natives began to surrender, I was attacked on the right bank of the Kwilu River by a small group of Kashinsi, who belong to the Batshoko race.[7] The attacks continued from December 18 till December 26. One day I was attacked five times, and even on Christmas Eve, while a nice and friendly village waved to us for rest and peace, we were suddenly attacked from the left side. A young brave soldier got shot in both his legs. And so on Christmas Day, while at home they were preaching the gospel of peace, we were engaged in a fight with the great black children. They suffered heavy losses, but some of that has already been forgotten, and their women and children are coming toward us now, and they nearly start to play with me. Unfortunately, I have some wounded soldiers in my ranks, but nobody was killed this time.

In the meantime, reinforcement has arrived. Boma[8] sent me hundred soldiers and two whites. I have grown used to being alone, though, and I don't like their company that much, even though I can't live without it in Europe. Today I plan to continue my journey toward the Portuguese border where, so it was reported to me, military posts have been built along the upper river. It is also said that there are cities as big as New York over there, but no people — I mean Belgians- have yet been there, so it is probably fantasy. (...)'

Until November 1913, Sörensen continued to occupy and 'gain new land', as he called it, and defend Belgian interests against Portuguese intrusions along the border. As much as possible, he mapped out the area in more detail, documenting and correcting, where necessary, the borderline that Grenfell and Sarmento had drawn out on paper without, however, knowing the actual terrain well. As Sörensen remarked in a letter he wrote from the border on 26 November 26, 1913:

> 'Nobody seems to have followed the border since Grenfell and the Portuguese lieutenant Sarmento regulated it, and they don't seem to have been along the whole distance. Because I discovered, or rather found out, that the Kombo River, which along a considerable distance forms the border between us and Angola, does not flow into the Uovo River but rather into the Tenduala.[9] I can well understand why they were mistaken: they mixed up a tributary of the Kombo River with itself. The result: a new border regulation.'

Sörensen often did not exactly know where he was either, and at times his rendition of his mapping activities in the mountainous area along the border reads more like a comic strip, even through real danger and violence were never far away:

> (...) for my map I also needed the name of the rivers. As I told you, we were close to the border and I wanted to know more exactly where I was. Very early the next morning I sneaked across the border and luck was on my side because, even though this is an uninhabited region, I could see a convoy of travellers approaching. I hid in the woods and when the caravan passed, I rushed towards them with my two soldiers, shouting: 'Hands up! Your life or the name of the river!' I was lucky that they didn't start to shoot at me because out here people are all carrying guns. I told them not to be afraid, and I did get the river's name, which pleased both me and my soldiers. (...) Later, on many occasions, our situation looked quite bleak, but we were always able to handle it.'

And so he slowly progressed along the border in an easternly direction, crossing the Wamba River and making his way into the area that today's local Lunda population refers to as *Mabeet* (the valleys, or literally 'the holes'):

> 'Mountains and ravines, ravines and mountains. The poor carriers! Sometimes we had to slide down some steep slope and then climb up on the other side on all fours. But it was a beautiful and great land, so all of us were in great spirits.'

It is in this 'land of holes' that Sörensen made the 'discovery' that was to put his name on the map literally; he stumbled upon a mountain 'of 1500 metres' in height. The highest peak of what colonial cartographers referred to as the 'Crystal Mountains' was officially baptised 'Pic Sörensen' shortly afterwards. And so, for decades to come, the District Commissioner's name was perpetuated on the official maps of Belgian Congo (cf Maquet 1939).

If, on a certain level, the tale of the Congolese postcolonial era might be told as a history of holes (the potholes in Kinshasa's streets and the graves on its abandoned

cemeteries, the giant holes of industrial mines that have left the face of Katanga and Kasai pockmarked and disfigured, and the pits that are dug by Congo's numerous artisanal miners to often also end up as graves), it is the figure of the mountain that seems to encapsulate and summarise the story of its precolonial worlds and subsequent colonial intrusions with their accompanying processes of seizure, occupation, domination and control.

When Sörensen 'discovered' his mountain, the Lunda royal village of Nzofu was already established in its vicinity. Nzofu is situated thirty kilometres southwest of the mountain and its village infrastructure is still very similar to that in Sörensen's days.[10] By now, the road that a few decades ago still allowed a car to reach Nzofu has deteriorated beyond repair, and the royal village itself only consists of some thirty mud huts with thatched roofs, which lack even the most basic electricity and water facilities (as, in fact, do all other villages in the remote region of the *Mabeet* valleys). Yet, in spite of minimal material infrastructures, the royal Lunda village with its political and symbolic importance as the heart of a vast tributary regional political network cannot be overestimated. Then as now the royal title of Nzofu counts as the most important Lunda title in the region's traditional political geography, and the Lunda king's authority is recognised across a large part of Kwango and the Angolan province of Lunda Norte. On the Angolan side, the Nzofu title is represented by a second royal court, headed by a different clan of the same royal lineage. The whole of this vast area is considered Nzofu's political territory or *ngaand*; the king rules over this territory in his capacity of 'lord of the land' (*mwaant mwiin mangaand*) .

The Lunda have something in common with the Belgian intruders: they are also colonisers. The Lunda royal genealogy, recited on an almost daily basis at the Nzofu court, narrates how Nzofu and a number of other Lunda titleholders started to migrate sixteen generations ago from what is referred to as *kool*, the Ruund core land in the southeast of Congo (near the Nkalaany River, in what is today the province of Katanga). From this heartland, some Lunda groups moved south and east, but the group that was led by the Nzofu titleholder started to migrate west, until they finally settled in the *Mabeet* area. Here, they subjected the area's autochthonous populations to their political rule, a subjection that did not necessarily come about in a peaceful way and often involved violent and bloody battles that were still ongoing at the end of the nineteenth century . The Lunda thus coercively exported their own political system and replicated it along an expanding political frontier, superposing the architecture of their own political institutions onto the local worlds they encountered. Typical of this system of Lunda occupation, and in spite of the often violent nature of its rule, is that the Lunda tended to leave the ritual powers of local landowners intact in an attempt to incorporate these powers into their own political structure and thereby strengthen the latter in the process. While these land chiefs were politically colonised and dominated by Lunda overlords, who redefined them as subordinate vassals within the dominant overarching Lunda court system, they often continued to maintain a special ritual and spiritual relation to the land; a relation that the Lunda occupants, lacking ancestral ties with this land, could not possibly claim and for which they remained ultimately dependent on these local chiefs' spiritual powers. As a result, authochtonous land chiefs often continued to play an important role in rituals within the newly established Lunda polity.

In his court, numerous dignitaries assist the Nzofu paramount titleholder. They mainly consist of relatives representing the interests of the king's own patrilineage, while others represent the clans into which the king is married, or embody political relations and ties with the different autochthonous groups that came under the domination of the court. Next to the court, the political superstructure of the *Mabeet* valley area consists of thirteen major sub-regional titleholders or vassals (*ayilool ajim*), each with their own court structure. According to the Lunda history that is orally transmitted in all of these local Lunda courts, these men accompanied the Nzofu titleholder during the migration from *kool*, the Lunda heartlands, and are therefore considered to be 'children of kool' (*aan a kool*), that is, they belong to the oldest and most important descent groups surrounding the dynastic lineage. It is important to stress that although the Nzofu king is identified with the land of his political territory (*ngaand*), he does not

Nzofu Kateend II in the royal compound at Nzofu village, October 1987.   145

'own' it. The paramount titleholder is said 'not to have the land, he has *ayilool*.' In his function of *mwaant mwiin mangaand*, the paramount titleholder allocates parts of his political territory to his sub-regional titleholders, who then administer the land thus 'given' to them in their capacity of royal vassals and delegates. Most importantly, this function authorises them to collect tributes (*milaambw*) from the inhabitants of the area they oversee. At set times, the *ayilool* hand over to the paramount titleholder a small but highly valued part of these tributes, which may include palm wine, meat from the hunt, and first crops.

It is the paramount titleholder who invests all these sub-regional titleholders, distributes the regalia at their enthronement and offers them kaolinite clay (*lupeemb*) to symbolise the fact that he has delegated his powers to them just as he himself was anointed with kaolinite and thereby enthroned by the *mwaant yaav* sovereign whose court is located in western Katanga, in *kool*, and who thus embodies the very origin and source of the Lunda political power. All these major titles, as well as those of the numerous minor local titleholders, called *ayilool akeemp,* are distributed according to a combined system of perpetual kinship (which fictionally maintains 'original' blood ties between the various titleholders) and positional succession (which identifies the actual titleholder with the original holder of the title) (see Cunnison 1956). In this way, use of land and political administration are linked to perpetual titles that are defined in terms of real, putative or fictive consanguinity and further strengthen the typical Lunda tributary network (see Bustin 1975), thereby linking the various layers of the smaller segmentary authority structures into one integrated whole.

While there is a vast network of men united by an expanding web of 'kinship' that integrates all these titles and of which the Luunda royal title constitutes the epicentre, it is important to keep in mind that the same system is built on a structural tension between *dominium* and *imperium* (see Crine 1963); this is the distinction between political chiefs who hold the political and judiciary rights as well as the right to the tribute, and land chiefs without important political functions but with real ritual ties to the land. And even if the Nzofu king officially combines both these roles, as sovereign paramount political ruler (*mwiin mangaand*) and as *mwiin mavw* (literally 'lord of the soil'), he remains ritually dependent on these original landowners to perform the second role and take on the ritual responsibility for the land's more cyclical and regenerative elements that enable the *ngaand*'s fertility and fecundity, and subsequently its social and physical reproduction and its material welfare.

It is this structural dependency on autochthonous ritual powers over ancestral land that made of the mountain that Sörensen subsequently 'discovered' one of the most important and strategic symbolic spots within the political geography of the *Mabeet*'s precolonial universe. It was not by coincidence that the Lunda colonisers deliberately chose to establish their royal village at the foot of the mountain when they moved into the area. The mountain goes by various different names in the various languages spoken by the different ethnic groups of the Kwango and Kwilu, but in *uLuund*, the local variant of the Lunda language spoken in Katanga, it is known as *mukiindw wa ngaak*, the 'mountain of the grandfather (or ancestor)'. Despite what is suggested by its colonial name, Crystal Mountain, there are no diamonds or crystals to be found in the small *mukiindw wa ngaak* mountain range. But it does have a natural resource that represents, at least for the Lunda chiefs, a far more precious material: kaolinite deposits in a small lake on top of the *mukiindw wa ngaak*. It is this very kaolinite or *lupeemb* clay that is used in the enthronement rituals of all the political titleholders in the Kwango, including the powerful *kyaamvu* or Yaka paramount of Kasongo Lunda, who the Nzofu king regards as a younger and therefore subordinate brother. Maquet (1939) reports how emissaries from all these regional courts, including the *kyaamvu*'s, would travel to Nzofu in order to obtain this with kaolin clay, which represents the historical Lunda heartland of *kool* in Katanga and the political power that emanates from the royal court there. By controlling access to this most crucial ritual substance, the court of Nzofu thus controls the regional distribution of political power, thereby establishing itself as the most senior and powerful political authority of all. But to make this possible, Nzofu himself has to rely ultimately on the ritual authority of Ngandu, an autochthonous Holo land chief whose village forms the gateway to the lake. In his capacity of ritual guardian of the lake and of all the spirits and powers that reside in the mountain and under the water's surface, Ngandu is the one and only person who can act as an intermediary between the realms of the living and that of the spirits. Only Ngandu can enter into the lake in order to extract kaolinite from it. Politically subservient to Nzofu, Ngandu's ritual powers are thus indispensable to underpin Nzofu's claims to political supremacy.

Inevitably, the Lunda colonisers' complex conceptualisations of power, with their careful balance between political dominance and ritual authority in relation to land, were bound to clash with the Belgian take on what colonial dominance meant. The Pic Sörensen became the stage on which the encounter between these two radically opposing and incompatible worldviews was played out most strongly. It stands out as the ultimate battleground on which two different histories of colonisation and two different notions of occupation meet without merging. When Sörensen put 'his' mountain on the colonial map, he must have been very much aware of its ritual and political importance for the local populations he was trying to subjugate. It could not have taken him long to recognise its powerful potential and appreciate the larger strategic and symbolic implications of his mapping move, and it is no mere coincidence that he uses the 'mountain' image to comment upon the accomplished colonising work in a letter he wrote to Jürgensen from Bandundu on 26 February 1921, during his second and final term as the Kwango's District Commissioner. At that point Sörensen's health was weakened by a severe bout of malaria and its subsequent arsenic treatment. He would retire from active service four years later. Looking back on his career, it was the 'mountain' image that came to his mind to describe the past decades of colonising efforts. Using it as a *pars pro toto* for the whole Kwango area, which was by now increasingly under colonial control, he commented:

> 'As Erasmus Montanus says: we now have some folk here on the mountain.'[11]
> The big world company 'Lever Brothers – Sunlight, Soap, Pears Soap'[12] has established a big oil mill at the confluence of the Kwengo and Kwila[13] rivers. Furthermore, there are still three other mills in the district, though this one is the biggest. A little over twenty whites are working there, as well as thousands of black people, not including those natives who are collecting the palm nuts. It is a very big business. It is odd for an old Congo hand like me to see smoking chimneys here in our silent jungle, to hear the sound of the machines and see the white light beaming into the night. It is like an adventure.'

His account of the civilising mission, the bringing of 'white light', is unmistakably tinged with a feeling of nostalgia for the bygone world of the 'silent jungle' in which he himself had felt so comfortable. But in the end it is the topos of 'his' mountain that prevails. It stands out as a powerful image, an ideological figure, emblematic not only of the cultural superiority of Belgian colonialism, posited at the pinnacle of progress and civilisation, but also of its political and military supremacy. Sörensen's peak literally shows the fact that colonial rule came out on top in its confrontation with the 'great black children', as he calls the Congolese in one of his letters.

In this way, the Belgian colonisers wrote their logic of occupation, subjugation and domination into the landscape and onto the bodies of those that came under the control of the colonial state. A new order was thus established in which the older local meanings of the mountain were overwritten and, at least partially, erased. And indeed, Sörensen's occupation of the *mukiindw wa ngaak* irreversibly drew the world of Nzofu into the colonial orbit. From the 1920s onwards, the colonial administration started to strengthen its grip on this unruly part of the Belgian Congo. In 1920, Nzofu is mentioned for the first time at some length in the local colonial administration's reports.[14] The first Catholic and Protestant missionaries (Belgian Jesuits and American and Canadian Mennonites) arrived in the area shortly afterwards. The *Unevangelised Tribes Mission* set up a first pioneer mission post in nearby Kamayala in the mid 1920s. Overlooking the mountains and valleys of the *Mabeet*, another important mission station was built in the early 1930s in Kajiji, near what is now the small town of Kulindji. In 1954, after the dissolution of the *Unevangelised Tribes Mission*, this station was handed over to the Mennonite Brethren. Sha-Musenga, Kahemba's first Jesuit mission, was founded in 1938 (cf. Denis 1943).

Throughout those years the Belgian administration made various attempts to reform the local chieftaincies by actively intervening in the succession of chiefs, ensuring that only candidates perceived to be loyal to the colonial cause were installed. It promoted chiefs of minor rank and placed them as *chefs médaillés* on the same administrative level as the Lunda king of Nzofu. This interventionist policy had, in fact, already been started by Sörensen in 1912-1913, but was now being implemented on a larger scale and in a more systematic though often rather unsuccessful way.[15] In the meantime, the military wing of the colonial machine continued its attempts to neutralise remaining pockets of occasionally fierce, armed resistance against the Belgian presence. Two hundred kilometres east of Nzofu, in the hinterlands of Kahemba, a town where the colonial administration set up office in 1912, some Lunda and Chokwe chiefs, such as the locally still legendary Shautale, continued to fight the colonial presence until well into the 1930s. These continuing conflicts between the colonial authorities and their colonial subjects reached a dramatic apotheosis in 1936, when a certain Kamoyo, a local man from the nearby town of Kulindji who had been recruited as census taker by the Belgian colonial administration, arrested an unknown but, according to local accounts, large number of villagers. The latter had refused to cooperate with the Belgians, who were attempting to set up a system of forced agricultural labour through-out the region at that time. This plan met with widespread foot-dragging resistance.[16] Shackled and chain-ganged in groups of two and four, the arrested recalcitrants were deported to Kahemba, sentenced by the colonial authorities and locked up in the town's main prison. Shortly afterwards, during the night, the prison building caught fire and burnt down to the ground. Chained in their cells, none of the prisoners survived the inferno.

This and other events illustrate to what extent the local worlds that were being brought into the orbit of colonial 'civilisation' continued to radically resist the often harsh Belgian rule. As Sörensen's letters and the episode above have made abundantly clear, the colonial violence was often of an overtly brutal, physical nature. It is no coincidence that the colonial period is still remembered by the former colonial subjects as the time of the *chicotte* or whip, for example. But the forms of violence that the coloniser exposed the colonised to were also of a much more covert, subtle and symbolic nature, as is illustrated by the planting of the Belgian Congo's flag on top of the *mukiindw wa ngaak*, a mountain that was so very central to the social, political and cosmological worldview of the region's inhabitants. Symbolically destroying that world's order in the act, Sörensen's claiming and naming of the mountain paved the way for the subsequent administrative but also missionary reconfiguration of the *mabeet*, introducing new concepts of time and space, new notions of labour, new moral matrixes, and new beliefs and cosmologies that deeply impacted on local conceptualisations of the meanings of power, land, work, value, ownership and personhood.

The colonial transformations undeniably altered local worlds in deep and radical ways, but the ruptures and breaches they caused never fully erased older underlying meanings and action schemes. For example, the symbolism of the colonisation of the mountain was soon countered and the peak itself was turned into a counter-hegemonic figure of resistance against the mainly Protestant attempts at evangelising the area from the mid-1930s onwards. In this way, the late 1950s witnessed the birth of a local messianic cult with an openly anti-colonial message.[17] Operating from the mountain site, it managed to rally local support for a while but by the 1970s it had run out of steam. Yet in 1987, when I arrived in Nzofu for the first time to carry out a long-term field research in the area, the mountain's back appeared not to have been fully broken. Just a few years before I arrived, a cross had been planted on top of the mountain by Jean Carrer, a zealous Catholic missionary belonging to the French congregation *Société des Missions Africaines* (SMA). It did not take long before the Holy Cross was struck down by a lightning bolt, a fact that was interpreted at the time by the Nzofu court as a clear sign that the spirits inhabiting the mountain lake continued to be stronger than the faith imported by the white missionaries.

In many other ways, the mountain has continued to be the locus of conflicting claims over land between the *Mabeet* inhabitants and intruding outsiders. Whereas on one level, some of these conflicts continue to unfold very much according to the same logic that also characterised earlier colonial land intrusions and occupations, the contemporary arena in which these conflicts emerge is an even more global one; the corporate interests and capital flows that shape the current encounters of the *Mabeet* inhabitants with the external world have become even more complex, volatile and unpredictable than earlier colonial inroads into their world.

In the early 1990s, for example, during the final years of the Mobutu regime, Thierry Fraselle, a Belgian citizen and owner of Elma Diesel, a well-known repair shop for 4x4 diesel pumps in Kinshasa, acquired a land concession from the Zairean state in the *Mabeet* territory, near the Tundwila River that Sörensen mentioned in his letters to Jürgensen. Fraselle set up a large-scale diamond prospecting operation in the vicinity of Mansabu village, not far from Kulindji. Mansabu, an important vassal of the Nzofu paramount, told me how he had authorised Fraselle to make an airstrip on the village common land and made a request for some gifts in return. In 1994, as in Sörensen's days when signing a treaty with a local chief, these gifts still consisted of goats, a gun, mirrors and beads. Fraselle's operation was financed by South African investors based in Cape Town. They produced satellite imagery of the area's fluvial geomorphology and provided expatriate drilling, diving and pitting experts to assist Fraselle on the ground with his prospecting activities. However, when Kabila's army roamed through the area in 1997, the entire mining equipment was looted and destroyed. Fraselle's financers dropped the project while he himself moved to Tanzania, where he started to work as a safari guide until his death in Dar es Salaam in 2003. It remains unclear if diamonds were ever found.

It took another decade before more powerful new players arrived on the scene. In May 2007, Indian geologists employed by Jindal Rex Exploration, a subsidiary branch of the Indian industrial giant Jindal Steel and Power Limited, were brought to Pic Sörensen by helicopter. There they set up a pilot plant. Around that time, Jindal Rex Exploration Pvt. Ltd. was incorporated under a joint venture with Rex Diamond Mining, a company with headquarters in Canada and an operational centre in Belgium. This joint venture allegedly invested 30 million US dollars to finance its prospecting activities (pitting, drilling and trial mining for diamonds) on Pic Sörensen and in the nearby Tundwila River. On the ground, the airborne operation was run by a Lubumbashi-born former Belgian citizen with a South-African passport, a Jean-Claude Van Damme lookalike who lived officially in Durban and had previously worked for Charles Taylor in Liberia and for an American security firm in Baghdad. When I met him in Kahemba in 2007, he was waiting for heavy excavators and other tilling and trenching equipment to arrive so as to start digging off Sörensen's mountain with the intention, or so he said, to level it down to the ground. However, lack of success meant that in April 2008 the Jindal geologists left the mountain and moved their operation to Nzofu, where their helicopters descended in May causing a panic amongst the villagers who fled into the bush, thinking that they were being invaded by the Angolan armed forces.

Even though this venture ended as unsuccessfully as Fraselle's earlier attempt, the Jindal diamond prospection by no means remained an isolated event. In the same period, BRC Diamond Core, a Canadian-South-African merger domiciled in Canada and listed on the Toronto Stock Exchange, also obtained an option over eight prospecting licenses along the Kwango River, between the towns of Tembo and Kasongo Lunda. In 2007 it started a large diamond prospecting project that covered an area of nearly 2,300 km². There too, all the exploration work was serviced by helicopter. In September 2010, I personally witnessed how an Australian company, operating under the name DMA (Diamond Mining Australia), was prospecting for diamonds in the Kwilu district, near the Jesuit mission station of Kisanji, some 200 kilometres north of Kahemba town. Although they were allowed to prospect in the nearby Kasai area, they had no authorization to do so in Kisanji. As in the case of the Jindal geologists, they too left the area in a helicopter, reportedly after disputes with the local authorities.

151

5. Corpus Vile: Death and Expendable Youth in Kinshasa

CORPUS VILE (plural: *corpora vilia*):
From Latin **CORPUS** ('body') and **VILE** ('worthless'). A person, animal or thing treated as expendable, to therefore use as an experimental subject regardless of whatever loss or damage it may suffer as a result. Figuratively: the subject of an experiment.

'Shadows are widows of the light. Death too is a widow.' (Breytenbach 2009: 15)

The other day, I was picturing myself
In my dreams, while I was asleep
And I was thinking of the day I'll die
Who will mourn me on the day I die?
I do not know.
Therefore, let me weep for myself.

Will death come to me in the forest,
Or will it come in the village?
Will death come with illness,
Or will I drown?
Oh mother, the day I'll die!

The day I'll die, me, the poor man,
I'll think of Ida, my wife.
I'll think of the kids I leave behind.
And I will be happy to leave
The misery of the world
Behind me
On the day I'll die!

The day I'll die, me, the rich man,
I'll think of all the money that I leave behind.
I'll think of all my belongings and my cars.
And I'll think of all the children I sent to Europe.
Ah, the day I'll die!

The day I'll die, me, the drunkard,
I'll think of my palm wine.
And I'll think of the end of the month,
When I used to drink with my friends.
Oh mother, the day I'll die!

The day I'll die, me, the prostitute,
I'll think of my wig.
I'll think of my clothes.
And I will only regret that the music
Of Africa Fiesta continues without me.
Oh mother, the day I'll die!

(Seigneur Tabu Ley Rochereau
in *Mokolo Nakokufa [The day I die]*)

INTRODUCTION:
DEATH AS A DE-FAMILIARIZING TECHNIQUE

Focusing on another site in the city of Kinshasa, the cemetery of Kintambo, this chapter further explores the socio-materialities and diffuse nature of localised everyday 'politics of the urban' that pervades the city as a whole.[1] In this particular case, urban action takes the form of volatile 'street politics' that informs a particular kind of effervescent 'political street' (Bayat 2012), a street where urban wrongs are played out and addressed along generational lines far more than along class lines. As I noted before, class is perhaps not the best analytic category to understand and explain the tensions and fault lines of city life in the Congolese context. As elsewhere in Congo, and indeed Africa (cf. Cole 2011; Cole and Durham 2007), the nature of intergenerational dialogue has become extremely complex in Kinshasa, and as this chapter will illustrate, the very possibility of intergenerational transmission is openly questioned. In combining an urban anthropology with a focus on youth (as a relational concept), my reading of the cemetery and its specific 'situated urban political ecology' (Lawhon, Ernstson and Silver 2014) will evolve around the nexus between (corporeal) intimacy, violence and violation, and the possibility for the production of political and moral criticisms and claims made by young Kinois. More concretely, I will focus on the ways in which, in this urban site, the vitality of the youthful body and the 'life of the corpse', to borrow a phrase from Mexican artist Teresa Margolles (cf. Kittelmann and Görner 2004), are made to collude and collide in today's urban setting. Youth and death are two categories that usually exclude each other, but they have become intimately connected in Kinshasa since the early 1990s (Vangu Ngimbi 1997). And it is the nature of this connection that

prompts us to think about the seemingly counterintuitive ways in which young people, who face powerful societal problems, articulate their sociality and their 'law' out of the very source of their own desperation and even their own deaths. By eliding life and death, by placing the city as a whole in the presence of death, Kinois youth remove the distance we would normally place between ourselves and the dead. When Kinshasa's young denizens forcefully take over funerals and turn their own dead bodies into a powerful medium to re-focalise the refracting histories and experiences of death within the urban site, and when they use death as a 'technique' of 'de-familiarization'[2] and convert it into a presence of estrangement that constantly de-centres the taken-for-granted nature of local experiences of the urban, they then successfully manage to position themselves in the public eye, establish a highly conspicuous presence and forcefully assert and stake out a place for themselves in this city that very often refuses to acknowledge their right of access.

After an ethnographic description of some of the complex ways in which death continues to be dealt with in Kinshasa's rural hinterlands, followed by a summary description of the material infrastructure of Kinshasa's cemeteries, and the mourning rituals and funeral events unfolding around them, the remainder of this chapter offers an attempt to understand what using death as technique of de-familiarization or estrangement exactly entails.

<< REW: 1987

In 1987, I started my first long-term field research at the foot of Pic Sörensen, in a remote rural area known as *Mabeet* ('The Holes' or 'Valleys'), situated in the southernmost point of the DR Congo's Bandundu province, on the border with Angola (see Chapter Four). This vast area of wooded savannah and gallery forest is home to a number of dispersed village communities, ethnically dominated by Lunda and Chokwe groups.

Three weeks after my arrival in the area, I attended a mourning ritual at a nocturnal wake in Nseej, a small hamlet roughly three hour's walking distance from Nzofu, the larger and more important Lunda village, where I lived for almost two years during my first field research. It was already night when I emerged from the narrow bush path and stepped into the clearing of the Nseej hamlet, which consisted of nothing more than three or four huts. In front of one of these modest grass-thatched mud houses, two small groups of men, women and children were sitting around two fires. The groups included the deceased's wife (*mufidi* or *mufiil*), some of the deceased's children, nephews, nieces, maternal uncles, older brothers and a number of in-laws representing the widow (usually her [classificatory] father and/or one of her maternal uncles), as well as a ritual specialist [*mbuki*] and his assistant [*nsadi a mbuki*]). They were all quietly singing song lines from the *munem*, a complex mourning song cycle consisting of hundreds of

155

sayings and proverbs.[3] Now and then, their singing was interspersed by the women's ritualised weeping and by improvised vocalizations of some of the male elders, who, following the *munem* rhythm, continued to duel vocally with each other throughout the night, hinting at the possible causes of death, and making subtle accusations and references to the outcome of various divinatory sessions that had been carried out after his death. In front of the deceased's house, a shelter (called *chisaambw* or *kachikuumbw ka mufiil* in the local Lunda language: 'the little house of the widow') had been erected, for the widow of the deceased is no longer allowed to enter the house of her deceased husband until the first mourning period is officially ended, some forty days after the actual burial. She is to spend this whole period under this shelter, seated on the door of the house that has now become a *chimboonzu*, the house of the dead. During these weeks, another widow keeps her company and acts as a caretaker (*chikolkol*), prepares her food, sleeps together with her at night and consoles her (she 'pours water on her heart', — *meem angwichiil kambuny*).[4]

Sitting with the Nseej villagers around the fire, I learned that the actual burial had taken place some 40 days earlier, and that this mourning night (called *kutoongam* or *kunoomish mufidi*) marked the official closure of the first, and most important, period of mourning, thereby allowing 'the lifting of prohibitions and food taboos' (*kusumik*) that apply to the village as a whole (for example, the prohibition to have sex during the nocturnal wake) and to the widow herself. The latter has to observe several rules throughout the whole period of mourning.[5]

In this particular case, the ritual was quite complex because the widow had already lost two other husbands, and an elaborate purification ritual was needed to cleanse her of the stench of death and take away the cause that set off this chain of consecutive deaths. Earlier on, it had been established in a number of divinatory sessions that the widow was possessed by a spiritual entity (*haamb*) called *muf* ('corpse' or 'dead person') and that it was this spiritual force (or 'shade' as Victor Turner called it) that was responsible for her husbands' deaths. In the ritual universe of many people in the Central African savannah belt spanning Southern Congo, Angola, Zambia and beyond, these *mahaamb* 'spirits', shadows and shades (an open-ended class containing up to thirty different spiritual entities)[6] continue to play an important role even today. These spiritual force fields frequently interfere in people's lives in ways that may be benevolent or malevolent. A specific cult exists for each *haamb*. To appease them, it is important to erect a cult shrine and make offerings to them from time to time.

The ritual that was performed to close the widow's mourning period is known as *kadiaang mukeew*. It centres on the ritual purification of the widow in order to reinsert her into the normal flow of social life by severing her ties with the deceased and appeasing the *muf* spirit that was believed to have caused the death of the three husbands. During the period of mourning, a widow is not allowed to eat cooked cassava paste.

Her meals consist exclusively of uncooked groundnuts, cassava roots and corn. Nor is she allowed to wash herself after she has been covered with ashes from the kitchen fire, which is extinguished on the day of her husband's death (only to be lit again at the end of the mourning period). Throughout this period she is to wear a loincloth only, tied together with a cord and folded between her legs like a baby's diaper. This dress code (called *mwiinkaank*) signifies the fact that the widow has become like a small child (*mwaankaank*) again, and is in need of care.

At daybreak after the night of mourning, the ritual specialist started to prepare on a fire a herbal potion (*lukosh*) to 'wash' and purify the widow. This act of purification took place in front of the deceased's house after they had dismantled the shelter under which the widow had spent all of her days and nights since the burial. While a fire was lit inside the house for the first time since the funeral, the widow was seated on the door that had been placed in front of the door opening. The healer then received a gourd of palm-wine from a representative of the deceased's parents (usually one of his [classificatory] parents or maternal uncles), whereas the widow's relatives offered him a chicken, together with a small sum of money called *nseew*.[7] The chicken was then nailed onto the door with bamboo pegs, and the herbalist started to apply the herbal mixture[8] onto the chicken as well as the widow's body, sprinkling the mixture with a brush made of leaves onto the head, breast and arms of the widow, who was still crouching on top of the door. This is called 'dispersing the charcoal ashes' (*kumwaang makal*),[9] in reference to the fact that, at this point, the widow's caretaker and one of the deceased maternal uncles sweep together all the ash and remaining charcoal of the fires that had been lit during the night and throw them away near the house of the deceased, at a spot to remain a secret from the other family members who are present during the wake.

After the herbalist had cleansed the widow, the woman who acted as her caretaker smeared her with the remaining 'medicine' (*moon, chikosh*) and then taking her by the left hand, they started to run together around the house. The two women were closely followed by the healer, who, using some twigs of the *mwiinzoomb* tree,[10] sprinkled them both once more with the herbal preparation. The whole sequence was repeated several times, accompanied by the singing of the bystanders. The widow was made to run around the house to 'wake her up' and make her alert, and to chase off the 'image' or shadow of the deceased that was still sticking to her body and mind. That is why the chicken, as well as the widow, had to be treated by the herbalist. The deceased's shadow and smell, i.e. the very memory of him, still clung to his wife's body and by cleansing her with a brush, the healer then transferred with the same brush the deceased's shadow onto the chicken.

Accompanied by her caretaker, a few of her female relatives as well as a female representative of her husband's family, the widow was led to a nearby stream by the healer after this purification ritual. She emerged from the water clean and pure, while the gourds, pots and brush used for the preparation and application of the medicinal materials were left behind in the river to drift away downstream. Walking back to the village, she was not allowed to turn her head and look back so that all ties with her past should be severed, a past that was also ritually burnt when all the women present lit a fire near the riverbank with a specific kind of grass, brought for the purpose.

Back in the village, the widow's head was shaved by a male relative of the deceased,[11] after which the healer fed her a ritual meal consisting of some food stuffs she had not been allowed to eat during the mourning period, such as cooked cassava mush and pieces of a small spotlessly white fish (*mpaanv*) included in the meal to illustrate the fact that the widow, like the fish, had re-entered normal social life as a clean, spotless 'white' person. The remains of the meal, together with the widow's hair, were deposited on the door and then carried out of the village by the widow on her head. Accompanied by the healer and the female caretaker, who sang *munem* songs throughout the trajectory, the widow walked along a path leading to the west of the village (i.e. 'downstream' to the setting sun, the location of *kaluung*, the underworld, where the dead are transformed into ancestors). Stepping off the path, she had to break through three 'gates' (two of which consisted of two long leaves of grass, knotted together by the healer) with her right foot.[12] The last 'gate' was not made of grass but consisted of a new tree shoot that had been bent. Here, the healer made a small puppet out of grass leaves, called 'image/resemblance of the corpse' (*chifaanish cha muf*), a representation of the *haamb* shade considered to be the source of all the widow's troubles. He anointed the widow's breasts with with kaolinite clay (*mpeemb*) while addressing the *haamb*: 'Go away with all your dead people and your diseases, and leave me alone.' He then untied the knots that held together the puppet representing the spirit of the 'corpse' so that the puppet fell to pieces. This ritual is called 'closing the door' (*kupat chiiy*), and is meant to sever once again the links between the widow and the entity that had been causing her misfortunes. Finally, the widow carried and deposited the door in front of a *kapwiip*-tree, a tree that is often used as a ritual depository of 'evil' and witchcraft.[13] The tree itself was also smeared with kaolinite.

From there, the widow proceeded to another tree,[14] once more 'breaking' two more 'gates'. At the foot of this tree, which had been bent and tied to the ground to form a third gate, the healer had previously installed a sculptural relief made of earth in the shape of a man lying on his back with his arms and legs spread wide open conspicuously displaying his genitals. The healer covered the entire figure with kaolinite. He made another grass 'corpse' puppet to the right of the figure's head, while the chicken, which had been used in the cleansing ritual in the village and to which the deceased's shadow had been transferred, was nailed to the ground left of the earthen figure. Food offerings (corn, beans, cassava and groundnuts) were strewn around the figure while the widow, standing in front of the sculpture, put the second 'corpse'

puppet between her legs and pushed the puppet's penis into her vagina.[15] By means of this transgressive act of copulating with the *haamb* shade, she had lifted its curse, while the caretaker hit the ground with a stick in another act of ritual cursing in order to prohibit the widow from remembering her deceased husband. Having thus once again cut the ties linking her to death, the widow then covered the sculpture with the loincloth she had been wearing during the mourning period and tied a new cloth, which she had brought for that purpose, around her waist.[16] Thereupon she returned to the village, but not before being cleansed one final time with tree bark by the healer to wash off the impurities of the world of the dead she had entered and now left.[17]

Upon their return to the village, the healer presented the widow to her affines, because they were the ones who had hired him for his services. The widow's in-laws then handed her over to her father (or his representative), but not before asking the healer to state publicly that the whole ritual had been carried out correctly, thereby averting possible future accusations from the widow's lineage in the case that she falls ill or dies later on. Finally, the in-laws also offered a meal to all those present.

Later on during that day, the deceased's house was burnt down. After such a final and irreversible rupture, the widow normally re-integrates with her own matrilineage, together with the children who are still under her care. These may be reclaimed by their father's family later on, after the compensatory payment of a goat (*mpeemb wililish*) to the widow's father or her mother's brother.

>> FF: DEATH AND THE CITY: CEMETERY INFRASTRUCTURE

'Ah, Maman Chantal! No kidding, if someone tells you that you are ugly, you ought to thank him, and tell him: 'Why do you call me ugly? You want to know what ugly means? Have you ever been to a morgue? And did you see how corpses are put on top of each other there, like parcels? And seeing all these dead bodies, didn't your heart cringe and didn't you want to run away?' Some have their eyes wide open, some corpses are already rotting, their mouths hang open, ah, really, the human body is ugly!'
[Part of a conversation between two women, recorded during a *matanga* nocturnal wake, Camp Luka, Kinshasa, March 2008]

This vivid description of corpses in Kinshasa's morgues was made in a casual conversation during a nocturnal ritual of mourning. It stands in sharp contrast with the careful, ritualised treatment of death as it was carried out, and to some extent still is, in Kinshasa's rural hinterlands, as exemplified in the Lunda ceremony described above.[18] Deaths, mourning rituals and funerals still mobilise a great deal of social capital in an urban context such as Kinshasa's, but, as elsewhere in Congo (Noret & Petit 2011), the emotional contents of death, its ritual handling and the affective dimensions surrounding its occurrence have radically changed. These changes are due to several factors.

Firstly, the very nature of the city's material infrastructure has brought about important changes in the way urban residents are forced to handle death. Few morgues in Kinshasa operate well enough to prevent a corpse from decomposing for more than a couple of days, and the overall poor standard of public utilities does nothing to help to improve the situation. The history of the city's built form and its material, physical infrastructure must be taken into account if anyone wants to understand the ways in which urban residents deal with their dead today. As I pointed out before, Kinshasa was for many decades, especially after 1960, a city where formal urban planning and architecture was practically non-existent and this remains the case to a considerable extent today. Therefore, a significant part of the city's material infrastructures and all public utilities such as water, electricity, roads and public buildings (administrative buildings,

schools etcetera) still rely on what was put in place during the colonial era. However, most of these colonial infrastructures exist nowadays as a disintegrating conglomeration of decaying fragments and rotting material, a distant echo of what once existed. Urban residents are thus constantly confronted with the ensuing shortcomings and deficiencies in the city's infrastructures. These have become very apparent in the city's graveyards.

During the colonial era, which formally lasted from 1908 to 1960, large plots of land within the city were set aside by the Belgian colonial administration for the construction of cemeteries. These graveyards were modelled on typical nineteenth-century European cemeteries and inscribed the landscape with a Christian (mostly Roman Catholic) topography. They were thus the immediate result of a colonial intervention that created a novel type of space within the new urban context that was emerging in Congo in the first half of the twentieth century. In Leopoldville's urban planning, most of these cemeteries were situated in empty zones and no-man's-land, which (as mentioned in Chapter Two) rendered the lines of colonial colour bars visible in the urban landscape

Many colonial cemeteries were rapidly engulfed by living areas after 1960 because after independence formal urban planning ground to an almost complete halt and the demographic explosion that Kinshasa underwent in the second half of the twentieth

century only increased the pressure. This often resulted in an ad hoc and makeshift form of slums and camps, which has to a large extent continued to define the material outlook, sensory feel and the generally poor quality of life in the city as it has emerged since 1960. This chaotic city is often referred to by Kinois as a *cité cimetière*, a cemetery city 'that has died' (*mboka ekufi*), a necropolis where the material infrastructure has become totally 'cadaverous' (*cadavéré*)[19] and life is constantly rhythmed by the inescapable presence of death. This is a city where the omnipresent Mercedes 207 taxi-buses are usually called 'spirits of death' (*esprits de mort*) due to the many fatal car accidents they cause, and where the mechanical controls and inspections the city tries to impose on the owners of these often dilapidated, unroadworthy vehicles are known as 'moratorium' (*moratoire*). This is a city where the governor is whispered to frequent a famous 'marabout' by the name of Mort-Mort; where the nocturnal crowds at concerts and in nightclubs are thought to consist of zombies and returning dead who refuse to let go of life; where widows and widowers continue to be bothered at night by their deceased spouses (the so-called *époux/épouses de nuit*); and where death has become a model for collective social and political action, as in the case of the *journées ville morte*, which the UDPS opposition party regularly called for throughout the 1990s .

Cemeteries in Kinshasa and its periphery include Kimbanseke and Gombe (named after the municipalities where they are located), Kinsuka and Kimwenza (both in the Mont Ngafula municipality), Kisenso (between the Mont Ngafula and Matete municipalities), Kingampio, SIFORCO ([ex-SIFORZAL] in Masina, near the international airport), Mikonga (on the road to Maluku) and Gombe Lutete. Some of these cemeteries (the cemeteries of Kingampio, Kimwenza, Mikonga and Sans Fil in Masina, for instance) were originally traditional burial grounds belonging to the Teke-Humbu, the local landowners and original inhabitants of what is now Kinshasa. Many of the older colonial cemeteries within the city have since been abandoned and closed down by the urban authorities, mostly because they greatly exceeded their capacity to take in more corpses. Some of the older city cemeteries, such as Kintambo and Kasavubu, were already closed in the late 1980s. Other centrally located cemeteries such as Gombe, in the very centre of the city, and more peripheral cemeteries such as Kinkole and Kinsuka, were officially closed in 2010 by the city's current governor, André Kimbuta. Some colonial cemeteries such as Kasavubu have been converted into gardens and fields, and some have been left as they were, such as the large cemetery of Kintambo. Some cemeteries such as Kanza, Sans Fil and Makala have also ceased to exist in the meantime, while others are threatened by the uncontrolled and rapid urban sprawl (Kinsuka, Kisenso). Some cemeteries (such as Kisenso and Kintambo) are also vulnerable to erosion, a constant problem in many neighbourhoods in and around Kinshasa, which is partly built on unstable sandy hills.[20] New cemeteries were — and continue to be — laid out in the eastern and western peripheries, such as Mbenseke and Mitendi (on the road to Matadi and the Lower Congo) and Kinkole (in the municipality of Nsele). *'Nécropole — entre terre et ciel'* (Necropolis — between heaven and earth) would have been a fitting nickname for Kinshasa as a whole, but it is the official name of the city's most recent (2010) cemetery, a public-private joint venture on the city's easternmost outskirts in Nsele. Finally, numerous burial sites in and around Kinshasa are not officially registered or even known to the city authorities.

————————

Let us take a walk in the cemetery of Kintambo. Extending across two of Kinshasa's municipalities, Ngaliema and Kintambo (both part of the Lukunga district), the cemetery is located close to the place where Stanley founded his first trading post, the Stanley Pool station, and signed a 'friendship treaty' with Ngaliema, the chief of Kintambo village in 1881. Kintambo cemetery thus takes us back to the early colonial origins of the city, even though the densely populated municipalities of Kintambo and Ngaliema no longer resemble the fishermen's villages of the end of the nineteenth century,[21] and even though the cemetery in its current form only emerged long after 1923, the year in which the colonial authorities decided to move the colony's administrative capital from Boma to Leopoldville, a transfer that was completed in 1929 (Toulier, Lagae and Gemoets 2010: 35).

In use since the mid 1950s, Kintambo cemetery was one of the largest and most centrally located graveyards of the colonial city. Today it still is the city's most emblematic cemetery, even though there are very few reminders of the colonial order that once marked this space. In total disarray, the cemetery epitomises instead the full extent of neglect and decay to which the colonial infrastructure of most of Kinshasa's public utilities has succumbed. Already by the late 1980s, the urban authorities had decided to close this cemetery down because it was literally overflowing with corpses. However, in spite of two more official attempts to close it during the following decades, the inhabitants of the neighbouring *quartiers*, the densely populated slum areas of Camp Luka, Quartier Congo and the slightly more upscale Jamaïk, have continued to bury their dead there. Every day, more corpses arrive and a lot of burials still take place in Kintambo cemetery, even though it has long (at least officially) been abandoned by the city authorities. At the *Division Urbaine* of Kinshasa, the administrative unit responsible for all the city's cemeteries, no official statistics are kept about the yearly number of burials in the city. However, between 2002 and 2005, the head of the *Service d'inhumation* kept a personal record of the number of reported burials,[22] and arrived at an overall average of 21,968 deaths per year for this period. The cemetery of Tsuenge (at Masina SIFORCO) seemed to absorb more bodies than any other cemetery in and around the city, but Kintambo still ranked second, with 25.17% of the city's burials in 2002, 24.34%

in 2003 and 21.47% in 2004. And 23.65% of all the deceased in Kinshasa during this period were buried in cemeteries that no longer exist.[23]

As the cemetery is not kept up or taken care of by the urban authorities anymore, it has become, in the words of the Kinois, 'a forest where snakes lay their eggs'. The cemetery's original ground-plan has disappeared totally. Its formerly asphalted streets and carefully maintained alleyways have given way to lush vegetation that has overgrown this thanatopolis completely, as if the dead needed a second and more final burial. Here indeed, as people often remark, one dies twice: tombs and coffins are often simply carried away by floods during the rainy season's torrential storms and by heavy erosion and mud slides from the hills of Ngaliema that partly surround the cemetery. In this way, corpses often disappear as rapidly as they were buried. A few months after a burial, any cheap cement cross on a grave is usually removed or destroyed by the cemetery's gravediggers, thereby allowing them to recycle and resell unmarked graves. Since space is a scarce commodity in this cram-full graveyard, different corpses are frequently buried on top of each other's coffin. Tombs are also regularly destroyed by the inhabitants of the surrounding neighbourhoods in their search for a good spot for their illegal housing constructions. In this dense urban jungle, the living and the dead are often engaged in a fierce competition over land. Like many other cemeteries in the city, such as Kinsuka and Kisenso, Kintambo cemetery is under constant threat from the uncontrolled rapid urban sprawl eating away at its borders and making it increasingly difficult to maintain the already blurred dividing line between the living and the dead (De Boeck 1998b). As Kinois say: 'We [the living and the dead] have all become the same' (*biso nionso bato moko*).

In Kintambo and other cemeteries in Kinshasa, the living and the dead indisputably live in close proximity, and their lives seem intimately entwined. Even if many people perceive the cemetery as just another festering wound on the city's already pockmarked face, for many others it offers openings and promising prospects. Through a spontaneous commoditization of death, the cemetery has become a marketplace to satisfy a person's 'thirst for money' (*lokoso ya mbongo*). Not only do children play football between the decaying graves[24] but they also try to make a small profit out of the burial ground. They burn the vegetation that grows there in the dry season in order to hunt for bush rats, which may then be sold as food. They fill sacks with sand from the small river that runs through the cemetery in the hope of selling some to nearby construction sites. Tombstones along the road are used to display second-hand clothes or plastic bowls made in China and vendors call out their loud sales pitches to passers-by. Other tombs are turned into makeshift bars and *malewa* restaurants, where one might rest a while, eat some food and drink a bottle of freshly tapped palm wine.

The greater part of the cemetery's surface has been converted into fields and kitchen gardens. Women harvest the cassava, corn and groundnuts that they planted and sowed on and between graves and now sprout and grow from the bellies of the dead. Mortuary houses in the cemetery are used as shelters by *shege* street children (whom Kinois more generally refer to as *société morte*, 'dead society'), while local *kuluna* gangs hold their meetings to drink, smoke, talk, sing and dance in the less accessible parts of the graveyard.[25] Other groups of young men spend their days loitering on the road that goes through the cemetery hoping to be hired as singers and drummers at a funeral. Others offer their services to gravediggers who occupy and control the cemetery and have transformed tombstones along the main road into their personal office space where they wait for clients.

Forming a loosely-structured association of different groups or 'stables' (*écuries*) that offer specific services (digging graves, manufacturing cement crosses, maintaining the tombs and so on), these self-appointed gravediggers also supervise access to Kintambo cemetery and keep an eye on what goes on there. All the gravedigger groups consist of a few more senior men and a fluctuating number of younger men and boys,

some as young as seven or eight years of age. Most of them live in the surrounding neighbourhoods of Camp Luka and Quartier Congo on the slopes of the Ngaliema hills, although some also regularly spend the night in the cemetery itself.

Their association is called *Shamukwale*, the name of a Congolese village near the Angolan border, some 200 kilometers east of Pic Sörensen and Nzofu. During the years that UNITA controlled the Lunda Norte diamond fields along the Kwango River (roughly between 1991 and 1998), this village constituted one of the main points of access into Angola for tens of thousands of young Congolese men and women, many from Kinshasa, eager to try their luck in clandestine diamond mining and trafficking activities.[26] With the ironic humour that is so typical of the people of Kinshasa, the gravediggers thus turn dead bodies into diamonds, and interpret their own digging work as a form of clandestine artisanal diamond mining. In this way, they refer, for example, to the digging of a grave as *zolo (na) zolo*, a phrase that literally means 'nose to nose' but that is also the name given to a specific form of artisanal alluvial mining carried out by divers or *zolmen* during the dry season, when the water-level is at its lowest and the riverbed's gravel may be reached more easily.[27]

In many ways, their work is certainly 'illegal', even though their presence in the cemetery is extremely visible. The Shamukwale association consists of twelve semi-autonomous smaller groups, including *Écurie Bana cimetière*, *Écurie Etat-Major* or *Camp Kawele*, *Écurie Camp PM* (Military Police) and *Écurie Camp Police*. Each *écurie* or 'stable' functions as a territorial unit that occupies, controls and works in a specific part of the cemetery according to an often challenged and continually contested hierarchy that is established on the basis of 'firstcomers and latecomers' rights. These rights cede certain groups control over more profitable parts of the cemetery (close to the main road, for example), while other will have to make do with the less accessible and thus less profitable areas.

None of them is officially employed by the city, although there is a great deal of connivance and complicity between the members of the association and the urban authorities. Until 2010, for example, the gravedigger that most of them acknowledged as the 'president' of the Shamukwale association was a man in his early forties from neighbouring Camp Luka. He also happened to be the older brother of the director of the administrative unit that represents the urban authorities in the graveyard. He was later replaced by his younger brother while he himself became the head of the administrative agents in the cemetery. Unlike gravediggers, these agents are officially appointed by and receive a salary from the *Division Urbaine*, a subdivision of the urban administration that is headed by the governor of Kinshasa. However, due to the recent process of decentralization and reform of the Congolese administration (cf. Trefon 2009a), the provincial minister of interior affairs now also has a say in the management of the city's cemeteries. Consequently and in spite of the fact that the cemetery no longer exists officially, the city's civil servants continue to hold office in what remains of the once small administration building, which only has one wall still standing today. That they are there at all, even though the cemetery is closed, is explained by the fact that people who can prove to be the rightful owners of a collective family grave still have permission to bury their family members in Kintambo *cimetière*. Sitting at a small improvised table in the ruins of the former office building, the administrative agents thus continue to authorise and register burials, and they are supposed to control whether a burial will indeed take place in a collective family grave. In return, the deceased's family receives a *jeton*, a small cardboard ticket with an official registration number, for which they have to pay a fixed sum. Once this registration fee is paid, they can contact an *écurie* of gravediggers, negotiate the price and location of the tomb, and proceed with the funeral.

It is easy to see how this procedure might set in motion a complex shadow economy and an endless carrousel of trade-offs between a whole set of actors with interlocking interests (deceased's family members, gravediggers, civil servants in the cemetery and various other actors at more important echelons of the city's administration, to whom a significant part of the earnings of the cemetery office is transferred, and who, in return, shield the gravediggers and ensure that they are not chased off the cemetery). Similarly to the case of the Building (see Chapter Three), this is not as if the state is absent, but rather that it has to negotiate and stake out its place within a much wider web of different stakeholders who all share interests that overlap, at the very least temporarily, and are therefore all mutually interdependent. The mutual trust that is needed for these interdependencies to function smoothly and to endure over time, as in this case, is often built on kin- or clan-based ties and therefore on a shared sense of ethnic affiliation which, here as elsewhere in Africa, still constitutes one of the most trusted 'pathways to accumulation' (Geschiere and Konings 1993).

By means of such makeshift operations and fragmented constellations, and their often unravelling, defracturing and refracturing, horizontal and vertical interdependencies, the city, the multiple users of the cemetery and the gravediggers manage to shape the cemetery as a provisional public sphere, even though its order remains very precarious and its rules and laws come easily undone. Not only do funerals introduce a new public, different orders, laws and sets of ownership during the day but the nocturnal time-space also generates other owners, alternative rules and territorialising manoeuvres in the dark. After nightfall, a different set of people takes over the cemetery. They may be lovers in search of privacy, for example, but very often the activities of the people frequenting the cemetery at night are less benign, and the sense of insecurity during these hours is so strong that the inhabitants of Camp Luka tend not to use the access road to their neighbourhood after nightfall, for this road leads straight through the cemetery. This also means that Camp Luka's inhabitants are de facto living under a state of curfew that keeps them in their homes after sunset. Even street children who live in the cemetery during the day tend to abandon the area at night in search of safer places to sleep. The rumoured domain of vagabonds and thieves, gangs and assassins, rapist soldiers and harassing policemen, the cemetery becomes a place of even more clandestine activities at night. In the evening, bands of young thieves come together in the cemetery to split the earnings from their day's 'work' at Kinshasa's central downtown market. It is also at this time that groups of young people start to offer their services for more clandestine burials. People who cannot afford to finance a burial are very often forced to bury their dead in a secret and non-official way. This happens more frequently when the deceased is a young child. In 2007 and 2008, I observed how a small group of male adolescents, members of an *écurie* known as *Tshico*, would often gather along the dusty road that cuts across the cemetery. They were waiting to be contacted by parents who wanted to bury their child at night, unseen by the authorities and without officially registering the burial. Other youths were waiting for the cover of darkness to dig up and steal the coffins of those who were buried during the day. These coffins are subsequently resold (cf. De Boeck and Plissart 2004: 136). Still others were waiting for nightfall so that they could pillage graves in the hope of laying their hands on clothes, jewellery and gold teeth.

MOMENTS OF MOURNING: THE AFFECTIVE TURN OF DEATH AND THE MORALITY OF 'DISORDER'

The song I started this chapter with, *Mokolo Nakokufa* ('The day I die'), is a classic song from the great songbook of Congolese rumba, a musical genre that started to emerge at the same time as new urban infrastructures and the novel experience of an urban lifeworld under Belgian colonial rule. Composed in 1966 by Seigneur Tabu Ley Rochereau, it offers a timeless philosophical reflection about human mortality and has become an inextricable part of the collective musical memory of Kinshasa. One of the reasons behind the huge success of this song is the fact that Tabu Ley conjures up a kaleidoscopic view of an urban collectivity as pieced together from the fragmented perspective of different individual voices, all imagining in the first person singular the day of their own death: the singer himself, a poor man, a rich man, an alcoholic, a prostitute...

It is no coincidence that in this famous song mortality becomes the prism through which different splintering perspectives and identities are turned into a collective experience; In Congo, death has always been the spectral lens through which people imagine themselves as a shared social body. Still to this day, the dead body remains an important social infrastructure in a megalopolis such as Kinshasa, even though kinship ties, clan and lineage identities, and other forms of social belonging that reference a shared pre-urban past, have often lost much of their cohesive power or have been thoroughly reconfigured. Likewise the *matanga* (nocturnal mourning rituals preceding

the actual burial) remain important social events that engender communal moments of encounter and generate opportunities for wide-ranging social networks to be made and regenerated from one *matanga* to the next. These occasions to meet around death bring about what Elyachar has termed the 'semiotic commons', a commons created through the 'phatic labour' (Elyachar 2010) of the words that sustain the city's social infrastructure, with its specific communicative channels, its *Radio Trottoir* small talk and gossip. As Durham and Klaits (2002: 778) remark with regard to funerals in Botswana, 'people find themselves connected in their very physical well-being through emotional states and sentimental connections recognised and forged in public space'. What partly produces this connectedness among all those present is the sense of shared, collective *Trauer Arbeit*, formed during the night of mourning and an intimate, often very corporeal and tactile, always emotionally-charged relationship with the body and spirit of the deceased.

Relatives, neighbours and friends are brought together in moments of mourning during these nocturnal wakes, which last all night and well into the next day to culminate in the procession to the cemetery and the actual burial of the corpse. Once the

corpse is retrieved from the morgue, it is taken 'home' and laid in repose for public viewing in the family compound, or then in the street or any available public space if the compound does not have enough room, as is often the case. The physical presence of dead bodies in the street has profoundly reconfigured the access and use of public space in the urban setting. Some decades ago, it would have been unconceivable to place the body of a deceased person in the middle of the street in Kinshasa. In the 1960s and 70s, mourning rituals took place inside the compounds, while children and young-sters were barred from any direct contact with death itself. If a funeral procession passed through the street, mothers would call their children indoors: children were not supposed to come into contact with death, since they represent the beginning of life and should not be contaminated by its end. Today, however, the body of the deceased is often placed upon a bier in the middle of the street, under a funeral chapel or *cataphar*[28] around which people gather to mourn the deceased and hold nocturnal wakes open to all. To mark the presence of a corpse, streets are blocked and palm leaves are placed at their entrance. As a result of this and also because they have become so numerous, the dead have quite literally taken possession of the street. For the duration

of the mourning period, they tend to 'privatize' the urban public space and in doing so, they constantly redraw the cartography of a street and neighbourhood, redefining its meaning, its use and accessibility in the process.

People gather around the dead body to weep, sing, talk to the deceased, touch and embrace the body, dance around it and take care of it until the actual moment of burial, which takes place the next day. *Matanga* also provide entertainingly ludic moments as they invariably offer occasions for laughter, amusement, flirtation and excitement; they hold out the promise of new encounters, and the pleasure of meeting up with old friends and acquaintances. But, at the same time, *matanga* remain very weighty occasions in which existing hierarchies and power relations within and between families, lineages and clans are reaffirmed or challenged. In most cases, maternal uncles of the deceased are the ones in charge of the funeral. They decide on the time and place of burial, and they also raise the necessary money, hire chairs, contract an orchestra and/or choir, contact the authorities, take care of the formalities for the burial, deal with the cemetery authorities, supervise the course of action of the mourning period until the burial, assemble the deceased's family (on the mother's and father's side, and

the in-laws as well), conduct the palavers involving heritage and funeral contributions, and, most importantly, establish the cause of death, definitely in cases where witchcraft is suspected to be at the origin of the death.

Death thus remains an important group event, and a focal point to bring people together and re-imagine and replenish the social weaving of relationships in the urban context. *Matanga* continue to set the rhythm and pace of social life in the city. They function as important motors for the reproduction and renewal of social networks, offering a nocturnal space-time in which the social landscapes that open up between people during the day are constructed. Yet, in recent years, *matanga*, as ritualised forms of a shared, collective labour of loss, also seem to have lost a lot of their socially constructive force. Partly as the result of the corrosive impact of decades of political mismanagement and state neglect that have heavily impacted on the quality of social life in general, the transformations surrounding death in the urban setting also epitomise increasingly divisive new societal tensions. Among other things, these are caused by the exponential population growth of the city, as well as generational imbalances that accompany this spectacular demographic increase.

Although female fertility rates in Kinshasa have dropped dramatically since the 1970s (cf. Shapiro and Tambashe 2003), Kinshasa's yearly growth rate currently exceeds 5%, which still makes it one of the largest and fastest growing urban centres on the continent. A closer analysis of the available (though somewhat unreliable) demographic data for Congo reveals that 65% of the total Congolese population is under the age of 25, and that this figure is probably higher for Kinshasa. Although the official life expectancy at birth for the Congolese population as a whole has risen from 47 years in 1960 to 54 years in 2010, Congo has also gone down from its 106th position in the WHO world health rankings in 1960 to the 163rd position in 2010 according to the WHO statistics.

In the past few decades, urban centres such as Kinshasa have experienced an undeniably excessive mortality rate. Due in part to AIDS, the high death rate must also be blamed on the overall harsh conditions of life in the city, where exponential growth and exponential decay go hand in hand. Death has thus become omnipresent in daily life and has started to restructure urban living in many fundamental ways as it also has elsewhere throughout the continent.[29]

That death and the dead body itself become increasingly important 'means of

re-imagining the social' (Nuttall 2013: 418) is also indicative of the hardship that is so much part of life for many Congolese. Given the city's demographics, young people are affected by death in significantly larger numbers than their elders.[30] In 1966, it would not have occurred to Tabu Ley to include in his song a young person's voice pondering about the day of his or her own death, but today the categories of 'youth' and 'death' have become inextricably linked. As a result, in every Congolese urban centre, and most strongly pronounced in Kinshasa, young people have made death and funerals central elements to express themselves and stake out their place in the city. This is certainly the case in Camp Luka, an overpopulated slum that started to grow out of an illegal squatting area in the early 1970s on the border of Kintambo cemetery and has been growing ever since. The name 'Camp Luka' became popular in the 1990s when its inhabitants, with typical Kinois humour, named their slum after Luka Camp, a concentration camp run by Bosnian Serb armed forces in Brcko, Bosnia-Herzegovina, during the Bosnian war.

Camp Luka inhabitants also refer to it as 'The State' (*Leta*) and its young people therefore refer to themselves as 'children of the State' (*Bana Etat*). They also call themselves 'children of disorder' (*bana désordre*) because they are the ones who impose the order of disorder on the cemetery and indeed the rest of the city. Disorder is what characterises their 'law', the unruly rule of their own strange, raggedy state, and this law of disorder is implemented in often animated ways, at once ludic and violent, during mourning rituals and funerals, and through the materiality and aesthetics of the medium of the body — their own as well as that of the dead.

As already stated, the fathers and uncles of the deceased are normally the ones in charge of a funeral. In recent years, however, the city has witnessed a powerful reversal of the standard norms and rules that regulate intergenerational dialogues in the spheres of kinship and public life. Children and youngsters are increasingly taking over control of mourning and burial rituals. This is especially true when a young person dies, and, as previously indicated, premature deaths have become the rule rather than the exception. The demise of a young person is an emotive moment of crisis, an affective turn that triggers a lot of anger and foments strong rebellious sentiments amongst the deceased's age-mates. This anger is mostly directed at older generations. More specifically, the parents and elders of the deceased are the first ones to be blamed for this death. In such cases, youngsters invade the ceremony: they single out fathers, maternal uncles and other elders and accuse them, normally using the available vocabularies of witchcraft that pervade the urban site, of having 'eaten' their young relative or friend, (*balei ye*, *babomi ye*: they [the elders] 'ate' him, they killed him). Such accusations of witchcraft usually tend to alter radically the course of the funeral itself. The *matanga* mourning rituals almost invariably 'turn into disorder' (*matanga ekomi désordre, pito-pale*) and become an intergenerational battlefield.[31] And when that happens, the deceased's friends, classmates or just any youngster living in the same neighbourhood, are very likely to take control over the *matanga* and the funeral rituals themselves. These groups of young people, sometimes in collaboration with local *kuluna* youth, start to throw stones at everyone present at the place of mourning. They might uproot the trees in the compound or attack the deceased's parental home, often destroying or burning it down in the process, while beating up, chasing away and sometimes even lynching or burning to death the parents, uncles, aunts, priests and preachers who gathered there to mourn the deceased. The family of the deceased sometimes tries to appeal to the police to regain control over the corpse during the funeral procedures, but the police often refuse to get involved. And when they do, their intervention often leads to the situation deteriorating even further. On several occasions in the recent past, youngsters have been hit by police bullets and even killed, provoking yet another round of violent funerals.

Whatever the case may be, the general atmosphere quickly becomes chaotic and often very violent. This sense of unease and violence is augmented by the youngsters' singing and dancing, as well as their copious use of marihuana and locally brewed alcohol (*lungwuila, chichampa, lotoko* or *supu na tolo,* 'breast soup'). On invading the scene of mourning, they single out certain elders and sing: *Tango mosusu ndoki ye oyo ye oyo* ('Maybe the witch is this one or that one'). After having chased the family off the compound, they proceed to carry away the dead body. They sometimes also block the neighbouring street and erect a 'road barrier' (*barrière*), forcing passers-by to make a monetary contribution. If the latter refuse, they run the risk of being dirtied — at the very least — with a mixture of burned rubber and palm oil. The money that is extracted in this way is often spent on the burial itself.[32]

Under these circumstances, the funeral itself almost inevitably turns into a totally chaotic event as well. Minibuses and cars are randomly commandeered in the street by youths. Sitting on a car's rooftop or hanging out of its windows while singing and shouting, and flashing their buttocks or breasts, they use these hijacked cars to drive to the cemetery at high speed. More often, the coffin with the corpse is paraded through the streets, carried by the deceased's friends and surrounded by boys and girls as they dance and sing songs full of sexual license: 'Today the vagina no longer works, today, the vagina will rot away' (*Lelo libola etuli, lelo libola ekei kopola*). Other songs further develop this theme: 'Here [the cemetery] it is a hotel. You come, you make love, and from the very first shot, it is: 'Goal!' (*Awa ezali hotel. Oyei, osali, ya premier coup ezalaka direct*"), or: 'Water, men's water, water from the backbone [sperm], water, water! When I catch you, I will put my penis inside you, the penis, the penis, I will fuck you!' (*Mayi! Mayi! Mayi mibali, mayi mayi mikongo, mayi mayi! Soki nakangi yo nakocha yo etsubeli, etsubeli, etsubeli! Nakosiba yo!*). While performing these songs, young boys and girls sit down on top of the coffin and putting it between their legs, they make copulating movements as if they were having sex with the corpse.

During the funeral processions towards the cemetery, the lyrics of songs often also become outspokenly political, attacking in no uncertain terms the political leaders of the city and the country, or else the elders and other authority figures such as priests and preachers [33] in general: 'We go, we go to the mourning ritual. We refuse to acknowledge the councillors [i.e. the elders' authority]. If you want to preach, preach to your believers. If you want to preach, preach to your own children. If you want to preach, preach in your own house.' (*Toyei, toyei matanga, toboyi baconseillers, soki olingi koteya, teya bandimi na yo. Soki olingi koteya teya bana na yo. Soki olingi koteya teya na ndako na yo*). Other songs openly voice youth's discontent with the state of the nation: 'Children with a diploma sell water, children with a diploma sell sausages. A rich country, but where is its dignity?' (*Bana na diplome bakei koteka mayi, bana na diplome bakeyi koteka boudin. Pays riche lokumu ezali wapi?*). Finally, some songs bluntly criticise the country's current leadership. Sometimes they even give voice to a sense of nostalgia for the former Mobutist regime: 'Mobutu ever since you left, we only eat rice [i.e. we are hungry]' (*Mobutu Mobutu tango okenda loso na loso.*)

177

While all this squabbling, dancing and singing can set a rather ludic tone to the unruly funeral processions to and inside the cemetery, young people carrying the body also engage in the far more serious business of performing a divinatory ritual on the corpse; a performance that is liable to erupt in extreme acts of violent retaliation. By tapping the left and the right foot end of the coffin with a stick, they ask the dead person to point them to those responsible for his or her death (left for the maternal and right for the paternal elders respectively). In response, the coffin with the corpse starts to 'dance' and leads the carriers to the house of the person responsible for 'eating' the dead person. Here, the girls in the funeral procession play a very active role, because they are often the ones who articulate suspicions of witchcraft by addressing the suspected culprits directly and bringing their name out into the open, while encouraging the dead person to reveal the truth about his or her death:

Now that you have eaten X, watch out!

(To the corpse:)

Even if it is someone from the father's side
Even if it is someone from the mother's side,
Follow those who ate you
Track them down
Lead us to their hiding place
So that we can kill them
Track them down during the night
Track them down during the day
Find them, even if they hide in the water
Open your eyes and your face
Even if they take a bus, follow them
Don't let them escape
Even if they hide in the fields, follow them
Even if they hide in the forest, follow them
Even if they are more than ten
We know the witch,
We know the village he comes from.
Those who killed X are known!

It is in this manner that the coffin with the corpse guides the crowd to the house of an elder. This, in turn, typically leads to the house being destroyed and the person that the corpse denounced as the witch being publicly beaten or even killed by the mob. And when, at the end of this chaotic disorder, the funeral procession eventually arrives at the cemetery with the corpse, the young people following the coffin usually destroy tombs and often attack gravediggers, or even bystanders, who happen to be at the wrong place at the wrong time.

'Copulating' with the corpse. Camp Luka, Kinshasa, March 2007.

Funerals have become much more than moments of political contestation for rebellious urban youths. Funeral rites are used to address civic wrongs, but the violence and rage that are unleashed during these events spring from another place, from somewhere deep inside, far beyond the level of official state or church politics. The aggressive display of the disorder of affect (and the affect of disorder) touches on deeply moral issues, and is related to the much more intimate domains of young people's own bodies and lives. Their actions pose fundamental questions with regard to the possibility of inter-subjective relations; they address possible reconfigurations of what kinship might mean, and attempt to redraw the dividing lines between insider and stranger; and they question the very definition of the notions of ancestrality and sacrality, and the feasibility of continued intergenerational transmission of social knowledge. These are some of the issues that I will explore in the next section.

CORPORA VILIA: EXPENDABLE YOUTH AND THE NOTION OF SACRIFICE

If, as Lévi-Strauss famously remarked in the concluding pages of *Tristes Tropiques*, cities are machines, 'instruments intended to create inertia, at a rate and in a proportion infinitely higher than the amount of organization they involve' (Lévi-Strauss 1974 [1955]: 413), Kintambo cemetery does seem to be the right place to redefine anthropology as *entropology*, 'the discipline concerned with the study of the highest manifestations of this process of disintegration' (Lévi-Strauss 1974 [1955]: 414). But is this what is really going on in Kinshasa's burial grounds? It is not very difficult to read spaces such as the cemetery of Kintambo, with all their infrastructural degradation and the breakdown of cultural norms and longstanding notions of social order that accompanies this material decay, as a general metaphor for the zombified state of a city and a country that, in the words of Kinois, 'died' or 'rotted' a long time ago (*mboka ekufi, mboka ebebi*), or are perceived as terminally ill and *cadavéré*.

But are notions of entropy, chaos, disorder and dissipation of energy adequate tools to understand the dynamics of a place such as the cemetery of Kintambo? Do these notions have sufficient explanatory power to capture fully the meanings embedded in the new mourning and funeral practices that have developed around it? It is indeed tempting — and perhaps even too obvious — to understand Kinshasa's postcolonial cemetery as a mere zone of social abandonment, to use Biehl's term (Biehl 2005), and a territory with specific Agamben-esque connotations, in which the law is in force but no longer has substantive meaning (Agamben 2005). The cemetery of Kintambo and its surrounding slums offer an almost camp-like infrastructure (as the Bosnian origin of Camp Luka's name itself indicates), which exemplifies the state of exception that has become the rule in postcolonial Congo and beyond (cf. Norris 2000).

This abandonment fully illustrates to what extent Kinois are turned into *homines sacri*, collectively reduced to the specific forms of raw, bare life, i.e. a politicised form of natural life, a life exposed and subjugated to death, placed outside both the divine and the profane law. Kinshasa's young inhabitants strongly sense that they have become the *corpora vilia* of a (post)colonial experiment called Congo, that they are the expendable subjects of a ruthless necropolitical form of governmentality (Mbembe 2003),[34] a thanatocracy that is controlled by previous generations who, by reducing their own children to becoming 'animals', have 'sacrificed' them in the process. The phrase 'We live like animals' (Lingala: *tokomi kovivre lokola banyama*) is often heard in the streets of Kinshasa. But although young people in Kinshasa invariably speak about themselves as a generation that has been 'sacrificed' by its own elders, the sacrificial aspect is, strictly speaking, absent from the way in which the state produces death (and, as Agamben reminds us, under Roman law the *homo sacer* could be killed with impunity, but could never be sacrificed). Indeed, there *is* no sacrifice here, but only 'eating', a witch-like killing devoid of any meaning or sense of sacrality. The act of killing an animal, for example, may only be called sacrificial if a form of identification between the sacrificer and the sacrificial object is made and then unmade during a ritual process (cf. Cartry 1987: 8). In the Congolese setting, however, this sense of identification is totally absent. Not only does the state constantly outlaw its own youth, excluding it from any real rights to the city and expelling (and often even physically eliminating) it from the public sphere in general, but the city's older generations, the parents of these young people, have also completely 'de-solidarised' themselves from their own children.

This act of de-solidarisation has radically transformed the nature, and the very possibility, of intergenerational transmission in Congo's urban worlds. Kinshasa's neo-Pentecostal and other Christian fundamentalist churches have significantly contributed to this trend of parental unlinking, or 'de-parentalisation' (Tonda 2008). Preaching a radical break with the autochthonous ancestral past, which is constantly demonised (Engelke 2010), these 'churches of awakening' (*églises de réveil*) have been contributing greatly to an ongoing redefinition of longstanding Central-African landscapes of lineage and kinship affiliation, and they do so by propagating a move away from the extended family and its accompanying kin-based model of solidarity. They have re-centred the focus towards the more 'western' model of the nuclear family and its related forms of singularisation, as well as individual rather than collective subject-formation. Finally, they have traded the gift logic of reciprocity and kin-based solidarity for a monetary- and capitalist-oriented logic, and everything this entails (a new work ethos, new notions of accumulation and maximalisation of profit, new forms of self-realisation and individualism) (De Boeck 2005b; see also Meiers 2013: 142ff). This explains why preachers in prayer movements such as Mama Olangi's, for example, often state that 'family is witchcraft'. Given the neoliberal notions of selfhood that are promoted by these churches, those family members (nephews, nieces and other dependents) who could always turn to maternal uncles for help within the gift-based logic of kinship solidarity are now not only being reformatted as 'strangers' but also redefined as 'witches' when they appeal for help, because for a true and authentic Christian, it is 'by the sweat of your brow that you will eat your food until you return to the ground' (Genesis 3:19).

Profound changes such as these processes of de-parentalisation have provoked dramatic shifts in the city's social realm, as attested by new forms of witchcraft accusations directed against 'witch-children' (*bana bandoki*). This is the inevitable collateral damage produced by these new definitions of relatedness. It is the flip side of what happens to elders during funerals. It is the missing other half of the increasingly impossible intergenerational dialogue, in which young and old accuse each other of being witches. Since the early 1990s, and coinciding with the continent-wide rise of Pentecostal and charismatic religious movements, children in Kinshasa and elsewhere in the country are increasingly being blamed by their parents and elders for all the mishaps, misfortunes, illnesses and deaths that occur in their families. As an immediate consequence of these accusations and the often genuine fear of elders that they will be 'eaten' by their own offspring, thousands of children have been expelled from their homes and left in (mostly Pentecostal) churches in order to be exorcised (see De Boeck 2008b, 2009b). As a result of such newly emerging processes of exclusion, children regularly end up in the street. The more their numbers grow, the more these street kids or *bashege*, as they are commonly known, are regarded as a real nuisance and a danger to the city. Nowadays, they are deemed no different from the many *kuluna* street gang members that are increasingly terrorising the city neighbourhoods (and who have partly sprung from the ranks of this growing army of street 'rats') (see also Chapter Three). In public opinion, both categories (street children and gang members) have merged (also because both are associated to a certain extent with the space of the cemetery, often the space in which they live or from where they operate). And both categories are not only held responsible for the increasing sense of insecurity in the city but also for the profound banalisation and desacralisation of death within the urban context. Most adults in Kinshasa are deeply shocked that children and young adolescents 'no longer respect the dead'. They are extremely troubled by the fact that children and young people eat and sleep on tombs in the city's cemeteries, and that they have turned funerals into a '*bêtise*' — some ridiculous nonsense —, a happening that takes no notice of former ancestral beliefs and moral frames of reference, and mocks long-standing gerontocratic orders and gendered structures of authority. Elders are equally appalled that their 'children' have converted corpses into a mere 'toy' or game (*eloko ya jeu*), and that coffins have become 'like footballs' to be kicked around during the football 'match' that the funeral has become. For them, this development or 'match' is 'bad' (*match eza mabe*).

The same sense of moral indignation is also generally conveyed by Kinshasa's numerous TV stations (in recent years Kinshasa has seen the birth of an unprecedented number of TV stations, most of which are privately owned) (Frère 2007). *Lingala Facile*, for example, is the name of a widely watched TV programme. Conceived by the Congolese star journalist Zacharie Bababaswe, this programme comes in the form of a 'proximity account' (cf. Pype 2011). The visual equivalent to *Radio Trottoir*, it offers a platform for spectators to send in their own images and witnessed accounts, usually filmed with a mobile phone. This footage tells of what exists and happens in the capital's streets and neighbourhoods. In this way, the whole of Kinshasa is frequently subjected to amateur footage showing, amongst other things, the material decay of the city's graveyards. Similarly, Kinois regularly report on ill-functioning morgues and their rotting corpses; they document and comment on the life of children in the cemetery and show and denounce the chaotic, violent yet effervescent nature of a young person's burial. The widespread use of mobile phones has greatly contributed to a further intensification of the mediatisation of death's penetration of the public sphere.[35]

Again, as in Tabu Ley's song, death in its enhanced visibility reveals itself to be a central focal point of urban life in which different converging views come together. A divisive yet also unifying presence, it engenders simultaneous multiplicities while also constituting the unique lens through which the city's obverse and reverse points of view come together. In this way, death seems to offer one of the few vantage points from which the possibility of initiating an intergenerational dialogue might be envisaged, even if that dialogue often turns into a dialogue of the deaf. In the eyes of their (grand-) parents' generation, most youngsters act as if death signifies the end; as if there is no afterlife beyond death, as if one just disappears. In sharp contrast with longstanding autochthonous beliefs in ancestrality (see also Kopytoff 1971), elders find that, in the minds of their children, the production of ancestors has come to a standstill. And yet, their children constantly exclaim: 'How can we still believe in ancestors if our own elders don't respect them?!':

> 'Our elders are the ones who should uphold tradition, who tell us about the important place of ancestors, but when you see how *they* cope with the dead who become ancestors, when you observe how corpses are put in the street, how they are buried hastily, how they are left to rot in morgues, how can we continue to believe that these corpses will turn into ancestors one day? Our elders have turned the process of dying into a *fait-divers*, and they have started to treat the dead with disrespect. So why should we still respect the elders?'
> [Excerpt from an interview at the cemetery of Kintambo, September 2005]

In this way, funerals have not only become a means of political contestation against a generation of post-independence politicians that has squandered the future of the following generations and refuses to make room for them. In a much broader sense, death has also become an occasion for this urban youth to criticise the role of parents and elders who in their eyes have *démissioné*, 'stepped down' and given up: elders no longer seem to be capable of playing their roles and fulfilling their promises; their moral authority has vanished; and while they 'eat' their children, they accuse their children of 'eating' them. In the light of this failure of gerontocracy, 'corpses have become the responsibility of the young people of the neighbourhood' (*bibembe ekoma ya bana quartier*). It is out of necessity, therefore, that the young, in their own words, have become the 'directors' (*bazali kodiriger*). They take over the control of the dead because elders have abused their power and authority, have squandered their wisdom and therefore 'have become little children' (*bakomi bana mike*).

Young Kinois have thus designed a new architecture of urban survival. By invading so visibly and violently the fabric of life, death and the sheer materiality and aesthetics of the dead body now serve as an inspirational force, a structural support, a framing device for negotiating social relationships and constructing identities. In a world where mourning has reconfigured meaning, where cemeteries have become dwellings for the living, and where coffins are likened to footballs that boys kick about, the only way to live is to reframe death into something else. For young Kinois who deal with dead bodies on a routine basis, dying is no longer a departure from life. Instead, it has become that which gives life its significance, density and directionality. Life, in fact, cannot be lived, spoken about or even imagined outside the space of death. Youth's instrumentalisation of death, as the single surface of a prismatic form, has thus transformed corpses into points of a strategic retroversion or retroflexion, a curving or bending back onto themselves of elders' discourses, and of the city's own fascination and disgust. For this is what these urban young do: by means of their funeral raids, they offer a mirror in which the city's moral indignation about its children is turned against itself by forcing the city to behold itself and reflect on its own nature and future.

Paradoxically, however, this opening up of ways to reflect on the conditions of urban living and to think about the possibility of alternative collective futures, always goes hand in hand with the reintroduction of pre-urban ritual forms and dynamics that reframe the urban 'enactment of moral sentiment' (Livingston 2008: 293) in very specific ways. As my long ethnography of a Lunda mourning ritual at the beginning of this chapter illustrates, urban youth's lewd songs, their insults and exposure of body parts, the whole play with the body's surface and its 'politics of undress' (Masquelier 2005), 'copulating' with the 'corpse' and the appropriation of rural divinatory practices that used to be the prerogative of elders really do constitute the playful, albeit also deadly serious, replays of longstanding ritual syntaxes. This and not the breach with an ancestral past or the precolonial ritual vocabularies is what stands out in the end. This is also how one should understand the fact that youngsters ritually 'ridicule' and defy death and disease with comic performances and dances next to their dead friend's corpse, performances in which they imitate physically impaired people, for example. In doing so they connect with older ritual vocabularies to keep death, disease and misfortune at bay. Similarly, during the *matanga* and funerals, young people of Camp Luka also recycle and incorporate other regional ritual traditions. A good example of this is the manner in which young men have taken over dances such as *musangu*, a stylised sword dance characteristic to the Lunda and Yaka political aristocracy (cf. also Mayasiwa Luveya 1986/1987) and normally exclusively performed in the rural context by elders on important political occasions, such as a titleholder's enthronement, court festivities or at the end of a *mwiingoony* (or *mungonge*) initiation ritual. Village elders' capacity to dance the *musangu* in a fittingly fierce and upright manner is an inexhaustible topic of conversation among men in this rural context. In its erectness, 'hardness' and virility, the dance is seen as the ultimate corporeal enactment of idealised notions of masculine pride.[36] In an urban context, however, this dance is enacted by the deceased's young friends. In this way they not only salute and honour him but also allow themselves to question and invert the gerontocratic orders they criticize, to restore a sense of pride to their own masculinity and to construct themselves as elders in an urban context that treats them as outcasts. Kinois youth thus shape a future for pre-urban ritual forms of which they often possess no firsthand knowledge (none of these young men that dance the *musangu* was ever initiated into a *mungonge* cult, for example), but which they nonetheless employ anew in an urban context and in a creative act of local *actualisation* — a specific form of what Mudimbe calls '*reprendre*', to resume or take up again (Mudimbe 1999). Seen in the context of contemporary African art and the position of the African artist, Mudimbe understands this *reprendre* to be a combination of three movements: first, it means taking up an interrupted tradition not out of a desire for purity, which would testify only to the imagination of dead ancestors, but in a way that reflects the conditions of today. Secondly, *reprendre* suggests a methodological assessment through which the artist evaluates his tools, means and projects within a social context transformed by colonialism and, later, by influences from abroad. Finally, *reprendre* implies a meditation on the meaning of the two preceding exercises.

Through similar acts of *reprendre*, Kinois youth impose their body scale, its mobility and temporal and relational logic onto the city. Using their bodies, they introduce their own moral frameworks against the 'order' as imposed by the state and church, which promote what remains essentially a very colonialist modernity. They give their own private and intimate corporeal realms an infrastructural importance by turning it into a public stage, something that is epitomised to the full by the famous Congolese *sapeurs* (members of the SAPE movement– the Society of Tastemakers and Elegant People; cf. Gondola 1999), who often use the graveyard's tombstones as a catwalk during their fashion competitions, and thereby playfully turn the urban nightmare into oneiric lines of flight.[37] And by using corpses and tombs as alternative political platforms to speak out, they present death, which is so omnipresent in the urban context, as a powerful tool for self-making and for exercising their critique against those figures of authority that are held responsible for the debacle of life in the city today. In this, they seem to exemplify and confirm the observation made by Jewsiewicki and White (2005: 1): 'As death seems increasingly present in the lives of people in many parts of Africa, emerging forms of social mourning echo the need for new political futures, and mourning shows itself as an important terrain for the social production of meaning.'

Whereas some have interpreted these reterritorialising youth strategies, which the *kuluna* violence pushes to the extreme limit, as forms of 'low intensity insurgencies' against the state,[38] they have not as yet crystallised into a more formally organised and institutionalised political youth movement. Neither have they sparked off a Central-African Spring (and it should be noted that it was a corpse, the burned body of Mohamed Bouazizi, a young Tunisian street vendor, that set off the Arab Spring in 2010). In part this is due to a number of structural factors within this urban context (such as the lack of a widespread middle-class that could sustain such a movement), but partly this is also because Kinois youth's criticisms transcend, in the end, the mere political level. Theirs is essentially a moral criticism of the world they live in. The outside world, that is to say the urban public sphere, is criticised, dismantled and tentatively reshaped by positing it against its opposite: the intimate corporeal space of inner self and intersubjective relations. By means of a discourse and songs that refer to love-making, sexuality and play, and through a powerful and transgressive act of symbolic copulation between two bodies (on the one hand, the strong and youthful body and on the other hand, the corpse with all its rotting, disintegrating, malodorous immediacy), young people are shouting out a basic question at Kinois society in general: what does it mean to be human (and to be human together across generations) in the light of the constant threat of sudden disappearance and annihilation in a context of systematic abandon, generalised infrastructural decay and material as well as spiritual insecurity? In view of the omnipresence of death and the constant threat of being annihilated and forgotten, the corporeal dimension of youth's vocabularies of self-realization powerfully posits the city in the immediate time-frame of the moment, the immediate now, so as to celebrate its vitality and life and offer an alternative to the degradation. This urban life, which is saturated with a sense of deadness that numbs everything and everyone, stands paradoxically against what is shown as the generative dimension of death, that is, the power of death not simply to mortify and degrade life but in fact to *breathe life into* it. At the same time, the strange alliance between youth and death forces the city to stare into the face of its own death, and thereby into the darkest corners of its own modalities of existence. Young bodies, whether dead or alive, appear here as lucid, ludic and also subversive sites and frontiers of re-territorialisation, not only of official cultural and political programmes but also of the much deeper and darker sides of what constitutes humanity in this urban setting. They struggle to redefine the *vie nue,* with all of the horror and disgust that comes with it, and to reanimate this bare life with new forms of profane *and* divine law. By exploring the possibility of turning their own bodies into sacrificial bodies they attempt to inject elements of sacrality into the banality of dying. That is also the new meaning of the graveyard. It provides urban youth with a heterotopic space to express the crisis and find means to both *embody* and overcome the disintegration of their state, city, society and its moral values.

CONCLUSION: MOMENTS OF FREEDOM AND LINES OF FLIGHT

In this chapter, I have focused on the often perplexing ways in which young urban residents, through their cohabitation with death and a generation of new forms of mourning and of coping with dispersal and loss, endeavour to reframe the harsh conditions of urban living in Kinshasa into 'moments of freedom' (Fabian 1998), moments that represent possible lines of flight that offer the possibility for a 'de-centring' in Deleuzian terms. Not so much a matter of voluntary choice as a bare necessity, they create new possibilities, through language and practice, out of the destabilised meanings with which the social and infrastructural organisation of the city constantly confronts them.

Death makes youth visible in a city that otherwise condemns them to a peripheral and marginal existence. Death is a stone that the young throw into Kinshasa's pool, giving them an agency and a force to disturb, to de-familiarise and de-centre. Through an ethnographic description of their sometimes violent involvement in matters pertaining to death, I have examined specific local attempts by Kinshasa's youth to turn the aporia of a naked life-form into more euphoric solutions. In the process, I have argued that urban youngsters re-conceptualise the camp, the very territory of death itself, in terms of a more heterotopic space where death may be reconceived as sacrifice. This effort enables Kinois youths to contest and rethink the frameworks of the city, the state and the postcolonial political order, and in so doing express their longing for new communal futures. Firstly, funerals offer them the possibility to reject current official political and religious orders (all the more surprising given the tight grip the millennial churches have on all other aspects of public life in Congo today). It also offers them an even more powerful opportunity to redefine Congo's ongoing economic and socio-political crisis in terms of a primarily *moral* critique of the specific necropolitics that underpins the postcolonial state of exception. By replacing the law of the state, church, ancestor and elder with their own rule, which has been described as 'disorder', young Kinois thus make a powerful effort to reshape the moral (and religious) cartography of the urban public sphere.

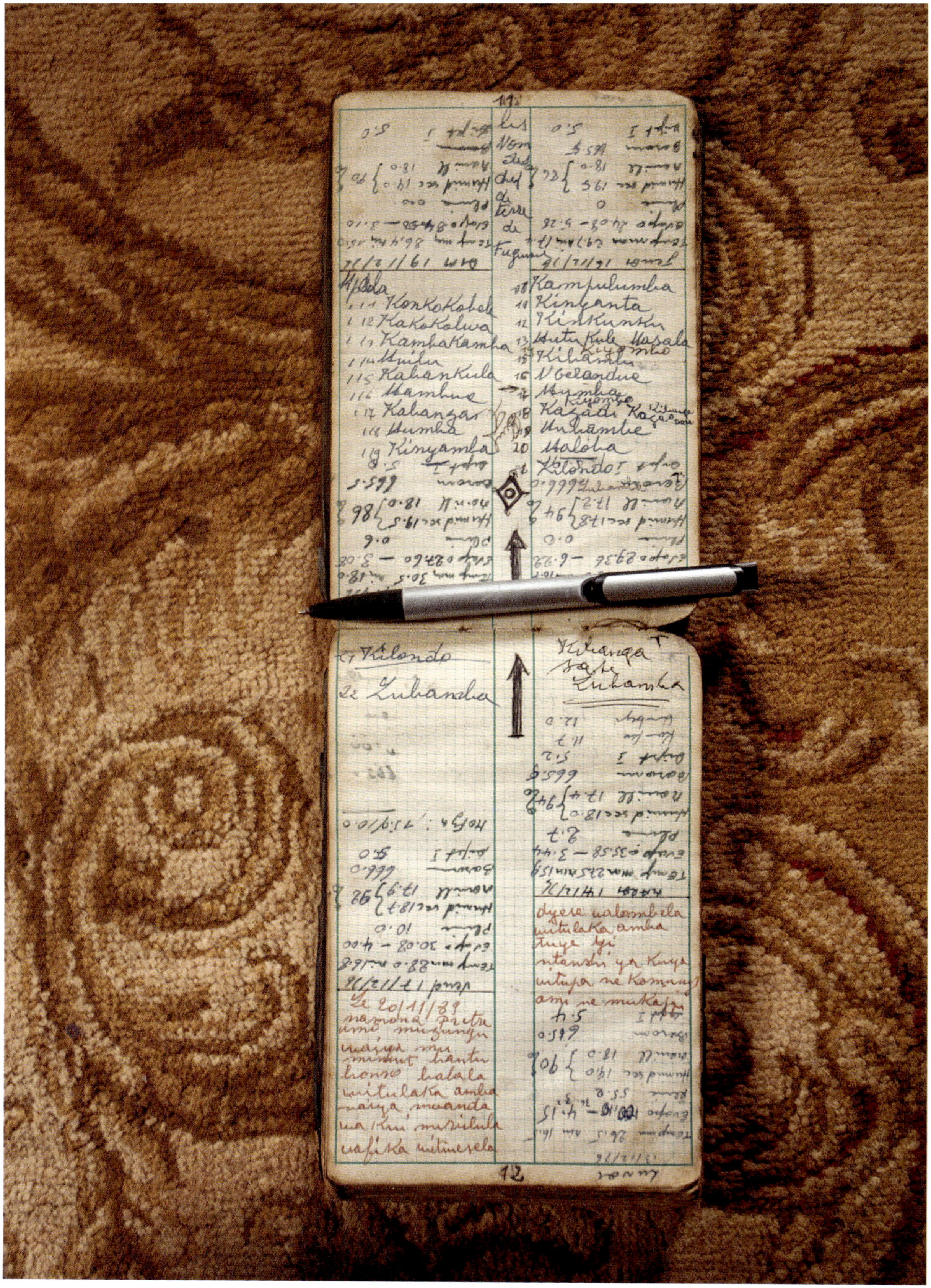
Kampulumba
Kilando
Lubanda

6. Mountains II: Pungulume

'And He said to them, "Because of the littleness of your faith; for truly I say to you, if you have faith the size of a mustard seed, you will say to this mountain, 'Move from here to there', and it will move; and nothing will be impossible to you.'" (Matthew 17:20)

SEPTEMBER 2013, KATANGA PROVINCE, IN THE TOWN OF FUNGURUME

Sammy and I are sitting in the living room of a large red brick house, somewhere on the outskirts of Fungurume, a small but rapidly growing mining town in the Dipeta River Valley 175 kilometres northwest of Lubumbashi, the capital city of Katanga province. Hills and mountain ridges form the valley's north-western crest. Like giant ribbons, horizontal ore bodies can be seen running through the mountain slopes, colouring them in different shades. The town itself is named after a mountain that the autochthonous Sanga population calls Pungulume. Mount Pungulume constitutes the geographical but also spiritual and ritual heart of this vast mountainous area that the Sanga consider theirs.

Today, Fungurume is rapidly expanding though in a rather chaotic and disorderly fashion. The dusty town stretches out along a poorly asphalted road that leads to the main road connecting the large mining centres of Kolwezi and Likasi. Heavy trucks filled with copper and cobalt ore are continuously passing by in the distance and from where we are sitting, we vaguely hear the thunderous noise of the powerful trenching and excavation equipment that is slowly but determinedly eating away the mountain tops surrounding Fungurume town. Further away still, as far as the eye can see, a landscape made up of more mountains and hills, forming one of the world's largest copper and cobalt deposits.

Fungurume's mineral resources still remain largely unexploited. People have always engaged in artisanal mining here, and even in precolonial times the area already was a major centre in a continental copper trading network. Large-scale industrial surface mining is of a more recent date. In the mid-1990s, during the final years of Mobutu's reign, the Canadian-Swedish Lundin group obtained concessionary rights from the Zairian state to mine most of the mountains around Fungurume, an area of 1500 kms², but it was not until 2006 and a major change in the holding company's ownership structure[1] that the new Tenke Fungurume Mining consortium (TFM)

started up its open-pit and oxide ore processing facilities. From 2009 on, TFM's mining activities have been in full swing, and the 2015 objective aimed at producing up to 500,000 tonnes per annum of copper by mining multiple deposits concession-wide.

The large rectangular living room we are sitting in is that of chief Mpala Swanage Pascal Musenge, the current land guardian of Fungurume, and one of the more important Sanga land chiefs in southern Katanga. His house, with its industrial red bricks, concrete floors, metal entry door and windows with glass panes, is decidedly bigger and better built than the shacks and mud huts that surround it. It was offered by the copper mining company as a 'replacement house' to Mpala Swanage's predecessor, chief Mpala Kibanga Sase, who died in 2009, to compensate for the fact that the latter's village had to be relocated in order to make way for the company's surface mining activities.

All along the living room's walls stand large club chairs. It is here that chief Mpala and his dignitaries hold court, welcome visitors, discuss family and clan issues, and look after the well-being of the *chefferie*'s inhabitants. Today, Sammy and I are Mpala's guests. When elders sit together in his court, local Sanga history is regularly brought back to life and we are here to record part of this oral history.

Sanga land chief Mpala Swanage Pascal Musenge. Fungurume, September 2013.

While we wait for chief Mpala to start, other visitors trickle in. Most of them are court elders who have been summoned by the chief to assist him with the historical facts. When everybody is finally seated, chief Mpala's voice starts to fill the room. With the aid of a little notebook in which the names of his predecessors are scribbled down, he takes us on a journey back in time, regularly interrupted and corrected by the court elders:

'We are Sanga. This is our home, we did not come from anywhere else. Our kingdom is "carried" by our family. It is from our family that our chieftainship issued. The name of the first chief is Mpala Konkokobele. He is the first "king", and many more followed him. Konkokobele was succeeded by Kakokolwa, and after Kakokolwa came Kambakamba, and then there was Mwilu, and then Kabankula, and Mambwe, and Kabanza, and Mumba, and Kinyamba, and Kapulumba, and Kinyanta, and Kikunku, and Mutukule Masala, and Kiyombo, and Kibambi, and Ngerendwe, and Mumba [who is also known as Mulawa Nyama], and Kazadi, and Mubambe, and Maloba, and Kilondo, and finally Kibanga Sase, who is also known as Lubamba. They are all dead now. Today our chief is Mpala Swanage Pascal Musenge Kayambwe.'

'Mpala Konkokobele was a chief who came from the land of the Ruund.'

'No, it is not like this, Mpala Konkokobele was already here when the Ruund [the Lunda] came and installed their power base. But they encountered chief Mpala Konkokobele who was strong, and they gave him the *mikundula* [royal bracelet] and a crown symbolising royal power in the Ruund kingdom, and they [the Ruund] went to Kasenga in Zambia instead.'

'The chiefs of the old days always settled in the river valleys, but after the death of one of them, Konkokobele built his village on top of a mountain, and from there he organised his power and his army, because on this mountain cattle could graze and chickens were plentiful. Isn't that so, father?'

'No, that was not the reason. The chief went to live on the mountain because of the wars, to be able to see from where our enemies would approach to attack us. Another advantage of settling on top of the mountain was because of its rich soil. There, chief Mpala had enough space for large fields. He could feed his cattle there, as well as control and oversee all the corners of his kingdom.'

'We fought many wars against our enemies who approached us from all sides. From the north, east, south and west, they came from everywhere, but from the south there were fewer attacks from the baYeke because they were stopped by

the Sanga of chief Mpande.[2] This is why the baYeke[3] came as friends to Mpala and flattered him: "You are a real man, we will live in peace with you." So none of our chiefs died in battle, as Mpala's court could count on many powerful skilled warriors. In those days chiefs mainly died as a result of witchcraft. They won all the battles, for example, those against the baLuba and against the Chokwe. They were all defeated by us.'

'But there is the story of a Belgian general who came to our land accompanied by baYeke warriors, and Chief Mpala opposed their arrival because he did not want to live under Yeke domination. When the Belgians arrived in Bunkeya, they allied themselves with the baYeke to fight Mpala, who resisted colonial rule. So they attacked us, and these attacks went on for seven years. In the seventh year, they gave a bag of sugar to one of our villagers and in return he betrayed us and gave away the location of the secret place where the chief and his family members would go into hiding at times of war. When threatened by an attack, the royal family and the villagers would seek refuge in a large cave in one of

the mountain sites of Fungurume, in the vicinity of Mulumba. We started to hide our women and children in this way after the Yeke began to raid our villages and to decapitate our children and mutilate our women's genitals. This was their strategy to discourage our warriors before battle. So every time the Belgians and the baYeke would attack, everybody fled to the secret cave. But this time, the attackers followed them. They blocked all the exits and lit large fires to smoke them out. Three days later, all those inside the cave were dead, except for five people. Chief Mpala Mumba Mulawa Nyama survived because he was not in the cave.'[4]

'If we follow our history further, there is the story of the royal village of Kyamakela, the village that was located near Mount Kwetebala, close to Mount Pungulume. At that place the soil was phosphorous and rich in minerals, and there were lots of natural caves in the mountain. That is where our people would hide during wartime. Mount Kwetebala was the first hill we conquered. That is the origin of our village. When we arrived on the hilltop, we called it

Kwetebala, which means 'to appropriate the field'. We conquered the hill and built our village there and started to work on the fields. The other mountain we colonised was Pungulume, the mountain that gave its name to the town of Fungurume today. In fact, the Belgians could not pronounce the word 'Pungulume' correctly and they misspelled it as Fungurume. In our language *pungulume* is the name of a sacred animal that we consider an ancestor of ours. It plays an important role in our rituals. When we address the mountain spirits, it is Pungulume we invoke, because Pungulume lives in this mountain. It does not show itself very often, only during the most important rituals. On those days, the Mpala land chief observes strict ritual dietary restrictions and eats and sleeps alone in seclusion in his *mbela* hut in order to prepare for the ritual incantations that he then addresses to the ancestors and the mountain spirits.'

'Other hills and mountains, such as Mount Goma [now called Tenke], also play an important role, for example in meeting with strangers. These meetings were held outside the village so that these outsiders would not know the exact position of our warriors. Our land consists of 258 hills, all rich in copper. Many of them were named according to the way the different copper veins coloured the hill surfaces. Others were given the names of wars, the names of specific historical meetings that took place there, or the names of specific families and clans. Some families held exclusive rights to certain hills, and therefore others could not settle on these hills. Some hills were sometimes also given to a single individual who was thereby linked to the mountain in question and could no longer build his house elsewhere.'

'Today our territory has been much reduced by the state. Our kingdom used to be much vaster. It stretched all the way to Mutombo (the current Yeke chief in Bunkeya) and to Mpande, for we were given land after every victorious war. But then the Belgians arrived, and after them Mobutu, and we gradually lost our land for they all wanted the land of Mpala, which was rich in copper and salt. The Belgians divided the land to create the province of Katanga, the districts, the territories and the *chefferies*. The Belgians seized our land by killing our land chief and exterminating our village. The kingdom of Mpala formed an independent state. We were self-sufficient, we had our fields and we lived off hunting, producing copper crosses [5] and selling our salt. None of our neighbours, the Luba, Chokwe, Kaonde, Ruund or even our brothers at Mwasha, had salt. We were rich. We not only had salt but also sugar and other things that we obtained from our brothers in the south, those from Zambia who came to buy salt from us. That is why there are still so many Kaonde in this area. They all came here to buy salt.'

'The name of each mountain and each river is linked with a specific moment in our history. Chief Mpala finally left Mount Kwetebala to settle where he now lives in order to better control and oversee all the land in his custody. For his land had become so vast and there were so many riches: animals, fields and salt. Large blocks of salt were carried to the markets of Kolwezi and Lubumbashi to be sold there, and we made lots of money. The salt came from a place we call Kabo, and this salt vein leads all the way to Nguba. There the salt needs to be dug out of the earth, but at Kabo it is out in the open. People could just gather this salt from the surface in order to sell it, but then the Europeans started to mine for the underground salt at Nguba. To that end, they constructed large basins into which the salt would be channelled by means of water. The name of our salt was *macho* and our children would be called the children of *macho*, 'the children of salt'. But the name we gave ourselves was Bayogalo. It was a political name that indicated that our power did not derive from the Ruund or Yeke, but that power issued from our own family.'

'Chief Mpala Kilondo had a lot of difficulties with the colonial state. One day, policemen came and got drunk in our village and started to beat up our children. This started a rebellion and the villagers fought the policemen who retreated to their headquarters. Thereupon, the chief police inspector sent troops to arrest all the villagers. This decision outraged chief Mpala Kilondo and he retreated at night to his *kapenda* [the house where all royal power objects are kept] to invoke the ancestors and the mountain spirits. A couple of hours later, it started to rain stones on top of the Chief Inspector's house. Early next morning, the police commander came to Mpala Kilondo to beg him for forgiveness.'

'Mpala Kibanga Sase died in 2009. He too had problems with the state because they tried to abolish his chieftaincy. When he was forced to abandon part of his land to a mining company in Fungurume, he travelled to Bunkeya and Kolwezi. Shortly after his arrival, the provincial governor wrote a letter to the mayor of Kolwezi asking for chief Mpala to be removed from the city of Kolwezi. So chief Mpala was sent back.'

'I am Mpala Swanage. I am the current chief and my place in history is still in progress. I know the borders of all my land. Some borders are kept by my sub-chiefs who were given some of Mpala's land. These borders are marked by wooden sticks to prevent others from stealing our land from us.

With the Basangwa people we share the Kubitwe River; with the Kuyamba we share the Kamimbi River; with the Kamungu we share the Kubulebi River; and we share the Kubusele River with the Mutaka. So that means that all this land around the Dipeta River [the main river running through Fungurume valley] and its affluents belongs to Mpala and his sub-chiefs. This is the land that Mpala demarcated with a *muwara* [traditional land marker] upon his arrival and that he claimed as his. This is how we protect our land, but we live in constant fear because the state wants to seize the riches of our land, and the arrival of the whites prevents us from accessing our own mountains. Because everybody knows that the mountains of Mpala contain a lot of mineral resources, and that is the reason why the big mining companies are fighting Mpala.'

If there is one thing that Mpala's tale reveals, it is to what extent the Sanga, as political titleholders and ritual land guardians, identify with their land, its mountains and the different spirits inhabiting each of them. At the same time, these oral histories have also started to falter and fade in a rapidly changing and disintegrating landscape in which

their historical caves, sacred sites and the very mountains themselves are being destroyed by large scale mining activities and can therefore no longer be relied on to anchor one's sense of identity and belonging. Mirroring the mountains' physical destruction, Sanga oral history has itself become a site of dislocation and loss, with uncertain gaps and disparate memory laps, questioning silences, and nostalgic displacements that betray an increasing sense of alienation.

As Mpala's unravelling tale of Sanga political history, memory and identity reveals, the disruption of the Sanga memory landscape was a tale long foretold. It is a tale of precolonial warfare with neighbouring ethnic groups, of a European colonisation that brought violence of an even more overt nature and enhanced scale, and of a subsequent and equally disruptive violence introduced through an increasing administrative and political subjugation during the years of the formal Belgian colonisation. Mount Pungulume and its people were thus inescapably propelled into the orbit of a vast colonial and industrial complex that developed after the First World War as part of the larger Copper Belt area. During the Mobutu years, this industrialisation virtually came to a halt. But when the price of copper started to soar in the first decade of the

new millennium, industrial mining picked up again throughout southern Katanga. The renewed demand for copper coincided with the neoliberal global capital investments that poured into the African continent in general and Katanga in particular, and this combination shifted Fungurume once more to centre stage in a new round of extractive colonisation.

In 1996, I was contacted by the newly-appointed manager of the Lundin Corporation at Fungurume. He wanted to know if I was interested in a well-paid job as consultant anthropologist. My task would consist in helping him with the relocation of 15,000 Sanga who had to make way for the planned new Fungurume mining site, a large-scale infrastructure that included the construction of a whole new city, an airport, labour camps for the workers as well as large processing plants and a number of other industrial facilities. I politely declined the offer.

Meanwhile, some of their planned infrastructure has been built. Fungurume now sports a large airstrip, surface mining has been in full swing since 2009, and TFM announced in 2012 that it had put aside 67 million US dollars to pay a French developer to build a new urban site for 200,000 inhabitants.[6] Private-sector new city initiatives of comparable scale are being proposed throughout Katanga, although none has actually materialised. In the vicinity of the provincial capital of Lubumbashi, for example, two satellite cities are planned. The smallest one, Luano City, is financed by South African capital and will be more of a luxury gated community. The plan is to build it near Lubumbashi's Luano airport. The other, a much larger one, is Kiswishi.[7] Located on a land concession of 10,800 acres along the road to Likasi, it will eventually consist of high-end residences, commercial and light industrial activities and public services such as schools, churches and recreational centres. In 2013, all the houses of the three existing villages within the boundaries of the Kiswishi concession were marked for removal by large red numbers painted on the mud brick facades. So far, however, the villagers' huts are still standing, and only a recent asphalt access road shows that a new city might emerge here some day.

In Fungurume, by contrast, hundreds of houses have been bulldozed in the past few years, and many more are marked for demolition. Thousands of people are routinely forced off their traditional farmlands to make way for industrial mining activities, and many have been relocated more than once.[8]

One of the people in charge of the compensatory politics that accompanies these processes of expulsion and relocation is the man who took the job I declined so many years ago. Georgius Koppert is a Dutch anthropologist who previously worked as an evaluator of compensation and resettlement implementation policies for the Chad-Cameroon Petroleum Pipeline, a large World Bank project. For many years now, Koppert has been working as independent consultant in a TFM team that carries out social impact assessments and outlines and implements TFM's land access, compensation, and resettlement policy frameworks in Fungurume.[9] In this capacity, he is responsible for the distribution of land replacement allowances, livelihood restoration assistance and crop compensation. The land replacement facilitation fees (or *ententes*)[10] are distributed by TFM employees, such as Koppert, to individuals who have been affected, and fees are also distributed to their village and land chiefs. It was during one such transaction with chief Mpala in his courtyard that I briefly met with Koppert in March 2013. He had started to work for TFM years before and had managed to establish what he himself described to me as a good and friendly working relationship with Chief Mpala Swanage's predecessor, Mpala Kibanga Sase. The latter had also authorised Koppert to film, record and document Sanga songs, ritual invocations and dance performances. After Mpala Kibanga's death in 2009, Koppert continued to deal with the current chief Mpala Swanage, who was himself a TFM employee at that time. Quickly, however, the relationship between the two of them deteriorated as Mpala became increasingly critical of TFM's land replacement policy and the small amount of compensatory fees for land loss that he and his people were receiving. According to chief Mpala, the understanding between the two men became even more strained when

SARO SPRL INVESTIT POUR UN AVENIR MEILLEUR...

e vente spacieux, moderne et facile d'accès pour tous... Début du chantier en avril 2012, inauguration prévu pour 2013.

Mpala, who claims to hold a degree in mining engineering from the National University of Lubumbashi, was fired by TFM. In Mpala's version, this was because of his resistance to TFM's resettlement action plan, but other reasons I will not go into here might have come into play as well.

Around this time, the town of Fungurume was hard hit by torrential rains that caused a lot of damage. On Monday, 25 October 2010, Radio Okapi reported:
> 'Heavy rains cause havoc in Fungurume, Kolwezi and Pweto.
> One person dead and twenty injured, five of whom gravely, and over 600 houses have collapsed and a boat sunk. That is the assessment in Fungurume, Kolwezi and Pweto after last week's heavy rains in Katanga province. In Fungurume, situated 200 kilometres from Lubumbashi, it rained heavily last Saturday. The rain only lasted for an hour, but the material damage is considerable

Entrance to the planned new Kiswishi city. The billboard reads: To dream about it. To live in it.

according to *chef de cité* Clémentine Mutanda. Over 600 houses were destroyed. Nine school buildings, eight of them primary schools and one a secondary school, were not spared either. As a consequence, none of these schools opened its door on Monday. Two churches and a health care centre were also hard hit by furious rains. Fungurume's *chef de cité* estimates that over a thousand families are now homeless. She added that it is impossible for her to meet all needs after this disaster that has left twenty injured, five of whom remain in a serious condition. And in nearby Kolwezi, a woman was killed when a wall collapsed on top of her.' [11]

The rainstorm prompted further deterioration in the relationship between Mpala and TFM, in the person of Koppert. And in this escalating conflict, the spirit of Mount Pungulume started to occupy an increasingly central role. [12]

All over Katanga and far beyond across the whole of eastern Congo, beliefs in mountain and earth spirits are common and widespread. These spirits are entities that can act in benevolent or malevolent ways. They ensure people's good health, fertility, general well-being and material wealth, and cause the land to thrive and produce plentiful harvests. But when angered, they may also provoke illnesses, misfortune and death. As documented at length by Cuvelier (2011: 178ff), many of these (often female) spirits are also believed to control access to copper and other mineral resources and consequently also play an important role in mining activities. Among the Sanga of Mpala, it is believed that the female mountain spirit of Pungulume, together with her 'husband', the spirit of a smaller mountain nearby, controls access to copper ore bodies or else makes them invisible and inaccessible. Pungulume has the power to make copper flow or to block this flow. In this respect, control over ritual channels of communication with the mountain spirits is of utmost political *and* economic importance, and a land chief's power is constructed to a large extent around his capacity to converse with mountain spirits, engage in an intimate relationship with them, and keep them happy and contented so that they show their most benevolent side. In Mpala's mind, this also

gives him an undeniable advantage in the power play between himself and TMF, as his privileged access to the spirit of Pungulume provides him with the empowering means to turn his otherwise subaltern position into one of (occult and spiritual) control over the mineral resources that TFM wants.

The harm the violent rains inflicted on Fungurume in October 2010 was interpreted by chief Mpala as a clear sign that the spirits of Pungulume and her husband were angry. In his mind, the spirits' wrath and fury were provoked by TFM's gradual destruction of the mountain sites and the sacred caves in which the spirits dwell. Subsequently, immediately after the storm, Mpala held a nocturnal vigil during which he invoked the spirit of Pungulume in an attempt to restore ritually the balance between her and the world. To his great astonishment, he found that the spirits of Pungulume and her husband were no longer there: they had simply vanished. Further rituals revealed the underlying causes of their sudden disappearance. It was found that the spirits had been 'abducted' by Koppert. As mentioned before, Koppert had started to film and record Sanga rituals, invocations and songs, and it now dawned on Mpala that this had only been a pretext in order to steal the ritual technology that enables

land chiefs to converse with the spirits. This, in fact, had been the real underlying reason for TFM to hire an anthropologist in the first place. Mpala told me he believed that Pungulume and her husband had thus been tricked by Koppert and TFM into travelling to the American headquarters of Freeport-McMoRan, TFM's major shareholder and operating partner, where they were now being held hostage in an attempt to force them to reveal how to access Fungurume's copper ore reserves.

The spiritual warfare between TFM and Mpala did not end there. During our second trip to Fungurume in September 2013, Mpala told me how he had managed to free Pungulume's husband spirit and bring him back home by ritual means. Pungulume herself, however, continues to be held against her will in the United States.

'Katanga 20 October 2014 — ten people died in torrential rain in Kolwezi.
On Monday, 20 October, ten people died as a result of torrential rain that hit the city of Kolwezi, 343 kilometres west of Lubumbashi (Katanga). All the

victims came from Kasulo, a neighbourhood of the city that had been transformed into an artisanal mining site by its inhabitants. According to the *chef de quartier*, three artisanal miners were buried alive when a hole, which had been dug in the hope of extracting copper, caved in due to the rain. Their bodies are now at the morgue of Mwangezi hospital. The same source also confirms that four more were killed by lightning in three different parts of the neighbourhood, and that two others were carried away in the Dilala River on their way home from a wedding. When the rainstorm ended, another lifeless body was found in the street. The circumstances of his death remain unknown.'
[Reported by Radio Okapi on 21 October 2014]

7. 'Illuminating the Hole': Kinshasa's Makeovers Between Dream and Reality.

'Kabila left his trace. Our Congo does not want just words. Leave something tangible behind just like he did. Look at the roads he built, look at the new *Cinquantenaire* hospital,[1] look at the schools. The chief of all chiefs, Kabila Kabange, is leaving his trace. People will remember him. He demonstrated to Congo what is possible. Congo has become Europe, and Europe has become Congo. He stimulated our young people to build the New Congo.'
[*Kin-based singer Kas Kasongo in* 'Sisa Bidimbu', *a song Joseph Kabila used during the 2011 presidential elections as propaganda for his* 'Cinq Chantiers' *or infrastructural renewal programme, currently known as the* 'revolution of modernity'].

'Mirrors have a life too and that which gets caught in them continues existing there. Reality is a version of the mirror image. [...] Even though something can be inserted easily enough into the mirror, none of us knows precisely how and when it can be taken out again. Do mirrors have looking-glasses too, deeper layers, echoes perhaps incessantly sounding the fathomless?' (Breytenbach 2009: 66)

'A new radical politics must revolve around the construction of great new fictions that create real possibilities for constructing different urban futures. To the extent that the current post-political condition, which combines dystopian urban visions with a hegemonic consensual neo-liberal view of social ordering, constitutes one particular fiction (one that in fact forecloses dissent, conflict, and the possibility of a different future), there is an urgent need for different stories and fictions that can be mobilized for realization. This requires foregrounding and naming different urban futures, making the new and impossible enter the realm of politics and of democracy, and recognizing conflict, difference and struggle over the naming and trajectories of these futures. Urban conflict, therefore, should not be subsumed under the homogenizing mantle of a populist globalization/creative city discourse, but should be legitimized as constitutive of a democratic order.' (Swyngedouw, 2007: 59)

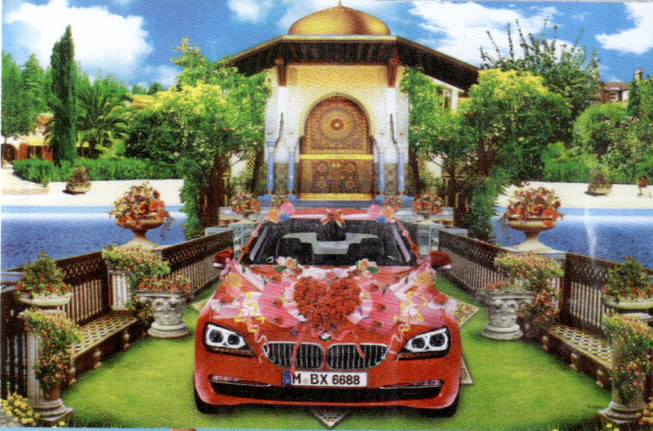

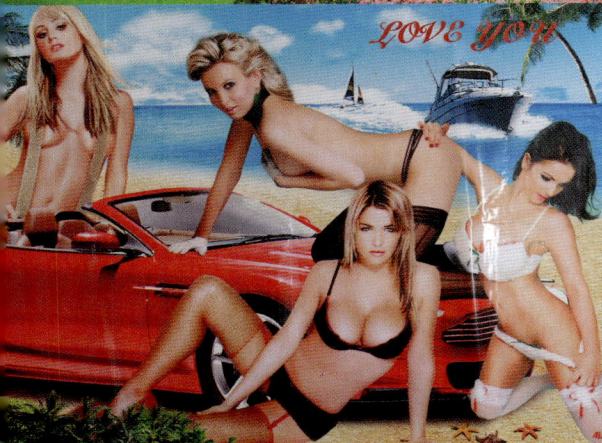

In her insightful chapter on 'noir urbanisms', Jennifer Robinson (2010) outlines the longstanding tendency within urban studies to conceive of contemporary African cities in dystopic terms. The present chapter attempts to do the opposite. Bringing together a number of themes that have been explored throughout this book, it examines if, where and how the inhabitants of Kinshasa reclaim hope and invent alternative futures for their city beyond the widely-shared and immediate desire for a 'western' house, a bourgeois living room, and the life-style that goes with it. Indeed, the models that were defined by colonialist modernity have never ceased to exert a strong attraction. Even if these colonial notions and ideas about what constitutes quality housing and infrastructure, and therefore a high quality of life, are beyond the reach of the average Congolese, they certainly continue to inform and format local notions of what the good life is all about. Everybody dreams of a 'proper' house, bathrooms with running water, sewage systems that do not stink or overflow whenever it rains, kitchens with electricity and roads without potholes. The built form with its 'durable' materiality of bricks and mortar continues to embody and define what decent living, material comfort and success are deemed to be about. Lubumbashi-based artist Richard Kaumba, known for his maquettes of colonial-style villas and mansions, illustrates this very well with the following statement he wrote on one of his creations in rather idiosyncratic French: 'The house is a machine to confront the good moment' (*la maison est une machine à affronter le bon moment*). What Kaumba calls the *bon moment* is the material and emotional life inside the house. In other words, the quality of one's house determines the quality of one's life. A house is wealth, peace and quiet.

The Chinese posters that have come to adorn the walls of many Congolese living rooms in recent years basically convey the same idea as Kaumba's maquettes do but translate it to a more contemporary reality, which so far has reached Congo principally in a visual form. These glossy posters of 'western' mansions and country houses, or the skylines of (often imagined and non-existent) 'modern' cities, update, and aesthetically repackage, the past colonial dreams of petit-bourgeois modernity, transposing them into the oneiric futures of more global and transnational spaces (see Hendriks 2013: 170ff).

Whether in the concrete or imagined materiality of the built environment by means of spectral images that advertise the arrival of the new global city on Congolese soil, or in the artistic utopian fantasies that I present in this chapter, all these material and mental spaces represent various forms of 'effective desire' (Crapanzano 2003: 6), each of which possesses a specific transformative capacity. I will reflect upon the current potential of the city to realise a new urban future for itself by focusing on what

a locally-produced skyscraper has in common with the creative work of Kin-based artist Bylex and the sprawling, new urban development area of the *Cité du Fleuve*. For better or for worse, the city is what it is and cannot escape itself; it depends on itself to fulfil its potential. But at least it has got '*de la gueule*' in that it enjoys a strong belief in itself. It has had a history of tenacious resilience and elastic flexibility, and the creative capacity not to submit but to distrust official vocabularies, to bypass institutional (non-)solutions and devise escape routes from what seem to be — when observed from the outside — obvious and inescapable dead ends. A complex and often problematic site of assemblage, multiplicity and social interaction, this bootstrapping city manages to suture and stitch itself together towards a future horizon by means of an always surprising and often unexpected inventive reworking of the fractures and frictions of its various pasts within the contours of a rapidly changing present. As will be illustrated in the last chapter of this book, such a future will necessarily have to take into account its own *longue durée* and include less visible though still very active histories and socio-political rhythms and architectures (in terms of a politics of land and kinship, for example) that continue to unfold and structure the urban landscape, thereby impacting upon the format of possible future urban trajectories.

UTOPIA 1: THE TOWER. A CONCRETE UTOPIA?

The Tower stands in the middle of the industrial zone of Limete, one of the more central municipalities of the city of Kinshasa. Part skyscraper, part pyramid, part citadel, this unfinished and ragged twelve-storey building sits strangely in the midst of warehouses, industrial plants, railroad tracks and new houses under construction that make up the built environment of *Limete industriel*. Soaring high above this desultory landscape in defiance of gravitational laws and urban zoning rules, this unusual architectural proposition is one of the city's strangest and most enigmatic landmarks. A giant question mark that begs profound reflection on the nature of the city, the heritage of its colonial modernist architecture, the dystopic nature of its current infrastructure and the capacity for utopian urban dreams and lines of flight that it continues to generate.

The proud owner and his wife are the Tower's only inhabitants. He is a middle-aged medical doctor who specialises in 'aeronautic and spatial medicine' and is known to all as 'Docteur'. In 2003, he bought a small plot of 109 m² and with the help of two architects, he started to build a four-storey building. But long before reaching the fourth floor, Docteur fired the architects and from then on and without a clear plan, he became his own architect. This is the norm rather than the exception in Kinshasa. Somewhere along the process, however, Docteur got carried away by his love for and preoccupation with space and skies, and soon what had started as a modest and rather conventional housing construction evolved into an increasingly megalomaniac vertical venture, reaching forever higher into the sky, and consuming ever more cement and concrete. After sacrificing his own finances, health and peace of mind to considerable length to bring about this 'vision', Docteur gradually lost control of the building site. Inspired by pyramid and ziggurat shapes,[2] the Tower took on and started to impose its own unstoppable approach to building itself to its logical conclusion, while Docteur became its hostage and visionary martyr. He hopes it will be completed by 'posterity' as he is very aware that he will probably not be able to see its completion in his own lifetime.

I contend that this tower should be understood as an idiosyncratic but also programmatic, even messianic, statement on the nature of a more ideal and liveable future city. First of all, Docteur stresses the functionality of the building, even though its functionality obviously leaves much to be desired from an infrastructural point of view. There is no running water or electricity inside the building, for example, and the plumbing for the many bathrooms and lavatories planned on every floor has simply been forgotten or ignored. But aside the level of its material infrastructure, Docteur envisages the still unfinished building to be a city in itself, a humanistic project that transcends the city while concurrently recreating it within its own confines, incorporating all kinds of people and activities. The tower sets the scene for a new vertical and autarkic urban community. A number of medical cabinets and operating rooms have already been installed on the first and second floor, even though patients are few and

far between. These rooms transform the base of the building into a hospital and an area for healing the sick and injured. The third floor is designed for lawyers' offices, the fourth floor will house an entire aviation school, and the sixth floor is to have a restaurant for all the tower's future inhabitants. Scattered throughout the labyrinthine building, there will also be rooms and offices for visiting philosophers, poets, inventors and scientists. Finally, high above the ground, on the building's windy top floor in the company of birds and close to God, is the place for soul healing. The spire on top of the tower invites you to pray, but also to contemplate the beauty of the natural world, the Congo River and Kinshasa's many surrounding hills. Looking out over the stage of the city below, it offers the perfect setting to reflect upon human nature itself, with all of its virtues and vices, its possibilities and shortcomings.

Situated at opposite ends of the tower, the healing of both body and soul thus brackets the owner's whole concept. From ground floor to spire, the tower offers a continuum extending from corporeal to mental matter. These two levels are architecturally connected by means of what Docteur refers to as an 'ergonomic' flight of stairs, precariously spiralling towards the top. Consequently, the tower's main function is to transform its urban residents into better, more fully integrated human beings. For the Docteur, the tower will therefore also function as a tourist site, a place to visit and retreat to, where people will be able to resource themselves before plunging back into the chaos of the surrounding city.

The tower does many other things as well. In Docteur's own words, which echo Kentridge's ideas on illuminating shadows (see Chapter Two), his tower is an attempt to 'illuminate the hole' (*illuminer le trou*). The tower is intended to transcend bare life and the mere level of survival that the city imposes upon its inhabitants. It is, for example, a perfect structure for the visual observation *and* control of life on the ground level. In its maker's mind, the tower is therefore also designed as a watchtower, a concept that, in the Congolese context, immediately takes on a religious meaning in reference to the South African branch of Jehovah's Witnesses and their Watchtower Bible and Tract Society, and the local Congolese Kitawala movement that originated from it in Katanga province in the 1920s. The Kitawala movement was characterised by its strong millenarian and anti-colonial message (Fields 1985), and the notion of (religious) sovereignty is powerfully conveyed in the image of the watchtower. But the same image of the watchtower also evokes notions of fortification and (military and colonial) control and domination. It is clear that Docteur's tower also incorporates these meanings as well. In his view, the tower offers 'a perfect vantage point to observe suspect movements and to warn of imminent terrorist attacks in the city'. And thanks to an intricate system of antennae, which has yet to be installed, the tower will also operate, in its creator's mind, as an air traffic control tower. If, for any reason, the infrastructure of Kinshasa's international airport should not work, airplanes will be able to use the tower as a beacon to ensure a safe landing. The tower is a solid, safe haven; a Noah's ark for Kinshasa's inhabitants in case of a flood, for example, or the more unlikely event of a tsunami. This is probably a less far-fetched notion than it seems at first for those who, like most Kinois, believe in the possibility of an apocalyptic end of the world. In fact, the tower functions as an overall protective device against all forces of nature. In this way, it also 'splits' the winds and storms during the rainy season, thereby protecting neighbouring homes. The fresh breeze that constantly blows through the tower's many rooms also makes it a welcome refuge to retreat to from the city's heat. In Docteur's mind, the tower thus offers a strong sustainable and ecological alternative when compared to most of the housing in the rest of Kinshasa. It provides a greener way of life in the city's polluted environment. The protruding cement roofs are designed to 'absorb' and 'breathe' rainwater out into the city's smoggy atmosphere. The rooftops themselves could be turned into gardens and areas to keep chickens and goats. And ideally, the tower will be powered by solar energy one day as Docteur hopes to cover its surface with solar panels.

THE FORESCOM TOWER: In spite of the tower's phantasmagorical character and the moralist and religious (as well as messianic and apocalyptic) notions that underpin it, Docteur's discourse about the tower, unhindered by infrastructural obstacles and shortcomings, actually reworks many of the propositions made earlier by colonial modernist architects and urban planners. If, on a very general level, the vertical *topos* of the mountain as the physical site of domination, control and subjugation may be considered colonialism's basic geographic feature (it was no coincidence that Stanley's first trading post was built on top of Leopold Hill), then colonial modernist architecture subsequently incorporated and translated this idea of the mountain into built vertical

Léopoldville
Building Forescom.

statements of power. These were gradually emerging in the urban landscape of the 1940s and 1950s. For example, the Forescom tower, located in what is now Kinshasa's downtown district of Gombe, became one of the early landmarks of Belgian colonial modernist urban architecture. Completed in 1946, and soon to be followed by other even more impressive high-rise buildings of tropical modernist signature (see Lagae 2002), the Forescom tower was Kinshasa's first skyscraper. With its ten storeys, it was one of the first of its kind in Central Africa.[3] As such, it was reportedly a source of pride for both colonisers and colonial subjects. For the former, it represented the success of the colonial enterprise, while it allowed the latter to dream of partaking of and being inserted into a more global modernity. The building was the tangible proof that Leopoldville was well under way to becoming the first *Poto moindo*, the first 'Black Europe'. Pointing towards the sky, the Forescom tower also pointed to the future. And because some of its architectural features made the building look like a boat on the banks of the Congo River, the tower also seemed to promise to set Leopoldville sailing to distant shores of other wider (and whiter) worlds beyond the horizon of the Congo River basin. The Forescom tower thus gave form to new hopes, prospects and possibilities. It materially translated and emblematically visualised colonialist ideologies of progress and modernity. Simultaneously, it should be added, it also embodied the darker repressive side of colonialism, with its elaborate technologies of domination, control and surveillance. The tower here was also a watchtower, the built extension of the panoptical colonial Big Brother. As such, the figure of the tower forcefully reminds us of the fact that the colonial urban landscape of Kinshasa largely came about as the result of a very intrusive history of both physical and symbolic violence and domination, marked by racial segregation as well as violent processes of dispossession and relocation.

THE HOLE: How liveable is the legacy of colonialist modernity in the contemporary urban setting? What remains of the colonial infrastructural heritage on a material level? What kinds of social lives and afterlives does it still enable, and what dreams and visions of possible futures, if any, does that colonial legacy still trigger for the residents of Kinshasa today?

As illustrated throughout this book, much of modernity's promises and dreams have turned into a nightmare in postcolonial Kinshasa. The city is littered with colonialism's broken infrastructural dreams, with fragments and figments of a modernity that has become part of an irretrievable past. And rather than referring to the ideal of the vertical, Kinshasa's inhabitants often seem to resort to the concept of the 'hole' to describe the urban infrastructure in which they live. On a first level, the notion of the hole (*libulu*) refers to the material holes and cracks that have come to scar the urban surface. There are the numerous potholes in the streets, of course, but also the hundreds of erosion points that are caused by heavy rainfall or by deficient water drainage. Swallowing houses and roads, these erosions cut through Kinshasa's hilly landscape and form a constant threat to the city's infrastructure. The largest erosion sites have even been given individual names, as if they were real persons, with their own character and temperament. This is the case with the *libulu Manzengele* in the municipality of Ngaliema, for example.[4] This particular erosion site became so well known throughout the city that even a Congolese nightclub in Bobigny, Paris, was named after it. In 2008, another large hole appeared in the erosion plagued area of Kindele, which is one of the city's troubled southern neighbourhoods on the slopes of Mont Amba, the mountain on which the campus of Lovanium, later re-baptised the University of Kinshasa [UNIKIN], was built. This particular hole in the city's surface was named *libulu Makaya*

('the cigarette hole'), and it became famous because of an onsite artistic intervention by the Kin-based artist collective SADI. [5]

But *libulu* may also refer to the dark hole of prison, for example, or the city's shadow economy. *Wenze ya libulu*, 'market of the hole', is the name of a particular marketplace in the municipality of Barumbu, but more generally *wenze ya libulu* may also refer to an 'informal' market where things are sold below the official price (see Lusamba Kibayu 2010: 314). The concept of hole is often used as well to make ironic comments upon the state of things in Kinshasa and Congo generally. A couple of years ago, a Kinois businessman opened a dance bar next to the Forescom tower and called it *Le Grand Libulu*, 'The Big Hole'. The formula proved successful and the owner opened two more bars with the same name in more distant parts of the city. In the meantime, the name has also been adopted by other more informal small pubs and dancing bars throughout the city, inspiring a typical Kinois response to the subject of holes: 'If we have to live in a hole, we might as well dance in it!'

But even if holes have emerged as Kinshasa's generic type of infrastructure as well as a kind of meta-concept to reflect upon the degradation of the colonial infrastructure

and upon the closures and often dismal quality of social life that followed the colonial city's physical ruination, there is still the question as to how the gap between colonial mountain/tower and postcolonial hole is filled in the experience of Congolese urban residents. Except for dancing, what other possible answers do Kinois come up with in response to the challenge presented by these holes? If the city has transformed towers into holes, how can holes be 'illuminated' and become 'towers' again?

UTOPIA 2: BYLEX AND THE MODEL OF THE TOURIST CITY

As noted before, the inhabitants of Congo's urban landscapes have been turning away from former colonial models and have redefined the spaces of colonialism on their own terms ever since independence. Kinshasa's residents reworked the legacies of colonialist modernity by appropriating the former colonial housing infrastructure, for example, and by reassembling and translating it in ways better suited to local social life. Using their own bodies as infrastructural building blocks and imposing the rhythms of their own forms of mobility onto the city, Kinois have designed alternative maps and architectures for Kinshasa. Through music and words, they have invented new acoustic urban landscapes, and in doing so they have also moved away from French, the coloniser's language. And there have been many moments of collective rebellion in which the mirror of colonialist modernity has been violently smashed and destroyed.[6] And yet somehow, Kinshasa constantly returns to and remains hypnotised by images reflected in the mirror of colonialist modernity. This fascination is often expressed in playful ways that manage to transcend, thanks to their ludic and parodying nature, a merely mimetic reprise of the colonial legacy and former metropolitan models. For example, think about the *sapeurs'* playful appropriation of western designer clothes, or consider the fact that Bandalungwa and Lemba, two municipalities in Kinshasa, are currently engaged in a well-humoured (but also deadly serious) dispute over the ownership of the names 'Paris' and '*ville lumière'*, even though (or precisely because) they are constantly hit by power cuts and have to remain in the dark for days on end. The mayor of Lemba even painted the slogan 'Lemba is Paris' above the entrance to the municipality's administrative headquarters. Similarly, on Facebook, one finds several pages called *Lemba c'est Paris* or *Bandal c'est Paris*.[7] Here, mimesis becomes a poetry of the possible that, as argued by Newell in relation to urban youth in Abidjan, offers a form of playful appropriation and transformation of the realities of modernity (Newell 2012).

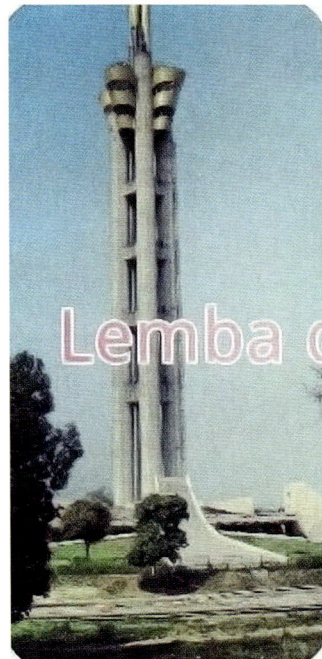

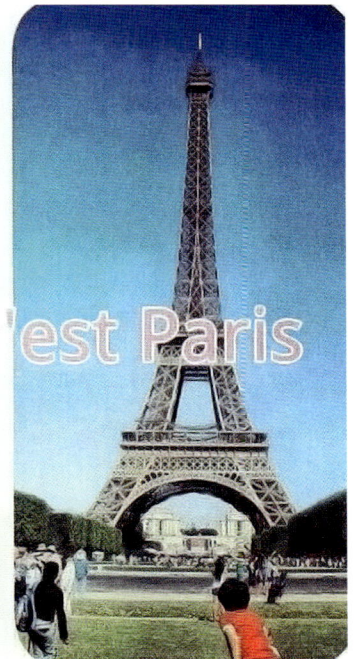

But even when approached critically, or with humour and irony, modernity's propositions continue to fascinate and enchant. This fascination comes across in the work of Kinshasa-based artists such as Kingelez Bodys Isek (1945–2015) and Bylex (b. 1968). Both are known for the utopian urban visions that emanate in their artistic work, and especially in pieces such as Kingelez's *Ville fantôme* (Phantom City) and his *Projet pour le Kinshasa du troisième millenaire* (Project for Kinshasa of the Third Millenium), or Bylex's *Cité Touristique*, (Tourist City).[8] Whereas the original maquettes that gave form to the colonial urban plans of the 1950s are slowly decaying (as are the neighbourhoods that they gave birth to), the models of these two artists revive and rework many propositions of modernist urban planning, albeit with a specific twist. In different ways, the emancipatory and humanitarian preoccupations of colonial modernity, its religious overtones, moralising framework, authoritarian and totalitarian nature as well as obsession with security issues and control, return incessantly in the form and content of the ideal city that they propose in their artistic oeuvre. What is striking in these propositions is the fact that the ideal city is not viewed as an entity to inhabit on a permanent basis, but as a prolegomenon, a place to counterbalance existing cities, a place to visit and resource oneself. In their view the ideal city is, in a way, a resort.

SUN CITY AND THE CHINESE PAGODA OF NSELE: The prototype in Africa of the 'city as resort' model is undoubtedly Sun City, South Africa's most famous high-end tourist centre, which brands itself a 'kingdom of pleasure'. In Kinshasa, this idea of a resort-like 'kingdom of pleasure' materialised most strongly in Mobutu's presidential site of Nsele, east of Kinshasa's national airport along the Congo River Basin. In the late 1960s and throughout the 1970s, Nsele and the neighbouring fishermen's village of

Kinkole were developed into sites that fully symbolised the ambitions of Mobutu's *Mouvement Populaire de la Révolution* (MPR). It was in Kinkole that Mobutu launched the country's new currency, the Zaire, on the 24 June 1967. And it was on the *Place du Zaïre* in Kinkole that many of the MPR's historical political rallies and meetings were held and Mobutu gave some of his most legendary speeches. The newly built *cité* of Nsele, some fifteen kilometres east of Kinkole, was the 'citadel of the political life of the Mobutist regime' (Fumunzanza 2011: 236). It was here that the MPR was founded on 20 May 1967 and it was also here that its ideological charter, the historical 'Manifest of Nsele', was issued. From 1966 onwards, the 8,000 hectares of the nearby Nsele domain were developed as a private presidential agro-industrial farm. Later on, the presidential domain was turned into a tourist site and made accessible to the inhabitants of Kinshasa. In 1980, when the presidential domain of Nsele had already gone bankrupt, Mobutu donated it to the state, which meant the beginning of the end for the Nsele resort. But for a while, it attracted many Kinois, especially after Mobutu built the palace of Nsele, an oriental fantasy dominated by a huge pagoda and constructed with the help of the Chinese. A kingdom of pleasure indeed, the palace of Nsele was at the centre of a

grandiose tourist infrastructure, with an Olympic-size swimming pool, tennis courts, a conference centre, a large restaurant and hotel complex (2,000 beds and hundred VIP suites), with villas, bars and bungalows (cf. Fumunzanza 2011: 237). Nsele became the stage where the madly decadent and hedonistic side of the Mobutist regime, with its theatrical but corrupt magnanimity and all its grandiose dreams, displayed itself most fully. It also provided the setting for the inevitable end to Mobutu's dictatorship. It was here that Mobutu, in a historical and emotional address to the nation in April 1990, announced that the one-party system and twenty-three years of dictatorial regime had reached an end. Today, the palace is an abandoned ruin.

Unlike Sun City and other 'pleasure' resorts such as that of Nsele, Bylex's maquette of the 'Tourist City' is a more reflexive resort that forces us to use our minds and ponder. The Tourist City occupies an almost mythical place in his thinking and embodies his uncompromising striving for a better, universal world. And again, the main protagonist is the tourist.

KINSHASA, A STORY OF IMPERFECTIONS: But first a word about the artist Bylex (born Pume). Bylex is a researcher, a godlike architect and an inventor of concepts. A true demiurge who creates order out of chaos. He investigates in an almost scientific way the invisible laws and processes of the world. As an artist, Bylex is not interested in the day-to-day reality of Kinshasa but turns his attention to what lies beyond the horizon of the visible and the tangible. He penetrates what he refers to as 'the mysteries of the invisible' in order to create his own universe with its own laws of nature: a world with perfection and harmony at its centre. The visual language of his objects, drawings, costumes, furniture and models is immediately recognisable. The titles of his works, as enigmatic as they are poetic, refer to one great indivisible universe: *Les mystères de l'oeil caméra* (The Mysteries of the Camera Eye), *Le hibou menacé* (The Threatened Owl), *Souris métallisée* (Metallised Mouse), *Papillon vampire* (Vampire Butterfly), *Montre Bylarti* (Bylarti Watch), *La chaussure croissante* (The Growing Shoe), *Voiture Bassai* (Bassai Car), *L'humanité prise en ôtage* (Humanity Taken Hostage), *Escartes, Blue Bird Perroquet* (Blue

Bird Parrot), *Cité Touristique* (Tourist City) and many others. All of these objects are always accompanied by written texts that act as guidelines offering interpretive grids to read the objects' hidden meaning.

Bylex grew up and still lives in Petro-Congo, a neighbourhood in the municipality of Masina. A long dusty dirt road leads to his compound, a tiny plot of land with a small house on a street corner at the edge of Malebo Pool. I vividly remember my first visit to this house over ten years ago. The room in which Bylex welcomed me was dark and oppressively hot. Petro-Congo had been without electricity for several days, and the fan and television set in his modest living room were standing idly by, while a tiny light bulb hung purposelessly from the ceiling. As a result, conversation inevitably turned to the limitations and impossibilities of life in Kinshasa, its shortages and deficiencies, and the constant decay and breakdown of its infrastructure. It was not long, however, before Bylex diverted our conversation to the question of how to overcome these problems. In his view, this obviously demanded an intervention on an immediate material level. Who doesn't want a refrigerator that refrigerates, a television that displays images or a fan that rotates and cools the air? But more importantly, according to Bylex, the chaos of Kinshasa also invites you to engage in a mental exercise that triggers an even more compelling inner need to overcome imperfection.

SEEING BEYOND THE HORIZON: What really interests Bylex is not so much the banal reality of daily life, the *lived-in order* of everyday existence (the *parole* or the *performance*, so to speak) but a more mental order of things, a *thought-of order* that Lévi-Strauss would undoubtedly have called *pensée sauvage*; that is to say, the world's underlying universal order, the untamed thought processes (the *langue* or the *competence*) that sustain the world before being tamed by the social or cultural context in which they happen to be expressed. In the case of Bylex, this 'taming' occurs within the context of Kinshasa, but for him this is something of secondary importance. In his view, this fact is no more than a rather annoying coincidence although Kinshasa is unquestionably present in his work, albeit often indirectly or by contrast (as the *Cité Touristique* example below illustrates). Bylex sees himself living and working just as easily in New York, Paris or Tokyo and ultimately the question of 'where' makes no real difference. Bylex remains unperturbed by these accidental twists of fate.

In a sense, Bylex is essentially a conceptual artist. He is as much a *chercheur* (researcher) and *concepteur* (inventor) as an artist. He is, as he puts it, as concerned with words and ideas as with the making of objects. Bylex's work is marked by thorough, almost scientific, research work into the invisible laws and processes that underlie the visible reality of the material world. He thus turns his gaze resolutely to that which lies beyond the horizon of the visible and immediate experience. 'To see beyond the horizon' (*voir plus loin que le lointain*) is what Bylex invites us to do. He ask us to say what cannot be said, to think what has never been thought before and to give form to something that has never had a shape before; in sum, he wants to enable the invisible to become visible.

In this spiritual universe, where lucidity and insanity come together and touch, God serves as the great safety net. In this, Bylex is a true Kinois as well: someone for whom God is an ineluctable reality.

MYSTERIES OF THE INVISIBLE: It is from this imaginary — but no less real — place in his head that Bylex set off on a voyage of discovery many years ago in search of what he calls 'the mysteries of the invisible' (*les mystères de l'invisible*). From within this personal imaginary space, a mental platform between art, science and the spiritual, Bylex began his ongoing expedition in search of the laws of that invisible, perfect universe beyond the imperfect empirical reality of the visible world. And he regularly reports on this mental journey in the form of sketches and models of objects and buildings, often constructed out of photo paper and enclosed in small, glass boxes:

> 'Inspiration is a mystery. And a mystery is something that the eye cannot see. My own universe, my own distinct world, my inner spiritual mechanisms cause the Bylex body and the Bylex mind to invent. Sometimes, when one is asleep, one dreams. And sometimes, one conceives of a work of art by using one's mind. Meditating is an activity which takes place in one's brain, inviting one's cells to coordinate one's dreams. Thoughts have a labyrinthine structure. One tries to travel in one's mind. And one's thoughts make one reflect and meditate about the world. Starting from these thoughts, one generates images in one's memory. My brain constantly generates a lot of images. And these images allow me to translate the invisible into something that is visible and palpable. My hands are there to help externalise and put onto paper the ideas which live in my mind.' [9]

The drawings, plans and objects that he brings back from his travels through his mind attempt to render the invisible visible, but ultimately they are no more than a few stones, a bit of grit and dust, unsteady pointers to the trail he is blazing through the crystals of the mind. They merely are, as it were, humble fragments, imperfect shadows of the unattainable — divine — perfection.

L'ESPRIT EST LIBRE (THE MIND IS FREE): As far as Bylex is concerned, the exercise of transcending and overcoming the obstacle of materiality is performed on a daily basis within his head. Every head and certainly his own, says Bylex, contains a marvellous instrument, which is a brain. And in this brain dwells *l'esprit*, the mind. This mind works according to a process that Bylex calls *adaptation magnétique* (magnetic adaptation): certain things feel drawn to one another, belong together, while others do not.

You are free in your head to reinvent that magnetic attraction between objects and even devise new connections. You can classify things according to your own rationale and can design, think and create an alternative, albeit invisible, mental world as you see fit. In other words, in your head you can cut yourself loose from the world and be freed of its material manifestations. 'The mind', says Bylex,

> 'is not limited like the body. Your mind does not need to take public transport. Your mind does not have to get on a plane to return to your room in Kinshasa or Brussels when you are somewhere else. The mind is free, and even in captivity it cannot be confined. Consider a prisoner. Lock him up in a cell somewhere. What do you see? If the prisoner feels the need to see his house or his room, he doesn't need permission from the guard. A guard would never allow my mind to see my room! But my mind can get out even without the guard's permission, and go to see my room. By this I mean that the mind is the basis, for in your mind there are relations far more complex than those outside, in the visible world. That is the power of the mind, and this power is a victory.'

It is this spiritual flexibility that gives Bylex the ability to construct a worldview with universal ambitions amid the difficult circumstances that characterise life in Kinshasa. His work is made up of models and objects that become exact expressions of an imagination transformed into images. Bylex's work can certainly be regarded as one long exercise in the visionary rethinking of the impossible. This transcendence in and through the mind of the imperfection of empirical reality is important in a city such as Kinshasa, where the potholes along the road can be very deep indeed, and where the stench of the sewers is often unbearable. Bylex's oeuvre thus unfolds as an exercise in designing another, more ideal world. A world that is pure, crystal clear and hard as rock, monolithic and solid, consistent with the laws of the mind rather than the daily caprices and worries of life in a city such as Kinshasa.

WITH GOD AND SCIENCE IN SEARCH OF PERFECTION: Bylex's quest is subsequently a continual, radical and absolute search for 'perfection'. The objects he makes are copies of an ideal and idealised world within his head. In this world, reason is of crucial importance. It is no coincidence that Bylex called one of his costume designs *Escartes* or *Esprit Cartésien* (Cartesian Mind). Reason appeals to him because of its absolute and almost divine nature, which suggests an attitude of unmistakable Romanticism. In Bylex's quest for *reine Vernunft*, we not only find reflections of a form of Kantian idealism, but also of the reaction that this idealism sparked in the Romantic period. The artist is an autonomous subject ('*Je suis quand même le maître de mon esprit*,' [I am master of my own mind] Bylex says) but at the same time he is also an instrument of the Divine. Bylex's work moves, as does his life, in a space between reason and religion that many of us would no longer recognise but that undoubtedly would have been familiar to people of the early nineteenth century. It is not hard to imagine that the things Bylex sees through his mind's eye are not so different in their nature from what Caspar David Friedrich perceived when he painted *Wanderer above a Sea of Fog* or *The Polar Sea*: a perfect, frozen, silent and sublime world in which God's hand is present — a seemingly paradoxical marriage between a sublimated Enlightenment and the god-like Sublime (cf. Gamwell 2002). God and science go hand in hand in Bylex's work, as they seemingly do in Docteur's mind with his tower, and very much in the way they did in that of nineteenth-century painters, natural philosophers and scientists for whom, partly as a reaction to Kant and the German Idealists, scientific rationality could perfectly well coincide with a mystical, pantheistic longing for the essence and totality of things. As *artiste-chercheur-concepteur*, as Bylex likes to describe himself, and as a man of God (for Bylex is also very active as a preacher in one of Kinshasa's many neo-Pentecostal movements), his quest for perfection is indeed highly religious in nature, for God is perfect and will choose only the perfect on the Day of Judgment. And the perfection He seeks is beauty. Hence Bylex devotes a great deal of attention to understanding *la beauté*. Like a mantra, the phrase 'Beauty is neither colour nor size, it is form' (*la beauté, c'est ni la couleur ni la taille, c'est la forme*) returns time and again in Bylex's explanations.

'INDIRECT EMOTION': BYLEX, MATHEMATICS AND THE REINVENTION OF FORDISM: In order to convey the religiously based idea of perfection underpinning his artwork, Bylex talks about the rules of the modern manufacturing process, or the order of numbers and figures. His artworks are made according to the principle of industrial production. For Bylex, all the objects he makes must be reproducible on a large scale, like industrial products, and manufactured by what he describes as 'indirect emotion', in other words, through Abstraction and Reason, reproducible independently of the person of the artist himself, and therefore more perfect than artworks that are made by 'direct emotion' (although both are needed in order to succeed in the creative process):

> 'There is direct and indirect emotion. When we speak of *direct emotion*, we deal with thoughts that are produced without being thought. That means that you don't think about them. Rather, they are generated intuitively, and on the spot. *Indirect emotion*, on the other hand, is something that is reflected upon and thought about for some time. That is indirect emotion. I can give you an example of such indirect emotion. When I use a typewriter to write, I produce letters that were already pre-existing. These letters are like indirect emotions, they existed previously to my typewriting. The letters already existed before I pressed them down on my typewriter. Direct emotion, on the contrary, is something that is realised on the spot. It is like saying "yes" or "no" on the spur of the moment.

The same applies to works of art. When an artwork is created by means of direct emotion, it means that its realisation was not part of the process of reflection. For example, I can say: "Here I intend to use the colour 'blue', but in the process of creating the work of art, I suddenly change my mind and I tell myself to use the colour 'green' instead of blue'." The colour green is the expression of a direct emotion, a sudden intuition which announces itself without premeditation and without reflection. But indirect emotions are conceived of well in advance. They are premeditated, less immediate. I think about what to do in advance: "This is what I will do, this is the size of the object", and then I stick to what I thought about before making it. That's indirect emotion. Take for example the inventor of cars. When one starts to make a car one can say: "This will be a BMW of this particular type or series". As such, this specific car can be endlessly reproduced. One can make ten thousand cars of this particular BMW type. That is what indirect emotion means: it is conceived beforehand, imprinted. But, during its production, it is also possible to change from the original concept, put in other chairs for example, or shape it in other forms, and give it other colours. At that moment, the original idea changes. It becomes an instantaneous creation, a direct emotion rather than something premeditated, imprinted and pre-registered.'

In Bylex's world, the search for perfection has close ties with mathematics. This 'mathematics' is symbolised in his work by the recurrent motif of little black and white squares. For Bylex, the square represents the perfect form because it has four equal sides. And black and white are 'perfect' colours because they exist in themselves and not as blends. White also represents balance, while red in the Bylex universe signifies hope:

'In the Bylex art, the square symbolises a certain equilibrium. Bylex always works according to the norms and rules of basic geometry. I also work a lot with the colour "white". For Bylex, this colour represents purposefulness and determination. I will give you an example of this: Doctors are dressed in white to show people that they have the will power to accomplish their job in spite of all the difficulties they might encounter. Some people are already dying when they arrive at the hospital, but this does not discourage the doctors. They will surmount this difficulty to heal the patient in question. This goes for me as well. Sometimes I encounter great difficulties while I am working on an object, but I try to surmount this difficulty to arrive at the best possible result. This is why I use the colour "white", to illustrate my determination to make the best possible artworks. I also use the colour "red". In the Bylex language this means that there is always hope, no matter how insurmountable the difficulties. I have always been hopeful that I will succeed one day. This is also the meaning of the word

Byl. Byl is the man who doesn't acknowledge the impossible, the man who always finds a solution and demonstrates that anything is possible.'

The name *Byl* also brings us back to numbers. Like the square or the colour white, numbers and figures have the same ideal purity that points us to the true nature of the Divine Plan. In Bylex's work, mathematics and figures not only stand for modernist reason, but also for 'science' in the sense that alchemists must have used it (and the alchemical tradition lives on in Kinshasa, partly under the influence of Rosicrucians).[10] For Bylex numbers are the bearers of an almost kabbalistic symbolism that gives meaning to the Divine Plan. Numbers represent both science and mysticism, the irresistible nature of Reason as well as the incomprehensibility that lies within religious experience. Therefore, the artist's utopian code name is *Byl*, a name composed of three letters: *b* — the second letter of the alphabet, *y* — the twenty-fifth letter and *l* — the twelfth letter. Together the numbers of these letters add up to thirty-nine, which is to say: 39 = 3 followed by 9 and then 9 = 3 times 3. This formula applies to Bylex himself (for he is his father's third son) as well as to Christ (who died at the age of 33). The *ex* at the end of *Bylex* stands for *exhibition*.

AN ENCOMPASSING TOTAL WORLD: The name Bylex embraces an entire creative programme, as well as a method for transforming the private individual, Pume the imperfect human being, into a public personality, the ultimate form of Bylex. The Bylex personality is a conceptual project in which the artist, in his quest for perfection, ultimately becomes God himself and, in creating his own world, becomes one with Him. That is why Pume constantly refers to Bylex in the third person and why he gave his daughter the name Lorbyl (a combination of 'Lord' and Bylex). It is this aspect that also explains the authoritarian and totalitarian, all-encompassing and monolithic nature of the Bylex universe. The world of Bylex is, in a sense, the world of monologue. Bylex thinks, lives, breathes and creates in his own world; a world in which there is little room for dialogue, difference, and openness. Undoubtedly, this is something of a protective reaction of a man who lives in a cannibalistic urban space that is forever invading the lives of its inhabitants and constantly forcing its way into their field of vision, penetrating their intimate spaces, bodies, ears, pores and noses, and compelling them to submit to its whims. Hence, no doubt, his obsession with safety issues (as illustrated by his Tourist City project — see below).

Against this indomitable Kinshasa, Bylex juxtaposes an all-encompassing total world with its own, equally compelling aesthetics. In contrast to the world out there, Bylex is the lord and master of his own world: he controls and surveys its contours, and imposes his own will and order on it. To free himself from the many limitations and restrictions that Kinshasa forces upon its inhabitants, Bylex thus creates his own maniacal utopia. He does this on a grand scale in a city plan such as the Tourist City, and also on a smaller scale, right down to the details: with his models of individual houses, cars, furniture, clothing, shoes and even watches and tiepins, he designs his own urban environment.

THE CITY'S VERBAL INFRASTRUCTURES: Bylex's authoritarian and totalitarian manner of speaking, thinking and designing is undeniably also a characteristic of the Congolese capital itself. For Kinshasa is the city that was permeated for decades by the Word of the Dictator, and the all-pervasive aesthetics of the Mobutist *animation politique* which accompanied that Word. It is no coincidence that this totalitarian political discourse was laced with references to God and marked by a constant religious transfiguration of the political field. In daily broadcasts on the Zairean state television, Mobutu descended from heaven with a halo around his head, without a hint of irony. In today's Kinshasa, that legendary Hegemon has been replaced by the Old Testament God. With the help of the thousands of churches and prayer groups active in Kinshasa, the inescapable voice of Yahweh foists itself in just as authoritarian a way upon the public urban space in order to turn it, through the light of His Word and Will, into the City of God, the new Jerusalem. And in this city where the Holy Spirit manifests itself at every moment of the day in the form of glossolalia, and where the trance-like prayers of the faithful are continually charged with the power of the Divine, it is not very difficult to believe in the potential of words to represent and redesign the city in a new way through the construction of rhetorical architectures. Their speech, prayers and songs form an unremitting attempt to subdue the rapture of urban madness, to comprehend the living thing that is the city, to build and to govern the unmappable world of people's journeys through the city's perilous and transitory ground, and to conjure up new possible futures for it. Even though, as I have argued earlier, the city often disrupts the links between signifiers and signified, and corrupts the meaning of words in the process, speech nevertheless remains one of the most important building blocks with which to conquer and alter the city. *In the beginning was the Word* (John 1:1). This is a profound belief that Bylex shares with his fellow citizens and transposes onto his own universe. Through language Bylex ceaselessly redesigns the city to enable its rebirth in an unremitting attempt to subdue, comprehend, build and govern it in order to convert its chaos into an alternative order. And through the creation of a whole library of Bylexian neologisms, he tries to impose a new linguistic order on the urban world in order to seize the city and imbue it with a new, more liveable meaning.

IMPROVISATION AND LAUGHTER AS THE KEY TO IMAGINATION: The totalitarian longing for a controllable universe, the demiurge-like impulse to create a perfect world — and become oneself a god — stands in stark contrast with the imperfect, chaotic, irrational and totally unpredictable city that Kinshasa is. This is why all Bylex's artworks, be they grandiose plans and construction projects or small models of objects such as visionary armchairs, clocks, shoes or wristwatches, are enclosed in their own space and shielded from the evil exterior world in glass boxes, almost as if Bylex is aware that his poetic propositions are too fragile to survive the contamination of the urban chaos without extra protection. In fact, the city incessantly forces Bylex to leave the high plane of reason and return to 'direct emotion'. This 'direct emotion' is essentially none other than the capacity for improvisation. As illustrated throughout this book, Kinshasa naturally compels its residents to improvise. Confronted with human mistakes and infrastructural shortcomings, you are forced to improvise in order to bridge the constant hiatus that exists between words and deeds, or between ideas and their practical implementation in the everyday business of urban life. And like every other resident of Kinshasa Bylex also knows how to give the quality of improvisation its due:

> 'Sometimes I need direct emotion, at other times indirect emotion. I combine both to arrive at something that is complete. When I make something, the indirect emotion might change, the form might change. The same happens to ideas. When you want to construct a house, for example, you picture it as having three bedrooms, a living-room, a kitchen and a bathroom, but while building it you run out of money. This forces you to change the original concept: two bedrooms instead of three, and a living-room and kitchen but no longer a bathroom. So the concept adapts itself to the circumstances, and this thanks to direct emotion. The decision made on the spot, this is direct emotion.'

One of the basic elements of improvisation is laughter, and this playful laughter is also an important bridge between Kinshasa and Bylex's work. In Kinshasa, jokes, jibes, parody and the derisory often constitute the ultimate 'weapons of the weak' with which the downtrodden thumb their noses at the rich and powerful. Similarly, it is laughter that teasingly breaks open the enclosed, totalitarian world of the city from which, all too often, no escape seems possible. Humour generates the oxygen and openness necessary to save the self-referential urban world from suffocating, and in similar ways it opens up the closed system of the Bylex universe. Bylex proffers this relativising laughter in a mocking and understated manner. It is often by means of an ironic joke disguised as scientific seriousness that Bylex pulls the viewer's leg. The viewer can never be entirely sure that they are not being taken for a ride, or when Bylex's statements are meant to be taken seriously or not; for instance, when he explains the name one of his children, Dane, as an acronym meaning *densité d'analyses normales experimentées* (density of normal experimental analyses), or when he distinguishes between *vraie* and *fausse folie*, true and false madness. A bicycle trying to pull a truck is one of the examples Bylex gives of 'false madness'.

It is in this playful but also completely serious way that Bylex navigates the many contradictions in which he lives. His gaze pierces the city, sometimes with touching naïveté, at other times with 'scientific' originality, but always with humanity and engagement. In a compulsive effort to perceive beauty, he provides, in a single stroke, both an analysis and a synthesis of the urban world. In this sense, his work is one long exercise in learning how to 'see' anew; in reflecting upon the visible, muddy reality in which urbanites have to live, and in extending one's gaze beyond the theatre of the everyday to capture the invisible laws on which this incomprehensible reality is founded. In the end, Bylex offers you the opportunity to return to the child-like capacity to be astonished by the world and imagine it as a better place.

THE TOURIST CITY: Let us now turn to the model of the Tourist City itself. The Tourist City is a utopian urban project which condenses the core of Bylex's *Weltanschauung*. With the Tourist City, Bylex seems to question not only the 'true' objectives of architecture but also of politics. Within the generalised condition of economic and political crisis that marks the global world today, and speaking from a city where the physical life of that crisis is omnipresent in very tangible ways, Bylex makes a strong plea for a new universal humanism, and offers us a language to re-imagine, re-invent and rebuild the very premises of the urban world that we all inhabit. Implicitly or explicitly, Bylex suggests that the basis itself, the necessary premise for any form of political and architectural thinking about the city, is situated within the urban dwellers themselves. Bylex's Tourist City is therefore a relevant, though mostly indirect, comment on the political, because the conceptual architecture and visual language of this centrepiece provides an emancipatory space to express alternative social ideals and ethical concerns in the real world.

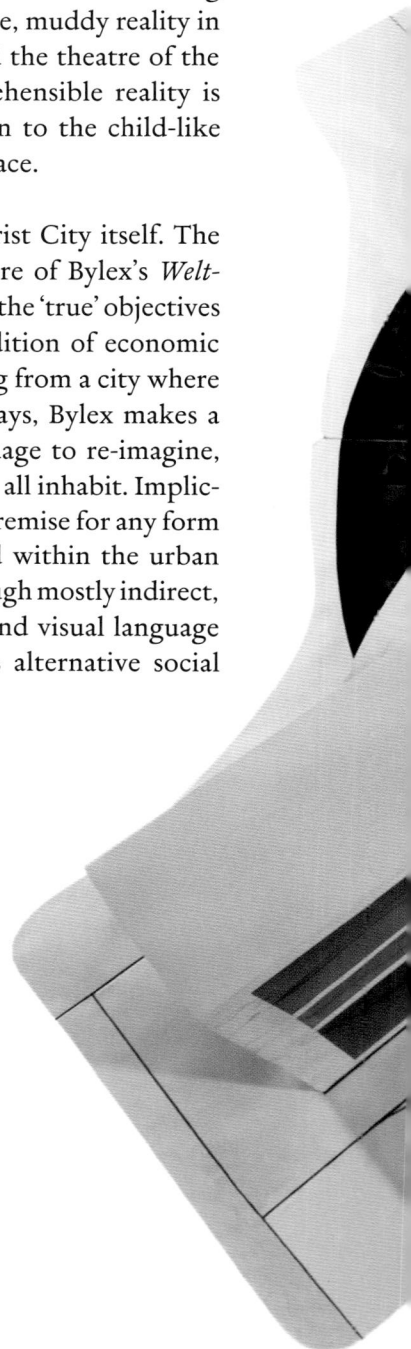

The architecture of the Tourist City is entirely and unmistakably marked by the central presence of the Royal Dome. This Dome is not only a 'Temple of the Spirit', as Bylex likes to call it, but also the Temple of a humanity without God, or rather, the Temple where Man, in typical Bylex fashion, becomes his own God. The 'Tourist', the figure of the Wanderer, is called to this cupola-shaped Temple in order to induce contemplation and reflection about himself:

'In the middle there is the Royal Dome representing a king's crown. To the left there are hotels. We see the passage of a tunnel running through this building, and the black and orange parts represent the asphalt highways. To the right we see three swimming pools located on the commercial square. All of the buildings around it represent the commercial centre. On the other side there are three more pearl-shaped swimming pools, in red and blue, and a bit further there are again three more swimming pools. So that makes for nine swimming pools in the commercial centre.

We also have cylindrical pillars which are put there for security reasons, with radars and solar cameras. These cameras work with different systems, they are multidirectional and will work 24 hours a day to assure the tourists' security.

But let us return to the Royal Dome. You see the Dome and its passageway tunnelling through it. The colour yellow is that of the synthetic lawns. There will be yellow grass, crystal-coloured grass, as well as sapphire blue grass. A bit lower, we see the shape of the windows in the hotel buildings of the Tourist City. These are anti-kamikaze buildings. As we have said, there will be a central nucleus and then these external glass-shaped structures that stop bullets. Continuing our way around the city we arrive again at the Dome. To its left there is another hotel, in red this time, which also has an anti-kamikaze security system.

The centre is the most important part, it is like a kingdom. Around the king are his subjects, but it is the king who gives his orders to the others. Therefore the Royal Dome is the city centre and there is something special that sets it apart. The other buildings do not have a large amount of synthetic lawns, but the royal dome is surrounded by a multitude of colours, a veritable amalgam of colours. It is as if to say: it is the Royal Dome that took all the colours and distributed some to the other buildings. It is the centre giving the example to the other buildings, as if to say: "It is I who guide the commercial part, the hotels, the asphalt roads." That is why the city's central part is its human heart: through this centre people get access to the different parts of the city (the hotels, the commercial part, the swimming pools, the circulation, the city's higher and lower points) to finally reassemble in the Royal Dome, the point of interrogation. After having visited the whole city, people return to this part of the city that enables reflection and meditation, asking themselves: "What purpose does this city serve?" That is the role of the Royal Dome, which is also some kind of museum. A museum is a place of meditation. One can walk through different rooms and observe different objects and things. It is as if one was walking through a temple. And in a temple one has to be respectful. In a temple one does not behave as in a bar, and you have to make sure to say and do the right thing, or walk the right way, because it is a place for meditation. It is like going to a cemetery. There you do not behave like a barbarian either, do you? Once there you wonder: "And what if I die? How am I going to be buried? How is it going to work? Where will they put the flowers? What is life after death going to be like? Who is going to stay behind?" In short, you put yourself in the deceased's place, and this reflection induces a sort of discipline, a kind of silence, a feeling of calm and quiet. In conclusion you tell yourself: "I am not going to make any noise. Instead I will listen to my inner thoughts. What does my heart tell me or reproach me?" And the Royal Dome is this heart, it is the heart of the whole city.

After having visited the city and its hotels, and after having walked on the city's roads, you finally end up in a huge universal temple. And there you will be told: "This is not only a place where Buddhists enter, or Catholics, Protestants etcetera, but it is a place where everyone is welcome." Some people pray without a church, because the real church is the heart! It is not a building, it is not a priest. Inside oneself there is a conscience. It is like a black hole. In this hole you will question yourself, your own words, because inside yourself you are all by yourself. No wife, no kids, just you... That is the real temple. So when you arrive at the Royal Dome you enter a state of self-reflection. You tell yourself: "Here I am, I visited all the places of the Tourist City, but what did I learn from this visit? Did it do me any good? What will the relationships that I established here bring me?" It starts a process of interrogation before leaving the city again: "What have I learned?" That is *the* question! Everything that one might have thought about the nature of the city will turn out to be relative. As if Bylex wanted to erect a universal temple where one does not have to worry about what is normal and what not. In this temple a Buddhist can meet a non-Buddhist or a Protestant, people who are different from me, but who all want this state of peacefulness.

What is the reason for making such a city? It is surely not to lead other people onto the road to Evil, no! The Tourist City is about universal cohesion. Everyone has his place in it, everyone is equally important. I am not the only important one, but all those around me are important too. Even if they are different and not like me, they too are important and should be safe. That is the Tourist City's ideal! It is a city where one learns about morality. Not a morality learned from books, but a morality automatically instilled in you by the environment. An automatic learning process: you enter the Dome, and there you know: "This is the creation." And in the white part of the city you tell yourself: "I can't stain this whiteness with impurity, here the person and the light have to become one." Within the Tourist City one takes care not to dirty the City. It should be kept clean, because long after me other generations will visit it and cherish its cleanliness. This is what perfection and harmony are all about. The Tourist City is the perfection of harmony!'

In some respect, and in spite of the Dome's royal adjective and its religious epitheton 'Temple of the Spirit', Bylex seems to be close here to the more secular humanist ideals of the Belgian visionary and peace activist Paul Otlet (1868-1944), famous at one time for his Mundaneum and World City projects (cf. Levie 2006). The Mundaneum, or World Palace as it was originally called, aimed at gathering all the world's knowledge in one single classificatory system, which would then form the basis for a new 'world city'. In a rather similar way Bylex's Temple of the Spirit proposes the notion of a 'global' museum that will bring together all knowledge ever generated about the world in one encyclopaedic heart, the Royal Dome. As such, a visit to the Dome will serve as an impetus, not so much as to create a new city but to rebalance the existing urbanscape, as I will further argue ahead.[11] This museum of knowledge and beauty is open to all humanity. It immerses the visitor in an atmosphere of peace and quiet, thereby stimulating the 'tourist' to ponder and philosophise. Bylex wants the Royal Dome to prompt existential questions in the tourist. By assuming that such contemplation has the power to transform the tourist into a more reasonable and moral human being, Bylex also expresses his strong belief in the power of architecture as a universal instrument of political, social and ethical emancipation. The Dome is the built form of a *Bildungsideal*. By its very form, it influences, inspires and re-educates people and illuminates the 'black hole' of their conscience.

Simultaneously, Bylex uses architecture as a sort of totalitarian system of control (and here he echoes some of Docteur's preoccupations with his tower). Bylex trusts that the design of the buildings and the perfection of the architectural form itself will convey his universalist message and his quest for Order, Perfection and Enlightenment in an empathic manner. At the same time authoritarian undercurrents are never far away. In this respect, Bylex's oeuvre can easily be placed within the context of the post 9/11 era, which has defined the beginning of the 21st century and also forms the inevitable backdrop for Bylex's own work. However naive the model of the Tourist City might seem, the hotels and offices, with their bulletproof 'anti-kamikaze' glass windows and their security cameras, show a world where perfection and harmony are under constant threat and need to be safeguarded through the iron logic of defensive measures. To a certain extent, Bylex's utopia might be said to have much in common with contemporary Singapore, for example, where the state runs the city as if it were a gated community.

Although the model of the *Cité Touristique* at first sight seems to be a rather crude translation of a modernist belief in the tabula rasa, that is, the possibility of leaving the existing city behind in order to start from scratch somewhere else, it is really a much more complex and hybrid combination. It brings together Christian Messianic idealism, Russian Constructivist ideas about social control and condensation, the profane (German) *Bildungsideal*, the modernist ambition to create a sanitised and 'bright' architecture based on social equality and formal perfection, as well as neoliberal ideals of the charter city (and as we will see below, one is currently being built on Bylex's doorstep).

In a way, this puzzling mix is what Bylex offers us, but he adds his own specific twist to it. By exploring the language and metaphors that Bylex proposes and by immersing ourselves in the utopian dimension of his urban paradise, we, as 'tourists', wanderers and spectators, start to understand under what set of axioms the aesthetic discourse might become political. For Bylex, the utopian city still has a *practical* (and political) role to play as a major scene of and for change. Even though the Tourist City is an imaginary space outside the reality of any existing city, it still provides the urban subject with a potential for emancipation in the real world. No matter where you live or what your actual urban background is, the Tourist City's social ideals may be expressed and achieved there. Subsequently, the model of the Tourist City is not meant to exist independently. The Tourist City is an analogous city; it is an exordium, an introduction to the city. It is not conceived as a city to be lived in on a permanent basis, but it provides a model of the city as a refuge in order to reflect upon and counterbalance the imperfections of existing cities. In this, it is not an African escapist alternative to Disney World or other theme parks and resorts such as Sun City, but rather an honest attempt to deal with the shortcomings of the existing city as a universal form with universal urban problems. Bylex is not running away from the real world with its political and economic realities. For example, Bylex's Tourist City does not start from the premise of Homo Ludens and the idea of an economy which has freed people from labour, as is the case of New Babylon, the urban utopia proposed by the Dutch artist Constant. Bylex's Tourist City, on the contrary, is all about cities where architectures may be positively instrumental, even if these cities are encapsulated in and marked by the inequalities of a neoliberal capitalistic system. The tourist is not a pleasure seeker, but someone in search of inner growth. After a trip to the Tourist City, the tourist always has to return to the imperfections of the real city that he calls home. But now replenished with fresh inspiration, creativity, reflexive capacity and imagination, the tourist is ready to brave the urban dystopia on the ground and bring the existing city, whether its Kinshasa, Johannesburg, Tokyo, Paris or New York, back into balance again, thereby making it a better place for all.

SPECTRAL KINSHASA: Bylex's utopian alternative Kinshasa strongly resonates with Docteur's vision (and in many ways the latter's tower forms the logical material realisation, the heterotopic translation of Bylex's artistic cardboard and coloured paper utopia). Similarly, the tower and the vision of the Tourist City are in tune with a number of urban developments that claim to announce the birth of the new Kinshasa.

The promise of financial reward and material benefit that neoliberal capitalism holds out (a promise that is magnified in the discourses of religious entrepreneurs who run the numerous 'miracle' churches that have sprung up all over Congo) also propels the pauperised population of Congo's cities, towns and villages into imagining the possibility of a future that magically converts their nightmares into utopian dreams. Whereas many Congolese are often not in the position to bridge the divide between today and tomorrow, let alone plan much further ahead in time (and therefore frequently seek to escape from the present by having recourse to nostalgia for a re-invented colonial or precolonial golden era), the teleologies of today's global neo-liberal frameworks address and convert the otherwise uncertain future in strongly utopian terms, turning today's hardships and disillusions into the possibility of hope and 'change' in the process. This is the attraction and strength of visions of the future that private investors, real estate companies and government alike hold up to the urban residents of Congo. Almost every main street of Kinshasa, and other major Congolese cities such as Lubumbashi, is lined with huge billboards that either promise new gleaming apartments, condominiums and entire new towns for a middle-class whose emergence still remains rather hypothetical, or else they announce the construction of new conference centres, shopping malls, five star hotels, and skyscrapers with names such as 'Modern Paradise'[12], 'Crown Tower', or 'Riverview Towers'. These advertisements proclaim the

coming of a new and modern city and with it a 'new standard of life for Kinshasa' (*un nouveau niveau de vie à Kin*, as one billboard has it) and as such they also offer a spectral and often spectacular vision of Congo's reinsertion into the global oecumene, even though this remains highly speculative and very volatile. While some of these projects are actually being built or have been completed, many continue to exist merely as 'ocular ground' (McCarthy 2002: 542), almost as if the image in itself was sufficient materialisation of the dream. Simultaneously, the same image constantly reveals the tensions and disjunctures between these mirages of the new city and the histories and temporalities of the lives currently lived in Kinshasa by most people. In February 2010, for example, I was struck by two adjacent billboards on one of Kinshasa's main avenues. One presented a picture of a new shopping centre, complete with fountains and gardens, while a poster right next to it advertised a new brand of Aladdin lamp, still the most important device for many Kinois to help them light up their nights because large parts of the city are no longer or not yet, or then only at random moments, connected to the city's failing electricity grid.

THE MODERN TITANIC: In the sustained politics of '*visibility*' that the Congolese government brands as its 'revolution of modernity' (see Chapter Two), many advertisements that have popped up since the early 2010s sport a portrait of President Kabila

246

alongside the declaration that Congo will soon become 'the mirror of Africa' again. In other words, Kinshasa is again looking into the mirror of modernity to fashion itself, but this time the mirror no longer reflects the earlier versions of Belgian colonialist modernity. Instead Kinshasa's political elites are eager to capture the aura of Dubai and other hot spots of the new urban Global South.

Of all these billboards, the most striking appeared in 2010 near Ngobila Beach, Kinshasa's main port, not very far from the spot where, in Conrad's novella, Kayerts and Carlier watched over 'the fetish', the storehouse containing the capitalist spirit of civilization. However, Ngobila Beach is a sorry sight nowadays. It has become an industrial wasteland. The riverbank itself is hidden from view by semi-sunken boats that no longer offer possible lines of flight. Instead, the carcasses of these rust-eaten boats just lie there stranded, stuck in the mud and surrounded by floating carpets of water hyacinths. It is in this very same spot that a building company calling itself 'Modern Construction' chose to erect a new conference centre. In 2010, it put up a huge billboard that also displayed a photo of a smiling Kabila. On his left and right, you could see a computer generated picture showing the new international conference centre in the form of a giant cruiser, complete with a rooftop terrace and restaurant. Kabila seemed to be telling the Kinois that this new building, reminiscent of the boat-like architectural elements of the Forescom tower — the material emanation of the triumph of colonialist modernity —, was offering the nation a new start and promised a prosperous voyage *en route* to a more global modernity. Even if, rather cynically, the project developers at the time had provided the building with the name 'Modern Titanic'[13], the image of the ship setting sail towards a new future for Kinshasa proved powerfully seductive. Although there was no doubt in anyone's mind that the odds against the Titanic *not* sinking remained overwhelming, and although many urban residents in Kinshasa knew that they would never gain access to this new future, this naval image inspired irresistible hopes of a better future and new and more advantageous ways to cruise through life and navigate the city. Even those who count themselves amongst the president's political adversaries could not help but exclaim: 'If only this were true', or 'And what if it turned out to be real this time?'. Although utopias usually remain locked within the realm of pure speculation and material impossibility, Kabila's *chantiers* seemed to awaken new hopes and rekindle a dormant capacity to 'believe' and to dream against all odds.

LA CITÉ DU FLEUVE: Nowhere does the *speculum* of neoliberal global modernity conjure up the oneiric more spectacularly nor reveal its exclusionist logics more strongly than in the much debated *Cité du Fleuve* construction project, which, as the developer's website states, 'began as a dream in 2008'. Contrary to many other projected new 'cities' in and around Kinshasa,[14] *Cité du Fleuve* is currently underway although its infrastructure turns out to be far more banal, less spectacular and on a much smaller scale than the advertisements and promotional videos promised. *Cité du Fleuve* is being built on land reclaimed from sandbanks and swamps in the Malebo Pool, a small distance from Port Baramoto, another one of the city's sorry harbours, adjacent to Ngobila Beach. As mentioned in Chapter Two, in its final phase *Cité du Fleuve* will be 600 hectares in size, and include over 200 villas and 10,000 luxury apartments, 10,000 offices, a marina, schools, cinemas, restaurants and conference rooms. It will be connected to the rest of Kinshasa by two bridges and a transit road. Self-sufficient in water and electricity supply, *Cité du Fleuve* aims to offer potential buyers a luxurious lifestyle and secure land titles. In this respect, the developer's website states:

> 'One of the many factors that make *La Cité du Fleuve* unique in Kinshasa is that no land titles have existed on this property before (as it will be built on reclaimed land, where until now there has been a swamp along the Congo River. When you buy land at *La Cité du Fleuve*, you can rest assured that there are no possible claims on your property.'

According to the developers' website, *Cité du Fleuve* will thus provide a 'standard of living unparalleled in Kinshasa and will be a model for the rest of Africa'; it will be a haven of 'modernity, sobriety, friendliness and the pleasure of living', 'a white water lily', 'a satellite floating on the riversides of the majestic Congo river' that will 'showcase the new era of African economic development' and constitute Kinshasa's major 'tourist focal point'.

Parallels with the Bylex vision are obvious. *Cité du Fleuve* and the Tourist City share the same glossy, bright aesthetics and the same preoccupations with security and cleanliness. Moreover, neither *Cité du Fleuve* nor the Tourist City is, by any standard, a real and living city: they are tourist attractions, offering opportunities to break away from the real city. But whereas the *raison d'être* of Bylex's Tourist City is premised on a return to the real urban world, *Cité du Fleuve* makes no such claim. On the contrary, it aims to keep the real city at bay. The utopian idea of a tabula rasa has always been at the heart of much modernist urban planning, but the materialisation of these modernist dreams has always involved an endeavour to include different social classes. In India, for example, Le Corbusier's Chandigarh was conceived of as a city where both rich and poor could belong, and its zoning plans envisioned a place for all. As a matter of fact, Jawaharlal Nehru commissioned this capital city not only to showcase the newly independent India's modern, progressive stance but also to offer an alternative city model that reached beyond the strictures of class and caste (Kalia 1999). Similarly, Brasilia was an attempt to transform the class structure of Brazilian society, even though these principles became subverted in the process (cf. Holston 1989).

Contrary to the original inclusive ideal of the modernist city, or to the universal humanism of Bylex, satellite cities that are currently being constructed or planned in Kinshasa and in many of Congo's major urban areas seem to have given up on this ideal of a broader collectivity. Conceived as huge gated communities that are run by means of specific bylaws, the new segregationist cities for the emerging African middle class, the supposed beneficiaries of the new economic Afro-optimism, profoundly redefine the meaning of the current urbanscape.

The reality is that most people living in the city will never be able to set foot on the two islands.[15] If all goes according to plan, *Cité du Fleuve* will probably be accorded the administrative status of a new municipality and then be subject to its own special bylaws. Operated as a huge gated community, *Cité du Fleuve* will inevitably redefine what is Kinshasa's centre and edge. Consequently, it reflects many of the ideas behind concepts such as Stanford economist Paul Romer's 'charter city'; that is, a special urban reform zone that allows local governments, in partnership with global investors and other actors of 'extrastatecraft' (Easterling 2014), to adopt new systems of rules and establish cities that are supposed to drive economic progress in the rest of the country. At the same time, *Cité du Fleuve* also replicates the segregationist model of *Ville* and

Cité that proved so highly effective during the Belgian colonial period. It is clear that the islands will become, at least in the minds of their makers, the new *Ville* while the rest of Kinshasa, with its ten million inhabitants, will be redefined as its periphery. In this way the new city map will redraw the geographies of inclusion and exclusion in radical ways, and relegate — conceptually if not materially — its current residents to the city edges.

Undoubtedly, this re-urbanisation process regularises Kinshasa and ends its 'exceptionalism' in the sense that Kinshasa's dynamics of urban growth has now started to resemble that of other world cities in the Global South such as Dubai, Mumbai, Rio and the urban conglomerations of Southern China. Simultaneously, however, Kinshasa joins the shadow-side of that global process of urbanisation, a side that reveals itself in the increasing *favela*-isation and more difficult access and right to the city for many of its current inhabitants. Here, the spectral dimension of the marvellous inevitably merges with the more dismal dimensions of violence and terror, expressed through the processes of repression, 'sanitation', expulsion and forced relocation that have always been an integral part of the politics of urbanisation in this part of Central Africa.

This nightmarish aspect is repeated in these new spectral topographies and forms the tain, the tinfoil backing of the mirror that increasingly also attends the process of urbanisation worldwide (cf. Sassen 2014).

In spite of this, projects such as *Cité du Fleuve* have generated remarkably little conflict. When I started to follow the construction of the first island in 2008, I expected major clashes between the government, the developers and the inhabitants of the Malebo Pool's southern riverbank, including a number of fishermen, who had to or will have to make way for this project. Two of the fishermen's villages in the marshlands of the Pool have already been removed to make room for the expanding *Cité du Fleuve* islands. A number of inhabitants in the Kingabwa neighbourhood have undergone a similar fate. Their shacks were demolished to make way for the construction of the access and transit road currently connecting *Cité du Fleuve* to the city. Yet their eviction only generated short-lived clashes with developers and the authorities, and at no point did these evictions engender more sustained collective action than people's initial anger.[16] Protest quickly came to a halt when (small) financial compensations were made to (some of) the evicted inhabitants of the riverbank shacks. In the rare cases where individuals continued to put up a fight, it was not so much to protest against their removal but to demand a higher compensation rate.[17]

In the meantime, hundreds of farmers currently cultivating land in the riparian area are in danger of being evicted from their fields as well (also see Chapter Eight), but so far they have shown little or no solidarity with those already evacuated. Here as well, dissent largely remains 'atomised' (Harms 2012). As I discussed in Chapter Six, similar processes of eviction have equally failed to generate a strong organised collective resistance elsewhere in the country.

I will further analyse some of the possible reasons for this lack of organised collective (political) protest in the next chapter. But clearly one reason is already to be found in the absence of, or in the difficulty to construct, a formally constituted public realm as previously illustrated. Another and perhaps equally important reason certainly has to do with the fact that Kinshasa's residents and their leaders not only share the same longing for a better future city but they also remarkably often share the same dream of what that city should look like. When I asked the farmers in danger of eviction whether they were aware of what awaited them, they said: 'Yes, we'll be the victims, but even so, it will be beautiful, it makes one dream!' *(C'est beau quand-même, ça fait rêver!)*. Notions of beauty, as Harms remarks in relation to similar emerging urban zones in Saigon, reproduce rather than challenge the core ideals that legitimise such exclusive building projects despite their counter-hegemonic potential (Harms 2012). In other words,

people who will not be granted access to the new 'Mirror of Africa' often revel just as much as the ruling elites in this dream of the modern city and the forceful promise made by this 'aesthetics of arrival' (Kaur and Hansen 2015), even though the dream of a new future for the city simultaneously generates very tangible forms of ever more pronounced segregation and of new topographies of inclusion and exclusion, of propinquity and distance, of haves and have-nots. In spite of this, the expectations of both groups are remarkably similar and seem to reflect a far more widespread yearning for the right of inclusion in a global society.

Subsequently, a site such as *Cité du Fleuve* is not a utopia in the strict sense of the word, it is something else. Unlike utopian visionary dreams, it does not generate or offer hope. Instead, it offers Kinshasa a new heterotopia, a novel space that escapes from the real order of things, from its standard forms of classification and accumulation, if only because it conjures up the marvellous through an appeal to the imagination and the aesthetics of the oneiric that is apparently irresistible.

In the end, this is also why it seems almost not to matter whether the new city is physically built or not. In any case, it remains unclear whether the government itself cares or believes that the new polis will emerge in any lasting way. The Kinois are not easily fooled either: they know very well from past experiences not to trust or believe in official discourses or outcomes of government policies. For all they know, the new city might well prove to be as chimerical and volatile as the speculative capital, and the hedge and vulture funds that will supposedly finance and build it. There is something indeed 'magical' about the non-transparent, speculative and volatile nature of these forms of capital production, profit-making and wealth accumulation. The sources of that wealth are never revealed and remain very opaque, 'mystique' and unpredictable, and therefore they are easily explained in terms of the cultural discourses and practices of the occult that people continue to use to 'capture' (Lingala: *-zwa*) extravert sources of material well-being [18] as well as to understand their own predicament and exorcise the abyss of material and spiritual insecurity that constantly opens up in their everyday life. In fact, hedge funds, money market funds and other investment vehicles that constitute the dark money of the global 'shadow banking system' (SBS) seem to be defined as much by uncertainty as the everyday lives of the Congolese. Even though this shadowy world of global finance is ideologically driven by modernist teleologies that have become so impossible in daily life, it is attracted to cities such as Kinshasa precisely because of that genomic or systemic similitude that illustrates that the unpredictable is not only located in the figure of 'the African city' but also in the global scape. It is in this spatial vector that local actors and the forces acting upon them meet and jointly generate the same velocities and accelerations while sharing the same aspirations and futurities.

In summary, a project such as *Cité du Fleuve*, which is 'emerging from nowhere' (*surgissant du néant*) as a government propaganda magazine put it (Mobateli 2014), reveals the occult qualities of volatility and unpredictability that cause speculative capital and city to be mutually attracted to each other. In a way, the occult thereby constitutes one of the city's main assets and seems to generate its main financial opportunities. That the new city will ever materialise is unpredictable and uncertain in the eyes of many Kinois. The invisible and speculative nature of the crisis capitalism that finances these new urban projects, as well as the fact that this financial capital in a place such as Kinshasa defines itself as the fetish that Conrad already understood it to be, further contribute to these uncertainties. The 2008 global banking crisis and the subsequent 2012-2013 Cypriot financial crisis only heightened this feeling of uncertainty. Due to the global stock markets crisis, many satellite city projects were cancelled or postponed. In this way Lubumbashi's Kiswishi City project mentioned in Chapter Six was postponed until further notice. This large new city project was originally planned by Renaissance, a Russian investment company that has since shape-shifted into various other identities with different names.[19] Similarly, in the case of *Cité du Fleuve*, construction was considerably slowed down for a while because of cash flow problems. The project was supposed to be completed within eight years, a time span that is likely to be expanded much further into the future. In addition, there is a huge difference between the spectacular images used to promote the idea of this new city, and its actual materialisation. In reality, rather than making Kinshasa a new Doha or Dubai, *Cité du Fleuve* amounts to nothing more than banal suburban housing infrastructure. Somewhere between dream and reality, prices keep going up in all kinds of mysterious ways indeed.

In the end, these new cities short-circuit any real tangible roadmaps for the construction of a better urban future in spite of their capacity to engender dreams about a future that emerges as a kind of anticipation inscribed in the present (de Abreu 2013; Guyer 2007; Nielsen 2011). In the face of this spectral politics of images on billboards and advertisements in which the hyper-real city seems to appear out of nothing and might well disappear again into nothing, the only place where the city can be inhabited, and where it is constantly being built, is the Hole, the living city that projects such as *Cité du Fleuve* so desperately try to keep at bay.

8. Ngaliema's Revenge. Urban Expansion, Chiefs, and Land.

'Inst. 2.1.22: "If an island arise in the sea, an uncommon event, it is open to occupation for it is regarded as belonging to no one" (*nullius enim esse creditor*); Dig.41.30.1.4: "If I build on an island arising in the sea, it is mine forthwith; for what belongs to no one is open to the first taker" (*quod nullius sit, occupantis fit*).' (Fitzmaurice 2014: 54, footnote 91)

1882. April 9, Leopoldville.
'He [Chief Ngaliema - FDB] will tell you with equanimity of what will happen when he is dead; how he will be swathed in cottons and woollens and silks and satins, and, after many days of continued fusillading, will be buried in an honoured grave. Indeed, from the pleasure he takes in reciting all this, he seems to you as a person whose life is devoted to prepare for the great event of death. The part of dying is hateful, because it involves pain; but the period after death will be glorious. All those robes, and silken stuffs, and velvet cloaks that I have given him, will adorn his body as it is conveyed in state, followed by chanting warriors, and multitudes of female mourners loudly lamenting, while the youths of all the surrounding villages will fire incessant volleys of musketry for many days and nights. "Ah," says Ngalyema admiringly shaking his head, "that is what I call grand, and worthy of a king!" from which I gather that, in his opinion, life does not become a king half so well as death.' (Stanley 2011 [1885]: 392-393)

If the current pattern of urban expansion in Africa is marked by the development of 'oceans of poverty containing islands of wealth', as stated in the 2010 UN Habitat Report on *The State of African Cities* (UN Habitat 2010), then it is becoming clear that these islands are under constant threat of being sucked straight back again into the unstable sludge of the urban swamp. There is no escaping the overwhelming whirlpool of the living city's generative but sometimes self-destructive energy. The lack of organised collective political protest that I commented upon in the previous chapter does not mean that the city fails to resist. On the contrary, the 'hole' of the living city strikes back in all kinds of ways and often uses all the decentring power it can muster to force us to reconsider categories we take for granted and common definitions we tend to use in order to figure out the qualities and shortcomings of urban life in Central Africa. In the living city, these decentring forces and energies spring from various (including pre-urban and precolonial) pasts that, even when ruptured, mutilated and mutated by the city, continue to strongly resonate underneath the surface of the 'modern' city. In the process, the urban is remoulded into something else.

As illustrated by various of the 'acupunctures' throughout this book (see Chapter Five on the cemetery of Kintambo, for example), the genealogy of contemporary urban space is shaped not only by forces of colonialist modernity, and more recently the workings of neo-liberalism, but also, and to a considerable extent, through continuations and adaptations of older, longstanding, less discernible though very present social and cultural infrastructures, habituses, moral matrixes and ideas about what constitutes social well-being, for example, or power, wealth, property and collective identity. These are histories of specific modes and forms of mobility and of particular logics of seizure, occupation and distribution. They originate from precisely the kind of social and cultural worlds that (post-)colonial city-planners and investors have tried to ban from the urban surface. Yet, it is this *longue durée* perspective that continues to impact strongly upon the city, that gives it a soul, drives it forward and enables it to grow and expand. Illustrating the need to theorise the urban present beyond the idea of modernity or the 'new' (Robinson 2013), this chapter will look into some of the forms in which these pasts continue to haunt and enchant the urban present and to impact upon the shape of its possible futures.

AUTOCHTHONOUS NOTIONS OF 'COMMONS' AND CONTEMPORARY URBAN GROWTH

April 2013. It is a hot afternoon and Sammy and I sip our Primus beers on the rooftop of a decrepit bar somewhere along Boulevard Lumumba in Masina. We are at a rehearsal of a local Yaka band. Kas Kasongo, the orchestra's young and charismatic lead singer briefly gained national recognition in 2011 with his song *Sisa Bidimbu* in praise of Kabila's 'revolution of modernity' and the new Kinshasa that it promised. Today, Kas seems to have forgotten that he once showered Kabila with praise. The orchestra starts to play an energetic tune that is based on the rhythmical pattern of a standard Yaka folk song, and then Kas's incantatory voice breaks into the rhythm. *Kinshasa ebeba*, he sings, 'the city has rotted', 'And you who live in the village, don't pity yourselves / The Kinshasa that we have migrated to has become a village full of suffering, problems and contradictions / Ah, poor me, Kinshasa has completely deteriorated / And the way to Europe is also closed.'

The next song at the rehearsal is called *Meni N-Yaka* ('I am a muYaka')[1] in which Kas Kasongo relates how 'the baYaka founded Kinshasa':

It is me, the muYaka who created Kinshasa
Kinshasa, the city that feeds young and old
First I settled in Angola
Then I also settled in Lunda [2]
When I noticed that our village had become too crowded I left
Now I am close to the Beach [Kinshasa's port]
I built a canoe to cross the river
[…]
I came to Kinshasa on foot, I did not have an airplane
I came to Kinshasa on foot, I did not have a truck
On my way to Kinshasa I passed the Mount Mangengenge
And I settled in the village of Kintambo
I am the son of the lion and the leopard [3]
When I arrived in Kinshasa there was nobody
The muTeke lived on the other side of the Congo River
The muTeke came from the other side to sell his fish
[…]
In the old days, the White Man asked me: 'What is the name of this place?'
I answered: 'It is Kinshasa.'
'What is this?'
'It is Kinshasa', said the White Man
Kinshasa, the city that feeds young and old
[…]
Me, muYaka, when I went to the Round Table [4]
They covered my eyes with a black tissue
They put three boxes in front of me:
The first one contained gold, the second silver, and the third sand
I chose the sand
Me, King Kyaamvu Panzu, I chose the sand, I chose the land
Land is the thing that young and old revel in

The historical claims that Kas Kasongo makes in this song are somewhat shaky: the original land-owners of what has become Kinshasa were a number of Humbu and Teke chiefs, such as Ngaliema. They, and not the Yaka, were the ones who signed land treaties with Stanley upon his arrival in the Malebo Pool in the late 1870s and early 1880s. But the song does not aim to be a truthful historical account. As an anamnestic exercise in collecting, recollecting, recalling and transforming the tracks of faded pasts, the song is meant to reveal something else. This is the fact that for many people in Kinshasa, and perhaps young people more than anyone else, the available frames of reference to claim an identity and a place for themselves inside the city not only come from the current world of neo-liberal globalisation (and this in spite of the current urban pimping that I described in the previous chapter) but are often rooted in much older local worlds. We are very much used to imagining the city as the hard core of modernity, although perhaps still unfinished at its fringes. In reality, however, many of Kinshasa' inhabitants conquer and domesticate the city, navigate its spaces and infuse it with their own modes of place-making and their own registers of power, value and wealth. These register have little to do with the rationality of modern city planning. Instead they often find their origin in the logic of a sort of pre-urban notion of 'commons', a notion that strongly hinges on, and is deeply rooted in, a precolonial politics of land (*mabele*). It is this notion that structures the city in terms that somehow continue to resonate more strongly than the more alienating official frameworks imposed by state and finance.

In this chapter I want to take a closer look at what this autochthonous notion of 'commons' might still mean in the city today. The city is expanding at an alarming speed, and those who drive that expansion are no longer, or no longer exclusively, the *ya mbala* or the *ya ngwe*, the villagers who migrate from the rural hinterland to the city. Although their influx continues to contribute significantly to the city's rapid expansion, processes of urban growth are also increasingly driven by internal migration within the city. People in the more central parts of the city have now started to move from these older urban centres to the city's fringes. If they own a house in central areas, they may well sell it and build a new house in the periphery in order to escape from all the social and ecological pressures that have become part and parcel of life in the over-populated and promiscuous older parts of the city. A minority of wealthier Kinois may also decide to keep their first house in the city and build or acquire a second or even third property in the new zones of expansion.

The migratory movements from the countryside to the fringes of the city, or from the inner city to the periphery, have given rise to a vast 'peri-urban' landscape (Trefon 2009b) that in terms of its material hardware is often defined by its very generic outlook. Here the city replicates itself in a seemingly endless process of segmentation. The result is a new semi-urban landscape that consists of repetitive but often scaled-down re-runs of the more standardised architectures and general lay-out of older and more established parts of the city. In fact, the emerging new neighbourhoods reference the colonial *ville* less by replicating the architecture of the already existing city, and more by recycling the names of its neighbourhoods, squares, streets, bars and other common points of reference, as if to stress that the new zones of habitation in the merging peri-urban belt are as 'urban' as Kinshasa's colonial heart.

Most of the new constructions in the urban periphery conform to a very rudimentary plan, which mainly entails four walls and a corrugated iron roof. In the emerging peri-urban fringe some parts are in higher demand than others, because they are accessibly located near a main road, for example, or less prone to soil erosion. This is the case for popular areas such as Kinkole, Bibwa and Mpasa, and here you might occasionally also encounter larger walled compounds containing more luxurious housing structures. As mentioned, these often belong to wealthier Kinois from within the city, such as politicians and high-ranking government officials, and increasingly also to Congolese who live abroad. But inevitably, they will not only have to share their new street and neighbourhood with rural newcomers but also with a large, growing group of people who have been pushed out of the inner city because they can no longer afford the rent and the expenses of living there, or simply because they cannot find a space where to live.

To a large extent this process of urban expansion is made possible by Kinshasa's numerous land chiefs who, as the descendants of the original custodians of the land on which the city is built, continue to hold on to large portions of land around the city. These chiefs play a crucial role in the 'opening up' of the urban periphery, a process that is taking place on a vast scale at the city's eastern, southern and western outskirts.

KINSHASA'S LAND CHIEFS AND COLONIAL RULE: Given the history of Kinshasa's land guardians in the last hundred years, it is quite surprising that their presence has endured at all and that they have been able to continue to exert such a strong, though not always officially registered or recognised, influence on the city and its possibilities for spatial expansion. It has been a turbulent history, strongly marked by a colonial politics of repression, by various forms of expulsion, displacement, and forced relocation, as well as by unpredictable administrative reforms aimed at severing land chiefs' ties with their local power bases.

To my knowledge, a comprehensive history of Kinshasa's land chiefs remains to be written, even though the evolution of some of these chiefships has been documented in a rather fragmentary way by some authors (most recently de Saint Moulin 2012; Toulier, Lagae and Gemoets 2010).

The more the land chiefs were engulfed and swallowed up by the city, the less visible and the more marginalised many of them became within the urban fabric. Nowadays, many of the villages and chiefly courts that once constituted the precolonial power landscape of the Pool's southern bank have simply vanished. But in spite of these erasures, the history of the original Humbu and Teke inhabitants of the Pool has never been fully obliterated. Spectres from the past still exist everywhere in Kinshasa, if only because many of the names of former chiefs and villages continue to live on in the city's memory and in the names of its municipalities and neighbourhoods. For example, the neighbourhood of Mombele in the Limete municipality is named after Pierre Mombele, who by claiming direct descent from Ngaliema became the chief representative of all the Teke chiefs of Leopoldville at the Brussels Round Table Conference in 1960.[5]

Limete and numerous other municipalities such as Ngiri-Ngiri, Yolo, Kingabwa, Ngafula and Selembao, have retained the names of local landowning lineages and clans whose villages existed well before the origin of the colonial city.

Often the names no longer correspond with the original historical setting of these villages. This is mainly due to the impact of the colonial politics of urbanisation that was responsible for relocating many of the precolonial villages. In fact, the ongoing expulsion of fishermen's villages due to the building of the *Cité du Fleuve* in Kingabwa merely echoes much earlier forced evacuations and resettlements on a much larger scale in the first half of the twentieth century. In this way, Teke villages along the banks of the Malebo Pool such as Limete, Ngiri-Ngiri and Kingabwa-Mvula had to make way for expanding industrial and port infrastructures. They were relocated by the colonial authorities to other parts of the city. In 1922, for example, Ngiri was forced out of the Kingabwa riverine area and relocated by the colonial urban administration into what became known as *Mboka Sika* or *mboka ya sika*, the 'New Village', a neighbourhood that later became the centre of Ngiri-Ngiri, a new municipality created in the late 1950s. Shortly after Ngiri's removal, Kingabwa suffered the same fate. Following upon the death

Teke land chief Jean Daniel Bambory Popo Mwinkwa,
Mombele neighbourhood, municipality of Limete. March 2015.

of Chief Mvula of Kingabwa in 1939, his village was moved to Mboka Sika by the colonial authorities in 1942, only to be relocated to the Mombele neighbourhood later on.[6]

In spite of the disruptive processes of expulsion and relocation that brutally severed these chiefs' ties with the ancestral lands that constituted the source of their moral and political authority, many nevertheless continued to play a role of some importance within the new urban environment. On various occasions over the past few years, I have seen how some of these chiefs, after so many decades since their removal from the Kingabwa river bank, have continued to be called upon to act as judges in disputes over rights to fishing grounds in the Pool, for example.[7]

Notwithstanding certain continuities, the forced relocations that took place in Leopoldville throughout the period of colonial occupation had a profound impact upon local power balances amongst chiefs and villages during that period. From the earliest days of colonial presence, intrusive colonial land politics caused a great deal of tensions, even outright urban warfare, among the Humbu and Teke clans, who started to fight each other over territorial control of certain areas in the new and alien environment of the city.

Teke land chief Kingakati Mbo (middle) from the clan Musey, *chef de groupement* of Kingakati, on Kinshasa's eastern periphery bordering on the Bateke Plateau. February 2013.

The historical land treaty that Stanley signed with chief Ngaliema is a good example of this. Ngaliema came from the once powerful royal court of the Teke king, Makoko Iloo, on the opposite side of the river.[8] Many years before Stanley's arrival in the Pool area, Ngaliema and other Teke emissaries connected to King Makoko's court had started to cross the river and settle along the Malebo Pool's south bank. The main reason for this Teke colonisation of the southern part of the Pool was to secure Teke fishing rights on both sides of the river and strengthen trading positions along the Pool as well as diplomatic and political relations with local Humbu chiefs who were already occupying this part of the river basin. The Teke had interacted and traded goods and people with these Humbu settlements long before the arrival of the coloniser. Through intricate and still ongoing policies of Humbu-Teke matrimonial alliances, Ngaliema and other Teke chiefs were rapidly integrated into the political, social and economic system of the Pool's southern bank.[9] In this way Ngaliema was incorporated into the court of Ngako, the Humbu chief of the important village of Kintambo (or Ntamo, as it was also called). But when Ngaliema took control of Kintambo after Ngako's death and signed a land treaty with Stanley in August 1881,

Humbu land chief Doona Henriette Nsona Nsasa from the Nzinga clan,
chef de groupement of Lutendele, in the municipality of Mont Ngafula. March 2015.

this angered many of the autochthonous Humbu inhabitants.[10] In their eyes, Ngaliema's authority was subordinate to that of the Kintambo lineage, which in turn owed allegiance to the area's most important Humbu authority, the Makoko (or chief) of Lemba, whose village was situated further inland and later gave its name to one of Leopoldville's main municipalities. These tensions escalated into a series of violent clashes between the Teke and the Humbu. At the end of 1891 or early 1892 and at the height of the Humbu-Teke conflict, the village of Kintambo was sacked and destroyed. A few years previously in 1888, various Teke had already started to seek refuge on the Pool's northern banks, even though French military operations against noncompliant Kongo and Teke villages were in full swing there at the time as well.[11] After the destruction of Kintambo, Ngaliema and many of his Teke followers also crossed the Pool to Brazzaville. And with the world as he knew it rapidly falling apart around him, Ngaliema himself died in exile shortly afterwards in 1892, in the same year as Teke king Makoko Iloo. To my knowledge, no records or witness accounts exist of Ngaliema's funeral, but I imagine that he was buried in a far less glamorous manner than he had imagined for himself.

Teke chief Mikala, sub-chief of Kingakati, at his home in the neighbourhood of Kinkole, municipality of Nsele. March 2013. On the medal (called *mpalata*) he wears is written in French and Flemish: *sous-chefferie indigène Congo-Belge / inlandsche onder-hoofdij Belgisch-Congo* (indigenous sub-chief Belgian Congo).

Ten years after Ngaliema's death, Leopoldville had completely swallowed whatever was left of Kintambo village. It disappeared as if it had never even existed, and today only the baobab in the garden of Bibi's Place, a local dancing club near the *Kintambo Magasin* roundabout, is a reminder of this troubled past.

And yet, the new city did not manage to completely erase the older political histories of its original inhabitants. Conflicts and fights between Humbu, Teke and other ethnic groups about the territorial control of the city and the Pool continued well into the twentieth century, and added yet another layer to the already considerable history of violence that the colonial presence had initiated. In fact, the colonial policy that was responsible for the removal of chiefs along the Pool's south bank also created a local power vacuum that was perceived by other ethnic groups from upstream areas along the Congo waterway, such as the Bobangi and the Banunu from Bolobo and Ntsei, as an opportunity to gain control over the old trading networks in the Pool. The Bobangi had been trading smoked fish, slaves, pottery and iron implements with the Teke of the Pool long before the arrival of Stanley, and the big men and chiefs of these two groups were related to one another through ritual ties of blood brotherhood and alliances.

Humbu land chief Bernard Mapesa of the clan Nvula-Nene (Kimvula), neighbourhood of Mitendi, municipality of Mont Ngafula. March 2015.

But until 1892, the Teke alone had set the trading rules in the Pool. For a while, they even managed to successfully bar the Bobangi from selling ivory to Europeans (cf. Vansina 1973b: 428). But after Ngaliema's death and the Teke's weakening territorial grip over the Pool due to colonial interference, clashes between Teke and Bobangi became increasingly frequent in Leopoldville, especially between 1920 and 1940.

The relocation and resettlement policy of the colonial ruler was responsible for the fact that many of Leopoldville's original landowning lineages gradually lost control over their land resources, even though they still consider this land to be rightfully theirs nowadays, as we will see further ahead. However, they are rarely able to produce proper records of land ownership to substantiate these claims. This is hardly surprising seeing that the absence of land title deeds in itself results from a long and brutal history of colonial and postcolonial land reforms.

These reforms have also dramatically complicated the very notion of 'traditional' precolonial commons. Prior to the arrival of Stanley and his men, a land chief, who was often the head of the longest established lineage in a village, exercised authority over land allocation in a village and the villagers held usufruct rights to the land, which they

Teke land chief Ima Ngande Munke from the clan Inkianu,
chef de groupement of Nguma, in the municipality of Maluku. March 2013.

used in frequently complex systems of shifting cultivation. These systems are still very much in place in large parts of the country, but colonial rule in the Congo Free State (1885-1908) and the Belgian Congo (1908-1960) profoundly altered the legal principles that organised and underpinned access and entitlement to land before the arrival of the colonisers. During the colonial era, new land law systems were established to favour the exploitation of the country's natural resources by the new rulers and redefined large parts of the country as 'vacant land', a label that was never clearly defined and often ignored the hunting and gathering rights of local groups of inhabitants. Moreover, lineage lands that local villagers purposefully allowed to lie fallow for future farming were often considered to be 'vacant' by the colonial system. This allowed the colonial authorities to annex this land, thereby radically reducing the political authority of land-owning lineages across the colony, while creating the possibility of relocating and shifting entire populations around.

POSTCOLONIAL LAND REFORMS: In addition to these profound changes introduced during the colonial period, the controversial Bakajika land reform of 1966 further

268

Humbu land chief Mutsendi Dimasa Rima, clan Mpanzu Kaba, of the *groupement* Mbenseke-Mfuti, on Kinshasa's western periphery. March 2015.

complicated land matters. In June 1966, the Congolese government promulgated the Bakajika Law, which was aimed at undoing colonial concessions granted before independence. The new land law foreshadowed Mobutu's anti-colonialist 'return to authenticity' campaign and was heavily promoted at the time by the emerging regime's propaganda machinery as an attempt to break the former coloniser's continuing hold over land,[12] but in reality it did nothing to return land ownership to local autochthonous groups, who continued to regard this land as part of their ancestral heritage. On the contrary, the Bakajika Law was the first in a series of postcolonial laws designed to ensure stronger government control over land and mineral resources. The new land law system effectively continued the colonial system of land control, which enabled state ownership of all wealth 'above and below' the ground thereby ensuring that public mineral rights went to the government. The new laws did not fully abrogate pre-existing customary land rights, and as a result of the new legal framework, customary law as codified under colonial rule formally ceased to be a legitimate source of land rights. The new legal framework also left the future concessionary status of these lands very unclear (Kisangani and Bobb 2010: 36-37). In the end, the Bakajika legislation further alienated

Humbu land chief Martin Lusala Mayindu, *chef de groupement* of Kimwenza Matadi Mayo together with his sister (doona), in the municipality of Mont Ngafula. March 2015.

local populations from their lands and paved the way for a great deal of legal uncertainty.[13]

As mentioned earlier, what continues to complicate matters greatly even today is the fact that privately owned land is rarely properly registered. This is as true in Kinshasa as it is in the rest of the Democratic Republic of Congo. Tenure remains a very precarious thing in Congo because of the fact that clear and effective land titles have almost never been established.[14] This makes it difficult to use land as collateral for a loan, for example, and it has discouraged farmers from investing capital on essential land improvements needed to increase agricultural production. As noted by Meditz and Merrill (1994: 171), the land situation in the 1980s and 90s was exacerbated by the limited government resources available to embark on a large-scale land registration as well as the common practice among concession holders of bribing local officials to postpone indefinitely investigations of further development activities on the concession.

This observation remains as true today as it was in the early 1990s. Political interference has also exacerbated land disputes and obstructed their resolution, while the theft or disappearance of documents and files relating to land disputes by corrupt government officials, judges, army officers, businessmen and family members of land

Humbu land chief Ngandu Ndola Mabela, *chef de groupement* of Mikondo, at his home in the municipality of Kimbanseke. March 2013.

chiefs is another common practice that has added to the number of unresolved land disputes (see below). This is clearly illustrated in recent evictions and land conflicts in the Kingabwa marshlands, an area under pressure because of the opportunities that the construction of the *Cité du Fleuve* will supposedly bring.

MATRILINEAL PRINCIPLES UNDER PRESSURE: The state is not alone in complicating land matters. Land chiefs themselves often challenge each other's authority, and the fact that the boundaries of their lands have never been clearly demarcated further intensifies conflicts between different land-holding lineages. However, what most debilitates the notion of 'traditional commons' is the frequent infighting amongst relatives within many of the Humbu and Teke chiefly lineages. The title of land chief is normally passed down along matrilineal lines, usually from mother's brother to sister's son, although in Humbu landowning lineages, it is not uncommon for a *doona*, that is, a sister of a deceased land chief, to inherit the title temporarily if no suitable candidates are available among the chief's sister's children. However, in the city today, these principles of matrilineal inheritance have come under increasing pressure.[15] More often than not,

Humbu land chief David Ebalavo, head of the Mbuku
Mvemba Mavuba clan. Municipality of Lemba. March 2015.

such rules are contested by the chiefs' own children, who believe that they, rather than their matrilineal cross cousins, should have a right to the title of land chief. Apart from the already considerable intergenerational tensions that currently exist in Kinshasa (cf. Chapter Five), we can see a major switch from a matrilineal to a more patrilineal system of *de facto* inheritance in which elders are constantly overruled by their own offspring. The latter frequently start to sell land on their own account, even if they do not have the right to do so according to standard Humbu/Teke hereditary kin-based mechanisms of land control and 'ownership' rights. What this boils down to in practice is that the same plot of land might be 'sold' several times by different individuals from one land lineage to several different buyers. Local police officers and administrative agents who have to register the land sales are often part of the game, as it offers a chance to increase their meagre wages. It is not hard to imagine to what extent this evolution forms the basis of lasting land disputes and adds to the already existing general confusion and legal insecurity surrounding land and property ownership.

Let me illustrate this with the case of Samuel Mandefu Bie, the current chief of the old Teke-Humbu landowning lineage of Kimbangu village, one of the most important precolonial villages together with Kintambo and Kinshasa. Although the village itself has been completely eaten up by the city, chief Mandefu still lives in the same compound where the first colonisers encountered his predecessor at the end of the nineteenth century. This compound is located slightly to the east of Kingabwa, in what is currently known as the Petro-Congo neighbourhood of the municipality of Masina.

It is only a short distance away from Bylex's house (see Chapter Seven) and not very far from where the small Tshangu River enters the mighty Pool. The chiefly court is easy to find on Kimbangu Avenue because of a giant baobab tree, which is said to have been planted by Stanley's men [16] and grows in the centre of the compound. Local oral history also has it that the prophet Simon Kimbangu, who was arrested by the colonial authorities in June 1921 but managed to escape, rested under this tree while on the run. [17] At the back of the compound is a small cemetery where former chiefs lie buried.

One of these former chiefs was Paul Imbali. As one of the informants of the Jesuit demographer and academic Léon de Saint Moulin, parts of his biography have been relatively well documented (cf. de Saint Moulin 2012). During Paul Imbali's reign, the colonial state requisitioned a large portion of his lineage's land. It was on this land that the international airport of Ndjili was built in 1953. However, even after the construction of the airport, Imbali continued to sell parts of the same land to various other parties. As a result, he was sentenced to several years in jail, which he spent in various prisons throughout the country. During his absence, the colonial administration replaced him with a certain Louis Mbimi. But when Imbali eventually returned home shortly after independence, he took up his chiefly position again until his death in the mid-1980s. After his death, the title of chief was supposed to pass on to his sister, a certain Mama Mambwala, but the latter refused to take on this responsibility and handed the title to another member of the family instead. This new chief was called Jacques Kwe, but he drowned in the Congo River only a short time after his investiture.

Paul Imbali, Masina Petro-Congo, early 1970s.

Daniel Ngangwele.

273

Thereupon, Mama Mambwala, in her position as power broker and king maker, decided to give the title to Daniel Ngangwele, one of Imbali's four official children, even though Imbali was not Daniel's biological father. Daniel's mother had previously been married to a man who had died shortly after his son's birth. Daniel's mother had then married Imbali and moved into his polygamous household with her son.

The fact that Daniel Ngangwele was only chief Imbali's adoptive son was not, however, the primary reason that Imbali's other children (two sons and a daughter, Bibiane Ngamayele) disputed Mama Mambwala's choice. The real reason might have been that, towards the end of his life, Imbali himself disinherited his adoptive son. He apparently took this decision when it was discovered that Daniel had been having an affair with one of his father's wives.

Whatever the reason may have been, Daniel's enthronement was the start of a struggle between Daniel and his two brothers, who both died in the 1990s, as well as with his sister, Bibiane. When Daniel Ngangwele himself died in 2009, Mama Mambwala, a very old woman by then, managed to outmanoeuvre Bibiane, who considered that the title should finally become hers, by handing it instead to

274

Daniel Ngangwele (far right) with Joseph Kabila and other land chiefs from Kinshasa (such as chief Kingakati to the far left).

Samuel Mandefu, one of Paul Imbali's sisters' sons. Samuel Mandefu had been Daniel Ngangwele's chauffeur for years and had been very close to his uncle. His enthronement therefore made a lot of sense in the eyes of many, because it also meant a return to the standard matrilineal succession procedure that had been upset by Daniel Ngangwele's own succession to the title. But while Mandefu's enthronement conformed to recognised rules of succession and was formally endorsed by the urban authorities in 2010, it did not succeed in ending the family conflict. On the contrary, both Bibiane Ngamayele and one of Daniel Ngangwele's own sons, Tati Imbali Mukoo, refused to recognise Mandefu as the legal heir to the title, and claimed the title as rightfully theirs instead. Early in 2010, Tati even set up his own parallel court in his father's compound, near the old baobab tree. Tati and several of his siblings also consigned the old and frail chief Mandefu, who until then had been living in the compound's main house, to a small shack at the back of the family plot. In fact, between 2012 and 2015, I visited the compound several times and each time Tati and his siblings made it impossible for me to speak to Mandefu. It was only during my last visit in March 2015 that I finally managed to speak to the old man himself while Tati was in jail because of a land dispute

Samuel Mandefu Biye. Municipality of Masina,
Petro-Congo neighbourhood. March 2015.

275

that opposed him to both Mandefu and Bibiane. At that point, Mandefu was in very bad physical shape for he too had spent several months in prison due to the same land affair in which Tati and Bibiane were involved. In fact, independently from each other, Bibiane and Tati had started to sell plots of agricultural marshland in the neighbourhoods of Mapela and Abattoir, land that they considered part of Daniel Ngangwele's 'heritage' but that had already been sold to a number of incoming settlers from the Brazzaville side of the Pool by Mandefu in the meantime. These simultaneous sales led to an internal family conflict that came to a head on 2 September 2010 when Tati was abducted in broad daylight at a bus stop in the Masina Petro-Congo neighbourhood by uniformed men. In the evening of the same day, the same uniformed men forced themselves into Samuel Mandefu's house and kidnapped him as well. Both men were taken to an undisclosed place, where they were tortured and robbed of their personal belongings before being released twenty-four hours later. Tati subsequently took the matter to court. There it was found that the uniformed men, who claimed to be members of a non-existent Joseph Kabila Special Intelligence Service (*Division special de renseignements de Joseph Kabila* – DSRJK) and to have acted

Tati Imbali Mukoo. Municipality of Masina, Petro-Congo neighbourhood. March 2013.

on direct orders of the president's immediate entourage (the *Domaine de la Présidence*), had actually been hired by Bibiane. In spite of this evidence, Bibiane won the court case and was acquitted. In the following years Tati and Bibiane continued to contest each other in court, which finally lead to the arrest and imprisonment of both Tati and Mandefu in 2014.

It is clear that Bibiane could not have pulled this off without some serious backing from a number of other, more important actors. As we will see in the next section, these included high ranking army officers and members of the public administration who were powerful enough to successfully bribe court judges. All of them were using Bibiane's (unrightful) claim to the status of chiefly heir to cash in on her illegal land sales. And while Bibiane skilfully manipulated these contacts and networks to triumph over the other family members, it also catapulted her into a different and more dangerous power game with mightier opponents.

The following section will further use the case of Bibiane and her family to illustrate to what extent chiefly families continue to play a crucial but also very complex and ambivalent role in urban land issues and to show how the land claims made by (often internally weakened and divided) chiefly lineages become part of a much broader competition over land that characterises the ways in which politics of space is played out on a large scale in Kinshasa more generally.

COMPETING CLAIMS ON URBAN SPACE. THE COMPLEXITY OF LAND ISSUES IN KINSHASA'S MARSHES: The enforced removal of several Teke villages from the river banks of the Malebo Pool in the first half of the twentieth century freed up a great deal of space. Most of it was rapidly filled in by an industrial and port infrastructure, but many of the more marshy areas along the river bank remained unused until Emmanuel Capelle, the head of the colonial administration for the indigenous *cités* of Leopoldville between 1945 and 1952, suggested that a green belt, a *ceinture agricole* (Capelle 1947: 52), should be created around the city to promote peasant horticulture there. This, Capelle strongly felt, was needed to feed the rapidly expanding city, while it would also keep part of Leopoldville's booming population busy and check their 'idleness'. To this end, from 1954 onwards, plots in the marshy area where the Ndjili River enters the Pool were allotted mainly to unemployed women who had recently migrated from the rural hinterlands to the city. A number of kitchen gardens was set up in an attempt to put these women to work.

After independence, the colonial project of peasant horticulture was resuscitated and expanded (Mianda 1996:93). Promoted by the Department of Agriculture and Rural Development and with the support and co-operation of the French, the scope of the initial colonial project was considerably extended during Mobutu's reign (1965-1997). At the end of this period, horticulture in the Pool encompassed most of

the marshlands between Kingabwa and Ndjili airport, and vegetable production in this area started to play an important role in Kinshasa's economy, providing fresh vegetables to markets throughout the city.

Ever since then, the Malebo Pool's south side has steadily transformed into a vast agricultural zone. In the 1980s, a South Korean agricultural company started to develop rice paddies in the Malebo Pool near Kingabwa, but this project was abandoned after widespread waves of looting that hit Kinshasa in 1991 and 1993. After the Koreans had left, the local population quickly moved in to occupy the rice paddies, and it did not take long before they started to expand them, often empoldering the Pool's marshes with very basic tools such as shovels, and even their own bare hands.

In this fashion, the inhabitants of the neighbourhoods along the Congo River, from Kingabwa all the way to Nsele and Mikonga, have continued to convert large parts on the DRC side of the Pool into arable land. By now, in certain areas such as the mouth of the river Tshangu near the Ndjili airport, the empoldered area is already reaching several kilometres into the Malebo Pool (De Boeck 2011).

As Mianda reports, even after the introduction of the Bakajika land law that

abolished customary kinship rules determining access to land, these rules continued to co-exist with the new state law. 'As a result', she states, 'those who wish to undertake garden production in Kinshasa must first negotiate with the chiefs and then acquire the title to the land from the civil authorities' (Mianda 1996: 93). This remains the case even today in that access to a piece of horticultural marshland often needs to be negotiated with local chiefs, although in theory it is the urban, provincial and national administration that has the right to allocate the land to farmers, and although the farmers themselves have started to contest both the chiefs' and the state's authority over these polders. According to the farmers, this is land that had not previously existed but that was created by means of their own labour and efforts, which therefore gives them every right to occupy it and consider it to be their own property. (In fact, their argument of ownership through the principle of what is called *creatio ex nihilo* in Roman Law is also used by the *Cité du Fleuve* management: since they created the islands out of nothing, they feel that Kinshasa's land chiefs' claims — that given that the islands are built in the river, which is ancestral territory, they should therefore be compensated by the *Cité du Fleuve* for the occupation of this territory — fails to make any sense.)

However, the farmers' claim is contested not only by land chiefs but also by urban authorities. From the National — and since the administrative decentralisation reform (see Trefon 2009a) increasingly from the Provincial Ministry of Agriculture to the Governor and all the way down to the municipal level, these various administrative organs have been making attempts to impose a legal framework in order to direct, control and, above all, tax these new farming activities on often previously non-existent land. Each farmer is supposed to make a payment of $200 to the land registry office of the province of Kinshasa.[18] This is the prerequisite in order to obtain a *contrat d'exploitation* ('operating contract') from the Urban Division for Rural Development ($10), and a *permis d'exploitation agricole* ('agricultural operating license') (another $10) from the Inspection of Rural Development and Agriculture, a unit on the municipal level. Only after meeting all these administrative measures can someone officially acquire the usufruct rights to a small horticultural plot (usually no more than two to six acres) for as long as they want on condition that they can prove it is continuously cultivated. In theory, the municipality is supposed to send an inspector to check on this once a year. In practice, however, none of these regulations and procedures is

applied in any straightforward manner. The inspector rarely comes, and since none of this land is shown on any official map, the authorities in many cases have no knowledge of which surface area of land should be taxed.

In fact, the Pool's huge garden belt is organised outside any clearly defined form of government control on the ground. The actual 'ownership' of these gardens is in the hands of some eighty farmers' associations that represent more than a thousand farmers, most of whom are women. These associations have divided the riverine farmlands into fourteen *secteurs* (Kingabwa sectors 1, 2 and 3, Rail 1 and 2, Tshangu, Mapela / Abattoir, Mafuta Kizola, Lokali 1 and 2, Tshunge-Masina, Tshunge-Nsele, Mikonga 1 and 2) which, in turn, are sub-divided into a varying number of *blocs* or 'squares', each consisting of hundreds of tiny garden plots that, as mentioned before, rarely exceed two or six acres. A *président de secteur*, who officially represents the level of the municipality but in reality acts totally independently, is aided by a number of *chefs de bloc* and oversees the farming activities in each sector. He also organises and oversees the contacts with the thousands of women who each day buy up the gardens' produce and ensure that vegetables are distributed throughout a large part of the city's numerous markets.

Farmers within each 'square' and sector all know each other well, hold regular meetings and regularly collaborate with one another, but these structures of cooperation and solidarity can also easily unravel. Garden plots are in high demand and holding on to one is a relentless struggle. Maintaining a claim to a garden plot requires constant physical presence and occupation. If, due to illness or some other reason, a farmer fails to show up for a couple of days, her co-farmers will not hesitate to rent it out to another person who will immediately take over her place and hold on to it for as long as possible. As with the examples of the market women under the Building, the men repairing potholes (see Chapter Three) and the Kintambo cemetery gravediggers (Chapter Five), one can never be sure of 'ownership' of a strategic spot or place. As these other examples reveal, while the extreme atomisation and morcellation of space makes it possible for someone to claim a spot as their own, this also complexifies this ownership because of the constant need to negotiate their presence with a multitude of others who make similar claims. If presence is an absolute must to stake out a claim, it is also determinedly contested. This in turn regularly results in disputes and conflicts.

Skirmishes, confrontations and contestations of this kind not only take place on

this 'micro-scale' (Ansoms, Wagemakers, Walker and Murison 2014) but also spread out to other levels. Again, the riverine fields provide a good example. Since agricultural land is in high demand in Kinshasa (cf. Wagemakers and Makangu 2011; Wagemakers, Makangu, De Herdt and Kitshiaba 2011), the creation of new arable land in the Malebo Pool has led to innumerable and sometimes violent clashes in which the parties involved contest one another's ownership and right over previously non-existent land.

In the riverine area under consideration, these conflicts are mainly played out first between the farmers' associations and the Teke and Humbu land chiefs, such as the family of chief Mandefu, as was mentioned before. Let us therefore return briefly to the case of Mandefu, Tati and Bibiane.

Mandefu and his family have basically run out of land to sell along the riverbanks of the densely populated municipality of Masina. As previously explained, a large part of the communal lands in the care of this lineage was confiscated by the colonial state in order to build the airport of Ndjili, and whatever land remained afterwards has long since been parcelled out. That is the reason why Mandefu, Bibiane and Tati turned to these newly available plots of horticultural land, claiming ownership rights over what

they themselves consider to be 'ancestral' land (even if that land was non-existent twenty years ago). All three of them started to sell large stretches of horticultural marshlands in the Mapela sector to individuals and families. They did so without the farmers' consent, even though the farmer associations of the Mapela sector had previously negotiated access to and 'ownership' of this land with chief Paul Imbali, the father of Bibiane and grandfather of Tati. All of this lead to a multi-sited conflict in which the farmers opposed not only Mandefu, Bibiane and Tati, who were already fighting amongst themselves, but also the various new 'owners' of these illegally sold plots. These new owners also started fighting one another, as the same plot had sometimes been sold simultaneously to two or more people. All these conflicts, however, did not discourage newcomers from moving into the Mapela area in their hundreds. The farmers' marshlands were thus transformed extremely rapidly into a shanty area, and in the process a large portion of the farmer's plots was destroyed. By 2010, a considerable number of shacks had emerged in what is essentially a very unhealthy swamp that is totally unfit for habitation as it lacks even the most basic infrastructure in terms of water, electricity and sanitation, and is regularly flooded.[19]

What complicated matters even more is that the farmers, the competing 'chiefs' (Mandefu, Tati and Bibiane) and the owners of the newly-constructed houses were each backed by various administrative and judicial actors on the municipal and the provincial level. This created a highly explosive situation leading to violent clashes among the various parties involved. In late 2009, for example, the farmers turned for support to the Provincial Minister of Agriculture and Rural Development, Mr Noel Botakile. He promised to help the farmers, even though in the meantime some of the exact same land in the Mapela/Abbatoir sector had been leased out by the office of the Governor of Kinshasa to a Chinese agricultural development project known as MAC (*Mission Agricole Chinoise*).[20] However, in response to the farmers' appeal to the Ministry, Bibiane successfully mobilised her military associates. As a result, a number of soldiers were posted in and around the expanding shanty area to protect shack owners from the attacks of furious farmers reclaiming 'their' fields. The conflict further escalated in early 2010 when these soldiers opened fire at policemen who were accompanying the provincial Minister Noel Botakile during one of his visits to the disputed site. The minister subsequently ordered the shacks to be destroyed. Bibiane retaliated by taking the farmers' association, MAC and the Ministry to court in order to secure her interests, as well as those of the army officers who were backing her behind the scenes. The first court hearing took place on 8 November 2010 at the *Tribunal de Grande Instance* (TGI) of Ndjili, in the presence of Minister Botakile himself.[21] Also present were Pierre Bukasa (the president of the *Union Nationale des agriculteurs, éleveurs et pêcheurs du Congo*) and two representatives of the city's public administration. It seems that Bibiane's lawyers successfully bribed the court instances because further hearings were postponed and to my knowledge the court has never reached a firm conclusion since then. To this day, Bibiane has not been ordered to return the illegally sold land to the farmers.

The complexity of this specific case, with its multitude of opposing actors and stakeholders on various interconnected formal and informal levels, is by no means unique in Kinshasa. A bit further downstream from the Mapela area, conflicts have been unfolding with a similar intensity and complexity. In some cases, land conflicts are fought out between rival politicians, as in a recent Kingabwa land dispute that was much covered in the local press and involved two high-profile politicians, Mr Mukonzo and Mr Gecoco Mulumba, who is also known as 'Papa Social'. Other conflicts over land have pitched farming associations, civil servants, land chiefs and private investors against one another in constantly changing constellations.

URBAN EXPANSION AND THE OPENING UP OF LAND IN THE CITY'S RURAL PERIPHERY: Land conflicts and disputes of this nature are common all over Kinshasa, but their level of intensity can vary greatly. In the Pool, where access to new land is limited and where the chiefs' control over land has grown extremely weak (a fact often exacerbated by the landowning lineages' internal crises and unravellings), the arrival of the *Cité du Fleuve* and of a number of other developments, including industrial ones, have undeniably raised the stakes and intensified the level of conflict.[22] This is the case to a far lesser extent in other and often more peripheral parts of the city, where land chiefs, such as several Teke and Humbu chiefs in the city's eastern and western periphery, have managed to hold on to their lands a great deal more firmly. Some of the chiefs in these areas have been assimilated into the fabric of the urban and provincial administration as *chefs de groupement*. Today, twenty-one chiefs in Kinshasa are recognised by the state as *chefs de groupement*, which means that they have official, albeit limited, administrative authority over land matters in their administrative *groupement* unit.[23]

However, numerous other chiefs are also active in each of the twenty-one *groupements* and two *chefferies* or chiefdoms that are recognized by the state administration across the territory of Kinshasa. Under the umbrella of the official administrative architecture that includes *chefs de groupement*, there remains a much broader hierarchical political network stretching across the whole of Kinshasa province and far beyond and with roots in a precolonial territorial politics defined by kinship and alliance. Whatever their legal status or official administrative function, all these other chiefs and subchiefs (*kapita*) within that wider web continue to exert their influence over land matters. Some of these chiefs are recognised by the state as *chefs coutumier*, a title that excludes them from any immediate administrative authority (as in the case of Mandefu, for example). However, many others are simply not recognised by the state at all, even though they too continue to play an active role with regard to land matters.

Chiefs still control large tracts of land particularly in the more rural parts of Kinshasa province to the south-west of the city in the urban districts of Lukunga, Funa and Mont Amba, and to the east in the urban district of Tshangu as well as on the Bateke Plateau.[24] It is no coincidence that these are also the areas of expansion for the city itself nowadays. In this process of rapid urban growth, these land chiefs play a far more decisive role than what may seem justified by their low or non-existent administrative status seeing that it is simply impossible for an individual, a real estate company or an industrial investor to obtain a piece of land without preliminary negotiations with them.

After negotiating with a chief over of a piece of land and making a first payment, which is defined in terms of a 'gift', the buyer receives a document, which is often a mere handwritten note signed by the chief or one of his representatives.[25] This note, which acknowledges the buyer's intent to settle on the land, is needed when the buyer presents himself or herself at the local police station and the office of the *chef de quartier*.

Once the chief's letter is made official by their stamping the document in question, the buyer can then start to legalise the property by going through all the different administrative levels and procedures, which go from the municipal level all the way up to the Land Registry at the *Hôtel de Ville*. This is a process that may take many years to complete and requires substantial sums of money to be paid at each level of the administrative hierarchy. Meanwhile back on the piece of land obtained from the local land chief, the buyer has to prove genuine intention to occupy it. The best way to do so is to start fencing the plot and building something on it. This needs to be done within three years after acquisition of the plot,[26] or else the land will automatically return to the chief and give him the right to sell it again to another party. Many chiefs, however, do not bother to wait that long and they resell the land before the end of this period, or else they sell the same plot to different buyers at the same time. In other cases, the chief's own children might sell the same plot to someone else without their father's knowledge or consent. All these instances trigger conflicts, litigations and legal suits that people can never be certain to win.

More importantly, however, chiefs will never interpret a land sale as being something final. It never severs their deep historical ties to that land. In their mind, therefore, they do not sell the land itself, but merely the usufruct right to that land. No matter what state law might have to say about this, as far as these chiefs are concerned the land is inalienable ancestral heritage and will therefore always remain theirs.

What 'selling' the land often means to them is not so much that it brings in money but that it represents a specific moment that sets in motion the possibility of exchange; it offers chiefs an opportunity to extend their own networks and reshape the city into an arena that allows them to generate 'tributary' dependencies with the person who 'receives' land and with the state who has to formalise the land sale. Rather than selling land, chiefs 'give' land. In this way, a land settlement is converted into a never-ending deal that will have to be renegotiated time and again by the occupant of the plot, and will have to be reconfirmed through the 'circulation of gifts' that strengthen the relational ties between the patron (the chief) and his client. Chiefs thereby infuse the space of the city with their own political economy and morality of gift exchange. This allows them to personalise the city's institutional level, and re-institutionalise the personal sphere into alternative networks and spaces of palaver, exchange and complicity that enable a circulation of commodities, money and people in ways with which these chiefs are more familiar and can better master and control. In this way, chiefs do not only recast their relationship with the new occupant of 'their' land, they also manage, in various degrees and with varying success, to redefine their relationship with the city and the state in terms of their own more personalised 'feudal' structures of deliberation, sharing of power and distribution of wealth. That, in the end, is the real value of land for these chiefs: it allows them to redefine a mere patron-client relationship with the state, in which they officially occupy the subordinate position, and turn it into a more empowering political economy of exchange in which these political and economic relations with the state can be shifted and turned around. A good illustration of this is the fact that even people at the highest levels of state power, including the president and the city's governor, are forced to take the existence of these chiefs into account if they want to acquire land. This fact was brought home to me in March 2012 when I accompanied a friend of mine to Bibwa, an old village located in the neighbourhood of Mpasa III (in the municipality of Nsele, on Kinshasa's eastern outskirts, near Mount Mangengenge) to negotiate the acquisition of a small plot of land under the care of the local land chief of Bibwa, chief Munziami Lita, an old man who is also a healer and renowned for his skills as a bonesetter.

We were guided to a small house where chief Munziami was treating his patients. When he finally finished, he invited us to his own compound, easily distinguishable because of an old baobab tree that overshadowed the chief's main house. At the back of the house, there was again a small cemetery that held the remains of some of Munziami's predecessors and other relatives. After offering the chief a standard opening gift, consisting of some kola nuts and salt, a piece of red loincloth[27] and a bottle of whisky, my friend started to negotiate the conditions of the sale, and before long he had reached an agreement with old Munziami. Afterwards, we walked to the allotment in the company of one of Munziami's grandsons, who mentioned how lucky my friend was to have been given this plot of land, because his new neighbour would now be Mama Olive, President Kabila's wife and Congo's First Lady. Apparently, she too had recently come to Munziami's courtyard with gifts to obtain land with a view to constructing a gated apartment community in this much coveted part of the city. After a brief negotiation, Munziami 'gave' her twelve plots adjacent to that of my friend. The fact that in order to access land, even Kabila's wife felt obliged to sit down with chief Munziami, who is not a *chef de groupement* and therefore has no immediate official function in the city's administration, is quite telling and indicates the chiefs' continuing hold over land; a hold that allows them to infuse the space of the state with their own political and moral economy of exchange, an economy still so powerful that it succeeds to force the state to adapt to its terms, and even manages to convert the president's wife into a client.

In the end, what this also means is that the postcolonial city is only capable of growing and expanding thanks to actors whose frame of reference is not that of the state, nor of colonialist modernity or postcolonial neo-liberal agendas. Instead, it is rooted in the kinds of rural and precolonial worlds that the coloniser tried so hard to eradicate and the city itself has wanted to expel from its surface. Paradoxically, an important way forward for the city to exist in the future seems to reside in a past that, upon closer inspection, has never stopped to invade and re-territorialise the space of the urban.

It is this paradox that ultimately constitutes Ngaliema's revenge on this city that not only wiped him out but also changed forever the precolonial autochthonous worlds that constituted the horizon of his life. More than ever, and against all odds, land chiefs continue to emerge as crucial figures in the making of the contemporary city. Holding the key to land they do not legally own but nevertheless consider theirs, they are the ones who open up a city yet to come. And it is in this capacity of land guardians that chiefs act as crucial safety and relief valves by means of which the city is capable of reducing the demographic pressures that would otherwise cause it to explode and make it totally unliveable.

At the same time, their position also remains fundamentally ambiguous and double-edged. Within the urban context, the figure of the chief is both respected and strongly contested. There is no denying the fact that the chiefs' continued involvement in land matters operates as a very efficacious form of urban sabotage that deeply disturbs, perverts and deregulates the city's functioning on the institutional level as well as in daily life. Triggering a lot of legal uncertainty and conflict, their presence engenders a range of shady deals and an endless carrousel of trade-offs and arrangements that make a more rational management of the city virtually impossible, thereby turning life in the city into a constant struggle. Of course, chiefs themselves are never in full control of the game either, and their power is also often reduced and weakened by the city. But on certain levels, the specific moral and political economy they inject into the city is powerful enough to force the state and the formal official political domain to adapt to its logic. Concomitantly, it also provides more inclusive openings for a large part of Kinshasa's inhabitants who feel abandoned by the state and excluded from the city. The social, moral, political and economic frameworks that these chiefs embody still resonate strongly with many of these urban dwellers, and as Kas Kasongo's song in the beginning of this chapter illustrated, they also continue to offer anchorage points of (ethnic) identification and belonging in the city that does not otherwise offer them a place.

Humbu land chief Munziami Lita and some of his sons.
Bibwa neighbourhood, municipality of Nsele. March 2015.

9. Coda:
Occupation and the
Politics of (Co-)Presence

Through text and image, and also by means of various 'urban acupunctures', this book has tried to capture the many ruptures and historical fault lines that run through Kinshasa, the many discontinuities that have marked and scarred the urban landscape and have sometimes left very visible, although always complex and never fully transparent, traces and marks on the skin of the city. These scars continue to inform the multilayered physical and mental landscapes that constitute Kinshasa today. At the same time, this book also explores the underlying continuities that link the present of Kinshasa to its various pasts and also inform the possible shapes of its future, although, here again, the lines that link past, present and future are never straight or uncomplicated.

What has emerged from this, I hope, is a city that is by no means a monolithic entity. Kinshasa is always a crowd, a multitude, an amalgamation of a great number of heterogeneous things and people. This is a city that was — and continues to be — shaped by endless, brutal and violent histories of oppression, suppression and repression. However, it has also received its form and force through equally long genealogies of hope, of powerful dreams and various lines of desire, of release and fulfilment, even though the latter rarely materialise in long and lasting ways. And every time the city revolts against the darker dynamics of its own coming into being (and, in the process, sometimes mistakes darkness for light and vice versa), it has a tendency to unravel, and then to reconstruct itself and unravel again. And each time, when the city tends to disintegrate and then vigorously piece itself back together, it does so in ways that are always unexpected and surprising, often unanticipated and never totally predictable.

The enormous capacity of the city to undo itself and then suture and stitch itself back together again from scratch is almost always rooted in spaces and through practices that are situated outside the spaces of officialdom and the spheres of formal and institutionalized action. An ever-changing giant jigsaw puzzle, the city thus feeds off the multi-layered shards of its own different pasts. The constantly changing constellations between all these different spatial fragments and splintering chronologies provide the city of today with a fragile and unsteady continuity and with some (semblance of) internal cohesion.

Simultaneously, these constant processes of splintering and suturing, of oscillating between zero and one, also constitute the city's initial disorder, its enduring opacity and pervasive lack of translucence and clarity. The city can never be taken for granted and its *mistik*, that 'mystery' so specific to Kinshasa, needs constant elucidation. That is how such a city generates its own identity, energy and drive: in its different public and more intimate or secret places and sites, and through the voices and practices of a wide variety of diverse characters that simultaneously give birth to the city and kill it, just like the city kills and gives birth to them.

As this book illustrates, the city here reveals itself not the product of careful planning or engineering, but rather the outcome of a randomly produced and occupied living space, which, as I have argued, belongs to whomsoever generates it, seizes and uses it. Fields, buildings, cemeteries, plots of land and even potholes in the street thus become sites of never-ending cycles of occupation. But occupation also always implies a letting go. In Roman Law, *occupatio* meant that ownerless things that were susceptible to private ownership could become the property of the first person to take possession of them. But in Congo's urban worlds, there never is such a 'first person', even though vocabularies of firstcomers and latecomers are constantly made use of to stake a claim or to argue one's right to occupy. In reality, however, there never is a *terra nullius*, a 'nobody's land', a ground zero, that can be occupied first. Inevitably, there is already an occupant, another history to be taken into account, another claim to be contested, another negotiation to be started up in the 'microphysics of contact' (cf. Pels 1999) that determines the possibility of presence and co-presence, of living and living with each other, in the city. Urban residents' claims are always simultaneous and competitive, and therefore constantly engender frictions and fractures, and upset and endanger the possibility of such 'living together'.

At a conference I attended in Copenhagen a couple of years ago, anthropologist Christophe Robert described how, similarly to Kinshasa, marginalized people in Saigon have started to occupy and squat some of the city's cemeteries, and according to him this occupation could be understood as a form of 'expectant citizenship' (cf. Robert 2014). However, by contrast, I believe that the young boys and girls who foray into Kinshasa's graveyards and occupy its tombs, and the women who carve out small garden plots for themselves in the Malebo Pool as well as the young men who 'occupy' potholes in Kinshasa's decaying asphalt roads by repairing them, would all find this a naive expectation. They know that random occupation of urban space almost always engenders new conflicts, and that such occupation, invasion, capture and seizure are always accompanied by (the threat of) expulsion and the necessity of retreat and letting go. And as was illustrated in various chapters throughout this book, the ultimate tool to engage in these movements of occupation and surrender is one's body, which is always with you, which can be thrown into the struggle and taken out of it again by moving away or by retreating (and eventually returning to reclaim what was relinquished if the circumstances allow it). Opposing more official vocabularies of colonisation and territorialisation, Congo's urban residents well understand the constituent role of the body as an autonomous tool for making urban dwelling possible. Here the body, as the city's basic infrastructural and relational building block (cf. De Boeck & Plissart 2004: 236ff), becomes the pivotal point of action in a pronounced politics of presence in which 'occupation as a *radical politics of infrastructure* thus revisions the city as a set of relations that take form as alternative *common* spaces for political action (...). To occupy, in this context, is to constitute the common(s) as a point of departure for rethinking how we come to think about and inhabit the city.' (Vasudevan 2015: 318-319)

In the end, occupation has less to do immediately with the formal claim of a political right to the city, in which notions of sovereignty or citizenship always remain unclear and unresolved anyway. This is not to say that occupation might not encompass such political claims, as recent street protests in Burkina Faso, Burundi, and indeed Congo, have shown. But in its very essence, the politics of occupation is part of an even more basic and fundamental (and therefore even more deeply political) claim: the simple claim to be, to stake out a place for yourself, to exist. *Tozali*, as one would say in Lingala: We *are* and we are here, with our bodies *and* our speech (for *occupation* is, after all, also a rhetorical device) we occupy the city, and because of this simple fact, our presence should be taken into account. This urgent demand for visibility and presence is, as W.J.T. Mitchell remarks in his essay on the meaning of the Occupy movement, 'a demand in its own right' and 'an insistence on being heard and seen before any specific political demands are made' (Mitchell 2013: 102). For him, this performance of *occupatio* 'refuses to describe or define in any detail the world it wants to create, while showing this world in its actual presence as a nascent community. It denounces the demand that it make specific, practical demands, while opening up a space in which innumerable demands can be articulated' (Mitchell 2013: 102-103). For Mitchell, such politics of presence is a reopening of what Hannah Arendt calls the 'space of appearance', a pre-institutionalised 'phenomenal' space 'where I appear to others as others appear to me' (Arendt 1998: 198), a world of spectacle that enables action, and ideally freedom, by making subjects visible to themselves and to a plurality of others; a public realm as stage or 'screen' (cf. Simone 2012a) that provides people with the opportunity to *appear* and to perform themselves in the whimsical immediacy of the encounter with others; a space to see and to be seen, to be actor and spectator at the same time. In this sense, a city such as Kinshasa, which I have described elsewhere as a theatrical and exhibitionist city (cf. De Boeck and Plissart 2004: 54), a spectacular city that constantly turns itself into a stage, a public theatre to perform oneself through the pronounced urban aesthetics of bodily display and public appearance as perfected most fully by the city's *sapeurs*, becomes one vast 'occupy movement', a relentless coming and going in which the city makes and unmakes itself at every moment. *Eza*, 'it is'...

August 2012, Kimbuta Boulevard in the municipality of Ndjili: I slowly walk away from the crowded and animated outdoor *terrasse* where I had been drinking a cool Primus beer with some friends. The sun is setting and I feel the heat of the day easing into a more bearable temperature. I stroll through the avenues of Ndjili, one of the old *cités* that the Belgians planned during the colonial period, in direction of Place Sainte-Thérèse. Approaching the sandy square, my attention is caught by the excited voices of a group of young children. Their backs are turned to the street as they gather around a TV screen that someone put out on the pavement. Curious to know what they are watching, I walk up to the group and stand in the back row. It is a Hollywood feature film and it does not take long before I realise it is Mel Gibson's *Apocalypto*. Even though I have always disliked this gruesome tale of raiders and refugees, colonisers and captives, I am sucked into the story. Blood splashes all over the screen, and every time Jaguar Paw, the main character, crushes the skull of one of his opponents, all the children cheer in excitement. Next to me stands a seven- or eight-year-old boy. During a particularly violent scene, I suddenly feel his hand in mine. I look down and he says: '*Papa*, don't be afraid, this is only fiction.'

Notes

1. Preface: Suturing the City. Living Together in Congo's Urban Worlds.

1. On this colonial museum read Vandenbossche 1955. For a comprehensive history of the IMNC, also see Van Beurden 2015.
2. Kimwenza was marked by a strong Catholic missionary presence from the early days of the colonisation. In 1893, the Jesuits were the first to found a missionary station and school on the Kimwenza plateau, and their example was followed by the Sisters of Our Lady of Namur in 1894 (Kavenadiambuko 1999: 93).
3. Sammy Baloji and Filip De Boeck, *Urban Now: City Life in Congo*. This exhibition took place in Wiels from May 8 to August 14 2016.

2. The Last Post: Congo, (Post)colonialism and Urban Tales of Unrest

1. Cf. 'Neoliberalism and the Genocide of 6 Million in Congo' The Real News Network (TRNN), 21 May 2013 (http://dissidentvoice.org/2013/05/neoliberalism-and-the-genocide-of-6-million-in-congo/)
2. See Sven Augustijnen's 2011 film *Spectres'* on the decolonisation process of the Belgian Congo, particularly the conditions under which the Congolese leader Patrice Lumumba was executed in 1961.
3. I mainly refer here to 'Discourse of Power and Knowledge of Otherness', the first chapter of *The Invention of Africa*.
4. Kalina was named after Lieutenant Kallina, an Austrian army officer who arrived in Congo in 1882 in the service of the *Comité d'Etudes du Haut-Congo* and drowned in the easternmost point of Ngaliema Bay in 1883.
5. On the colonial 'sanitary syndrome', see also Beeckmans 2013: 45-87; Lagae, Boonen and Liefooghe 2013. On the colonial urban planning history of Kinshasa more generally, see de Maximy 1984; De Meulder 2000; de Saint Moulin 2007; Kapagama and Waterhouse 2009; Kolonga Molei 1979; La Fontaine 1970; Lagae 2007, 2013; Lelo Nzuzi 2008; Pain 1984; Piermay 1997; Lagae and Toulier 2013.
6. In the preface, Stevelinck unwittingly reveals the racial realities and paternalism of the urban colonial context underlying this sanitary discourse when he warns the reader à propos the typography of his own book that '(...) many typographic rules have probably been broken. Composed by Blacks who danced in the light of the moon not even five years ago, these pages can evidently not aspire to the perfection which could have been attained if they had been printed by the elite craftsmen from the Metropole (...)' '[(...) il est possible que de nombreuses règles typographiques aient été violées. Composés par des Noirs qui dansaient à la Lune il n'y a pas un lustre, ces pages ne peuvent évidemment aspirer à la perfection que leur eût value d'être exécutés par l'élite des ouvriers métropolitains (...).']
7. It was no coincidence that the politics of the *cordon sanitaire* was implemented in the early 1930s, at a time when a growing number of traders and merchants, especially Greek and Portuguese, often with African wives and children of 'mixed race', started to build houses in the no-man's-lands between European and African neighbourhoods, thereby threatening and upsetting the colonial order of things.
8. *Debout Congolais* ('Arise Congolese') is the title of the official national anthem of the Democratic Republic of Congo.
9. Davis is an American Marxist writer, independent political activist and urban theorist. Liotta and Miskel are US defence policy and homeland security analysts, and Kilcullen is a counterinsurgency expert and a former Chief Strategist in the Office for Counterterrorism at the US State Department.
10. From: Observers.france24.com/content/20131220-police-street-merchants-congo-vendors

11 Journalist Laurel Kankole from the newspaper *Forum des As* uses this term in a press report dated 16 April 2014. The article reports the decision taken by General Célestin Kanyama, head of the National Police for the city and the province of Kinshasa, to make the sale of alcohol illegal before noon in the city's numerous outside bars (see http://www.forumdesas.org/spip.php?article856).

12 It is rather ironic, therefore, that on 15 May 2013, the provincial government of Kasai Oriental, inspired by the examples from Kinshasa and Lubumbashi, took the decision to go ahead with the construction of Lumumbaville, a new city in honour of the people's anti-colonialism hero, to be erected in the territory of Katako-Kombe, birthplace of Lumumba.

13 Its director, Hillary Duckworth, a former British army officer who became a banker, is also the founding partner, together with his brother Russell, of Hawkwood Capital, a British investment fund that initiated the *Cité du Fleuve* project through Hawkwood Properties and one of its majority shareholders, Mukwa Investment. The latter is a specialised investment fund based in Lusaka, Zambia, where the Duckworths own a number of family ranches and other companies.

14 http://www.congo-foret.com/community.html, accessed November 2011.

15 In urban policing and security vocabularies, a 'shadow evacuation' 'occurs when there is an evacuation directive for a specific danger zone, but people outside the danger zone evacuate when they do not have to.' (Doyle 2009: 198).

16 Some recent examples include Edensor and Jayne 2012; Obrist, Arlt and Macamo 2013; Murray and Myers 2006; Myers 2011; Parnell and Oldfield 2014; Parnell and Pieterse 2014; Pieterse 2008; Pieterse and Simone 2013; Simone and Abouhani 2005; Pinther, Förster, Hanussek 2012; Roy and Ong 2011; Simone 2004, 2010b, 2012b).

17 On the specific ways in which this 'worlding' shapes various real or imagined diasporic communities in the Congolese context, see De Boeck 2012a.

18 See http://mahindrahumanities.fas.harvard.edu/content/william-kentridge-drawing-lesson-one-praise-shadows

19 See for example Kentridge's animated film 'The Shadow Procession' (1999). For an overview of Kentridge's work, see also Alemani 2006.

20 For an interesting archaeology of the meaning of the line, see also Ingold 2007.

21 Trésor is a fictive name.

22 Again, Shayibunda is a pseudonym.

23 *Regedor*: administrative authority of a municipality or district. In Portugal, this function and title disappeared after 25 April 1974. It continues to be used in Angola as a way to integrate important chiefs and traditional title-holders (*sobas grandes*) into state bureaucracy (see also Heywood 2000 for a history of colonial administrative reforms in Angola).

24 http://www.clab.fi/information/architect/

25 http://www.clab.fi/information/architect/

1 'Chinese' as in cheap textile of poor quality.

2 2012 Country Reports on Human Rights Practices, US Department of State.

3 *Faire le branchement* (meaning 'to connect') is also used to refer to acts of corruption: a student looks out for a *branchement* or connection with a teacher in order to buy a diploma, for example. As such a *branchement* is also a more illicit version of what Kinois describe as a *cop*, an (informal) deal or bargain (*cop* from the French *coopération*, cf. Nzeza Bilakila 2004). The illicit, corrupt and therefore more hidden and invisible version of making such a bargain (*kobeta cop*) is also referred as *s(h)ida*, after the French acronym for AIDS, the 'invisible' disease. Other words and expressions that, in varying degrees, denote similar ideas of striking a deal through corrupt means are, for example, *kofina kanyaka* (to make a small gift, passing it from one hand to the other 'under the table,' unseen by anyone else) or *kofeinter* ('to lie, deceive').

4 The colloquial Lingala spoken in Kinshasa often expresses ideas of physical and mental well-being through the use of similar analogies. In this way, one can also be said to be *low-bat* ('have a low battery') when one feels drained of energy.

5 In 1984, Masina's total population was estimated at 162,000. In 2004, it had risen to nearly 600,000 (Fumumzanza 2008: 62), and it surpasses a million inhabitants today.

6 Together with the Bakongo from the Lower Congo province, the Yaka and other related ethnic groups (such as the Suku) from Kinshasa's adjacent Kwango district form a major demographic presence in Kinshasa.

7 Even today, rural latecomers to the city are nicknamed *ya mbala* (in kiYaka, *mbala* is the name given to the last boy to be circumcised during a circumcision ritual) or *ya ngwe* ('I refuse' in reference to their 'traditional' character and their 'refusal' to adapt to new modes of living).

8 In a report which was jointly presented by Unicef and the 'Commission Congolaise d'Aménagement du Territoire' in Kinshasa on 20 March 2014, it is stated that 30,000,000 people throughout the D.R.Congo have no immediate access to drinking water and only 9% has access to electricity.

9 In fact, REGIDESO and SNEL seem to be locked in an endless Catch 22 that nobody seems able to solve: Regideso says that it cannot satisfy the city's water demand because it does not receive the necessary electricity to do so, while SNEL claims that the Kinshasa power cuts, which it actually describes as 'intempestive', are due to the low water level of the Congo river in recent years. (Source: Radio Okapi, 21 March 2014: '*RDC : plus de 30 millions de personnes n'ont pas accès à l'eau potable, selon l'Unicef*'). Even the government has decided to bypass this endless gridlock. In April 2014, the *Agence congolaise des grands travaux* (ACGT) installed 3,600 light posts along Lumumba Boulevard between Ndjili airport and Masina Siforco. The light projectors work on solar energy, and thus are no longer dependent on the SNEL electricity grid.

10 Inspired by Hollywood Western movies, Billism (from 'Buffalo Bill') emerged in Kinshasa in the second half of the 1950s and deeply influenced the shape of the city's youth culture for decades to come) (see also De Boeck 2000; La Fontaine 1970; Geenen 2009; Gondola 2009; 2013; Pype 2007).

11 I have discussed the worlds of Congolese diamond diggers at great length elsewhere (see De Boeck 1998a, 1999, 2000, 2001, 2012b). On the current situation in Lunda Norte see Marques 2011.

12 In a highly informative blog post from 2010 entitled *Kuluna and Kuluneurs in Kinshasa: A Low-Intensity Urban Insurgency?*, Alex Engwete writes:'The modus operandi of *"kuluneurs"* is the following: either in broad daylight or at night, a pack of martial arts practitioners (called *"pombas"*) armed with clubs, machetes and other blunt objects raid and occupy a city square wherein they seize from passers-by and street vendors any valuable they can lay their hands on: money, watches, cell phones, merchandise, shirts, shoes, jewelry, etc. Victims who resist are hacked with machetes, clubbed or stabbed. Some victims have died from injuries sustained in those *kuluna* raids and many a warlord *kuluneur* has been gunned down by the *Police d'Intervention Rapide (PIR).'* (http://alexengwete.blogspot.com/2010/02/kuluna-and-kuluneurs-in-kinshasa-low.html).

13 See: www.banamputu.com/2013/03/20/kinshasa-les-kuluna-se-vengent-apres-la-mort-de-leur-ami-tue-par-la-population/

14 'Kinshasa: les Kulunas toujours actifs à la Tshangu.' Reported by Radio Okapi, 10 March 2014 (http://radiookapi.net/actualite/2014/03/10/kinshasa-les-kulunas-toujours-actifs-tshangu/). In fact, the *Likofi* operation, which the Ministry of the Interior had ordered, was the third of its kind since 2001 when Christophe Muzungu, who was Kinshasa's governor at the time, launched the *Kanga Vagabonds* ('Grab the Vagabonds') operation against street children (cf. Geenen, 2009). Because of its violent nature, the recent *Likofi* operation attracted a lot of international media attention, and even led Monusco and Unicef to issue a joint statement to protest against the many summary executions of (alleged) *kuluna* gang members in the streets of Kinshasa. In UN statements, mention was made of the execution of 20 youths (12 of whom were minors) during the first days of the *Likofi* operation.

15 On 15 September 2015, for example, a political rally of several opposition parties in the municipality of Ndjili was violently attacked by a large group of *kuluna*. According to Human Rights Watch and several news reports these thugs had been recruited by members of the ruling PPRD party to disrupt the meeting.

16 *Kipe*, from the French *occuper*, as in '*Occupes toi de tes affaires!'*

17 For other occupational categories see also Kamba 2008: 345-346; Dekossago, Bathwa and Namayele 2003-2004.

18 For a more detailed account of the violence generated in and by Kinshasa's *économie de la débrouille*, see also Ayimpam 2014a.

19 In medical terms, 'morcellation' means the division of solid tissue, such as a tumour, into pieces that can then be removed.

20 Obarrio (2014) observes a similar inflation of the juridical and a renewed hypostasis of the law in the Mozambican context.

21 For a similar analysis of infrastructure as 'divination device' in the Nigerian city of Jos, see Trovalla and Trovalla 2015.

22 On 20 March 2014, for example, overvoltage caused a fatal fire in Lubudi, a neighbourhood of the municipality of Bandalungwa known for its irregular electricity supply. One house on *rue Kasangulu* caught fire when, after weeks of darkness, the electricity suddenly returned with abnormal intensity. Several people of the household did not survive the incident.

23 Even the Pentecostal preachers themselves continue to seek help from diviners; a fact confirmed to me by a number of diviners during my interviews and conversations with them. The divinatory rituals I have been able to observe and document in the city over the years continue to build on longstanding autochthonous divination techniques, although the divinatory objects and the form of the consultation itself are sometimes adapted and transformed to respond better to the specific problems people face in the urban context, and to the open-endedness of the city itself. It should be noted that, in recent years, some forms of divination have (re)surfaced in very visible ways in the city. This is the case, for example, during funerals, especially if the deceased is a young person, the topic of Chapter Five.

24 The name Makila is a pseudonym.

25 The Suku are an ethnic group related to the Yaka (cf. note 6; see also Kopytoff 1988). On the forms and specific protocols of divination as practiced in this Yaka socio-cultural sphere see, for example, De Boeck and Devisch 1994; Devisch 2013. Depending on their cultural and ethnic background, diviners may also be women, as among the Yaka. However, whereas this is still the case in rural settings, or at least till very recently (see, for example, Dumon and Devisch 1991), it seems to have become much more of an exception in Kinshasa, where I have only encountered two female diviners in the past ten years.

26 That is why, during the divinatory séance, a diviner routinely smears his nostrils with red earth (*mukul*), in order to enhance his olfactory capacities and better 'sniff out' the problem in question.

27 It should be noted that acts of knotting and weaving in this particular cultural setting are, above all, about balance, rhythm and the (corporeal) rhythming of the world. This necessitates a more elaborate ethnography, but good starting points to ethnographically ground this idea would be Devisch 1993, for example, or Geurts 2002. See also You 1994.

28 For similar observations on the composition of divining tools in Northern Ghana see Cassiman 2013.

29 As mentioned earlier, the vocabularies of cell phone technology are commonly used in the urban context to refer to the state of one's physical and mental health.

4. Mountains I : Pic Sörensen

1   A detailed list compiled in 1931 by Major E.V. Larsen, the then president of the Danish section of the Association of Colonial Veterans of Belgium, contains the names of 315 Danes who participated in King Leopold's Congo Free State project between 1878 and 1908, the year when the CFS became a formal Belgian colony. Already in 1878, two Danish missionaries of the 'Livingstone Inland Mission' had started to work in Congo, and Stanley himself was accompanied by two young Danish officers, Albert Christophersen and Martin Mortensen. The latter died a year after his arrival in Congo. A large part of the Danish presence in Congo consisted of young officers like Mortensen (67 men in all), but there were also 88 steamboat captains and 90 mechanics of Danish origin working in the service of the Congo Free State.

2   *Kashinakashi*: a Chokwe word meaning 'old man'. It is also the name of a ritual sequence in the *mukanda* circumcision rituals that even today are still regularly performed in this remote part of rural Congo.

3   Currently named Boyoma Falls, situated along the Lualaba River between the river port towns of Ubundu and Kisangani/Boyoma.

4   Francis, Baron Dhanis (1861-1909) was an English-born Belgian civil servant and soldier in the service of the Congo Free State. He is remembered for his role during the Congo Arab war (1892-1894) and the Batetela rebellion (1897-1898).

5   This and subsequent citations from Sörensen's letters are from the Danske Udvandrerarkiv LM-1983-255, box 133:2 Jürgen Jürgensen. All translations are mine. *Bula Matari* translates as 'breaker of rocks'. Originally, it was the name the Congolese called Stanley, but it soon also started to denote the Belgian colonial rule as a whole.

6   'Batchoko': Chokwe.

7   'Kashinsi': Shinji, a small ethnic group that is part of the ethnic patchwork of the southern Kwango and Kwilu areas, together with the Lunda, Chokwe, Suku, Holo, Yaka, Pende, Sonde, Minungu and various other groups.

8   Boma remained the administrative and military capital of the Belgian Congo until 1923.

9   Known on today's official maps as Tundwala or Tundwila.

10   The village's actual location is no longer that of Sörensen's days, for every time a Lunda king dies, the royal village is moved a couple of kilometres to another location. The last such relocation of Nzofu took place in 1984/85, following the death of Nzofu Ntaambw Chingeendj. When his successor Nzofu Kateend II died in 2005, there was no such relocation, however, because two sons of Ntaambw Chingeendj have continued to fight each other over their right to the paramount title ever since. The ongoing dispute over the royal title has considerably weakened the court's regional influence in recent years.

11   The sentence is a quote from *Erasmus Montanus*, a satirical play about the introduction of civilisation in the backward rural Denmark of the eighteenth century. Written by Ludvig Holberg in 1722, the play was first published in 1723 and performed for the first time in 1747. The main protagonist is Rasmus Berg ('Rasmus Mountain'), who has been given a costly education in Copenhagen. When he returns to his village with all of his newly acquired knowledge, he has latinised his name as Erasmus Montanus and insists on speaking Latin with his parents, who are simple country folk. His conceited behaviour as a 'learned scholar' soon gets him into trouble with both his family and his fiancée Lisbet, who refuses to marry him if he does not stop to claim that the earth is round.

12   In 1884 the British company Lever Brothers started to produce Sunlight, the famous brand of household soap. As elsewhere in Africa (cf. Burke 1996), soap continues to be a powerful signifier of the new values and moral codes introduced by colonialist modernity.

13   Reference to the rivers Kwenge and Kwilu.

14   See the *Rapport d'enquête Zofu Kulinji* from 1920, in the dossier n° 8, *Chefferie de Nzofu*, archives of Kahemba district.

15   In this way, the Belgian administration also attempted to intervene directly in the succession of the Nzofu paramount titleholder after the death of Nzofu Kateend Mfumw a Nsaangw Mukanweesh in 1956. The colonial authorities succeeded in inaugurating a certain Chimbayeek, an elder from a rivaling faction within the royal lineage who, according to the court succession rules, had absolutely no right to the title. Only weeks after his enthronement Chimbayeek died, most likely from poisoning, and thereupon the title was returned (in 1963 or 1964) to the court's own candidate, Nzofu Ntaambw Chingeendj Kassom a Mbuumb.

16   Until the end of the Belgian occupation, for example, it was not uncommon for the *Mabeet*'s villagers to cross the border into Angola every time an agronomist or other colonial official was on tour in the region. There, people would await the colonial authorities' departure before returning to their village.

17   On similar religious movements elsewhere in the Kwango see Omasombo 2012: 125ff; Vansina 1973a.

5. Corpus Vile:
Death and Expendable Youth in Kinshasa

1   The cemetery of Kintambo is also the setting of *Cemetery State*, a documentary film that I directed (De Boeck 2010). Field research was mainly carried out between 2004 and 2008, with occasional visits since, most recently in March 2015 with Sammy Baloji.

2   'De-familiarization' or *ostranenie*, a notion I borrow from Shklovsky's seminal text 'Art as Technique' (2004).

3   This cycle of songs is normally part of the elaborate initiation rituals that take place when a member of the *mwiingoony* funerary association dies (see De Boeck 1991a).

4   This widow, a relative of the *mufidi*, should not have participated at another mourning night since her own husband's death.

5   In former times, the mourning period could take up to four months or even a year. Today, this period has been much shortened.

6   De Boeck 1991b. See also Wastiau 2000 on *mahaamb* spiritual entities among the Luunda-related Luvale of the Upper Zambezi, and Turner (e.g. 1968) on similar 'shades' among the Ndembu.

7   *Nseew* means 'arrow', and is also the name of a gift made by the wife-takers to the wife-givers in order to open marriage negotiations. In the mourning context, the gift signifies the fact that the widow is divorcing her deceased husband's family by ritually marrying into the healer's clan.

8   This mixture consisted of bark scrapings of the following trees: *mupach* (Dacryodis edulis), *muund* (not identified), *mujiw* (not identified) and *muleeng* (Uapaca guineensis, U. nitida). The scrapings are pounded on a large piece of bark from the *nsuumb* tree, and further mixed with leaves from *saansas*, *mbul a mulwalw* and *djaangudjaangu* plants (all unidentified). The resulting powder preparation is mixed with hot and cold water and used ritually to 'wash' the widow.

9   The same name is given to a subsequent nocturnal wake, some two years after the actual burial, when the deceased's own kin group (and thus without the widow and her relatives) will spend another night together, singing *munem* songs in memory of the deceased. The phrase 'dispersing the charcoal ashes' is also synonymous for 'dethroning a chief'.

10 Syzygium guineense, from the family Myrtaceae. This tree plays a prominent role in hunting rituals. Its wood is used to make rifle butts.

11 In this particular case it was her sister's son because a divinatory oracle had revealed he was partly responsible for triggering the anger of the *haamb* shade that had caused the husbands' deaths.

12 The three 'gates' referred to the three dead husbands. By 'breaking' the three gates with her right foot she ensured that her future husband would not die like the others.

13 For a more in-depth analysis of the different meanings of the *kapwiip* (Swartzia Madagascariensis, Leguminosae family) see De Boeck 1994b.

14 The *mukos* tree (Erythrophleum africanum or African blackwood, in the family Caesalpinacea). Its gum is used for purification, as the tree's name already indicates (-*kos*: 'to cleanse', 'to wash away').

15 At other performances of this ritual, I witnessed how the patient was made to copulate with the earthen figure as well.

16 Sometimes, the kitchen utensils and pots used to prepare food for the deceased are left on top of the *haamb* figurine as well. Usually, they are deposited on top of the deceased's grave, with the cooking pots turned upside down to 'block' and prevent the dead person from returning. Often, also, some personal belongings of the dead person are put on top of the grave as well.

17 This time the healer used the bark of the *musebe* (Vangueriopsis lanciflora, a species of flowering shrub in the family Rubiaceae), also referred to as the 'little one of *kapwiip*', to purify her from the *muf* spirit and the shadow of her deceased husbands, thereby 'whitening' her (returning her to life). As in many Lunda rituals, the whole ritual thus unfolded as a progressive movement towards 'whiteness', for this is the colour of life, while red, in all Lunda related cultures (cf. Turner 1967) is a much more ambiguous colour that may connote life-giving forces (as with the blood of birth-giving), but also death (menstrual blood, the blood of warfare and so on).

18 See also Devisch and de Mahieu 1979 for a detailed description of funerary rituals among the Yaka, who are the Lunda's northern neighbours in Bandundu province, and represent an important portion of Kinshasa's population ever since the early days of its creation (cf. also Roosens 1971).

19 The word *cadavéré* became a standard Kinois expression thanks to the 1984 hit *Ancient combattant* by Zao, a musician from Congo Brazzaville.

20 Especially in Mokali, Kimwenza and Mont Amba, the Cité Mama Mobutu, Camp Badiadingi, around UPN and elsewhere in Binza, many houses and neighbourhoods are threatened by various points of erosions (cf. Wouters and Wolff 2010; see also Radio Okapi, March 10, 2014: *Kinshasa : plusieurs quartiers menacés par les erosions*).

21 According to a 2004 census, the municipality of Kintambo had about 106,772 inhabitants (with a population density of 39,254/km²), whereas the larger municipality of Ngaliema was home to 683,000 inhabitants (with a population density of 3,046/km²).

22 Not only there are numerous burial sites in and around the city of Kinshasa that are not officially known to the city's authorities, but many deaths remain unreported because a significant part of Kinshasa's residents has never been registered in the city's civil registry.

23 I only had access to figures for the first 9 months of 2005, and none for later years.

24 In the months leading to the 2006 national elections, a local aspiring politician from Camp Luka tried to win some votes in his constituency by (illegally) carving out a football field amongst the graves in the middle of the cemetery. Although still used today by Camp Luka's youth, the football field has greatly suffered from erosion and has also caused further degradation to the graves, many of which have collapsed into the river that cuts through the cemetery and borders on the football field.

25 See also the film *Atalaku* by Dieudo Hamadi (2013).

26 It was only in 2013 that the Congolese and Angolan border authorities installed a customs office and officially opened the border in Shamajamo, close to the village of Shamukwale.

27 Similarly, artisanal miners in Lunda Norte compare their diamond digging activities to grave-digging. The mining holes are referred to as 'graves' (*majimba* in TshiLuba), hence the name for the diggers themselves: *majimberos*.

28 *Cataphar*: from the French *catafalque*, a raised structure on which the body of a deceased person lies or is carried in state. In Kinshasa, however, it mainly denotes the open plastic garden party tent that is put around the coffin.

29 This fact has not remained unnoticed by social scientists and historiographers. Although the classic topics of death and mourning have never ceased to be of importance in anthropology (see for a recent example Connerton 2011; see also Bloch and Parry 1982; Fabian 1972), increasing death rates throughout the African continent have given rise to the recent revival of anthropological and historical studies about funerals and mourning rituals in various African, and mostly urban, contexts (see for example De Boeck 1998b, 2005a, 2008a, 2009a; Dississa 2003, 2009; Grootaers 1998; Jewsiewicki and White 2005; Jindra and Noret 2011; Noret 2010; Noret and Petit 2011; Lamont 2009; Lee 2011; Vangu Ngimbi 1997; Vaughan and Lee 2008, 2012).

30 A 2013 radio broadcast from Radio Okapi, the UN radio station in the DRC, revealed, rather unsurprisingly, that child mortality is on the rise again in many parts of Kinshasa's vast periphery (Radio Okapi, May 4, 2013), while in the 2013 annual *State of the World's Mothers* (SOTWM) report 'Surviving the First Day', issued by the international NGO Save the Children, Congo occupies the world's worst position when it comes to the number of newborn deaths (see the Huffington Post 7 May 2013).

31 This change is already well reflected in a 1982 OK Jazz song by composer and singer Pepe Ndombe Opetun, a former pupil of Tabu Ley. In this song Opetun further develops the theme of Tabu Ley's 1966 song, while demonstrating the changes that have occurred in the city since: 'I do not know the day I will die, nor do I know how they will mourn me. Stretched out on the bed, nothing to worry about any longer, it is party time for everybody. This has become the norm in Kinshasa. The place of death has become a place to party. The women come to find a man, and the men come for a girl. It will be like that on the day I die. And they will drink and get drunk, and then they will start to brutalise everybody: 'Who killed this man' [implication: by means of witchcraft])?' (in Lingala: *Mokolo nakokufa nayebi te, ndenge bakolela nga. Na mbeto souci te, fête ya bato nionso. Kinshasa ekoma façon. Esika ya liwa ekoma fête. Bayeli nde mibali, mibali bayeli nde chéries. Mokolo nakokufa ekozala se bongo. Soki bameli balangwe, bayei kotutuka. Nani abomi ye?*)

32 By now the deceased's family members clearly no longer control the funeral, and often do not risk showing up at the funeral itself. Frequently, it is only after the burial has been completed that the responsibility for the dead person is handed over again to his or her family, after the latter has paid a fine to the youth that performed the burial. Often, this payment consists of the *muziku*, the amount of money raised by the *matanga*'s participants to finance the burial.

33 Surprisingly, given the Catholic and Protestant imprint that colonialism has imposed on the Congolese life-world, and also given the strong influence of prophetic movements such as Kimbanguism (cf. M'bokolo and Sabakinu 2014; Mélice 2011) or the more recent strong impact of new forms of Christian fundamentalism (Meiers 2013; Pype 2012), death is one of the fields that increasingly seems to fall outside of their hegemonic control. In recent years, Kinshasa has not only witnessed attacks against elders during funerals, but increasingly *kuluna* street gangs have also started to target churches and priests. In February 2012, for example, several Catholic churches in the capital were attacked by street gangs, and on 14 May 2013 the Church of Saint Augustine in the municipality of Lemba became the target of a *kuluna* attack. Some of these attacks are clearly ordered and manipulated by political factions in the city, as was the case in the June 2006 ransacking of the church of Sony Kafuta, one of Kinshasa's most prominent Pentecostal preachers, known for his pro-Kabila views. Other attacks seem to originate more spontaneously.

34 The assassination of the leading human rights activist Floribert Chebeya in Kinshasa in 2010 painfully reminded us once again of the necropolitical nature of Congo's governance.

35 Youtube, for example, contains numerous uncensored postings with raw footage showing mob killings during funerals in every gruesome detail. These posts also reveal that youth's appropriation of death has not only become common in Kinshasa, but has also become standard practice in other urban contexts in Congo, most notably in Lubumbashi.

36 In the Lunda context, a verb to describe the act of dancing *musangu* is *-funy*. The same verb is used to describe a title-holder's majestic stride with his flywhisk. The verb's causative form, *-funyeesh*, literally means: 'to cause to lift up what was bent down' and thus also 'to cause someone to honour himself.' (De Boeck 1991a: 174).

37 This is well illustrated by the photographic work of Congolese photographer Yves Sambu, who is known for his portrayals of *sapeurs* in Kinshasa's graveyards (see Sambu 2009).

38 See Alex Engwete 2010 in his blogpost on the *kuluna* phenomenon ((http://alexengwete.blogspot.com/2010/02/kuluna-and-kuluneurs-in-kinshasa-low.html).

6. Mountains II: Pungulume

1 In today's TFM ownership structure, Lundin Mining Corporation only holds 24% of the mining activities, while 56 % are owned by Freeport-McMoRan Inc., a US-based natural resources company. Another 20% is owned by *La Générale des Carriéres et des Mines* (better known as Gécamines), which is itself wholly owned by the DRC government.

2 Mpande is the most important royal Sanga court of Katanga. Today, it is situated in the mining town of Luambo, between Likasi and Fungurume (cf. Cuvelier 2011).

3 The Yeke reign was established under the warrior king M'siri, who dominated a large part of south-central Africa between 1850 to 1891 and controlled the trade route between Angola and Zanzibar from his capital in Bunkeya. M'siri's father was a Nyamwezi trader from what is now northwestern Tanzania. Between 1820 and 1850, Nyamwezi traders, such as M'siri's father, migrated in increasing numbers to Katanga in order to trade in copper, ivory, salt, iron ore, guns and slaves (cf. Legros 1996). They conquered and merged with Sanga chieftainships, such as Mpala, and managed to establish a powerful trading network across Central Africa. In 1891, M'siri was killed by Omer Bodson, a Belgian colonial officer who was a member of a punitive expedition against M'siri after the latter refused to submit to Belgian colonial rule. The baYeke still maintain a chieftainship in Bunkeya to this day.

4 According to Couttenier (2011), chief Mulawa Nyama in fact died in the assault. Mpala's story refers to an actual historical incident that took place shortly after Bodson assassinated M'siri. To fill the political void left by M'siri's death, the Belgians backed his son, Mukanda Bantu, in the hope of using the Yeke chieftainship to bolster colonial rule. At that time, the baYeke of Mukanda Bantu lived in conflict with Sanga chief Mpala Mumba. The latter refused to recognise Yeke domination, and consequently the rule of their Belgian allies as well. When the Lemaire expedition, a Belgian scientific exploratory expedition headed by Charles Lemaire, travelled through the area between 1898 and 1900, they were quickly drawn into this Yeke-Sanga conflict. It was not long before members of the Lemaire expedition organised a punitive campaign against Mpala Mumba, who was also known as Mulawa (or Mulowa) Nyama. In the ensuing fighting, Julien Fromont, one of the Belgian expedition members, was killed. Thereupon Mulowa Nyama and his villagers fled and hid in a cave. When they refused to surrender despite attempts to smoke them out, the entrance of the cave was blocked up. Three months later, troops entered the cave and found 178 dead bodies (cf. Couttenier 2011). The cave became an important commemorative site for the Mpala chieftainship (even though the soldiers had set off landslides to cover the cave and destroy all evidence). According to chief Mpala Swanage, the remains of some who died in the cave were excavated by an archaeological team some years ago. Chief Mpala claims that these remains are now stored in Lubumbashi's national museum. His repeated demands for the return of his ancestors' remains have fallen on deaf ears so far.

When, in September 2013, Sammy Baloji and I visited the museum together with Mpala, the museum director refused to see us. Reportedly, the historical cave site itself was recently destroyed as a result of nearby mining activities by TFM that caused it to cave in.

5 These X-shaped cast-copper crosses are also called *handa*. They where used as a form of currency in precolonial times.

6 In 2012, the population of the *cité* of Fungurume had already risen to 120,000 from 40,000 in 2005.

7 The developer of Kiswishi is Rendeavour, well-known for their plans for new urban centres in Kenya, Ghana, Nigeria and Zambia, none of which has yet been built (also see Chapter Seven, note 17).

8 According to TFM 2013-2016 Resettlement Action Plan, 1,500 people will be moved during this period. Some of these displaced people receive a replacement house, usually in a larger labour camp, while other receive compensation in cash.

9 The two most recent TFM's resettlements action plans can be consulted in full on the website of Freeport-McMoRan Copper & Gold, TFM's major shareholder. See *Land Access, Compensation and Resettlement Policy Framework, November 2012* and *Mitumba-Fungurume Hills Resettlement Action Plan (2013-2016)* at http://www.fcx.com/operations/AfricaTenke.htm.

10 As mentioned in TFM's own reports, these *ententes* do not apply to plots of land smaller than 2,500 m². In 2012, the fee was 200 US dollars per hectare.

11 http://www.radiookapi.net/actualite/2010/10/25/katanga-les-pluies-font-des-malheurs-a-fungrume-et-kolwezi-et-pweto

12 All of the following renders Mpala's version of events. I did not manage to ask Koppert about Mpala's interpretation and he might well be unaware of it.

7. 'Illuminating the Hole': Kinshasa's Makeovers Between Dream and Reality

1 *Hôpital du Cinquantenaire:* In 1954, the Belgian colonial authorities started the construction of a prestigious hospital building that was, however, never finished. Quickly taken over and squatted by Kinshasa's inhabitants, it remained a 'blight' on the urban landscape for the next fifty years. The ruins of the hospital building were rehabilitated as part of the 'Cinq Chantiers' programme, and the totally renewed hospital was inaugurated by Kabila on March 22, 2014. Operated by the Indian group *Padiyath Health Care*, the new hospital turns out to be rather unpopular with Kinshasa's inhabitants, mainly because the medical services it offers are considered far too expensive, with medical fees way beyond what the average Kinois can afford.

2 Several miniature replicas of the pyramids of Gizeh are displayed on Docteur's desk.

3 Also see De Boeck and Plissart 2004: 29 for a photo of the Forescom tower.

4 The Lingala verb *–zenga* means: to cut, to amputate.

5 Photographs of the Kindele holes were taken by SADI photographer Yves Sambu and shown as part of the exhibition *Tozokende Wapi? Tokokende Wapi?* at Halle de la Gombe, the French Cultural Centre of Kinshasa, in 2009.

6 One may refer here to the massive lootings that swept across the city and the country in the early nineties (cf. Devisch 1998).

7 On the notion of mimesis in the context of Kinshasa also see De Boeck and Plissart 2004: 20.

8 On Kingelez' *Phantom City* see De Boeck and Plissart 2004: 250-251. Also see Magnin 2003. On the *Tourist City* by Bylex see De Boeck and Van Synghel 2008; Van Synghel and De Boeck 2013. On Bylex more generally see Articlaut 2003; Pivin and Martin Saint Leon 2012.

9 This and all the following fragments in which Bylex speaks are excerpted from a series of long conversations that Koen Van Synghel and I had with Bylex in Kinshasa in September 2006. Part of these conversations were incorporated in a video film that came out with the book *The World According to Bylex* (De Boeck and Van Synghel 2008).

10 The Rosicrucian Order, which is also known as AMORC (from the Latin *Antiquus Mysticusque Ordo Rosae Crucis*), is a worldwide brotherhood dedicated to the study of the 'elusive mysteries of life and the universe'. Rosicrucianism was well established in Congo especially during the Mobutu years, and even today it continues to exert its influence, primarily among politicians, civil servants, soldiers and businessmen (see Lambertz 2015: 95ff).

11 The form in which Bylex imagines this is reminiscent of Le Corbusier's plans for the Mundaneum. Uncharacteristically, Le Corbusier designed a symbolically charged building in the form of a Ziggurat for Otlet's World City. But in contrast to the ancient Assyrian temple typology, which is related to the pyramids (and replayed in Docteur's tower), the form Bylex adopted for his Royal Dome borrows the visual language of later Christian churches built according to a central plan. I thank Koen Van Synghel for bringing Otlet to my attention.

12 Significantly, the people wandering about in the 3D poster image of this building were not Congolese but Asian.

13 In the meantime, this building is nearing completion and the construction company has changed its name. Today, the Modern Titanic goes by the more neutral name of the Congo Trade Centre.

14 These include *Cité Joseph Kabila Kin-Oasis* that aims to integrate 182 apartments and 33 villas in the municipality of Bandalungwa, *Cité du Millennium* (Millennium City) in Mitendi and *Cité de l'Espoir* (City of Hope) in Mikondo.

15 According to Robert Choudury, the manager of the *Cité du Fleuve*, most of his clients are Congolese. My own investigations reveal that the majority of people who have acquired real estate in the *Cité du Fleuve* are either Congolese who live abroad or politicians, such as government ministers, members of parliament and other members of the political elite, including the president and people belonging to the inner circle of power. Since the banking sector in Congo is relatively recent and not financially solid, it is ill-adapted to the newly emerging housing market. Until now, it has proven to be almost impossible for ordinary citizens to obtain a bank loan, and in the absence of an appropriate banking system, the acquisition of an apartment or house usually has to be paid for in cash. In contrast, certain categories of government officials and politicians have less of a problem to obtain bank loans because these are guaranteed by the Congolese state.

16 Cf. Thomas Fessy, *Congo River luxury condos cause Kinshasa controversy*, BBC News, Kinshasa, 20 August 2011.

17 As will be explained in the next chapter, when clashes about land occur, they often involve a different set of actors.

18 Here I use the notion of 'extraversion' in Bayart's sense as the local mobilisation of resources derived from what is often a very unequal relationship with the external global environment (Bayart 2000).

19 Today Renaissance is probably better known as Rendeavour. It is the initiator of several other new city projects elsewhere in Africa, including Tatu City near Nairobi, Appolonia near Accra, and King City in Takoradi, Ghana. Of these three only the King City project seems to move on, although at a much slower pace than announced — on Tatu see Van Den Broeck (forthcoming); on King City see Vannoppen (forthcoming).

8. Ngaliema's Revenge.
Urban Expansion, Chiefs, and Land

1 MuYaka, singular of baYaka. The Yaka, a dominant ethnic group in the neighbouring province of Bandundu, form a large part of Kinshasa's population today.

2 'Lunda': here this name is used in reference to Kasongo Lunda, the royal village of Mwene Putu Kasongo, the Yaka paramount chief who put up fierce resistance against the colonial intrusion into the Kwango area at the end of the nineteenth and the beginning of the twentieth centuries (cf. Marchal 1996: 200). The still existing court of Kasongo Lunda has strong historical and political ties with the Lunda paramount chief Nzofu, whose court is located further south in the Kwango district (cf. Chapter Four).

3 *Lion* and *leopard*: totemic animals that symbolise traditional political power.

4 The historical Round Table Conference took place in Brussels between January and May 1960 and brought together Congolese political representatives, traditional chiefs, and members of the Belgian political and economic establishment in order to negotiate the terms of Congo's independence. One of the thirty-nine traditional chiefs present at this conference was the Kiamvu, the Yaka paramount chief. Other traditional heads included Pierre Mombele who represented the Teke land chiefs of Leopoldville.

5 Upon his return to Congo, Mombele was appointed Minister of Education in Lumumba's government. Among music lovers, Pierre Mombele is also known as the father of Stervos Niarkos, one of the 'masters' of the SAPE, the *Société des ambianceurs et personnes élégantes*, a movement that was popularised in the 1980s by musicians such as Papa Wemba and King Kester Emeneya. Niarkos died in Paris in 1995 but continues to be venerated by Kinshasa's young *sapeurs* as the founding father of the cult of 'appearance', also known as Kitendi (the Lingala word for 'cloth'). A fashion contest in Niarkos' honour still takes place every year around his grave in the cemetery of Gombe.

6 Mfumu Mvula's grave is still located next to the *Camp des Forces Navales* (Port Baramoto), not far from the spot where the *Cité du Fleuve* is currently being built. For a photo of his grave, see Toulier, Lagae and Gemoets, 2010: 32.

7 Mfumu Jean Daniel Bambory Popo Mwinkwa is a Babali (Tio-Teke) chief and a direct descendant of Mfumu Mvula. He grew up and still lives in Mombele after Mvula was expelled from Kingabwa-Mvula in 1942. In March 2015, he had to interrupt the interview I was conducting with him to welcome a delegation of Kingabwa fishermen who came to pay their respects to 'their' chief and discuss fishing matters. (The Babali, a conglomerate of fourteen clans, are one of four different groups that, together with the Humbu, are commonly called the Teke or Humbu-Teke. The three other groups are the Banfinu, the Babwala and the Babintsa).

8 It was King Makoko Iloo (or Iloy) I who signed a first treaty on the third of October 1880 with Pierre Savorgnan de Brazza in Mbe, the location of Makoko's royal court at the time. The treaty allowed the French to set up a post at Nkuna, and it is this post that became Brazzaville in 1884.

9 Ngaliema himself married into the two important Humbu land-owning lineages of Lemba and Kimbangu (on the latter see also further in this chapter). Each of these controlled a considerable part of the land on which Kinshasa would later be built.

10 The 'Humbu' (a name that also designates a conglomerate of many different ethnic entities and clans) trace their origins to Kongo dia Ntotila, the Kongo empire of which Mbanza Kongo, nowadays the city of Sao Salvador in Angola, was the capital. According to their oral tradition, they left this Kongo heartland at the end of the seventeenth century and started to move towards their current location. The Teke, on the other hand, are believed to have originated in southeastern Gabon, and from there they steadily migrated to Congo-Brazzaville. It is around the Pool that the migratory histories of these two different groups collide. Before Stanley's arrival, the Teke had managed to establish themselves along the Pool and reduce the original Humbu inhabitants to the status of 'slaves', while gradually pushing them into the mountains to the southwest of the Pool (in what today is known as the neighbourhood of Binza in the municipality of Ngaliema). However, by the time Stanley arrived, Teke power had been considerably weakened due to a smallpox epidemic that had decimated the Teke population and had allowed the Humbu to get the upper hand again and reclaim the lands they had owned before. In the eyes of the Makoko of Lemba and other Humbu chiefs, Stanley's arrival could be useful in overthrowing the Teke. It is in this context that the Humbu discontent over the treaty signed between Stanley and Ngaliema must be understood. Angered, Humbu chief Makoko of Lemba, who controlled an important local market, closed the roads taking provisions to Leopoldville. In response, a punitive expedition was sent to Lemba in 1886 with the result that part of Lemba village was burnt down and some villagers were killed. In 1892, another punitive expedition was dispatched to Lemba because some of Makoko's subjects had killed a soldier and had attacked another local chief with whom the coloniser had negotiated a friendship treaty in the meantime. The chief of Lemba was sentenced to pay a large fine. He left his village shortly afterwards to resettle in Limete, where he died before 1907.

11 In 1885, the village of chief Ngampa at Djoué on the French side of the Pool was destroyed by a French military expedition, while the Teke village of Mpila suffered the same fate in 1887. In 1888, another French punitive expedition was launched against a Kongo village south of Brazzaville.

12 As part of this campaign, Franco and his orchestra OK Jazz, one of the leading bands in the Congolese popular music scene of the time, recorded the song *La loi Bakajika* in 1970. On the B-side of the record was a track called *Le pouvoir noir* (Black Power). In *La loi Bakajika*, Franco commented on the continuing hold over land by the colonial powers in South Africa, Rhodesia and the Portuguese colonies, and he compared this with the Congolese situation where, in his view, the Bakajika Law put an end to the colonial structures of land ownership.

13 On 31 December 1971, a constitutional amendment and the promulgation of a new land law empowered the state to repossess all land rights. In July 1973, the General Property Law was enacted to organise the country's new legal framework concerning land issues. With the enactment of the 1971 and 1973 laws, all lands now belonged to the state, and individual land rights had to derive from either state concessions or indigenous customary law (Meditz and Merrill 1994: 171).

14 This legal uncertainty is the topic of *Kafka in Congo*, a documentary film by Marlène Rabaud and Arnaud Zajtman (2010). Set in Kinshasa, it tells the story of a woman, Gorette, and her fifteen-year-long struggle to regain ownership of her house and land, unjustly taken from her with the help of corrupt government officials, lawyers and judges by someone also claiming to own the same plot.

15 This is the case of matrilineality more generally. Pentecostal discourses have also strongly impacted upon the redefinition of existing kinship landscapes along more patrilineally oriented lines (cf. De Boeck 2005b).

16 If that is the case, the baobab tree was probably planted by Anthony Swinburne, the head of the Kinshasa station at that time, who visited the village of Kimbangu in 1884 in order to conclude a number of land treaties with two local chiefs (cf.Fumunzanza 2011: 224).

17 As to the veracity of Kimbangu's passage there, see de Saint Moulin 2012: 66.

18 These were the official rates in 2010.

19 Heavy rainfall in late 2015, for example, caused this whole area to flood, leaving hundreds of people homeless. But even without such heavy rains the water levels in the Pool, a surface area of more than 500 km², are known to vary by as much as three meters over the course of a year.

20 In existence since the late 1960s, MAC is an agricultural development organisation that is financed and backed by the Chinese government and has a long history of agricultural projects (mainly rice cultivation) throughout Africa (cf. Diédhiou 2004: 236).

21 The daily newspaper *Le Phare* published an item about the court hearing on 7 December 2010.

22 Since its startup in 2008, the management of the *Cité du Fleuve* project (which will cover a substantial part of the horticultural marshlands if all goes to plan) has already been taken to court more than fifty times by a variety of other stakeholders and claimants (personal communication *Cité du Fleuve* management, February 2013).

23 Congo's administrative and territorial organisation consists of provinces and cities, both of which are organised in a slightly different manner. Provinces are subdivided into *districts*, *secteurs* and/or *chefferies*, *groupements*, and *villages*. Cities, on the other hand, consist of the following administrative units: municipalities (*communes*), *quartiers* and/or *groupements incorporés*. Kinshasa has a very complex administrative structure because it is both a city and a province (*ville-province*) and thus a combination of these two different layers of administrative organisation. The city of Kinshasa is not headed by a *maire*, for example, as other cities are in Congo, but by a *gouverneur*, the administrative head of a province. In the same way, the province of Kinshasa consists of districts (Lukunga, Funa, Mont Amba and Tshangu), but is also divided into 24 municipalities. Nine *groupements* are part of the administrative organisation of the city of Kinshasa (namely Ngimbi, Lutendele, Mbinza, Mbankana, Selembao, Kingabwa, Kimwenza, Mbenseke-Mfuti, Mikondo, Mikonga, Mvika Mikila and Kimpoko), but Kinshasa also consists of two *chefferies*, namely the Bateke *chefferie* (consisting of the Mbankana, Mongata, Mwe and Yuo *groupements*) and the Mbankana *chefferie* (consisting of the Nguma, Kingakati, Bu, Ngama and Kikimi *groupements*). These two *chefferies* are located in the eastern part of the province of Kinshasa and spread across the district of Tshangu and the Bateke Plateau, which continues into the neighbouring province of Bandundu. In short, Kinshasa's administrative structure is nebulous and opaque. Its different units and often conflicting levels of decision-making and authority constantly add to the chaotic and ungovernable nature of the city itself.

24 Especially in Kinshasa's eastern periphery along the Pool important Teke and Banfunu chiefs have been reigning over vast areas of land that their ancestors already controlled when Stanley arrived. These chiefs include Kingakati and Nguma. The latter resides at the entrance of the Pool in what is now Maluku, a Leopoldville outpost created in 1923 which has since become one of Kinshasa's municipalities. Nguma controls an active network of sub-chiefs such as Mikala, who lives in Kinkole. Kingakati, Nguma and Mikala still wear medals that they were awarded by the early colonial administration of the Belgian Congo in recognition of their status of *chef indigène*.

25 In some cases chiefs continue to use copies of title deeds used by the colonial administration.

26 This does not immediately have to be a house construction, for that involves financial resources that few people have at their disposal. Instead, the construction of a single wall, or even a pit latrine already suffices to demonstrate that people seriously intend to occupy this plot.

27 Red is a colour that symbolises traditional political power in this part of Central Africa.

References

Agamben, Giorgio. 2005. *State of Exception*. Chicago: The University of Chicago Press.

Agualusa, José Eduardo. 2009. *Barroco Tropical*. Alfragide: Publicações Dom Quixote.

Alemani, Cecilia. 2006. *William Kentridge*. Milan: Mondadori Electa.

Amin, Ash, and Stephen Graham. 1997. The Ordinary City. *Transactions of the Royal Geographical Society (Institute of British Geographers)* 22: 411–29.

Amin, Ash. 2015. Animated Space. *Public Culture* 27 (2): 239-258.

Amselle, Jean-Loup. 2001. *Branchements: anthropologie de l'universalité des cultures*. Paris: Flammarion.

Ansoms, An, Inge Wagemakers, Michael Madison Walker, and Jude Murison. 2014. Land Contestations at the Micro Scale. Struggles for Spaces in the African Marshes. *World Development* 54: 243-252.

Appiah, Anthony Kwame. 1992. *In my Father's House. Africa in the Philosophy of Culture*. London: Methuen.

Arendt, Hannah. 1998 (1958). *The Human Condition*. Chicago: The University of Chicago Press.

Arndt, Lotte. 2013. Vestiges of Oblivion. Sammy Baloji's work on Skulls in European Museum Collections. *Darkmatter in the Ruins of Imperial Culture* 11. [Online journal].

Articlaut, Francis. 2003. *Pume Bylex plasticien*. Montreuil: Les Editions de l'oeil.

Attali, Jacques. 2011. *A Brief History of the Future. A Brave and Controversial Look at the Twenty-First Century*. New York: Arcade.

Augustijnen, Sven. 2011. *Spectres*. Brussels: ASA Publishers. [Feature documentary, 104 minutes].

Ayimpam, Sylvie. 2014a. *Economie de la débrouille à Kinshasa. Informalité, commerce et réseaux sociaux*. Paris: Karthala.

Ayimpam, Sylvie. 2014b. The Cyclical Exchange of Violence in Congolese Kinship Relations. In: Jacky Bouju and Mirjam de Bruijn (Eds.), *Ordinary Violence and Social Change in Africa*. Leyden / Boston: Brill. Pp. 101-116.

Baloji, Sammy. 2007. *Mémoire*. [Video film in collaboration with Faustin Linyekula, 14 minutes].

Bayat, Asef. 2012. Politics in the City-Inside-Out. *City and Society* 24 (2): 110-128.

Bayart, Jean-François. 2000. Africa in the World: A History of Extraversion. *African Affairs* 99 (395): 217-267.

Beal, Jo and Sean Fox. 2009. *Cities and Development*. London: Routledge.

Beeckmans, Luce. 2013. *Making the African City. Dakar – Dar es Salaam – Kinshasa / 1920-1980*. Groningen: Rijksuniversiteit Groningen. [Unpublished doctoral dissertation].

Beeckmans, Luce and Johan Lagae. 2015. Kinshasa's Syndrome-planning in Historical Perspective: From Belgian Colonial Capital to Self-constructed Megalopolis. In: Carlos Nunes Silva (Ed.), *Urban Planning in Sub-Saharan Africa: Colonial and Post-colonial Planning Cultures*. New York: Routledge. Pp. 201-224.

Benjamin, Walter. 1972 (1934). A Short History of Photography. *Screen* 13 (1): 5-26.

Bernault, Florence. 2013. Carnal Technologies and the Double Life of the Body in Gabon. *Critical African Studies* 5 (3): 175-194.

Biehl, João. 2005. *Vita. Life in a Zone of Social Abandonment*. Berkeley: University of California Press.

Bloch, Maurice and Jonathan Parry (Eds.). 1982. *Death and the Regeneration of Life*. Cambridge: Cambridge University Press.

Bofane, In Koli Jean. 2008. *Mathématiques congolaises*. Paris: Actes Sud.

Bourdieu, Pierre. 1982. *Ce que parler veut dire. L'économie des échanges linguistiques*. Paris: Fayard.

Breytenbach, Breyten. 2009 (1984). *Mouroir*. New York: Archipelago Books.

Burke, Timothy. 1996. *Lifebuoy Men, Lux Women. Commodification, Consumption, and Cleanliness in Modern Zimbabwe*. Durham: Duke University Press.

Bustin, Edouard. 1975. *Lunda under Belgian Rule. The Politics of Ethnicity*. Cambridge, Mass. / London: Harvard University Press.

Butcher, Tim. 2007. *Blood River: A Journey to Africa's Broken Heart*. London: Chatto & Windus.

Capelle, Emmanuel. 1947. *La cité indigène de Léopoldville*. Léopoldville / Elisabethville: Centre d'études sociales africaines / Centre d'études des problèmes sociaux indigènes.

Cartry, Michel. 1987. Avant-propos. In: Michel Cartry (Ed.), *Sous le masque de l'animal. Essais sur le sacrifice en Afrique noire*. Paris: Presses Universitaires de France. Pp. 7-10.

Cassiman, Ann. (2013). *Journeys and Generations in a Diviner's Bag*. [Oral presentation at the European Conference on African Studies African ECAS. Lisbon, 26-30 June 2013].

Césaire, Aimé. 1966. *Une saison au Congo*. Paris: Seuil.

Chabal, Patrick and Jean-Pascal Daloz (1999). *Africa Works: Disorder as Political Instrument*. Oxford: James Currey.

Chalfin, Brenda. 2014. Public Things, Excremental Politics, and the Infrastructure of Bare Life in Ghana's City of Tema. *American Ethnologist* 41 (1): 92–109.

Castells, Manuel. 2000. *End of Millenium. (The Information Age: Economy, Society and Culture. Vol 3)*. Oxford: Blackwell.

Cole, Jennifer. 2011. A Cultural Dialectics of Generational Change: The View from Contemporary Africa. *Review of Research in Education* 35 (1): 60-88.

Cole, Jennifer and Deborah Durham (Eds.). 2007. *Generations and Globalization: Youth, Age, and Family in the New World Economy*. Bloomington, IN: Indiana University Press.

Comaroff, Jean and John L. Comaroff (Eds.). 2006. *Law and Disorder in the Postcolony*. Chicago: The University of Chicago Press.

Connerton, Paul. 2011. *The Spirit of Mourning. History, Memory and the Body*. Cambridge: Cambridge University Press.

Conrad, Joseph. 1961 (1898). An Outpost of Progress. In: Joseph Conrad, *Almayer's Folly. A Story of an Eastern River* and *Tales of Unrest*. London: J.M. Dent & Sons.

Conrad Joseph. 1983 (1902). *Heart of Darkness*. Harmondsworth, Middlesex: Penguin Books.

Conrad Joseph. 1962 (1917). *The Shadow Line: A Confession*. London: J.M. Dent & Sons.

Couttenier, Maarten. 2011. L'expédition scientifique du Katanga. In: Sammy Baloji and Patrick Mudekereza (Eds.), *Congo Far West. Arts, sciences et collections*. Tervuren: Royal Museum of Central Africa. P. 37.

Crapanzano, Vincent. 2003. Reflections on Hope as a Category of Social and Psychological Analysis. *Cultural Anthropology* 18 (1): 3-32.

Crine, Fernand. 1963. Aspects politico-sociaux du système de tenure de terres des Lunda septentrionaux. In: Daniel Biebuyck (Ed.), *African Agrarian Systems*. London : Oxford University Press. Pp. 157-172.

Cunnison, Ian. 1956. Perpetual Kinship: A Political Institution of the Luapula Peoples. *The Rhodes-Livingstone Journal* 20: 28-48.

Cuvelier, Jeroen. 2011. *Men, Mines and Masculinities: The Lives and Practices of Artisanal Miners in Lwambo (Katanga Province, DR Congo)*. Leuven: Catholic University of Leuven. [Unpublished doctoral dissertation].

Das, Veena and Clara Han (Eds.) 2016. *Living and Dying in the Contemporary World: A Compendium*. Oakland, CA: University of California Press.

D'Ascenzo, Fabiana. 2013. An African Metropolis: The Imploded Territoriality of Kinshasa. *Investigaciones Geográficas. Boletim de Instituto de Geografia* 80: 98-110.

Davis, M., 2006, *Planet of Slums*. London / New York: Verso.

de Abreu, Maria José A. 2013. Technological Indeterminacy: Medium, Threat, Temporality. *Anthropological Theory* 13 (3): 267-284.

De Boeck, Filip. 1991a. Of Bushbucks without Horns: Male and Female Initiation among the Aluund of Southwest Zaire. *Journal des Africanistes* 61 (1): 37-71.

De Boeck, Filip. 1991b. Therapeutic Efficacy and Consensus among the Aluund of Southwestern Zaire. *Africa* 61 (2): 159-185.

De Boeck, Filip. 1994a. 'When Hunger Goes Around the Land': Hunger and Food Among the Aluund of Zaire. *Man* 29 (2): 257-282.

De Boeck, Filip. 1994b. Of Trees and Kings: Politics and Metaphor among the Aluund of Southwestern Zaire. *American Ethnologist* 21 (3): 451-473.

De Boeck, Filip. 1998a. Domesticating Diamonds and Dollars: Identity, Expenditure and Sharing in Southwestern Zaire (1984–1997). *Development and Change* 29 (4): 777-810.

De Boeck, Filip. 1998b. Beyond the Grave: History, Memory and Death in Postcolonial Congo/Zaire. In: Richard Werbner (Ed.), *Memory and the Postcolony. African Anthropology and the Critique of Power*. London: Zed Books. Pp. 21-57.

De Boeck, Filip. 1999. 'Dogs breaking their leash': Globalisation and shifting gender categories in the diamond traffic between Angola and D.R. Congo (1984-

1997). In: Danielle de Lame and Chantal Zabus (Eds.), *Changements au féminin en Afrique noire: anthropologie et littérature (volume 1)*. Paris/Tervuren: L'Harmattan / Royal lmuseum of Central Africa. Pp. 87-114.

De Boeck, Filip. 2000. Borderland Breccia: The Mutant Hero in the Historical Imagination of a Central-African Diamond Frontier. *Journal of Colonialism and Colonial History* 1 (2): 1-43.

De Boeck, Filip. 2001. *Garimpeiro* Worlds: Digging, Dying & 'Hunting' for Diamonds in Angola. *Review of African Political Economy* 28 (90): 549-562.

De Boeck, Filip, 2005a The Apocalyptic Interlude: Revealing Death in Kinshasa. *African Studies Review* 48 (2): 11-32.

De Boeck, Filip. 2005b. Children, Gift and Witchcraft in the Democratic Republic of Congo. In: Alcinda Honwana and Filip De Boeck (Eds.), *Makers and Breakers. Children and Youth in Postcolonial Africa*. Oxford / Trenton / Dakar: James Currey / Africa World Press / Codesria. Pp. 188-214.

De Boeck, Filip. 2006. La ville de Kinshasa, une architecture du verbe *Esprit* 12: 79-105.

De Boeck, Filip. 2008a. 'Dead Society' in a 'Cemetery City': The Transformation of Burial Rites in Kinshasa. In: Lieven Decauter & Michiel Dehaene (Eds.), *Heterotopia and the City: Public Space in a Postcivil Society*. London: Routledge. Pp. 297-308.

De Boeck, Filip. 2008b. On Being Shege in Kinshasa: Children, the Occult and the Street. In: Michael Lambek (Ed.), *A Reader in the Anthropology of Religion (Second Edition)*. Oxford: Blackwell. Pp. 495-505.

De Boeck, Filip. 2009a. Death Matters: Intimacy, Violence and the Production of Social Knowledge by Urban Youth in the Democratic Republic of Congo. In: Antonio Pinto Ribeiro (Ed.), *Can There Be Life Without the Other?* Manchester: Carcanet Press. Pp. 44-64.

De Boeck, Filip. 2009b. At Risk, as Risk: Abandonment and Care in a World of Spiritual Insecurity. In: Jean La Fontaine (Ed.), *The Devil s Children. From Spirit Possession to Witchcraft: New Allegations* that *Affect Children*. Farnham, Surrey: Ashgate. Pp. 129-150.

De Boeck, Filip. 2010. *Cemetery State*. Antwerp / Amsterdam: Filmnatie / Viewpoint. [Documentary Film, 70 minutes].

De Boeck, Filip. 2011. Inhabiting Ocular Ground: Kinshasa's Future in the Light of Congo's Spectral Urban Politics. *Cultural Anthropology* 26 (2): 263-286.

De Boeck, Filip. 2012a. City on the Move: How Urban Dwellers in Central Africa Manage the Siren's Call of Migration. In: Knut Graw and Samuli Schielke (Eds.), *The Global Horizon. Expectations of migration in Africa and the Middle East.* Leuven: Leuven University Press. Pp. 59-85.

De Boeck, Filip. 2012b. Diamonds and Disputes: Conflict and Local Power on the Border Between Congo and Angola. In: Katja Werthmann and Tilo Grätz (Eds.), *Mining Frontiers: Anthropological and Historical Perspectives.* Cologne: Rüdiger Köppe Verlag. Pp. 73-96.

De Boeck, Filip. 2015. The Tower. A Concrete Utopia. Notes on a video-installation by Sammy Baloji and Filip De Boeck In: Holm, Michael Juul and Mette Marie Kallehauge (Eds.), *Africa Architecture Culture Identity.* Copenhagen: Louisiana Museum of Modern Art. Pp. 84-88.

De Boeck, Filip and René Devisch. 1994. Ndembu, Luunda and Yaka Divination Compared: From Representation and Social Engineering to Embodiment and Worldmaking. *Journal of Religion in Africa* 24 (2): 98-133.

De Boeck, Filip and Marie-Françoise Plissart. 2004. *Kinshasa. Tales of the Invisible City.* Ghent / Tervuren: Ludion / Royal Museum of Central Africa.

De Boeck, Filip and Koen Van Synghel. 2008. *The World According to Bylex.* Brussels: Koninklijke Vlaamse Schouwburg / Africalia.

De Boeck, Filip, Ann Cassiman and Steven Van Wolputte. 2010. Recentering the City: An Anthropology of Secondary Cities in Africa. In: Karel A. Bakker (Ed.), *African Perspectives 2009. The African Inner City: [Re]sourced.* Pretoria: University of Pretoria. Pp. 33-41.

De Herdt, Tom and Wim Marivoet. 2011. Capabilities in Place: Locating Poverty and Affluence in Kinshasa (Democratic Republic of Congo). *Journal of Human Development and Capabilities: A Multi-Disciplinary Journal for People-Centered Development* 12 (2): 235-256.

De Herdt, Tom and Jean-Pierre Olivier de Sardan (Eds.). 2015. *Real Governance and Practical Norms in Sub-Saharan Africa. The Game of the Rules.* London: Routledge.

Deibert, Michael. 2013. *The Democratic Republic of Congo. Between Hope and Despair.* London / New York: Zed Books.

Dekossago Kpalawele, Ben Bathwa and B.B. Namayele. 2003-2004. Les phénomènes bamamans manoeuvres, papa tactiques, bana mbwengi et bana kwata. Etude de la nature juridique de ces phénomènes. *Annales de la Faculté de Droit* XI-XXVII: 163-170. Kinshasa: Presses de l'Université de Kinshasa.

de Maximy, René. 1984. *Kinshasa, ville en suspens. Dynamiques de la croissance et problems d'urbanisme: etude socio-politique.* Paris: Editions de l'Office de la Recherché Scientifique et Technique Outre-Mer.

De Meulder, Bruno. 2000. *Kuvuande Mbote. Een eeuw koloniale architectuur en stedenbouw in Kongo.* Antwerp: Houtekiet / deSingel.

Demos, T.J. and Hilde Van Gelder (Eds.). 2012. *In and Out of Brussels. Figuring Postcolonial Africa and Europe in the Films of Herman Asselberghs, Sven Augustijnen, Renzo Martens and Els Opsomer.* Leuven: Leuven University Press.

Denis, Léopold. 1943. *Les Jesuites Belges au Kwango 1893 – 1943.* Bruxelles: L'Edition Universelle.

Derrida, Jacques. 2000. *Of Hospitality: Anne Dufourmantelle Invites Derrida to Respond.* Stanford: Stanford University Press.

Derrida, Jacques. 2013. Avowing – The Impossible: 'Returns,' Repentance, and Reconciliation. In: Elisabeth Weber (Ed.), *Living Together. Jacques Derrida's Communities of Violence and Peace.* New York: Fordham University Press. Pp. 18-41.

de Saint Moulin, Léon. 2007. Croissance de Kinshasa et transformations du réseau urbain de la République Démocratique du Congo depuis l'indépendance. In: Jean-Luc Vellut (Ed.), *Villes d'Afrique. Explorations en histoire urbaine.* Paris / Tervuren: L'Harmattan / Royal Museum of Central Africa. Pp. 41-65.

de Saint Moulin, Léon. 2012. *Kinshasa. Enracinements historiques et horizons culturels.* Paris / Tervuren : L'Harmattan / Royal Museum of Central Africa.

de Solà-Morales Rubio, Manuel. 2004. *The Strategy of Urban Acupuncture.* Presentation at the Structure Fabric and Topography Conference, Nanjing University, Nanjing, China, May 29-31 2004.

de Solà-Morales Rubio, Ignasi. 1995. Terrain Vague. In: Cynthia C. Davidson (Ed.) *Anyplace.* Cambridge, MA: MIT Press. Pp. 118-123.

de Villers, Gauthier (Ed.). 1996. *Phénomènes informels et dynamiques culturelles en Afrique.* Tervuren / Paris: Institut Africain-CEDAF / L'Harmattan.

Devisch, René. 1993. *Weaving the Threads of Life. The Khita Gyn-Eco-Logical Healing Cult Among the Yaka.* Chicago: The University of Chicago Press.

Devisch, René. 1995. Frenzy, Violence, and Ethical Renewal in Kinshasa. *Public Culture* 7: 593-629.

Devisch, René. 1998. La violence à Kinshasa, ou l'institution en negatif. *Cahiers d'études africaines* 38 (150-152): 441-469.

Devisch, René. 2013. Of Divinatory Co-naissance among the Yaka of the DRCongo. In: Walter E. A. Van Beek and Philip M. Peek (Eds.), *Reviewing Reality. Dynamics of African Divination.* Berlin: LIT. Pp. 25-58.

Devisch, Renaat and Wauthier de Mahieu. 1979. *Mort, deuil et compensations mortuaires chez les Komo et les Yaka du nord au Zaïre.* Tervuren: Royal Museum of Central Africa.

Diédhiou, Lamine. 2004. *Riz, symbols et développement chez les Diola de Basse-Casamance.* Quebec : Presses de l'Université Laval.

Diphoorn, Tessa G. 2015. *Twilight Policing. Private Security and Violence in Urban South Africa*. Berkeley: University of California Press.

Dissisa Vincent. 2003. Violence et funérailles au Congo-Brazzaville. *Bulletin de l'APAD* 25: 89-97.

Dississa, Vincent. 2009. Pouvoirs et chansons populaires au Congo-Brazzaville. Les funérailles comme lieu de la dénonciation politique. *Civilisations (Revue international d'anthropologie et de sciences humaines)* 58 (2): 81-95.

Doyle, Michael. 2009. Urban Mass Evacuation in the United States. In: Gary Cordner, Dilip K. Das and AnnMarie Cordner (Eds.), *Urbanization, Policing, and Security: Global Perspectives*. London: CRC Press. Pp. 195-201.

Duffield, Mark. 2002. *Global Governance and the New Wars: The Merging of Development and Security*. New York: Zed Books.

Dumon, Dirk and René Devisch. 1991. *The Oracle of Maama Tseembu: Divination and Healing among the Yaka of southwestern Zaire*. Brussels: Belgian-Flemish Radio and Television (VRT), Science Division. [Ethnographic film, 50 minutes].

Dunn, Kevin C. 2003. *Imagining the Congo: The International Relations of Identity*. New York: Palgrave Macmillan.

Durham, Deborah and Frederick Klaits. 2002. Funerals and the Public Space of Sentiment in Botswana. *Journal of Southern African Studies* 28 (4): 777-796.

Dyer, Geoff. 2012 (2005). *The Ongoing Moment. A Book about Photographs*. Edinburgh / London: Canongate Books.

Easterling, Keller. 2014. *Extrastatecraft. The Power of Infrastructure Space*. London / New York: Verso.

Edensor, Tim and Mark Jayne (Eds.). 2012. *Urban Theory Beyond the West. A World of Cities*. London / New York: Routledge.

Eliade, Mircea. 1952. Le 'Dieu-Lieur' et le symbolisme des noeuds. In: Mircea Eliade, *Images et symboles. Essais sur le symbolisme magico-religieux*. Paris: Gallimard. Pp. 120-163.

Elkjaer, Laurits. 2010. Interview with M. Casagrande on Urban Acupuncture. [http://alternativelegacybergen.blogspot.pt/2010/04/interview-witm-m-casagrande-on-urban.html]

Ellin, Nan. 2006. *Integral Urbanism*. New York / London: Routledge.

Ellis, Stephen. 2011. *Seasons of Rain: Africa in the World*. London: Hurst and Company.

Elyachar, Julia. 2010. Phatic Labor, Infrastructure, and the Question of Empowerment in Cairo. *American Ethnologist* 37 (3): 452-464.

Engelke, Matthew. 2010. Past Pentecostalism: Notes on Rupture, Realignment, and Everyday Life in Pentecostal and African Independent Churches. *Africa* 80 (2): 177-199.

Enwezor, Okwui (Ed.). 2002a. *Under Siege: Four African Cities: Freetown, Johannesburg, Kinshasa, Lagos*. Ostfildern-Ruit: Hatje Cantz Publishers.

Enwezor, Okwui. 2002b. The Black Box. In: Okwui Enwezor (Ed.), *Documenta 11_Platform 5: Exhibition Catalogue*. Ostfildern-Ruit: Hatje Cantz Publishers. Pp. 42-55.

Ernstson, Henrik, Mary Lawton and James Duminy. 2014. Conceptual Vectors of African Urbanism: 'Engaged Theory-Making' and 'Platforms of Engagement'. *Regional Studies* 48 (9): 1563-1577.

Fabian, Johannes. 1972. How Others Die: Reflections on the Anthropology of Death. *Social Research* 39 (3): 543-567.

Fabian, Johannes. 1998. *Moments of Freedom: Anthropology and Popular Culture*. Charlottesville: University Press of Virginia.

Fabian, Johannes. 2000. *Out of Our Minds. Reason and Madness in the Exploration of Central Africa*. Berkeley: University of California Press.

Fanon, Frantz. 1952. *Peau noire, masques blancs*. Paris: Seuil.

Fanon, Frantz. 1961. *Les damnés de la terre*. Paris: Francois Maspero.

Ferguson, James. 1999. *Expectations of Modernity: Myths and Meanings of Urban Life on the Zambian Copperbelt*. Berkeley: University of California Press.

Ferguson, James. *Global Shadows. Africa in the Neoliberal World Order*. Durham / London: Duke University Press.

Fields, Karen E. 1985. *Revival and Rebellion in Colonial Central Africa*. Princeton, N.J.: Princeton University Press.

Fitzmaurice, Andrew. 2014. *Sovereignty, Property and Empire, 1500-2000*. Cambridge: Cambridge University Press.

Foucault, Michel. 1995. *Discipline and Punishment*. New York: Vintage Books.

Frère, Marie-Soleil. 2007. Quand le pluralisme déraille : images et manipulations télévisuelles à Kinshasa. *Africultures* 71 (October issue): 47-55.

Freund, William. 2009. *The Congolese Elite and the Fragmented City: The Struggle for the Emergence of a Dominant Class in Kinshasa*. London: London School of Economics [Crisis States Working Papers Series N° 2].

Fumunzanza Muketa, Jacques. 2008. *Kinshasa: d'un quartier à l'autre*. Paris: L'Harmattan.

Gamwell, Lynn. 2002. *Exploring the Invisible. Art, Science and the Spiritual* Princeton / Oxford: Princeton University Press.

Garbin, David and Wa Gamoka Pambu. 2009. *Roots and Routes. Congolese Diaspora in Multicultural Britain*. London: Centre for Research on Nationalism, Ethnicity and Multiculturalism, Roehampton University.

Geenen, Kristien. 2009. 'Sleep Occupies no Space.' The Use of Public Space by Street Gangs in Kinshasa. *Africa* 79 (3): 347-368.

Geschiere, Peter. 2013. *Witchcraft, Intimacy, and Trust: Africa in Comparison*. Chicago: The University of Chicago Press.

Geschiere, Peter and Piet Konings (Eds). 1993. *Pathways to Accumulation in Cameroon*. Paris / Leyden: Karthala / Afrika Studiecentrum.

Geurts, Kathryn Linn. 2002. *Culture and the Senses. Bodily Ways of Knowing in an African Community*. Berkeley: University of California Press.

Goldstone, Brian. 2011 The Miraculous Life. *The Johannesburg Salon* 4: 81-96.

Gondola, Charles-Didier. 1999. Dream and Drama: The Search for Elegance among Congolese Youth. *African Studies Review* 42 (1): 23-48.

Gondola, Charles-Didier. 2009. Tropical Cowboys: Westerns, Violence, and Masculinity among the Young Bills of Kinshasa. *Afrique & Histoire* 7: 75-98.

Gondola, Charles-Didier. 2013. Le culte du *cowboy* et les figures du masculine à Kinshasa dans les années 1950. *Cahiers d'études africaines* 209 (1-2): 173-199.

Gordillo, Gaston R. 2014. *Rubble. The Afterlife of Destruction*. Durham / London: Duke University Press.

Graw, Knut and Samuli Schielke (Eds.). 2012. *The Global Horizon. Expectations of Migration in Africa and the Middle East*. Leuven: Leuven University Press.

Grootaers, Jan-Lodewijk (Ed.).1998. *Mort et maladie au Zaire*. Tervuren / Paris: Institut Africain-CEDAF / L'Harmattan.

Guyer, Jane 2007. Prophecy and the Near Future: Thoughts on Macroeconomic, Evangelical and Punctuated Time. *American Ethnologist* 34 (3): 409-421.

Guyer, Jane. 2011. Describing Urban 'No Man's Land' in Africa. *Africa* 81 (3): 474-492.

Hagman, Tobias and Didier Péclard (Eds.). 2011. *Negotiating Statehood: Dynamics of Power and Domination in Africa*. London: Wiley-Blackwell.

Hamadi, Dieudo. 2013. *Atalaku*. Kinshasa: Mutatu Productions. [Documentary film, 62 minutes].

Harms, Erik. 2012. Beauty as Control in the New Saigon: Eviction, New Urban Zones, and Atomized Dissent in a Southeast Asian City. *American Ethnologist* 39 (4): 735-750.

Hendriks, Thomas. 2013. *Work in the Rainforest. Labour, Race and Desire in a Congolese Logging Camp*. Leuven: University of Leuven. [Unpublished doctoral dissertation].

Herrick, Clare. 2014. Healthy Cities of / from the South. In: Susan Parnell and Sophie Oldfield (Eds.), *The Routledge Handbook on Cities of the Global South*. London / New York: Routledge. Pp. 556-568.

Heywood, Linda. 2000. *Contested Power in Angola, 1840s to the Present*. Rochester, NY: University of Rochester Press.

Hochschild, Adam. 1998. *King Leopold's Ghost*. Boston / New York: Houghton Mifflin Company.

Holston, James. 1989. *The Modernist City. An Anthropological Critique of Brasilia*. Chicago / London: The University of Chicago Press.

Honwana, Alcinda. 2012. *The Time of Youth. Work, Social Change and Politics in Africa*. Sterling, VA: Kumarian Press.

Howe, Cymene, Jessica Lockrem, Hannah Appel, Edward Hackett, Dominic Boyer, Randal Hall, Matthew Schneider-Mayerson, Albert Pope, Akhil Gupta, Elizabeth Rodwell, Andrea Ballestero, Trevor Durbin, Farès el-Dahdah, Elizabeth Long, Cyrus Mody. 2015. Paradoxical Infrastructures. Ruins, Retrofit, and Risk. *Science, Technology & Human Values*. [DOI: 10.1177/0162243915620017].

Hunt, Nancy Rose. 2013. *Suturing New Medical Histories of Africa*. Berlin: Lit Verlag [Carl Schlettwein Lectures vol. 7].

Hughes, Robert. 2013 (1981). *The Shock of the New: Art and the Century of Change*. New York: Alfred A. Knopf.

Iliffe, John. 1987. *The African Poor: A History*. Cambridge: Cambridge University Press.

Ingold, Tim. 2007. *Lines: A Brief History*. London / New York: Routledge.

Jackson, Michael. 2011. *Life within Limits. Well-being in a World of Want*. Durham / London: Duke University Press.

Jewsiewicki, Bogumil. 2010. *The Beautiful Time. Photography by Sammy Baloji*, New York: Museum for African Art.

Jewsiewicki, Bogumil. 2014. Denial and Challenge of Modernity: Suffering, Recognition, and Dignity in Photographs by Sammy Baloji. In: Ratiba Hadj-Moussa and Michael Nijhawan (Eds.), *Suffering, Art, and Aesthetics*. New York: Palgrave MacMillan. Pp. 51-74.

Jewsiewicki, Bogumil and Bob White. 2005. Introduction. *African Studies Review* 48 (2): 1-9. [Special issue on *Mourning and the Imagination of Political Time in Contemporary Central Africa*].

Jindra, Michael and Joël Noret (Eds.). 2011. *Funerals in Africa. Explorations of a Social Phenomenon*. New York / Oxford: Berghahn Books.

Jones, Sue and Nici Nelson (Eds.). 1999. *Urban Poverty in Africa. From Understanding to Alleviation*. London: Intermediate Technology Publications.

Jung, Dietrich (Ed.). 2003. *Shadow Globalization, Ethnic Conflicts, and New Wars: A Political Economy of Intra-State War*. London / New York: Routledge.

Kalia, Ravi. 1999. *Chandigarh: The Making of an Indian City*. New Delhi: Oxford University Press.

Kamba, Pierre. 2008. *La violence politique au Congo-Kinshasa*. Paris: L'Harmattan.

Kaminer, Tahl, Miguel Robles-Duran, and Heidi Sohn (Eds.). 2011. *Urban Asymmetries: Studies and Projects on Neoliberal Urbanization*. Rotterdam: 010 Publishers.

Kapagama, Pascal and Rachel Waterhouse. 2009. *Portrait of Kinshasa: A City on (the) Edge*. London: London School of Economics Development Studies Institute. [Crisis States Working Papers Series No.2].

Kaur, Ravinder and Thomas Blom Hansen. 2015. Aesthetics of Arrival: Spectacle, Capital, Novelty in Post-Reform India. *Identities: Global Studies in Culture and Power*. [DOI:10.1080/1070289X.2015.1034135].

Kavenadiambuko, Ngamba Ntima. 1999. *La méthode d'évangélisation des Rédemptoristes belges au Bas-Congo (1899-1919)*. Rome: Gregorian University Press.

Kentridge, William. 2005. *Black Box / Chambre Noire*. Berlin: Deutsche Guggenheim.

Kilcullen, David, 2013, *Out of the Mountains: The Coming Age of the Urban Guerrilla*. New York: Oxford University Press.

Kisangani, Emizet François and F. Scott Bobb. 2010. *Historical Dictionary of the Democratic Republic of the Congo*. Lanham, MD: Scarecrow Press.

Kittelmann, Udo and Klaus Görner (Eds.). 2004. *Teresa Margolles: Muerte Sin Fin*. Ostfildern-Ruit: Hatje Cantz Publishers.

Kolonga Molei. 1979. *Kinshasa, ce village d'hier*. Kinshasa: SODIMCA.

Kopytoff, Igor. 1971. Ancestors as Elders in Africa. *Africa* 41 (2): 129–42.

Kopytoff, Igor. 1988 (1965). The Suku of Southwestern Congo. In: James L. Gibbs Jr. (Ed.), *The Peoples of Africa*. New York: Holt, Rinehart and Winston. Pp. 441-478.

314

Krings, Matthias. 2015. *African Appropriations. Cultural Difference, Mimemis, and Media.* Bloomington / Indianapolis: Indiana University Press.

Künkel, Jenny and Margit Mayer (Eds.). 2012. *Neoliberal Urbanism and its Contestations: Crossing Theoretical Boundaries.* Basingstoke: Palgrave Macmillan.

La Fontaine, Jean S. 1970. *City Politics. A Study of Léopoldville 1962-63.* Cambridge: Cambridge University Press.

Lagae, Johan. 2002. *Kongo zoals het is. Drie architectuurverhalen uit de Belgische kolonisatiegeschiedenis (1920-1960).* Ghent: University of Ghent. [Unpublished doctoral dissertation].

Lagae, Johan. 2007. Léopoldville, Bruxelles: villes miroirs? L'architecture et l'urbanisme d'une capitale colonial et métropole africaine. In: Jean-Luc Vellut (Ed.), *Villes d'Afrique. Explorations en histoire urbaine.* Paris / Tervuren: L'Harmattan / Royal Museum of Central Africa. Pp. 67-99.

Lagae, Johan. 2013. Kinshasa. Tales of the Tangible City. *ABE Journal. European Architecture Beyond Europe* 3. [DOI: 10.4000/abe.378].

Lagae, Johan, Sofie Boonen and Maarten Liefooghe. 2013. Fissures dans le « cordon sanitaire ». Architecture hospitalière et ségrégation urbaine à Lubumbashi, 1920-1960. In : Maurice Amuri Mpala Lutebele (Ed.), *Lubumbashi, cent ans d'histoire : littératures, cultures urbaines, débats intellectuels.* Paris : L'Harmattan. Pp. 247-261.

Lagae, Johan and Bernard Toulier (Eds.). 2013. *Kinshasa.* Brussels: CIVA.

Lamont, Mark. 2009. 'Interroger les morts pour critiquer les vivants, ou exotisme morbide?' Encounters with African Funerary Practices in Francophone Anthropology. *Africa* 79 (3): 455-462.

Lambertz, Peter. 2015. *Divisive Matters: Aesthetic Difference and Authority in a Congolese Spiritual Movement 'from Japan'.* Utrecht: University of Utrecht. [Unpublished doctoral dissertation].

Laranjeira Rodrigues de Areia, Manuel. 1985. *Les symboles divinatoires : analyse socio-culturelle d'une technique de divination des Cokwe de l'Angola (Ngombo ya Cisuka).* Coimbra: Instituto de Antropologia Universidade de Coimbra.

Larkin, Brian. 2013. The Politics and Poetics of Infrastructure. *Annual Review of Anthropology* 42: 327-343.

Latour, Bruno. 2005a. *Reassembling the Social. An Introduction to Actor-Network-Theory.* Oxford: Oxford University Press.

Latour, Bruno. 2005b. From Realpolitik to Dingpolitik. In: Bruno Latour and Peter Weibel (Eds.), *Making Things Public: Atmospheres of Democracy.* Cambridge / Karlsruhe: MIT Press / ZKM Karlsruhe. Pp. 4-31.

Lawhon, Mary, Henrik Ernstson and Jonathan Silver. 2014. Provincializing Urban Political Ecology: Towards a Situated UPE Through African Urbanism. *Antipode* 46 (2): 497-516.

Lee, Rebekka.2011. Death 'on the Move': Funerals, Entrepreneurs and the Rural-Urban Nexus in South Africa, *Africa* 81 (2): 226-47.

Legros, Hugues. 1996. *Chasseurs d'ivoire. Une histoire du royaume yeke du Shaba (Zaïre).* Brussels: Editions de l'Université de Bruxelles.

Lelo Nzuzi, Francis. 2008. *Kinshasa. Ville et environnement.* Paris: L'Harmattan.

Levie, Françoise. 2006. *L'homme qui voulait classer le monde. Paul Otlet et le Mundaneum.* Brussels: Les Impressions Nouvelles.

Lévi-Strauss, Claude. 1974 (1955). *Tristes Tropiques.* New York: Atheneum.

Liotta, P.H. and James F. Miskel. 2012. *The Real Population Bomb. Megacities, Global Security and the Map of the Future.* Washington, D.C.: Potomac Books.

Livingston, Julie. 2008. Disgust, Bodily Aesthetics and the Ethics of Being Human, *Africa* 78 (2): 288-307.

Lund, Christian (Ed.). 2007. *Twilight Institutions. Public Authority and Local Politics in Africa.* Oxford: Blackwell.

Lusamba Kibayu, Michel. 2010. *Évolution des pratiques de sécurisation des conditions de vie dans trois quartiers populaires de Kinshasa: Enjeux et conséquences de la production spatiale et sociale de la ville.* Louvain-la-Neuve: Presses Universitaires de Louvain.

Lynch, David. 1997. *Lost Highway* . Paris: Ciby 2000 / Asymmetrical Production. [Feature film, 135 minutes].

Lynch, David. 1999 *The Straight Story.* Burbank, CA: Walt Disney Pictures. [Feature film, 112 minutes].

MacGaffey, Janet. 1987. *Entrepreneurs and Parasites: the Struggle for Indigenous Capitalism in Zaire.* Cambridge: Cambridge University Press.

Magnin, André. 2003. *Bodys Isek Kingelez.* Brussels: La Médiatine.

Malaquais, Dominique. 2011. Anti-Teleology. In: Edgar Pieterse and Ntone Edjabe (Eds.), *African Cities Reader II. Mobilities and Fixtures.* Vlaeberg, SA: African Centre for Cities / Chimurenga. Pp.7-23.

Mamdani, Mahmood. 1996. *Citizen and Subject. Contemporary Africa and the Legacy of Late Colonialism.* Princeton, New Jersey: Princeton University Press.

Maquet, Jacques J. 1949, The Modern Evolution of African Populations in the Belgian Congo. *Africa: Journal of the International African Institute* 19 (4): 265-272.

Maquet, Marcel-Alphonse-Joseph. 1939. Sur les flancs du Pic Sörensen, *Congo. Revue générale de la Colonie belge* 2 (3): 271-273.

Marchal, Jules. 1996. *L'État libre du Congo : Paradis perdu. L'Histoire du Congo, 1876-1900.* Borgloon : Editions Paula Bellings.

Martens, Renzo. 2009. *Episode III (Enjoy Poverty).* Brussels: Inti Films. [Video film, 90 minutes].

Marquez, Rafael. 2011. *Diamantes de sangue. Corrupção e tortura em Angola.* Lisbon: Tinta-da-China.

Masquelier, Adeline (Ed.). 2005. *Dirt, Undress and Difference. Critical Perspectives on the Body's Surface.* Bloomington / Indianapolis: Indiana University Press.

Mavinga Tsafunenga, Armand. 2011. *Cimetière de vivants. Poèmes.* Paris : L'Harmattan.

Mayasiwa Luveya. 1986 / 1987. Danses cheffales au Zaïre: le musangu (Yaka) et le sangila (Kongo). *Bulletin of the International Committee on Urgent Anthropological and Ethnological Research* 28 / 29: 89-98.

Mbembe, Achille. 1992. Provisional Notes on the Postcolony. *Africa* 62 (1): 3-37.

Mbembe, Achille. 2003. Necropolitics. *Public Culture* 15 (1): 11-40.

Mbembe, Achille. 2006. Variations on the Beautiful in Congolese Worlds of Sound. In: Sarah Nuttall (Ed.), *Beautiful / Ugly: African and Diaspora Aesthetics*. Durham: Duke University Press. Pp. 60-93.

Mbembe, Achille. 2014. The Zero World. Materials and the Machine. In: Sammy Baloji, *Mémoire / Kolwezi*. Brussels: Africalia / Stichting Kunstboek.

M'bokolo, Elikia and Kivilu Sabakinu (Eds.). 2014. *Simon Kimbangu. Le Prophète de la libération de l'homme noir*. Paris: L'Harmattan. [2 volumes].

McCarthy, Cormac. 2002. *The Border Trilogy*. London: Picador.

McFarlane, Colin. 2008. Urban Shadows: Materiality, the 'Southern City' and Urban Theory. *Geography Compass* 2 (2): 340-358.

McFarlane, Colin. 2011a. Assemblage and Critical Urbanism. *City* 15 (2): 204-224.

McFarlane, Colin. 2011b. Encountering, Describing and Transforming Urbanism. Concluding Reflections on Assemblage and Urban Criticality. *City* 15 (6): 731-739.

Meditz, Sandra W. and Tim Merrill (Eds.). 1994. *Zaire. A Country Study*. Washington, DC: American University.

Meiers, Bénédicte. 2013. *Le Dieu de Mama Olangi. Ethnographie d'un combat spirituel transnational*. Louvain-la-Neuve: Academia / L'Harmattan.

Mélice, Anne. 2011. *Prophétisme, hétérodoxie et dissidence. L'imaginaire kimbanguiste en mouvement*. Liège: Université de Liège. [Unpublished doctoral dissertation].

Mianda, Gertrude. 1996. Women and Garden Produce of Kinshasa: The Difficult Quest for Autonomy. In: Parvin Ghorayshi and Claire Béranger (Eds.), *Women, Work and Gender Relations in Developing Countries: A Global Perspective*. Westport, CT / London: Greenwood Press. Pp. 91-101.

Michel, Thierry. 1999. *Mobutu, roi du Zaïre*. Brussels: Les Films de la Passerelle. [Feature documentary, 135 minutes].

Miller, Jacques-Alain. 2012 (1966). Suture (Elements of the Logic of the Signifier). In: Peter Hallward and Knox Peden (Eds.), *Concept and Form. Volume One.*

Key Texts from the Cahiers pour l'Analyse. London / New York: Verso. Pp. 91-101.

Mitchell, W.J.T. 2013. Image, Space, Revolution. The Arts of Revolution. In: W.J.T. Mitchell, Bernard E. Harcourt and Michael Taussig, *Occupy. Three Inquiries in Disobedience*. Chicago / London: The University of Chicago Press. Pp. 93-130.

Mitlin, Diana and David Satterthwaite. 2013. *Urban Poverty in the Global South. Scale and Nature*. London: Routledge.

Mobateli, Angelo. 2014. Boom immobilier pour une ville de 10 millions d'habitants. *Kin la Capitale. Le magazine de la ville que nous voulons* 4: 32-33.

Moyer, Eileen. 2003. *In the Shadow of the Sheraton: Imagining Localities in Global Spaces in Dar es Salaam, Tanzania*. Amsterdam: University of Amsterdam. [Unpublished doctoral dissertation].

Mudimbe, Valentin Yves. 1982. *L'odeur du père. Essai sur les limites de la science et de la vie en Afrique Noire*. Paris: Présence Africaine.

Mudimbe, Valentin Yves. 1988. *The Invention of Africa. Gnosis, Philosophy, and the Order of Knowledge*. Bloomington and Indianapolis / London: Indiana University Press / James Currey.

Mudimbe, Valentin Yves. 1994a. *The Idea of Africa*. Bloomington and Indianapolis / London: Indiana University Press / James Currey.

Mudimbe, Valentin Yves. 1994b. *Les corps glorieux des mots et des êtres*. Montréal / Paris: Humanitas / Présence Africaine.

Mudimbe, Valentin Yves. 1999. *Reprendre*: Enunciations and Strategies in Contemporary African Arts.' In: Olu Oguibe and Okwui Enwezor (Eds.), *Reading the Contemporary: African Art from Theory to the Marketplace*. London: Institute of International Visual Arts. Pp. 31-47.

Mudimbe, Valentin Yves. 2008. What is a Line? On Paradoxes about Allegories on Identity and Alterity. *Quest. An African Journal of Philosophy* 21: 23-62.

Müller, Bärbel. 2009. Narrating Urban Acupuncture(s). In: Karel A. Bakker (Ed.), *African Perspectives 2009. The African Inner City: [Re]sourced.*

Pretoria: University of Pretoria. Pp. 207-216.

Murray, Martin J. and Garth A. Myers. 2006. *Cities in Contemporary Africa*. New York: Palgrave Macmillan.

Mususa, Patience. 2012. Mining, Welfare and Urbanisation: The Wavering Urban Character of Zambia's Copperbelt. *Journal of Contemporary African Studies* 30 (4): 571-587.

Myers, Garth. 2011. *African Cities. Alternative Visions of Urban Theory and Practice*. London / New York: Zed Books.

Nadeau-Bernatchez, David N. 2012. *La musique comme rapports aux temps. Chroniques et diachroniques des musiques urbaines congolaises*. Québec / Paris: University of Laval / Ecole des Hautes Etudes en Sciences Sociales. [Unpublished doctoral dissertation].

Naipaul, Vidiadhar Surajprasad. 1969 (1967). *The Mimic Men*. Harmondsworth, Middlesex: Penguin Books.

Neuwirth, Robert. 2006. *Shadow Cities. A Billion Squatters, a New Urban World*. New York / London: Routledge.

Newell, Sasha. 2012. *The Modernity Bluff. Crime, Consumption, and Citizenship in Côte d'Ivoire*. Chicago / London: The University of Chicago Press.

Nielsen, Morten. 2011. Futures Within: Reversible Time and House-building in Maputo, Mozambique. *Anthropological Theory* 11 (4): 397-423.

Nordstrom, Carolyn. 2004. *Shadows of War. Violence, Power, and International Profiteering in the Twenty-first Century*. Berkeley: University of California Press.

Noret, Joël. 2010. *Deuil et funérailles dans le Bénin méridional. Enterrer à tout prix*. Brussels: Editions de l'Université de Bruxelles.

Noret Joël and Pierre Petit. 2011. *Mort et dynamiques sociales au Katanga (République démocratique du Congo)*. Paris / Tervuren : L'Harmattan / Royal Museum of Central Africa.

Norris, Andrew. 2000. Giorgio Agamben and the Politics of the Living Dead. *Diacritics* 30 (4): 38-58.

Nuttall, Sarah. 2009. *Entanglement. Literary and Cultural Reflections on*

Post-Apartheid. Johannesburg: Wits University Press.

Nuttall, Sarah. 2013. Wound, Surface, Skin. *Cultural Studies* 27 (3): 418-437.

Nzeza Bilakila, Anastase. 2004. The Kinshasa Bargain. In: Theodore Trefon (Ed.), *Reinventing Order in the Congo: How People Respond to State Failure in Kinshasa*. London: Zed Books. Pp. 20-32.

Obarrio, Juan. 2014. *The Spirit of the Laws in Mozambique*. Chicago: The University of Chicago Press.

Obrist, Brigit, Veit Arlt and Elisio Macamo (Eds.). 2013. *Living the City in Africa. Processes of Invention and intervention*. Zürich: LIT Verlag.

Omasombo Tshondo, Jean (Ed.). 2012. *République Démocratique du Congo. Kwango, le pays des Bana Lunda*. Brussels / Tervuren : Le Cri / Royal Museum of Central Africa.

Pain, Marc. 1984. *Kinshasa: La ville et la cité (Etudes urbaines)*. Paris: L'Harmattan.

Pandian, Anand. 2014. Thinking like a Mountain. *Hau: Journal of Ethnographic Theory* 4 (2): 245-252.

Parnell, Susan and Jennifer Robinson. 2012. Re-theorizing Cities from the Global South: Looking Beyond Neoliberalism. *Urban Geography* 33 (4): 593-617.

Parnell, Susan and Sophie Oldfield (Eds.). 2014. *The Routledge Handbook on Cities of the Global South*. London / New York: Routledge.

Parnell, Susan and Edgar Pieterse (Eds.). 2014. *Africa's Urban Revolution*. London / New York: Zed Books.

Peffer, John. 2013. Flogging Photographs from the Congo Free State. In: Maria Pia Di Bella and James Elkins (Eds.), *Representations of Pain in Art and Visual Culture*. New York / Abingdon, Oxon: Routledge. Pp. 122-142.

Pels, Peter. 1999. *A Politics of Presence. Contacts between Missionaries and Waluguru in Late Colonial Tanganyika*. Amsterdam: Harwood Academic Publishers.

Piermay, Jean-Luc. 1997. Kinshasa: A Reprieved Mega-City? In: Carole Rakodi (Ed.), *The Urban Challenge in Africa. Growth and Management of its Large Cities*. Tokyo: United Nations University Press. Pp. 223-251.

Pieterse, Edgar. 2008. *City Futures. Confronting the Crisis of Urban Development*. London / New York / Cape Town: Zed Books / UCT Press.

Pieterse, Edgar. 2010. *Cityness and African Urban Development*. Cape Town: World Institute for Development Economics. [Research Working Paper, 42].

Pieterse, Edgar and Abdoumaliq Simone (Eds.). 2013. *Rogue Urbanism: Emergent African Cities*. Johannesburg: Jacana.

Pinther, Kerstin, Larissa Förster and Christian Hanussek (Eds.). 2012. *Afropolis: City, Media, Art*. Johannesburg: Jacana.

Piot, Charles. 1999. *Remotely Global. Village Modernity in West Africa*. Chicago: The University of Chicago Press.

Pivin, Jean Loup and Pascal Martin Saint Leon. 2012. *Pourquoi pas Bylex?* Pume. Paris : Revue Noire.

Pype, Katrien. 2007. Fighting Boys, Strong Men, and Gorillas. Notes on the Imagination of Masculinities in Postcolonial Kinshasa (DR Congo). *Africa* 77 (2): 250-271.

Pype, Katrien. 2011. Visual Media and Political Communication: Reporting about Suffering in Kinshasa. *Journal of Modern African Studies* 49 (4): 625-645.

Pype, Katrien. 2012. *The Making of the Pentecostal Melodrama: An Ethnography of Media, Religion and Mimesis in Kinshasa*, New York / Oxford: Berghahn Publishers.

Rabaud, Marlène and Arnaud Zajtman. 2010. *Kafka au Congo*. Brussels: Ekletik Productions. [Documentary Film, 59 minutes].

Rakodi, Carole. 2002. Order and Disorder in African Cities: Governance, Politics, and Urban Land Development Processes. In: Okwui Enwezor (Ed.), *Under Siege: Four African Cities: Freetown; Johannesburg; Kinshasa; Lagos*. Ostfildern-Ruit: Hatje Cantz Publishers. Pp. 45-80.

Rao, Vyjayanthi. 2006. Slum as Theory: The South/Asian City and Globalization. *International Journal of Urban and Regional Research* 30 (1): 225-232.

Reno, William. 1995. *Corruption and State Politics in Sierra Leone*. Cambridge: Cambridge University Press.

Robert, Christophe. 2014. Dead Zone: Pollution, Contamination and the Neglected Dead in Post-War Saigon In: Finn Stepputat (Ed.), *Governing the Dead. Sovereignty and the Politics of Dead Bodies*. Manchester: Manchester University Press. Pp. 53-74.

Robinson, Jennifer. 2010. Living in Dystopia: Past, Present and Future in Contemporary African Cities. In: Gyan Prakash (Ed.), *Noir Urbanisms: Dystopic Images of the Modern City*. Princeton / Oxford: Princeton University Press. Pp. 218-240.

Robinson, Jennifer. 2013. The Urban Now: Theorising Cities beyond the New. *European Journal of Cultural Studies* 16 (6): 659-677.

Roosens, Eugeen. 1971. *De Yaka van Kwaango: Een gevalstudie. Socio-culturele verandering in Midden-Afrika*. Antwerp: Standaard wetenschappelijke uitgeverij.

Roy, Ananya. 2011. Slumdog Cities: Rethinking Subaltern Urbanism. *International Journal of Urban and Regional Research* 35 (2): 223-238.

Roy, Ananya and Aihwa Ong (Eds.). 2011. *Worlding Cities. Asian Experiments and the Art of Being Global*. Malden, MA / Oxford: Wiley-Blackwell.

Samara, Tony, Shenjing He, and Guo Chen (Eds.). 2013. *Locating Right to the City in the Global South*. London Routledge.

Sambu, Yves. 2009. Why, When, How. *Transition* 102: 12-17.

Sassen, Saskia. 2014. *Expulsions. Brutality and Complexity in the Global Economy*. Cambridge, MA / London: The Belknap Press of Harvard University Press.

Scott, Ariel Osterweiss. 2010. Performing Acupuncture on a Necropolitical Body: Choreographer Faustin Linyekula's Studios Kabako in Kisangani, Democratic Republic of Congo. *Dance Research Journal* 42 (2): 11-27.

Sennett, Richard. 1994. *Flesh and Stone: The Body and the City in Western Civilization*. New York: W.W. Norton.

Shapiro, David and B. Oleko Tambashe. 2003. *Kinshasa in Transition. Women's Education, Employment and Fertility*. Chicago /London: The University of Chicago Press

Shklovsky, Viktor. 2004. "Art as Technique". In: Julie Rivkin and Michael Ryan (Eds.), *Literary Theory: An Anthology*. Maiden / Oxford / Carlton: Wiley-Blackwell. Pp. 15-21.

Silva, Sonia. 2011. *Along an African Border. Angolan Refugees and their Divination Basket*. Philadelphia: University of Pennsylvania Press.

Simone, Abdoumaliq. 2001. On the Worlding of African Cities. *African Studies Review* 44 (2): 15-42.

Simone, Abdoumaliq. 2004. *For the City Yet to Come. Changing African Life in Four Cities*. Durham / London: Duke University Press.

Simone, Abdoumaliq. 2010a. 2009 Urban Geography Plenary Lecture – On Intersections, Anticipations, and Provisional Publics: Remaking District Life in Jakarta. *Urban Geography* 31 (3): 285-308.

Simone, Abdoumaliq. 2010b. *City Life from Jakarta to Dakar: Movements at the Crossroads*. New York: Routledge.

Simone, Abdoumaliq. 2012a. Screen. In: Celia Lury and Nina Wakeford (Eds.), *Inventive Methods: The Happening of the Social*. London / New York: Routledge. Pp. 202-218.

Simone Abdoumaliq. 2012b. *The Social Infrastructure of City Life in Contemporary Africa*. Uppsala: The Nordic Africa Institute. [Discussion paper 51].

Simone, Abdoumaliq and Abdelghani Abouhani (Eds.). 2005. *Urban Africa. Changing Contours of Survival in the City*. London / New York: Zed Books.

Sluga, Hans. 2005. Foucault's Encounter with Heidegger and Nietsche. In: Gary Gutting (Ed.), *The Cambridge Companion to Foucault. Second Edition*. Cambridge University Press. Pp. 210-238.

Sohier, Antoine. 1949. Le probleme des indigènes évolués et la Commission du Statut des Congolais civilises. *Zaire, 3*(81): 3.

Spyer, Patricia. 2006. Some Notes on Disorder in the Indonesian Postcolony. In: Jean Comaroff and John L. Comaroff (Eds.), *Law and Disorder in the Postcolony*. Chicago: The University of Chicago Press. Pp. 188-218.

Standing, Guy. 2011. *The Precariat: The New Dangerous Class*. London: Bloomsbury Academic.

Stanley, Henry Morton. 2011 (1885). *The Congo and the Founding of its Free State. A Story of Work and Exploration. Volume 1*. Cambridge: Cambridge University Press.

Stearns, Jason K. 2011. *Dancing in the Glory of Monsters. The Collapse of the Congo and the Great War of Africa*. New York: Public Affairs.

Stevelinck, Henri. 1932. *Chroniques de Stinkopolis*. Léopoldville: L'Avenir Colonial Belge.

Stewart, Gary. 2000. *Rumba on the River. A History of the Popular Music of the Two Congos*. London: Verso.

Stoler, Ann Laura. 2008. Imperial Debris: Reflections on Ruins and Ruination. *Cultural Anthropology* 23 (2): 191-219.

Strathern, Marilyn. 1991. *Partial Connections*. Savage, Maryland: Rowman & Littlefield.

Strathern, Marilyn (Ed). 1995. *Shifting Contexts. Transformations in Anthropological Knowledge*. London: Routledge.

Swyngedouw, Erik. 2007. The Post-Political City. In: BAVO (Ed.), *Urban Politics Now: Re-imagining Democracy in the Neo-liberal City*. Rotterdam: NAI Publishers / Netherlands Architecture Institute. Pp 58-76.

Taussig, Michael. 1992. Culture of Terror – Space of Death. Roger Casement's Putumayo Report and the Explanation of Torture. In: Nicholas Dirks (Ed.), *Colonialism and Culture*. Ann Arbor: University of Michigan Press. Pp. 135-173.

Tipo-Tipo, Mayoyo Bitumba. 1995. *Migration Sud/Nord. Levier ou obstacle?* Tervuren / Paris: Institut Africain-CEDAF / L'Harmattan.

Tonda, Joseph. 2008. La violence de l'imaginaire des enfants-sorciers. *Cahiers d'Etudes africaines* 48 (189-190): 325-343.

Toulier, Bernard, Johan Lagae and Marc Gemoets (Eds.). 2010. *Kinshasa. Architecture et paysage urbains*, Paris: Somogy Éditions d'Art.

Trefon, Theodore (Ed.). 2004. *Reinventing Order in the Congo: How People Respond to State Failure in Kinshasa*. London: Zed Books.

Trefon, Theodore (Ed.). 2009a. *Réforme au Congo : Attentes et désillusions*. Paris / Tervuren: L'Harmattan / Royal Museum of Central Africa. [Series 'Cahiers Africains', n° 76].

Trefon, Theodore. 2009b. Hinges and Fringes: Conceptualizing the Peri-Urban in Central Africa. In: Franscesca Locatelli and Paul Nugent (Eds.), *African Cities. Competing Claims on Urban Spaces*. Leyden / Boston: Brill. Pp. 15-35.

Trovalla, Eric and Ulrika Trovalla. 2015. Infrastructure as a Divination Tool: Whispers from the Grids in a Nigerian City. *City: Analysis of Urban Trends, Culture, Theory, Policy, Action* 19 (2-3): 332-343.

Tsing, Anna Lowenhaupt. 1994. From the Margins. *Cultural Anthropology* 9 (3): 279–297.

Tsing, Anna Lowenhaupt. 2005. *Friction: An Ethnography of Global Connection*. Princeton, NJ: Princeton University Press.

Turner, Victor W. 1967. *The Forest of Symbols. Aspects of Ndembu Ritual*. Ithaca / London: Cornell University Press.

Turner, Victor W. 1968. *The Drums of Affliction. A Study of Religious Processes among the Ndembu of Zambia*. Ithaca / New York: Cornell University Press.

Turner, Victor W. 1975. *Revelation and Divination in Ndembu Ritual*. Ithaca / London: Cornell University Press.

UN Habitat. 2010. *The State of African Cities 2010. Governance, Inequalities and Urban Landmarkets*. Nairobi: UNEP Regional Office for Africa and the Arab States of the World's Cities 2010/2011.

Urdal, Henrik and Kristian Hoelscher. 2009. *Urban Youth Bulges and Social Disorder: An Empirical Study Of Asian And Sub-Saharan African Cities*. The World Bank Africa Region Post Conflict and Social Development Unit [Policy Research Working Paper 5110].

Van Beurden, Sarah. 2015. *Authentically African: Arts and the Transnational Politics of Congolese Culture*. Athens: Ohio University Press.

Vanden Bossche, Jean. 1955. Le Musée de la vie indigène, Léopoldville, Congo Belge. *Museum International* 8 (2): 82-87.

Van Den Broeck, Jan. Forthcoming. 'We Are Analogue in a Digital World': An Anthropological Exploration of Ontologies and Uncertainties around the Proposed Konza Techno City near Nairobi, Kenya. *Critical African Studies*.

Van Groenweghe, Daniel. 1986. *Du sang sur les lianes. Léopold II et son Congo*. Brussels: Didier Hatier.

Vangu Ngimbi, Ivan. 1997. *Jeunesse, funérailles et contestation socio-politique en Afrique*. Paris: L'Harmattan.

Vannoppen, Geertrui. Forthcoming. *'Documents are your Weapon': Mobilization of Paper in the Urban Context of Sekondi-Takoradi, Ghana*.

Van Reybrouck, David. 2014. *Congo: The Epic History of a People*. London: HarperCollins Publishers.

Vansina, Jan. 1973a. Lukoshi / Lupambula : Histoire d'un culte religieux dans les religions du Kasaï et du Kwango : 1920-1970. *Etudes d'histoire africaine* 5: 51-97.

Vansina, Jan 1973b. *The Tio Kingdom of the Middle Congo, 1880-1892*. Oxford: Oxford University Press.

Van Synghel, Koen and Filip De Boeck. 2013. Bylex's Tourist City: A Reflection on Utopia in the Post-political City. In: E. Pieterse and A. Simone (Eds.), *Rogue Urbanism. Emergent African Cities*. Johannesburg: Jacana Media. Pp. 83-90.

Vasudevan, Alexander. 2015. The Autonomous City: Towards a Critical Geography of Occupation. *Progress in Human Geography* 39 (3): 316–337.

Vaughan, Megan and Rebekah Lee. 2008. Death and Dying in the History of Africa since 1800. *Journal of African History* 49: 341-59.

Vellut, Jean-Luc. 1977. Rural Poverty in Western Shaba, c. 1890-1930. In: Robin H. Palmer and Neil Parsons (Eds.), *The Roots of Rural Poverty in Central and Southern Africa*. Berkeley: University of California Press. Pp. 294-316.

Vellut, Jean-Luc. 1987. Détresse matérielle et découvertes de la misère dans les colonies belges d'Afrique Centrale ca. 1900-1960. In: Michel Dumoulin and Eddy Stols (Eds.), *La Belgique et l'étranger aux XIXe et XXe siècles*. Louvain-la-Neuve: Presses Universitaires de Louvain. Pp. 147-186.

Vellut, Jean-Luc. 2006. Angola-Congo. L'invention de la frontier du Lunda (1889-1893). *Africana Studia. International Journal of African Studies* 9: 159-184.

Wagemakers, Inge and Makangu Diki O. 2011. Governance of Urban Agricultural Space: Struggle for Land in Kinshasa (DRC). In: An Ansoms and Stefaan Maryse (Eds.), *Natural Resources and Local Livelihoods in the Great Lakes Region of Africa*. Basingstoke: Palgrave MacMillan. Pp. 68-82.

Wagemakers, Inge, Makangu Diki O., Tom De Herdt and J.-M. Kitshiaba. 2011. Lutte foncière dans la ville : gouvernance de la terre agricole urbaine à Kinshasa et à Kikwit. In : Tom De Herdt (Ed.), *A la recherche de l'Etat en R-DCongo : acteurs et enjeux d'une reconstruction post-conflit*. Paris: L'Harmattan. Pp. 73-114.

Wainaina, Binyavanga. 2011. *One Day I Will Write About This Place. A Memoir*. Minneapolis, Minnesota: Graywolf Press.

Walker, Joshua. 2014. *The Ends of Extraction: Diamonds, Value, and Reproduction in Democratic Republic of Congo*. Chicago: University of Chicago. [Unpublished doctoral dissertation].

Wastiau, B. (2000). *Mahamba. The Transforming Arts of Spirit Possession among the Luvale-speaking People of the Upper Zambezi*. Fribourg: University Press.

Watson, Vanessa. 2009. 'The Planned City Sweeps the Poor Away. . .': Urban Planning and 21st Century Urbanisation. *Progress in Planning* 72 (3): 151–193.

Watson, Vanessa. 2013. African Urban Fantasies: Dreams or Nightmares? *Environment and Urbanization* 26 (1): 1-17. [DOI: 10.1177/0956247813513705].

Werbner, Richard. 2015. *Divination's Grasp. African Encounters with the Almost Said*. Bloomington / Indianapolis: Indiana University Press.

Wedel, Janine R. 2011. Shadow Governing: What the Neocon Core Reveals about Power and Influence in America. In: Chris Wright, Susan Shore and Devide Pero (Eds.), *Policy Worlds: Anthropology and the Analysis of Contemporary Power*. Oxford / New York: Berghahn. Pp. 151-168.

Weizman, Eyal. 2012. *Hollow Land. Israel's Architecture of Occupation*. London: Verso.

White, Bob W. 2008. *Rumba Rules: The Politics of Dance Music in Mobutu's Zaire*. Durham: Duke University Press.

White, Bob W. and Lye M. Yoka, 2010, *Musique populaire et société à Kinshasa. Une ethnographie de l'écoute*. Paris: L'Harmattan.

Williams, Raymond, 1977, *Marxism and Literature*. Oxford: Oxford University Press.

Wilson, Japhy and Erik Swyngedouw (Eds.). 2014. *The Post-Political and Its Discontents. Spaces of Depoliticization, Spectres of Radical Politics*. Edinburgh: Edinburgh University Press.

Wouters, Thomas and Eléonore Wolff. 2010. Contribution à l'analyse de l'érosion intra-urbaine à Kinshasa (R.D.C.). *Belgeo. Belgian Journal of Geography* 3 : 293-314.

Wrong, Michaela. 2001. *In the Footsteps of Mr. Kurtz. Living on the Brink of Disaster in Mobutu's Congo*. New York: HarperCollins Publishers.

You, Haili.1994. Defining Rhythm: Aspects of an Anthropology of Rhythm. *Culture, Medicine and Psychiatry* 18 (3): 361-384.

Young, Crawford and Thomas Turner. 1985. *The Rise and Decline of the Zairean State*. Madison, WI: The University of Wisconsin Press.

Index

Index of Illustrations

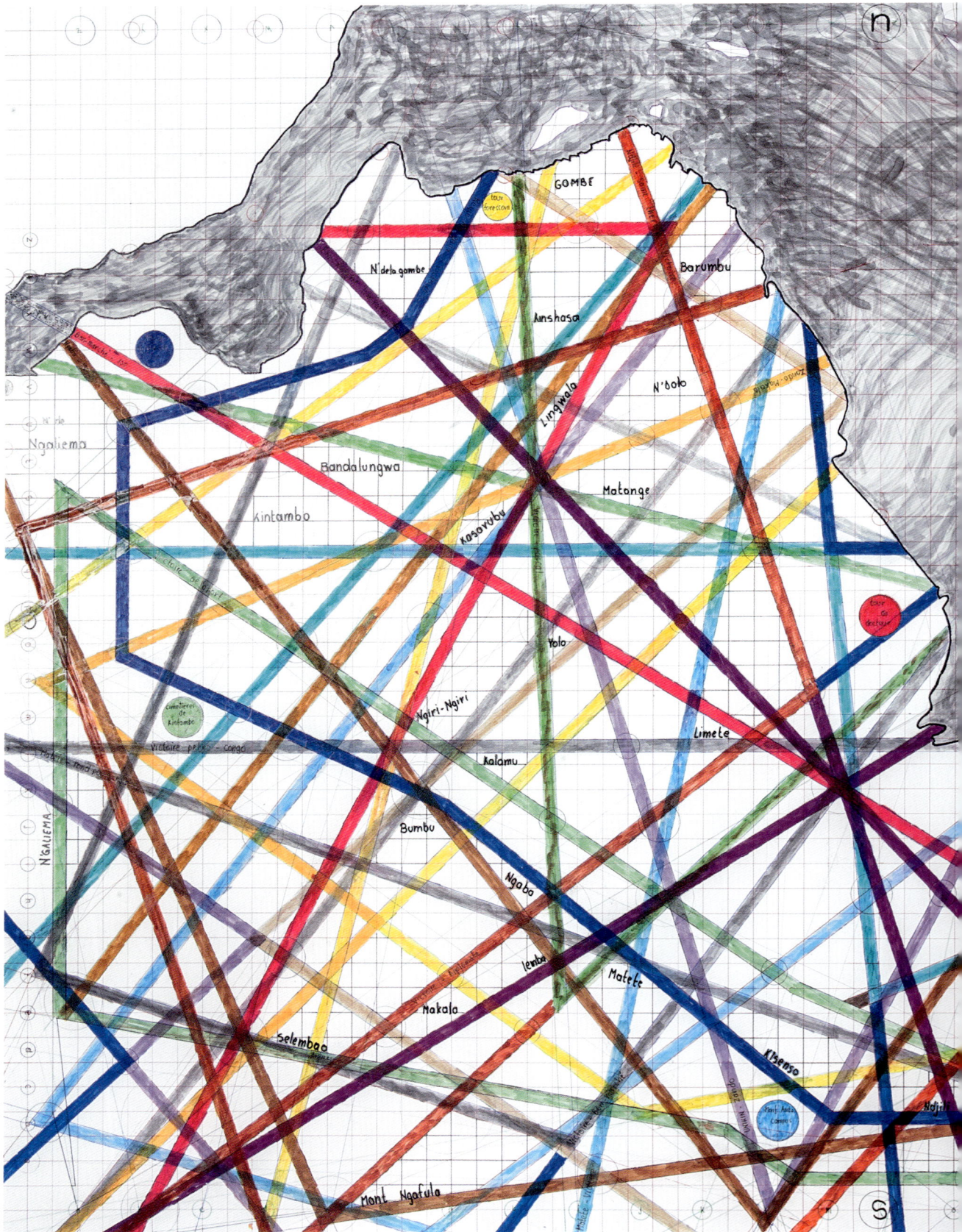

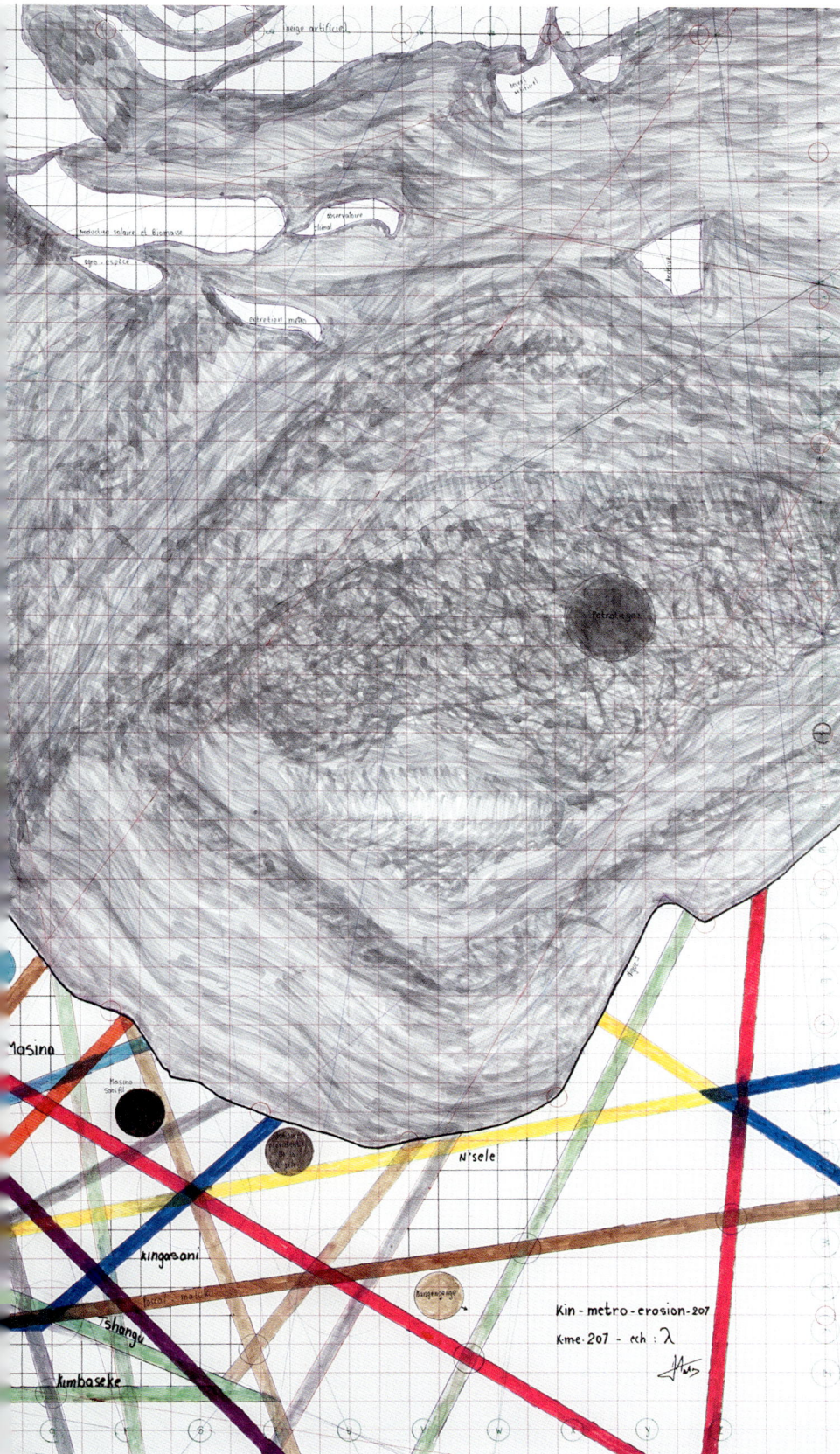

Kin – métro – érosion – 207
Drawing by Jean Katambayi 2016

Forescom Tower

Mount Ngaliema

The Doctor's Tower

Cité du Fleuve

Kintambo Cemetery

Kimbangu Village

The Building of Masina Sans Fil

Presidential Pagoda of Nsele

Mount Mangengenge

Mont Amba University Campus

Colophon

Published by Leuven University Press

© 2025 Authorized reprint by Leuven University Press /
Presses Universitaires de Louvain / Universitaire Pers Leuven.
Minderbroedersstraat 4, B-3000 Leuven (Belgium)
ISBN 987 94 6270 455 8 (print)
ISBN 978 94 6166 631 4 (ePDF)
ISBN 978 94 6166 643 7 (ePUB)
https://doi.org/10.11116/9789461666314
D/2025/1869/8
NUR: 764
www.lup.be

LEUVEN UNIVERSITY PRESS

Text © Filip De Boeck
Photographs © Sammy Baloji,
except photos p. 142–143, 145,
159, 245–247 © Filip De Boeck

© 2016 Autograph ABP

Originally published by
Autograph ABP in 2016,
with Publishing Partner:

Galerie Imane Farès
41, rue Mazarine, 75006 Paris – France
www.imanefares.com

in association with:

WIELS
Contemporary Art Centre
Av. Van Volxemlaan 354, 1190 Brussels – Belgium
www.wiels.org

and

The Power Plant
Contemporary Art Gallery
231 Queens Quay West, Toronto, ON M5J 2G8 – Canada
www.thepowerplant.org

Supported by Arts Council England.

Registered Charity no 1127712

Autograph ABP is a charity that works
internationally in photography and film, cultural
identity, race, representation and human rights.

Executive Editor: Mark Sealy MBE
Production: Jonathan Lewis / Essential Print Management
Digital Imaging: Ilan Weiss
Design: Dooreman

Acknowledgements

Autograph ABP would like to thank its staff and board:
Claire Antrobus, Steve Blogg, Adelaide Bannerman, Karin Bareman,
Peter Clack, Eric Collins, John Dyer, John Ellis, Rupert Grey,
Ron Henocq, Lucy Keany, Lois Olmstead, Renée Mussai, Declan
Pollock, Cherelle Sappleton, Mark Sealy, Mitra Tabrizian,
Holly Tebbutt, Iqbal Wahhab (Chair), and Tom Wilcox.

Special Thanks to:
Imane Farès, Dirk Snauwaert and Devrim Bayar (Wiels)
and Gaëtane Verna (The Power Plant).

AUTOGRAPH ABP   Galerie Imane Farès   WIELS   THE POWER PLANT   ARTS COUNCIL ENGLAND Supported using public funding by